Praise for
BEYOND THE GRAVE

"If you have a family you love, poured your soul into building a business, and hate the idea of seeing the lion's share of your estate go to the tax-man, you cannot afford to die without reading this book."

—Lou Richman, *Fortune*

"[*Beyond the Grave*] aims to show how proper estate planning leaves your family secure—not at war. . . . Condon's mission is keeping the family, and its assets, together through life and death, using proper inheritance planning." —*Los Angeles Times*

"The reader-friendly book deals with everything. . . . It thus behooves a parent with no plans for a coffer in his coffin to pay attention. . . . To find out what the authors have to say about the most common squabbles and conflicts that occur when parents die and children divide the inheritance, read *Beyond the Grave*, while you still have time to put its wisdom to use, that is." —*Saturday Evening Post*

"The book is necessary because, other than Ann Landers, no one has been dealing with the family side of estate planning. . . . Most books dealing with inheritances focus on the money side [and] the Condon's book deals with these issues as well." —*Santa Monica News*

"With good sense, humor, and authority, the authors provide a thorough look at inheritance planning with an eye toward maintaining good, stable family relations well after the estate has been settled. Presenting more scenarios than a season full of made-for-television movies, [the authors] consider the psychological and emotional aspects of leaving and inheriting money." —*Booklist*

"[*Beyond the Grave*], written in a reader-friendly manner reminiscent of an Ann Landers advice column, focuses on the most common family conflicts and problems that arise when ~~parents die and~~ their children divide the inheritance."

"In [Beyond the Grave], the Condons . . . discuss how to handle properly the allocation of assets after one's death and how to avoid possible problems [with] actual cases. . . . [Beyond the Grave is] a source of ideas and questions to ask one's lawyer when planning an estate."

—*Library Journal*

"It's not so much that [estate planning] rules have changed so dramatically—people have. . . . [Author Jeff Condon observes], 'Recognizing that you have an estate planning problem is 95% of its solution.' "

—*Fortune*

"The author correctly observes, perhaps no area of human relations is as fraught with emotion and misunderstanding as the transfer of money and property from one generation to the next." —*Orange Country Register*

"How to avoid money conflicts with our loved ones as much as possible, it offers insight into problems you might encounter with the almighty dollar, that you might not have even imagined . . . in an easy-to-read style. . . . The book is full of helpful advice, such as how to avoid probate court, give tax-free gifts while still alive, and deal with all the furnishings in your house to avoid fights among heirs. The Condons are straightforward, with a 'tough love' attitude toward fairness and responsibility. But the advice might save many heartaches after you are gone."

—*Fort Worth Star-Telegram*

Beyond the Grave

Beyond
the
Grave

The Right Way and the Wrong Way
of Leaving Money to
Your Children (and Others)

Revised and Updated Edition

Jeffrey L. Condon, Esq.

HARPER
BUSINESS

An Imprint of HarperCollins*Publishers*
www.harpercollins.com

This book is designed to provide accurate and authoritative information in regard to the subject of estate planning. It is sold with the understanding that neither the author nor the publisher is engaged in rendering legal, accounting, or other professional service by publishing this book. If legal assistance is required, the services of a competent attorney who emphasizes a practice in estate and/or inheritance planning should be sought.

HARPER
BUSINESS

BEYOND THE GRAVE. Copyright © 2001 by Gerald M. Condon and Jeffrey L. Condon; copyright renewed © 2014 by Jeffrey L. Condon. All rights reserved. Printed in the United States of America. No part of this book may be used or reproduced in any manner whatsoever without written permission except in the case of brief quotations embodied in critical articles and reviews. For information, address HarperCollins Publishers, 195 Broadway, New York, NY 10007.

HarperCollins books may be purchased for educational, business, or sales promotional use. For information, please e-mail the Special Markets Department at SPsales@harpercollins.com.

Originally published in hardcover in 1995 by HarperBusiness.
Revised edition published in paperback in 2001 by HarperBusiness.
Second revised edition published in 2014.

Designed by Joan Greenfield

Library of Congress has cataloged the previous edition as follows:

Condon, Gerald M.
  Beyond the grave: the right way and the wrong way of leaving
money to your children (and others) / Gerald M. Condon and Jeffrey L.
Condon.—[Rev. ed.]
    p. cm.
  Includes index.
  1. Estate planning—United States—Popular works. 2. Inheritance and succession—United States—Popular works. 3. Wills—United States—Popular works. 4. Living trusts—United States—Popular works. I. Condon, Jeffrey L. II. Title.
KF750.Z9 C66 2001
346.7305'2—dc21   00-140109
ISBN: 978-0-06-233622-4

HB 03.05.2024

To my dear, lovely, and age-defying mother,
Esther Condon. Thanks for giving birth to me.
With this dedication, we're now square.

J.L.C.

To my dear lovely and caring mother
Esther Gordon. Thank you for given birth to me
Wishing you come to more new shape

Contents

Acknowledgments xv
Preface, *or Even If You Usually Skip Prefaces,*
Make Sure You Read This One xix

Part I

Introduction

1: The Journey from Innocence to Cynicism 3
or You Really Don't Know Your Children—
Until They Divide Their Inheritance

2: Why an Inheritance Plan? 8
or Seven Challenges from Beyond the Grave

3: If You Do Nothing, the Law Will Do It for You 15
or Everybody Procrastinates—but Don't Wait Until You Are
on Your Deathbed

Part II

Preventing Inheritance Conflicts Between Your Children

4: The Unequal Inheritance 21
or If You Don't Want the Blame—Treat Your Children the Same

5: The Power Struggle 34
*or If Your Children Didn't Get Along Sharing Their Toys,
How Will They Comanage Their Inherited Property?*

6: Don't Die with Your Children Owing You Money 42
*or "I Asked for My Money Back—Now I Don't Get
to See My Grandchildren"*

Part III

Protecting the Inheritance from Your Child's Potential Problems

7: Protecting the Inheritance While It's in the Hands
of Your Child 57
or After Your Child Inherits—Will It Be There for Your Grandchild?

8: Protecting the Money for the Financially Immature Child 65
*or Will Your Daughter's Inheritance End Up at Nordstrom's
or with Her Newfound Friends?*

9: Protecting the Inheritance from Your Child's Spouse 76
*or Do You Really Want Your Money to Go to Your Son-in-Law's
Second Wife?*

10: Protecting the Inheritance for the Disabled Child 91
*or "Who Will Take Care of My Disabled Child When I Am
No Longer Able To?"*

11: Protecting the Inheritance from Your Child's Creditors 99
*or Whom Would You Prefer to Get Your Money—
Your Grandchildren or Your Son's Creditors?*

Part IV

Who Says You Owe Your Children an Inheritance?

12: Cutting Out a Child from Your Will or Trust 107
*or Now Is the Time to Begin to Defend the Lawsuit Your
Disinherited Child Will Bring After You Die*

13: How Much Inheritance Is Too Much Inheritance? 121
or Will Your Child's Inheritance Turn Him into a "Trust-Fund Baby"?

14: Are Your Children Spending Their Inheritance—and You're
Not Dead Yet? 129
or "That's My Son—the One Who Is Waiting for Me to Die!"

15: How to Control Your Child's Life from the Grave 136
*or "If My Children or Grandchildren Want My Money.
They'll Do It My Way—or the Highway"*

Part V

Who Will Hold Your "Problem" Child's Inheritance?

16: Who Should Be Your Child's Trustee? 145
*or You Can Let Your Sister Hold Your Child's Money—
but There Ain't No Policeman Looking over Her Shoulder*

17: Your Underage Child's Guardian 158
*or Your Children Are Terrific Kids—but Who Will Want Them Full-Time
If You Die?*

Part VI

How Will Your Children Divide Your Noncash Assets?

18: How to Leave Your Valuables and Household Contents
to Your Children 169
or "The First One to Mom's House after Her Funeral Wins"

19: Planning for the Succession of the Family Business 180
or When You Die, Will Your Business Die with You?

20: The Family Residence 192
or Be It Ever So Humble, There's No Place Like Home—
Until Your Children Fight over It After You Die

21: Dividing Your Real Estate Investments 207
or Your Investment Properties—Your "Pyramid" to Future Generations?

Part VII

Protecting Your Surviving Spouse's Ownership
and Control of the "Family Money"

22: The Three Issues You Must
Address to Protect Your Surviving Spouse 215

23: Protecting the Surviving Parent from "Grasping Children" 217
or "When Mom Dies—I'll Be Too Old to Enjoy My Inheritance"

24: Who Controls the Money and Property for the Incapacitated
or Incompetent Surviving Spouse? 230
or You May Not Want a Stranger to Control Your Surviving
Spouse's Money—but Are Your Children a Better Choice?

25: Does Your Wife Want to Manage the Family Money? 246
or "My Wife Says She Wants to Die First—So She Won't Be Left
with the Bookkeeping"

Part VIII

Will Your Surviving Spouse Divert the Family Money from Your Children?

26: You May Leave Everything to Your Spouse—but Will Your Spouse Leave Everything to Your Children? 255
or Preventing Your Money from Ending Up with Your Spouse's Bowling Instructor

27: The Potential Battle Between Children of Your First Marriage and Your Second Wife 265
or How Your Children Can Make a Difficult Life for Your Second Wife

28: If You Are on Your Second Marriage, Who Will Get Your Half If You Die First—Your Children or the Children of Your Second Spouse? 271
or "I Know My Second Spouse Will Do the Right Thing If I Die First, But . . ."

Part IX

Your Grandchildren

29: Grandparents to the Rescue! 283
or "If I Don't Help My Grandchildren While I'm Alive— Help May Never Come"

30: Including Your Grandchildren in Your Inheritance Plan 296
or "I Like My Children—but I Really Love My Grandchildren"

Part X

Pets and Charities

31: How You Can Die "Knowing" Your Pet Will Live Comfortably
for the Rest of His Life 311
or What to Tell "Fido" About His Inheritance

32: Leaving Your Money and Property to a Charity 318
*or Do You Really Want to Leave Everything to a
Charity That Clothes Naked Horses?*

Part XI

The Final Triangle: You, Your Children, and the IRS

33: The Permanent Repeal of the Death Tax 335
*or Well . . . That's Kind of a Vicious Lie. There's Still a
Death Tax . . . But Only If Your're Really Rich*

34: "How Does the IRS Know How Much I'm Worth
When I Die?" 345
or If Your Children Don't Tell—They May Go to Jail!

35: Pay the Death Tax or Fight Back—
Which One Sounds Like You? 352
or "I'm Not Crazy About My Kids—But I Hate the IRS Even More"

36: How to Leave More to Your Children and Less to the IRS 357
or Patriotism Does Not Require That You Pay More in Death Taxes

37: I Can Get Your Death Tax Wholesale 381
or You Never Paid Retail During Your Life—Why Start After You Die?

38: Your Money Is Taxed a Second Time
When Your Child Dies 386
or How to Prevent the IRS from Taking Two Bites of the Inheritance Apple

Part XII

Avoiding Probate

39: Using the Living Trust to Keep Your Children and Property
Out of the Probate Court 393
or Why Provide for Your Lawyer's Retirement Fund?

40: How Your Inheritance Instructions May Be Disregarded 401
or Do You Trust Your Children to Carry Out Your Inheritance Plan?

41: Don't Put Your House in Joint Tenancy with Your Child 407
or How to Lose Your House to Your Daughter's Creditors

Part XIII

Inheritance Planning and Government Entitlements

42: Can You Leave Your Child an Inheritance Without
Disqualifying Him from SSI? 421
*or How Your Child Can Inherit and Maintain
His Government Entitlements*

Part XIV

What Your Children Are Thinking . . .
and You Live and You Learn

43: The Most Pressing Concerns Your Children Have
About Your Will or Living Trust 429
*or Your Children Really Want to Ask About Their
Inheritance . . . but They Don't . . . Because They're Afraid
You Will Think They Can't Wait for You to Die*

44: Cautionary Tales from the Inheritance Arena 447
*or Read About . . . and Learn from . . . My Previous
Mistakes and the Mistakes of My Clients*

Final Thought:
"Should I Tell My Children about My Inheritance Plan?" 483

Index 487

Acknowledgments

In keeping with my lawyer-like penchant to compartmentalize, I shall break my acknowledgments into four separate and distinct categories.

For Those Without Whom This Revised Edition Wouldn't Exist

Colleen Lawrie. She is my incredibly industrious and seriously brilliant editor at HarperCollins, who championed the idea of this second revised edition. Not only is she the best book editor that ever lived, but a master of the lost art of editor-author diplomacy. Painful cuts and edits in my precious manuscript were almost made a pleasure with Colleen's pleasant and engaging manner. From now on, whenever bad news about anything has to be delivered to me, I want Colleen to be the messenger.

Margret McBride. She is my literary agent and has been with *Beyond the Grave* since before it was first published in 1995. Way back then, it was tough sledding for Margret to find a publisher for an inheritance book with a rough-shorn edge. (Remember the rejections we received because publishers wanted us to change "died" to "passed away"?) But Margret believed in us and found a toehold for this book with HarperCollins . . . an effort that literally changed the personal and professional lives of my father and me.

For Those Who Happen to Be My Children

Bradley. Hayley. Carly. Man . . . how did you get to be twenty-four, twenty-two, and sixteen, respectively? Wasn't it just yesterday that each of you was eight and actually *wanted* to hang with your old man? Well . . . it seems like yesterday to me.

Truly, the best thing for me about doing this revised edition is getting the opportunity to bestow some awesome fatherly advice to you in a printed format for everyone to see forever! And you don't have to listen to me pontificate (look it up, kids). You can read it right here at your leisure.

So here it is. The five "Greatest Hits" of my sage fatherly advice to you:

1. One day about twenty years from now you will turn around and wonder aloud, "What happened? Didn't I used to be younger than this? My dad warned me how time is fleeting when I was twenty-two and I refused to believe him." Well, guess what? It's true! As I sit here in my mid-fifties, I ask that question every single day. So, having been the first person to point out to you that life goes by quickly, I'll also advise you to look up from your electronic devices now and then. Glance around at your surroundings. Appreciate your daily existence. Tell yourself how lucky you are to have grown up and lived where you do, just minutes from the beach in Santa Monica. And recognize that the rewards you receive as you progress through life are directly proportional to your efforts.

2. As you get older and find yourselves mired in the conventional daily life—school, friends, profession, family, mortgage-paying—make sure you find time for service to humanity and the community. Whatever cause happens to float your boat.

3. The Golden Rule is not just a phrase we middle-aged folks spout off for fun. I conduct all aspects of my life by it. It's good Karma. Make it a fundamental building block for your lives and those of your future children.

4. While you engage in the thoughts and activities described above, try to find your joy in life. Whatever it is. A lot of folks go through life without knowing anything other than the daily grind. But just make sure that joy is legal. I am not sacrificing a morning swim workout to come to the police station at 5 a.m. and bail your asses out.

5. You have just *got* to watch more *Star Trek*. In all its versions and incarnations. Because *Star Trek* is good. It's really, *really* good!

For Those Who Made the Cut

In the Acknowledgments for *Beyond the Grave* in 1995 and for the 2001 revision, I had fun mentioning everyone with some connection to me. Distant relatives. Friends. Acquaintances. My children's friends. My children's friends' parents, coaches, and elementary school teachers. If I saw somebody once a week who had even a small role in my life or the lives of my children, they made it in.

Now, nearly twenty years after the original publication, those old social spheres are nearly gone, and I have practically no connection to most of those people. But I am so fortunate to have the ones that remain. These are the most meaningful people in my life, and they made me a happy (or at least, pacified) camper during the arduous process of writing this second revision. So if you happen to see your name down below, congrats! You made the cut!

My closest buddies since elementary and middle school: Bret Donnelly. Brad Wheeler. Mark Beede. Milton Stumpus. Eric Fonkalsrud. Paul Cooke.

My old law school buddies: Kenneth Aslan and Anthony Caronna.

My children's friends who have become part of my family: Hailey Sheridan. Kaile Nakao. Meghan Bradley. Karly Minderhout. Cianna Guerrero. Madeline Schulman-Clancy. Jordan Breuer.

My daughters' dedicated and hardworking softball coaches at Santa Monica High School: Debbie Skaggs and Dan Ramos.

My amazing and beautiful (inside and out) girlfriend, Kimberly Klaskin, and her daughter, Jenna.

My daughter's past and present softball team manager, who has been a voice of reason, calm, and quiet authority in the often tumultuous world of league and travel softball: Susan Croft.

My secretary, Marbellis Garcia.

My Atlanta cousins: Philip and Gilda Franklyn, and their reasonably well-behaved daughters, Stephanie, Rachel, Sarah, and Julia.

For Those Who Don't Know I Exist

I have acknowledged these two people in all prior versions of *Beyond the Grave* even though they don't know me from Adam. I'm just one guy in their respective legions of fans.

These gentlemen are the biggest cultural influences in my life, and it's *still* a thrill for me to have this platform and tell "the world" that I am a big fan. My previous mentions were more like short essays about their influence and effect on my life. For this version, I shall refrain from yet another river of praise, and simply mention names and brief attributes:

Mark Knopfler. Singer. Songwriter. Guitar virtuoso. My musical hero.

Sir Patrick Stewart. Thespian. Fun-loving and down-to-earth Brit. Owns the best portrayal of a captain of the *Enterprise*.

Once again, gentlemen, here's hoping that these Acknowledgments find you . . . because that may ultimately lead to my shaking hands with you before I die.

Preface

or

Even If You Usually Skip Prefaces, Make Sure You Read This One

There are so many professionals out there who are in the business of helping you accumulate money and property. Financial planners. Stockbrokers. Money managers. Insurance agents. Accountants. Business consultants. Arbitragers. You can't throw a stick without hitting at least one of them.

While those folks assist you with asset accumulation, I'll be the one to help you transfer those assets after you die. I am an attorney who is in the business of transferring your lifetime of accumulations to your children and/or other heirs after your death. In short, what I do is create inheritance plans.

An inheritance speaks for you from the grave. Often it will be in the form of a Will. Sometimes it takes the shape of a Living Trust. It could be as simple as a single sentence written on a cocktail napkin or as complex as a hundred-page instruction manual.

Whatever the form, an inheritance plan boils down to one purpose: It is your instructions for who inherits your money and property, when they inherit, and on what conditions they inherit.

My father, Gerald Condon, and I created thousands of inheritance plans for our clients over our combined seventy years of practice in the field. A lot of these clients have died. And being dead, they will never know the outcome of these plans. We, however, serve as their "periscope" from beyond. My father and I witnessed firsthand the impact of our advice and judgment calls on our clients' children, spouses, and other heirs.

As an inheritance-planning lawyer, I have seen a lot of these plans play out over time. Plans prepared years ago by my father, my colleagues, and me. And what have I seen? On most occasions, it is the smooth transition of money and property from client to heir, from spouse to spouse, from parent to child to grandchild. The client dies, the inheritance plan is read, the money and property are distributed, and life goes on.

Many times, however, I have seen an inheritance plan go sour, leaving bitter family legacies.

I have seen inheritance plans unintentionally result in battles between disgruntled heirs. I have watched helplessly as "sound" inheritance advice given years ago inadvertently creates chasms between children that may never be bridged. I have read inheritance instructions of Wills and Living Trusts that seemed well conceived on paper, but in practice left legacies of conflict and chaos.

And when the inheritance plan "goes bad," the lawyer who drafted that plan invariably gets pulled into the fray. As trite as this sounds, I got into this business to help people at a time when they need my kind of help. I truly revel in the feeling of being needed. But when I get sucked into the vortex of a family inheritance battle and see fingers of accusation and blame squarely pointed at me, I seriously ponder chucking this job and devoting my remaining years to my two passions: coaching youth softball and distance ocean swimming. (Yes . . . lawyers *do* have lives outside the office!)

What This Book Will Do for You

I have learned the hard way that there is a right way and a wrong way of leaving money and property to spouses, children, grandchildren, and other heirs.

You, however, do not have to learn the hard way. That is why I wrote *Beyond the Grave*, which I hope you will find invaluable. Its fundamental philosophy: **The recognition of any inheritance problem is 95 percent of the solution.** This book will open your eyes to a panorama of potential family conflicts and problems that often occur in the inheritance arena, most of which you never before considered. By identifying the potential problem areas now, you have the opportunity to establish an inheritance plan so that those problems will not arise after you die.

In other words, this book will prevent you and your family from becoming cautionary tales when you die and your money and property are divided.

Why I Wrote This Second Revised Edition

Since the original and first revised editions were published in 1995 and 2001, respectively, *Beyond the Grave* has become a rock-solid staple in the inheritance book genre. Ann Landers devoted an entire column to it. CNN and MSNBC used me as a "talking head" for segments on inheritance and estate tax matters. I appeared with Congressman Christopher Cox on John McLaughlin's *One on One* and guested on numerous "call-in" radio and television talk shows where I answered questions from studio and home audiences. I was interviewed for, or featured in, more than a hundred newspapers and magazines . . . from *Fortune* to *Dog World*.

At the time *Beyond the Grave* was published, several inheritance books already existed that had sold very well, and the conventional thinking had our book only receiving mild acceptance and sales. However, I wasn't at all surprised by its popularity. Inheritance issues are always relevant. The problems and conflicts that arise when money or an inheritance is involved are universal. It is simply human nature. This was true a thousand years ago, it is true now, and it will be true a thousand years from now.

Also, while most other inheritance-planning books concentrate on the money side, *Beyond the Grave* is the first book ever to incorporate into the inheritance equation human nature as its predominant focus—the family issues, problems, and conflicts that arise with ever-increasing frequency when spouses, children, and others inherit the family wealth. With *Beyond the Grave*'s fresh and human twist on a topic that is typically presented in a dry and numbers-based manner, it was bound to find a vast audience.

So . . . why this second revised edition? Well, it's a bit ironic. Although *Beyond the Grave*'s renown came from its human touch, the impetus for this second revision stems from changes on the numbers side of inheritance planning. Beginning in 2012, the "death tax" law went through a revolutionary change that effectively wiped out the death tax in America, and rendered obsolete much of my previous death tax advice.

Since I had to revise *Beyond the Grave* to make death-tax-related changes and additions, I decided to read it from cover to cover to ascertain whether it needed additional sprucing up. Before that read-through, I had not even looked at the book in more than a decade. It was truly surreal to read my own words years later, when my memory of writing them has long dissipated. Did you happen to see *Looper*, where Old Joe (Bruce Willis's character) has a sit-down in a diner with Young Joe, the past and younger version of himself (played by Joseph Gordon-Levitt)? For me, reading my book was just like that . . . past and present Jeff Condons meeting up and having a chat. Several times Reader Jeff could not help but exclaim to Author Jeff, "Buddy, you really nailed this one! Great job!" And Author Jeff was right there to respond, "Thanks, big guy! I remember writing that one. Came out well, didn't it?"

After talking to many readers through the years, however, it became clear that a new edition could benefit from two new sections: one that includes some cautionary tales (what not to do), and another that covers some of these important issues in a Q&A format for quick reference.

This Book Is an Easy Read . . . But Keep This in Mind as You Read It

Writing can be a very rewarding experience. But when the writing involves turning a subject as complex and tedious as inheritance planning into (one hopes) a lighthearted and entertaining read, it can also be exasperating. No one thinks of the estate lawyer as a tortured artist, but after multiple occasions of spending hours on a single paragraph attempting to be informative *and* witty, I felt like I was Van Gogh for nearly the entire combined five years I spent in writing the original and both revised editions of this book.

I can confidently say that *Beyond the Grave* succeeds in conveying invaluable inheritance information while still being an easy read. And the following, guidelines, disclaimers, and clarifications will further ease you into its content:

I Make Sweeping Generalizations

I am fond of broad and superlative statements that appear to be intended to apply universally to every reader. Of course, I know that for every person who embodies such an absolute, there is another for whom that absolute does not apply. Nonetheless, in order to help convey information and emphasize a particular point, a statement often comes across as somewhat dogmatic without reference to exceptions. Therefore, the sweeping generalization is a literary device I often employ in *Beyond the Grave*.

I Use Everyday Language to Explain Technical Ideas

Inheritance planning involves complex human and money issues. But discussing these issues in a legal manner would ensure this book's quick demise and bargain-basement status, as it would render it into a lackluster and uninteresting territory. Moreover, if I used fancy legal jargon, many readers would likely not understand what I was saying.

Therefore, I use nontechnical language to explain many technical concepts. For example:

The estate tax becomes the "death tax." Because the term "death tax" dramatically conveys the point that a wealth-transfer tax may be imposed when you die.

The person whom you appoint as your Successor Trustee to carry out instructions after your death becomes your "after-death agent." Because the term "after-death agent" conjures the image of the person you have appointed in your Living Trust who acts on your behalf after you're gone.

The special "sub-trust" known as the Qualified Terminable Interest Property Trust, which you establish in your Living Trust, becomes the "Surviving Spouse Life Estate Trust." Because the term "Surviving Spouse Life Estate Trust" simplifies the concept that this method funnels income and principal to your surviving spouse after your death.

And so on.

The Singular Means the Plural, Son Means Daughter—and Vice Versa

This book uses a question-and-answer format, with you doing the asking. Read each question as though you are sitting in my law office and addressing it to me. My response is written as though I am answering you personally.

In my responses to you, I often use the term "your child." But if you have more than one child, just mentally substitute the words "your children" where applicable. Similarly, any reference I make to "your grandchild" means *all* your grandchildren.

Likewise, when I refer to an heir in one gender, such as "he," "she," "daughter," "son," "grandson," or granddaughter," consider that reference to include both genders.

Husbands Statistically Die Before Wives . . . but Not Always

Throughout the book, particularly in parts 7 and 8, I discuss what happens when the first spouse dies and when the last spouse dies. But rather than repeat the term "first spouse to die" ad nauseam, I usually say, "when Dad dies" because Dad is, statistically, the first spouse to die. Likewise, because wives typically outlive their husbands, I use "when Mom dies" instead of constantly repeating "the last spouse to die."

However, do not be misled by this shorthand. What happens after Dad dies first *applies equally if Mom dies first*.

I Don't Tap-Dance Around Death Terminology

This book is not about death and dying. It is about recognizing and avoiding the most common problems and conflicts that arise when the family money passes from deceased parents to live children. However, any discussion of these issues necessarily involves the words "die" and "death."

Having practiced in the inheritance-planning field for my entire professional life, I know it is impossible to effectively communicate inheritance issues while tap-dancing around death terminology. Therefore, you won't see "passed away," "eternal rest," or "sent to Belize." (That last one is for us *Breaking Bad* fans.) But you will see "died." Too blunt and lacking tact? Perhaps. But ultimately, it is a more realistic and adult approach to inheritance planning.

I Am Not All Doom-and-Gloom

Throughout this book, I will make you aware of the impact of human nature, the human nature that causes the jealousies, conflicts, and rifts in "perfect families" when the inheritance is divided. Some may find this point hard to take because, well, sometimes the truth hurts.

As one client said, "Mr. Condon, why are you so doom-and-gloom? I came to you for a Living Trust, but all you've told me is that my kids can end up in conflict over my money. My kids love each other, but the way you're talking, you'd think they're constantly at each other's throats!"

If your children get along now—great! My job is to preserve that family relationship after you die. But to succeed, I must first open your eyes to the wide range of human emotions that surface in the inheritance arena. After recognizing a potential problem area, you can make an informed decision as to whether that problem needs to be addressed.

I do not criticize human nature in this book—I merely demonstrate that it is a force you must recognize when preparing your own inheritance plan.

"Money" Is Not Just Cash

Throughout this book, I use the term "the family money." It is not my intention that you limit that term to dollars or other cash assets. It is my shorthand way of describing any asset of economic value owned by Dad and/or Mom, including, but not limited to, real estate, bank assets, household furniture and furnishings, jewelry and other valuables, cars, stocks, bonds, brokerage accounts, paintings—anything you can put a price tag on.

Consult Your Own Inheritance-Planning Attorney

The book is designed to identify inheritance problems and conflicts that can arise when parents die and children divide the family money. However, because your set of circumstances may differ
from the scenarios and stories I describe, it is critical that you do
not include any of my suggestions in your own inheritance plan
without first consulting your own inheritance-planning attorney.

Part I

Introduction

1

The Journey from Innocence to Cynicism

or

You Really Don't Know Your Children— Until They Divide Their Inheritance

When I was a younger attorney, I was innocent in my approach to human nature. When my clients told me there would never be any inheritance conflicts between their children, I believed them. After all, who was I to dispute my clients' conclusions about their children?

Nothing, however, prepared me for the harsh reality of human conflict when my clients' "perfect" children divided their inheritance. Lawyers are not taught to recognize inheritance conflicts in law school. There are no "how-to" books or classes on this subject. The only way to learn about inheritance conflict is the hard way—from dealing with the children after both parents die.

Your "Perfect" Children

I typically hear this from people who attend my seminars: "Mr. Condon, I don't need this book. Your clients' children may do combat over their inheritance, but my children will not. They love each other. If an inheritance conflict comes up, they will work it out."

Let me respond this way. In every literate society, there is this saying about inheriting wealth: If you really want to know a person's true character, share an inheritance with that person.

This is sage advice. Having observed what happens between children following theirs parents' deaths, I have arrived at one indelible conclusion: Your children may be perfect—but you really don't know them until they divide your money.

Perhaps you will better understand my point after you read the story of Arthur and Hetty, the hallmark case in my journey from innocence to reality.

The Sad but True Tale of Arthur and Hetty

The voices of Arthur and Hetty are as clear today as they were twenty-five years ago. They said, "Mr. Condon, our children are absolutely perfect. They love each other, and there will never be a problem between them."

The inheritance plan I drafted for Arthur and Hetty was very basic. Everything they owned would be left equally to their three children: David, Mark, and Jennifer. About twenty years later, Arthur died; Hetty died a few years later, and their children came to my office to sign the documents that gave them their inheritance.

My meeting with David, Mark, and Jennifer could not have begun more pleasantly. They talked about how marvelous their parents were, how hard their parents worked, and how their parents sacrificed themselves and did everything they could do for their children and grandchildren. This was a conversation that would gladden the hearts of any deceased parents.

They ultimately came around to how wonderful Arthur and Hetty were to put David through Stanford undergraduate and medical school. With this comment, the room grew strangely quiet, and Jennifer's CPA husband stared off into some forlorn corner of my office.

Jennifer's husband wasn't admiring my office décor. He was making quick calculations in his head.

A few moments later, Jennifer's CPA husband announced that with books, tuition, rent, food, and fraternity dues for David's undergraduate studies, and with similar payments for medical school, Arthur and Hetty must have spent about $250,000 on David's education. On the other hand, Mark went to the local junior college and became a real estate broker. Jennifer never pursued higher education of any sort.

I sensed that the joyous and good feelings among the children were rapidly deflating. A silence ensued following the realization that Mom and Dad had spent almost a quarter of a million dollars on David's education—and literally nothing for Mark and Jennifer.

Jennifer finally broke the ice after this awkward moment. In a voice that can only be described as "cutesy," she said that if Dad and Mom had thought about it, they certainly would have equalized. They certainly would have left extra money or property to her and Mark to make up for their lavish support of David.

The implication Jennifer had made was this: If David was a morally upright person, he would now give a portion of this inheritance to his brother and sister to make up for their parents' failure to equalize.

But not a word was heard from Dr. David, and I noticed Mark and Jennifer staring at their brother. Finally, after a long, awkward silence, Jennifer's husband icily quipped to his wife, but loud enough for all to hear, "Well, I guess your parents just didn't love you as much."

So much for family loyalty and "perfect" children. To this day, David no longer speaks to his brother and sister. This chasm has transcended the generations, as David's children have no contact with Mark's and Jennifer's children.

And the grandchildren have no idea why.

The "Inheritance Gene"

If you have shared an inheritance with anyone, you may know of what I speak. Like Arthur and Hetty's "perfect" children, people simply behave differently in the inheritance arena. It is as if a special "inheritance gene" deeply recessed in the human body surfaces to change a person.

What is it about dividing an inheritance that leads to the most unpredictable and unforeseen conflicts between children? Why does dividing the inheritance breathe life into long-dormant irritations between children, daughters-in-law, and sons-in-law?

The answer came to me only after years of on-the-job training in dealing with my dead clients' children. After you are gone, your children may still be your children, but they are also people dividing your money.

And when money becomes involved, it is a whole new ball game.

Other Benchmarks on the Road to Reality

Inheritance planning is more than just preventing and resolving inheritance conflicts. It is also recognizing the numerous other inheritance problems that may rear their ugly heads.

When I started in this business, I simply could not fathom the myriad problems and risks that often surface in inheritance situations. At this point, after all the years of seeing what happens when wealth is transferred to heirs, I believe I have witnessed the entire Parade of Horribles.

I have seen the surviving spouse who lost the family money to the last caretaker.

I have seen the daughter who lost her inheritance to her husband in a divorce.

I have seen the son whose business creditors "ate up" his entire inheritance.

I have seen the son who casually disregarded the inheritance instructions made by his parents in their Living Trust.

I have seen the charity that used my client's money to buy Cadillacs for its directors.

I have seen clients' heard-earned money and property end up with their daughters-in-law's second husbands.

I have seen the children who had to give the IRS nearly one-half of their inheritance in death taxes.

I have seen the daughter who magnanimously bestowed her *entire* inheritance to a cult.

I have seen the son who was supposed to handle his disabled sibling's share of the inheritance but who instead put it in his own pocket and walked away.

As I am extremely fond of pointing out, recognizing a problem is 95 percent of its solution. In this book, I will open your eyes as mine have been opened during my transition from innocence to cynicism. I will show you the many fates that may befall your family in the inheritance arena. I will bring your attention to problems and issues in inheritance planning that you may not have otherwise considered. I will show you risks your money and property could be subject to once they are in the hands of your children, spouse, or other heirs.

By making you aware of these problems and giving you solutions, I hope to help you avoid the traps that so often hurt those whom you only sought to help.

2

Why an Inheritance Plan?

or

Seven Challenges from Beyond the Grave

Think of your Will or Living Trust as a computer—a very powerful computer. It is so powerful you can program it to send a rocket ship to the moon. But you use it only to write your checks.

My point is this: If you are like most people, you will fail to use your Will or Living Trust to its full potential. You will use it only to say who gets what. For example, if you have three children, your inheritance plan probably states that when you die, they will inherit one-third each. End of story. And when you die and your estate is distributed, your inheritance plan "dies" with you.

Your inheritance plan, however, should be more powerful than that. You should program it to live on after you die. It should be your "periscope from the grave" to accomplish the "Big Seven" goals of inheritance planning.

Goal Number 1: Program Your Inheritance Plan to Prevent Inheritance Conflicts among Your Children

Your plan should minimize the likelihood of conflicts, jealousies, bitterness, and after-death disputes between your children.

For example, take Arthur and Hetty, whom I told you about in chapter 1. They gave substantial dollars to one child for his medical education but failed to equalize between their other children. Had Arthur and Hetty used their inheritance plan to equalize, all their children might be on speaking terms today.

However, Arthur and Hetty never once gave any thought to equalizing among their children. They assumed, as do most of my clients, that each child and each son-in-law and daughter-in-law would act perfectly when they divided the inheritance.

Goal Number 2: Program Your Inheritance Plan to Protect the Inherited Money from Your Children's Potential Problems

If you are like most people, it is important to you to protect your money and property from risk. Accordingly, you have taken steps (or will in the future) to shield your assets from the human and economic problems that may arise in your life.

Doesn't it make sense to provide for the same protections once your wealth is in the hands of your children? Indeed, once your children inherit, your money and property become subject to the winds of their fates.

Your son gets a divorce? Your ex-daughter-in-law may wind up with a portion of your son's inheritance.

Your daughter runs into financial problems? Her inheritance may be "eaten up" by creditors.

Your son's business fails? His inheritance may fall into the hands of the bankruptcy trustee.

Your daughter causes an auto accident and has insufficient

insurance? The victim may look to her inherited money as a source to satisfy the claim.

Your son succumbs to a serious illness? With today's high cost of health care, the doctors and hospitals may eat up his entire inheritance.

Your son is addicted to drugs? His inheritance may end up with the pusher.

Your daughter is financially immature? She may lose her inheritance in bad investments, give it to her newfound friends, or blow it at Nordstrom's.

Losing your hard-earned money and property in any of these ways is not what you have in mind. To combat these possibilities, your Will or Living Trust should not die when you die. It must be your "periscope from the grave" to protect your money and property once it is in your children's hands.

The result will be that when your child dies, whatever is left of the inheritance will be around for your grandchildren (or other heirs).

Goal Number 3: Program Your Inheritance Plan to Ensure It Will Be Carried Out

Every inheritance plan requires you to name an agent who will carry out your inheritance instructions after your death. This "after-death agent" is your Executor (if a Will) or a Successor Trustee (if a Living Trust). You are free to choose whomever you wish as your agent. If you are like most of my clients, however, you will probably select one or more of your children.

But, what if the person whom you have entrusted to carry out your plan chooses not to do it your way?

You leave $20,000 to your son with the instruction to deliver it to your granddaughter when she reaches twenty-five. When your granddaughter attains that age, will the money be there for her . . . or will your son have used it for "family expenses"?

You leave your synagogue a share of your assets. Although

that is your wish, it may not be the wish of your daughter, who does not want to lose a portion of "her money" to a cause to which she does not subscribe.

You want your drug-addict son to receive his rightful share of the inheritance, but you do not want your hard-earned wealth to end up with his dealer. So you leave your son's share to your daughter with the instruction that she must manage it for his benefit. Using your son's money for his food, clothing, and medical needs certainly meets that requirement. But will she also decide that your son benefits when his money is used to pay for a trip to Rio during Carnival for her and her boyfriend?

There are many levels of inheritance planning. But whether you have a 200-page Living Trust prepared by the world's top lawyer or a Will handwritten by you on a cocktail napkin, upon your death all plans are equal. The effectiveness of any inheritance plan is entirely dependent on the choices made by the person you name as your after-death agent. If the person whom you have appointed to carry out your inheritance plan chooses—for whatever reason—to disregard your instructions, then you have no plan.

By becoming aware of this possibility, however remote it may seem, you can make an informed decision on who will serve as your after-death agent.

Goal Number 4: Program Your Inheritance Plan to Protect Your Assets for Your Surviving Spouse

If you are married, you and your spouse most likely hold title to your house, your stocks, your bank accounts, and your other assets jointly. It is your expectation that when you die, your half of those assets will automatically go to your surviving spouse.

But what will happen to your money and property after your surviving spouse dies? If you are like most people, you expect that it will go to your children (or other heirs). However, after thirty-five years in the inheritance-planning business, I can tell you with all confidence that this expectation often does not meet the test of reality.

Your surviving spouse may remarry and your half of the family wealth may end up with his or her new spouse.

Your surviving spouse may remarry and have additional children (or stepchildren), all of whom might share in your half.

Unscrupulous third parties may persuade your surviving spouse to part with the family wealth.

Your children may pressure your surviving spouse for an "early inheritance."

Your surviving spouse may become physically or mentally incapacitated, leaving him or her and the family wealth at the mercy of the "last caretaker" or the "final friends."

Your surviving spouse may not have the capability to manage the family wealth.

Once you become aware of these potential "surviving spouse" problems (no matter how remote they may seem to you now), you can incorporate the appropriate countermeasures in your inheritance plan.

Goal Number 5: Program Your Inheritance Plan to Reduce (or Eliminate) the Death Tax

When you die and your children inherit your assets, the IRS may make your children pay a special tax known as the "death tax." This tax is not imposed because you died; it is a tax on the *transfer of your wealth* after your death.

Throughout your life, you have paid more than enough income tax to your country, and perhaps to your state and your city. That you may have to pay more taxes when your children inherit your money and property is truly the final insult. If you are rich enough, the death tax may average 40 *percent* of all the assets you own when you die.

If you are like most of my clients, you want more of your money and property to go to your children and less to the IRS.

Goal Number 6: Program Your Inheritance Plan to Prevent the IRS from Getting Two Bites of the Apple

It is bad enough that the IRS may get a bite of your money and property when your children inherit it. However, it gets worse. When your children die, whatever is left of their inheritance will be taxed again. The result is, when your children die, the IRS could end up with 75 percent of your money and property, with only 25 percent passing to your grandchildren.

Planning to reduce the death tax only at your death is like getting two strikes in baseball or three downs in football. To have the most complete and effective anti-death-tax plan, you should take steps to prevent the IRS from getting two bites of the inheritance apple.

Goal Number 7: Program Your Inheritance Plan to Keep Your Children and Property Out of the Probate Court

The chief purpose of probate is merely to transfer your money and property after you die to your children (or other heirs). The probate judge is your "out-of-the-grave" agent who has one job: to authorize the transfer of your real estate and other assets after you die.

Probate, however, does not come cheap. Between the attorneys' fees, executor fees, court costs, publishing fees, filing fees, and appraisal fees, using the probate court to transfer what you own to your children can consume, on the average, 4 to 6 percent of your estate.

In addition, the probate process, like any court procedure, is time-consuming. The average probate process, if there are no problems, can last from nine months to two years.

Surprisingly, some people do not care whether or not their children have to go through probate. At my seminars, I never fail to hear at least one attendee say, "Why should I care if my children have to go through probate? After all, I will be dead. If they have to go through hoops to get their inheritance, then it will just be their problem."

Obviously, that attendee does not care. However, if you are like most people, you do care, and you want to spare your children the expenses and hassles of the probate process.

3

If You Do Nothing, the Law Will Do It for You

or

Everybody Procrastinates—but Don't Wait Until You Are on Your Deathbed

Why do so many people never get around to making their inheritance plan? More than a few people have told me such planning will bring them closer to their mortality. And many have said that paying a lawyer to do anything is evidence of a decaying society. But often, the reason is pure and simple procrastination.

If you do not have your inheritance plan, I have no "magic words" to get you to move to action. All I can tell you is the three consequences that will show up after you die.

Consequence Number 1: Here Come the Lawyers

Do not fear when your coffin is lowered into the cold, heartless ground. You will not be alone. Why? Because when you are buried, buried with you will be title to your real estate and all other assets you owned in your individual name.

How will your heirs get title out of your grave? They have to bring a lawsuit. This lawsuit is called "probate," and its sole purpose is to get the probate judge to authorize the transfer of your assets and wealth from you to your heirs.

Unless your heirs are versed in the particulars of the probate process, they will hire a lawyer to steer them through. This lawyer may charge, on average, 3 percent of what you owned when you died.

This is why lawyers call probate "the Lawyers' Retirement Fund."

Consequence Number 2: The Parade of Horribles

In chapters 1 and 2, I pointed out the parade of horribles that often occur in the inheritance arena. Being aware of these problems, you can use your Will or Living Trust to prevent any inheritance problems or conflicts from occurring in your family.

When you die without an inheritance plan, you have squandered this vital opportunity. Of course, you will not be affected, because you will be dead. However, your spouse, children, or other heirs will live on to witness the results of your failure to address and resolve these problems.

Consequence Number 3: The Law Tells You What Your Inheritance Plan Is

If you do not have an inheritance plan that says who gets what, the law will step in after you die and do it for you. In other words, by doing nothing, you have made a decision. You have decided to rely on the law to write your inheritance instructions.

Does the law know what you have in mind?

I remember my client Ruth, who was a widow with three children. Ruth's only asset was her home. She owned it with her first husband. When he died, it belonged entirely to Ruth. A year after her husband died, Ruth married Bert, and they spent the rest of their lives together living in Ruth's house. Although Ruth loved her second husband, she refused to put Bert's name on the title to her house. She maintained it as her separate property.

When Ruth contemplated an inheritance plan, she had to decide how she would leave her house. She had a number of alternatives. She could:

Leave her home to Bert, depriving her children of an inheritance.

Let Bert live in the home until he dies (or a shorter period of time), making her children wait before they get their inheritance.

Leave the home to her children, hoping they let Bert live there until he dies.

Ruth ran her mind ragged debating these alternatives. Finally, weary and fearful of offending either Bert or her children, she decided not to decide. She would do nothing. No Will. No Living Trust.

When Ruth died, the law made the decision for her. The law gave most of the title to Ruth's children, with Bert receiving only a small portion. Her children then went to court to force a sale of the house.

Bert spent the rest of his life in a retirement home.

Were Ruth's children cruel? Perhaps. Were her children wrong? Absolutely not. Her children were entitled to their money and they wanted it.

By not making a decision, Ruth made a decision.

Part II

Preventing Inheritance Conflicts Between Your Children

4

The Unequal Inheritance

or

If You Don't Want the Blame— Treat Your Children the Same

1. "My successful son tells me he and his wife will never forgive me if I leave him less because he is successful."

If you leave more to your "needier" child and less to your "successful" child, you may destroy any chance of maintaining family harmony between them after your death.

Rewarding Failure—Punishing Success

Mr. and Mrs. Wayne have two children. Their son is a successful medical doctor. Their daughter and her husband are employed but have difficulty making ends meet.

After a great deal of thought, the Waynes decided that because their daughter had a greater financial need, they wanted to leave 75 percent of their money and property to her and only 25 percent to their doctor son.

"Mr. Condon," said Mrs. Wayne with all confidence, "we believe this plan will achieve economic justice between our children.

After all, our son doesn't need the money, but our daughter does."

Good plan, right? Wrong! They had forgotten to consider what their son would think.

"Mr. and Mrs. Wayne," I responded, "unequal economic circumstances do not justify treating your children unequally. Sure, your daughter will be happy, but your son will be resentful. After both of you die, this plan may create a rift between your children—and they may never speak to each other again. And what's more, this conflict may transcend to your grandchildren."

The Waynes were very upset with my response. They were absolutely convinced their plan was right and nobody, not even the lawyer, was going to change their minds. And they let me know this in no uncertain terms.

"Mr. Condon, our children love each other," said Mr. Wayne in a harsh, adamant tone. "They would never let money come between them. They would never let money get in the way of family loyalty. Besides, this is our money and we can do whatever we want."

I could feel the Waynes' resentment of me growing by the second. But having seen what happens between children who are left unequal inheritances, I just could not stop myself from further comment.

"You are correct, Mr. Wayne. It's your money and you can do whatever you want. But let me put it this way. Pretend you are your son. In high school, you worked diligently to get good grades and were rewarded with a college scholarship. During college, you strived for high marks and worked part-time so you could enter medical school. Ultimately, you graduated college, graduated medical school, and became a successful doctor, bringing joy and honor to your parents.

"How would you feel, Mr. Wayne, if after achieving all this your parents left you less because you were successful? I'll tell you how you would feel. You would be hurt and angry. You would feel your parents had punished your success. And if you talk with your son about your plan, he would tell you the same thing."

The Waynes were unimpressed with my hypothetical situation.

They stood up, said they would get back to me after talking it over with their son, and abruptly walked out of my office. I, however, knew they would not return. They would find another attorney who would not question their inheritance plan.

A few hours later, Mrs. Wayne called me. The tone of her voice was no longer bold. It was sad. She and her husband had spoken with their son about their plan and were vastly disillusioned with his response.

Her successful son, she told me, was enraged with the idea that he would inherit less. "How could you even think of doing this to me," the son yelled at his mother. "I worked so hard for you. I studied when you asked me to study. I made something of my life. And now you want to punish my success."

Shattered Perceptions

Most parents want to do the right thing for their children and make them happy. And, naturally, parents want to help the child who they feel needs more help. But the successful child's argument is hard to refute. Why should his parents punish his success and reward his sister's failure?

(In addition, the economic disparity between children may change. The successful child could experience a reversal of fortune due to ill health, bad investments, divorce, remarriage, or for any other reason. And the needier child may someday climb the ladder of success.)

Mr. and Mrs. Wayne's perception of their "perfect and loving" children had been shattered. For the first time, they realized family love did not transcend the division of money. With their son's shrill voice still resonating in their ears, the Waynes reconsidered. In their inheritance plan, they left their children equal inheritances.

After Mr. and Mrs. Wayne died, I had the opportunity to speak with their daughter. She told me she was still "needy" and could have used a larger inheritance. But she agreed with her parents' plan. If she had inherited more just because she needed more, her brother, whom she loved dearly, would have never spoken to her again.

Do You Care?

Some people couldn't care less about the consequences of leaving an unequal inheritance to their children. Their attitude, basically, is, "I couldn't care less what happens after I'm gone."

But if you are like most parents, you do care. Whatever material things we have been blessed with, our children remain our most precious possessions. During our lives, we do what we can to help them maintain a warm and loving sibling relationship. And we also want to know that our children and grandchildren will remain "family" after we are gone.

Talk to Your Children First

If you plan to leave your children an unequal inheritance because of economic disparity between them, talk with them first.

Bringing this plan into the open allows them to ventilate their feelings and gives you the opportunity to gauge their reaction.

How will *your* needier child react? He will, of course, be happy to learn that he will receive a larger inheritance. But once he becomes aware of the family consequences, he may insist, to his detriment, that you treat all your children equally.

What will *your* successful child's response be? I assure you that nine times out of ten, it will be anger and incredulousness. If this occurs, you should reconsider your plan.

On occasion, clients will report back that I was wrong. Their successful child, in a beautiful gesture, agreed that the needier child should get more of the parents' wealth. That pronouncement, however, is usually nothing more than a "beau geste." Generously agreeing, while Dad and Mom are alive, to inherit less is not quite the same as the harsh reality of inheriting less after they die.

Solution: Treat Your Children Equally

If you care about maintaining family harmony after your death, leave your money and property to your children equally, regardless of their economic circumstances or their beau geste declarations.

Even the most seemingly harmless inequality can cause problems. One time, a medical doctor conferred with me about her own inheritance plan. During our meeting, she bitterly recounted how her sister wound up with her mother's engagement ring.

I am sure this ring was a trivial matter to the doctor's mother. Yet even though her mother had died twenty years before, even with the doctor's high level of education and personal discipline, her memory of this unequal treatment still generated feelings of anger and frustration. And because of this ring, she believes to this day that her mother loved her sister more.

These are the emotions of unequal inheritances that have not diminished with the passage of time.

Alternative Solutions

If you truly want your needier child to have more, there are methods you can employ to accomplish this goal that may be more palatable to your successful child.

Make Small Lifetime Gifts to Your Needier Child

While you are alive, give small amounts of cash or other property to your needier child. Chances are, making these small incremental gifts will not be an affront to your successful child.

Give an Insurance Policy to Your Needier Child

In your inheritance plan, leave your successful child and needier child an equal inheritance. But while you are alive, take out a life insurance policy on your life and give this policy to your needier child. When you die, your needier child will get the death benefits on top of the inherited assets.

Of course, this life insurance policy will result in your needier child getting more after you die. But because you pay for this policy while you are alive, and because your inheritance plan treats your children equally, this method may be less offensive to your successful child.

---

2. "We have a son and a daughter. We gave our son money so he could start a business. Our daughter, however, keeps asking us when she is going to get a similar gift."

As parents, we do not intentionally treat our children economically different during our lives. We help our children when we perceive they need help. We may give more to one of our children for tuition, doctor bills, business needs, car repair, a down payment on a house, or for any number of reasons.

Whatever the reason, we simply want to do the best we can for our children at the time their needs arise.

When we give money to our children, we usually do so without "keeping a scorecard." We do not think about giving the same amount to our other children at the same time. In fact, as time marches on, we may have long forgotten these money gifts.

Well, you may not have kept a scorecard. But who do you think did not fail to keep score?

Our other children, of course.

Our children's perception of equal economic treatment is not limited to what they inherit. They will measure equal treatment by what we have given them over the course of our lives.

I regrettably advise my clients that when we die, each of our children will look back at all the lifetime gifts we gave to him or her. Each child will add up these gifts and compare the total to the lifetime gifts we made to his or her siblings. If the overall tally does not result in roughly equal lifetime gifts to each child, our generous intentions may leave behind an unexpected, but nevertheless horrendous, conflict.

Failing to equalize lifetime gifts is one of the most significant sources of dispute between my clients' children. Why such emotional upheaval? One child explained it to me this way: "My parents must not have loved me as much as my sister. While they were alive, they gave more to my sister than to me."

Solution: Equalize During Your Lifetime

Step back and think about prior gifts of money or property you have made to your children. If you made more gifts to one child, I strongly suggest that you make rough equalization while you are alive. If, ten years ago, you gave your daughter $25,000, now is the time to give each of your other children a comparable sum.

If you choose not to equalize during your lifetime, gather your children (and their spouses) and let them learn of your reasons. Perhaps you cannot afford to equalize. Or perhaps there was some compelling reason for the gift to one child.

For the most part, children will act mature when confronted with this "confession" from their parents—and will understand this is simply "the way it is."

If you believe this news will distress your children, tell them anyway. No matter what their response is, you must not die with this issue unresolved. The problem will not go away; it will fester until your children no longer speak to each other.

If you raise the issue now, your children have the opportunity to ventilate their feelings. You can then defuse this potentially volatile situation.

---

3. "I gave $50,000 to my daughter to buy a house. My son tells me that I should give him a similar amount. I know that would be the fair thing to do, but I cannot afford it. To make it up to my son, I will leave him an extra $50,000 in my inheritance plan."

Clients who do not equalize during their lives often attempt to make up the difference after they die. If they made an early lifetime gift to one child of $50,000, they leave their other child an extra $50,000.

However, I have learned that equalizing after death simply does not work.

While I was interviewing Mr. and Mrs. Lawrence for their inheritance plan, they told me they recently gave $50,000 to their daughter, Jane, for a house down payment. They wanted to give their son, Dan, an equal amount but could not afford to do so.

I thought the solution was simple enough. The Lawrences would use their inheritance plan to equalize. When they died, Dan would simply inherit $50,000 more than Jane.

Twenty-five years later, both Mr. and Mrs. Lawrence had passed and Dan finally got his $50,000 gift. But when I met with Dan and Jane in my office, Dan bitterly complained to me that his parents had been terribly unfair. Inheriting $50,000 extra after his parents died was not the same as Jane receiving $50,000 twenty-five years before they died.

What Dan meant was this: Jane had the use of her $50,000 for twenty-five years. By the time both parents were dead, her $50,000 down payment had appreciated to $350,000. Had Dan received $50,000 at the time Jane received hers, he, too, would have a house or other investments worth $350,000.

Dan was right. His parents failed to foresee the impact of inflation and appreciation on Jane's lifetime gift. They should have left Dan an extra $300,000 to achieve true equalization between their children.

Dan ended his mathematical display with an offer to his sister. "Had Dad and Mom thought about it," Dan said, "they would have wanted fairness between us. But it's not too late, Jane. Fairness can still be achieved if you give me $300,000 from your share of the inheritance. That would put us on a level playing field."

I leave to your imagination Jane's response to her brother's suggestion. Dan and Jane, whose relationship the Lawrences described to me as loving and close, clashed over this issue and have not spoken to each other since.

Solution: Estimate How Much the Gift Has Appreciated in Value, Then Leave a Like Amount to Your Other Child

If you have made a gift of money or property to one child that has since appreciated substantially (or will appreciate in the future), how do you spare your other child from this type of conflict?

Quite simply, you have to predict the future.

Estimate the future value of the lifetime gifts you made to one child. This estimate doesn't have to be made with scientific, pinpoint accuracy. Your goal is to simply make an educated guess as to what the gift will be worth when you die.

Then, in your inheritance plan, provide that your other child shall receive this guessed amount off the top. The rest of your wealth will be equally divided between all of your children.

This solution will result in roughly equal treatment for all your children, but it may make no sense to the child who received your early lifetime gift. Having had the benefits of the gift so long ago, he may be left wondering why you have left him less. Therefore, consider discussing this plan with all your children now. Remind your children about the prior gift you made to one child and point out your goal of achieving fairness among all of them.

If You Cannot Afford to Equalize After You Die . . .

Sometimes, it may be impossible for you to achieve economic justice. If you gave $50,000 to your daughter twenty years ago, and inflation has since booted its value to $250,000, you simply may not have enough wealth to leave $250,000 to each of your other children.

If you do not have enough funds to equalize, the solution is to use someone else's funds. Let someone else pay your other children the like amount.

Who would this someone else be? The life insurance company.

Let the insurance company compensate your other children for the early (and now appreciated) lifetime gift you made to one child.

How this solution works is really quite simple. You give money to your other children so they can take out an insurance policy on your (and/or your spouse's) life. The amount of the premiums are modest compared to the death benefits. When you (and/or your spouse) die, the life insurance company will pay the death benefits to your other children tax-free.

4. "Most of my wealth is in two apartment buildings. To prevent management conflicts between my two sons, I plan to give each son a separate apartment property."

Leaving your children separate assets may keep them from hating each other. But fluctuating values of the assets after you die may result in unequal gifts.

I remember Mr. and Mrs. Kelly telling me about their sons, Tom and Robert, who disagreed on everything just for the sake of disagreement. The Kellys realized that leaving each son a 50 percent interest in each apartment property would create problems. Their sons' short fuses would render them incapable of making joint management decisions.

I suggested the Kellys consider a "one-for-Tom, one-for-Robert" approach. This plan would provide that when the Kellys died, apartment building A would go to Tom, and apartment building B would be left to Robert. Each son would have his own building free of the other's control.

About fifteen years later, both Mr. and Mrs. Kelly died, and everything could not have gone more smoothly. Each son became the owner of a separate apartment building. Each son managed his own property without sibling conflict. Each had a building of roughly equal value and equity. This one-for-Tom, one-for-Robert approach appeared to be the perfect solution.

So I thought.

Five years later, Tom engaged me to establish his own inheritance plan. During our exchange of pleasantries, I told Tom how pleased I was that his parents' plan had worked out so well.

Tom's response was not quite what I expected. Although he and his brother had disagreed occasionally, they always maintained a cordial relationship. But, he said, because of his parents' one-for-Tom, one-for-Robert approach, he and his brother became permanently estranged.

Tom explained that in the five years since his parents' death, his property doubled in value. Robert's property, however, only increased slightly. Because of this unintended unequal inheritance, Robert received the short end of the stick and became overwhelmingly jealous of his richer brother.

The Kellys' legacy of love became of legacy of animosity and bitterness. In their attempt to prevent one conflict, they inadvertently created another one. To this day, Tom and Robert, their wives, and their children no longer speak to each other.

Solution: Let Each Child Share the Risks and Benefits

As a general rule, do not leave a specific property to each child. What starts out as equal in value at the time you die may not remain equal years later. Instead, leave each child an equal share of each property so they will share the upswings and downswings of both.

This advice also applies to an inheritance of securities. For example, say you leave stock in Corporation A to your son and stock of equal value in Corporation B to your daughter. After you die, the value of stock B triples. The result is that your children unexpectedly end up with an unequal inheritance.

Exceptions

Like any general rule, there are exceptions. You may want to leave a certain property to one child because, for example, your child makes his home in that property. Or your children are like Tom and Robert and will simply not be happy co-owning their inherited assets. The exceptions are many, but whatever the reason, you may want to leave each child a separate property.

However, as noted above in the case of the Kellys, this plan can result in your children receiving an unequal inheritance. Is this risk justified? This is a judgment call you and your attorney will have to make.

---

5. "My Will leaves one rental property to my son and one rental property to my daughter. But last year, I sold the property that was going to my daughter."

If it's not there when you die, I assure you that you will have destroyed any relationship between your children.

Say your Will leaves property one to your son and property two to your daughter. You sell property two before you die and spend the sale proceeds.

What happens when property two is no longer there when you die? Depending on the inheritance laws in your state, you may have inadvertently cut your daughter out of her inheritance. In other words, you son gets his property and your daughter may end up with nothing!

Will your son generously give a portion of his inherited property to his sister? I doubt it. I have met at least a hundred children who were the victims of such circumstances. In all these situations, not once did the "non-cut-out" child share his inheritance with his "cut-out" sibling.

The result is you have created an irreversible inheritance conflict between your children.

How could you let this happen? How could you sell your daughter's intended property without changing your Will to make it up? It was easy. You forgot about the Will, or you procrastinated changing it, then you died.

Solution 1: Change Your Inheritance Plan Before You Die

If your inheritance plan leaves a certain property (or other item) to a certain child, and you no longer own that property when you die, you may have inadvertently cut that child out of an inheritance. To guard against this problem, change your inheritance plan so that your property goes to all your children equally.

Solution 2: The Backup Plan

Leaving a specific property or item to one child may eliminate co-ownership problems between siblings. However, there is the risk of inadvertently cutting out that child if you do not own that property when you die.

You can eliminate this risk by providing a backup plan in your Will or Living Trust. You provide that if a certain property you leave to one child is no longer there when you die, then all of your wealth will be shared equally between your children.

Solution 3: Substitute Cash for the Sold Property

If you leave a specific property to a specific child and you sell that property before you die, leave a cash substitute. The amount of the cash should be roughly equal to the value of the sold property.

5

The Power Struggle

or

If Your Children Didn't Get Along Sharing Their Toys, How Will They Comanage Their Inherited Property?

---

1. "Of my three children, I plan to make my oldest daughter the Successor Trustee of my Living Trust. Won't this make it easier to administer my Trust estate when I die?"

Probably not!

In your mind, making your daughter your "after-death administrator" makes perfect sense because too many cooks spoil the broth.

But what will your other children think about not being selected? Having excluded them from power, you have created a breeding ground for suspicion and jealousy. How is she managing the postdeath affairs? Is she doing it right? Is she taking some of the wealth for her own use? Is she charging a fee? If so, how much? And whatever she's charging, it's unfair!

Almost inevitably, your out-of-power children will want to assert some influence over your daughter. They may challenge every administrative action she takes and every decision she makes. If your daughter rebuffs her siblings, then come the conflicts, lawyers, litigation, and all you attempted to avoid in the first place.

And fanning the flames of these conflicts may be the feelings of your other children that you did not love them as much, you did not trust them as much, or you did not think they were smart enough to do the job.

Solution: Make All Your Children Successor Cotrustees of Your Living Trust (or Coexecutors of Your Will)

Avoiding these power struggles is simple. Appoint all your children as Successor Cotrustees. This allows each of them to participate in the trust administration. If a child does not wish to serve as Cotrustee, he has the right to decline, withdraw, or resign. Let the decision to serve be theirs rather than yours.

Having all your children as Cotrustees will not compound the complexity of the postdeath administration. In fact, it will do just the opposite. Why? Because your children are anxious to receive their share of the inheritance. All of them know that if they delay the process, it will delay getting their share. Cooperating with each other will get them in their money sooner.

Of course, many circumstances may justify appointing fewer than all children. For example, if you tell me your other child is mentally disabled, financially immature, a drug addict, or permanently estranged from the family, I will recommend that you not include that child as a Cotrustee.

A Geography Lesson

A client may readily accept my suggestion to appoint all his children as Cotrustees but may point out the difficulty of physically getting all his children to act together. As one client told me, "Mr. Condon, one child lives in Zimbabwe, Africa, while one lives in Vancouver, Canada, and the other lives close to us. Does the distance between them make it more sensible to appoint the closest-to-home child as our sole Trustee?"

No. Do not let geography prevent you from appointing all your children as Cotrustees. After all, they have to come home for the funeral. And even if they don't show up, time and distance can be eliminated by fax, telephone, or overnight mail.

Whatever problems distance and geography present, they are infinitely less serious than the divisiveness of choosing one child over the others.

What If the Other Children Say "It's Okay"?

Occasionally, a client's children all agree that one sibling should be the sole Trustee. There are many reasons for this, notably that one has more business experience. The issue, however, is not who would do the best job. The issue is, would this agreement eliminate the normal human suspicions and conflicts that arise when one child has sole power and the others are on the outside looking in?

If your children agree on one of them serving as sole Successor Trustee, I would still advise you to appoint them all. When you die, each child can then decide to participate in the post-death administration. If one child chooses not to participate, that child has the option to resign.

---

2. "My wife and I have one apartment building and three children. To prevent them from deadlocking over management decisions, we plan to make our oldest son the boss."

Mr. and Mrs. Greenfield had benefited from a surefire investment strategy: Buy real estate and live long enough. Shortly after World War II, they bought an apartment building with $25,000 down on a $100,000 purchase price. Forty years later, inflation had increased the value to over $1 million.

The Greenfields had three children and wanted to leave them the apartment building in equal shares. They also wanted a plan that would prevent their children from selling the building. They wanted to keep the building in the family bloodline and preserve it for their future generations. But this plan could be defeated if they left the building outright to their three children. Why? Because each child would be an owner of a one-third share. As an equal co-owner, each child would have the right to force a sale of the building through a court procedure, even against the wishes of his siblings.

But there was a way to achieve the Greenfields' goal. Instead of leaving the building outright to their children, they would leave it to a special Trust. This Trust would "live on" after Mr. and Mrs. Greenfield died, preserving the building in the bloodline until the death of the last Greenfield child.

As part of this inheritance plan, a Trustee would be in charge of the building after the Greenfields died. This Trustee, for all intents and purposes, would be the "boss" of the building. The Trustee would manage and operate the property and make the broad policy decisions.

Because of the children's past connection to the property, I assumed that each would serve as a Cotrustee. Mr. Greenfield, however, was adamant there be only one Trustee.

"I'm not a smart man, Mr. Condon," Mr. Greenfield said. "But there is one thing I do know: Too many cooks spoil the broth. There should only be one boss. Having three bosses in charge will only lead to deadlocks. And where there is deadlock, there are lawyers, courts, litigation, and lots of money out the window. With one boss, there is no deadlock."

There was wisdom in Mr. Greenfield's thinking. Getting three bosses to agree on any management decision could create problems. Why not keep it simple? Put one child in charge and avoid any potential deadlocks and complexities.

"The Boss"

The Greenfields wanted their eldest son as the Trustee of the apartment-building Trust. Sixteen years later, Mr. and Mrs. Greenfield died, and the eldest son became the sole "boss" of the building.

Initially, the other two children felt left out. But the oldest brother was not an uncompromising, power-hungry ruler. He consulted with his brothers on all management decisions. Eventually, all the Greenfield children became comfortable with this arrangement, until the day came when the eldest son wanted to borrow against the building for major improvements.

The others were against this decision. A bigger mortgage meant a bigger mortgage payment, leaving less net rental income. By this time, each child was counting on the existing level of rental income and did not want it reduced.

Ignoring his siblings' objections, the older son began the process of obtaining the loan. The other Greenfield children went to court to restrain their older brother from proceeding.

The problem that their parents had feared and hoped to prevent had come to fruition. The Greenfields believed making their eldest son the boss would keep their children out of the courtroom. However, their children spent two years in litigation and thousands of dollars in legal fees.

In order to end the lawsuit and save further expense, the brothers agreed to sell the property and divide the proceeds, a result completely opposite from their parents' wishes.

Solution: Share the Power

The Greenfields' case shows that you will not prevent sibling conflicts by delegating all management authority to one child. Inevitably, your out-of-power children may gang up on the child with the power. In fact, putting one child in charge in and of itself invites lawsuits by the out-of-power siblings.

The best solution is to simply make sure the power is shared equally. Put all your children in charge of the family real estate or business—and let there be majority rule. Having the opportunity to vote, your children will most likely accept and stand by the vote of the majority.

However, if there is no majority to carry a decision forward, or even if your children reach a majority, one dissatisfied child can still gum up the works through litigation. Hell hath no fury like a scorned sibling or business partner.

Therefore, do not assume your children can work it out themselves. If your children will co-own or comanage the family real estate or business, it is essential to help them resolve their conflicts without rushing to the courthouse. You can program dispute-resolution mechanisms in your inheritance plan that will force your children to arbitrate or mediate any dispute.

Your children may not be happy having to abide by the decision of a third party. But remember that inherent in any co-ownership or comanagement relationship is the potential for conflict and deadlock. Having a third party intervene is certainly preferable to litigating every dispute.

---

3. "My wife and I have two apartment buildings and two children who do not get along with each other in money matters. If they become co-owners of each property, we're certain it will lead to conflicts and lawsuits. To keep them from suing each other, we plan on leaving a separate building to each child."

In chapter 4, I related the story of Mr. and Mrs. Kelly, who had a similar concern. They had two apartment buildings and two combative sons, Tom and Robert. These parents feared if their sons became co-owners in each property, there would be constant deadlock. To prevent these sibling power struggles, the Kellys left one building to Tom and one to Robert.

The Kellys had intended their plan to preserve their son's relationship. Instead, it permanently drove them apart. The unintended consequence of that plan was that Tom ultimately received a much greater inheritance than Robert. When the Kellys died, each building had roughly the same value, but Tom's building later tripled in value while Robert's realized only a mild increase.

Exceptions: When to Share the Power

In the light of the Kelly case, I advise you not to leave a specific property to a specific child. However, there are a few exceptions.

For example, you have children with a history of sibling rivalry. They cannot agree on anything to save their lives. If they co-own their inherited property, even the simplest decision will be rife with conflict and deadlock.

Or, say your children have different economic goals. One child wants to sell the building and use the proceeds to buy a home. One child may wish to keep the building. Another may prefer stock investments over real estate. If they co-own their inheritance, none of your children can follow his dream.

If you believe these co-ownership problems may arise, then don't make your children co-owners. Instead, leave each child a separate property. With this plan, each child can manage his own property without sibling interference and follow his own economic destiny.

Do Not Forget About Equalization

Your properties may have roughly the same value or equity when you establish your inheritance plan. Do not assume, however, that the values will remain equal when you die. A lot can happen between the time you sign your Will or Trust and your death. Economic circumstances could drive one property up in value while only modestly increasing the values of the others. Or equities can change because you mortgaged or refinanced one of your properties.

If the values or equity are different when you die, you will have left unequal gifts to each child.

Equalizing Unequal Values

If one child will inherit a property with a higher value or equity, you can include methods in your inheritance plan to even up the difference in value.

One method is to provide that after your death, your children must hire a licensed real estate appraiser to calculate the difference in value between the properties. Then the child with the higher-valued property must even up this difference from his share of other inherited assets. You should also provide that if there are insufficient assets in your estate to equalize, the child with the higher-valued property must come up with his own "even-up money."

For example, your son inherits a property worth $100,000 more than the property inherited by your daughter. To equalize, your daughter must receive $100,000 from your other estate assets. However, if your estate has only $25,000 in other assets, your son must pay the remaining $75,000 value difference either in cash or an installment note.

6

Don't Die with Your Children
Owing You Money

or

"I Asked for My Money Back—Now I Don't Get to See My Grandchildren"

---

1. "Fifteen years ago, we loaned our son and his wife $50,000 for a house down payment. They guaranteed they would pay us back. For the first year, the checks were timely. Then payments started arriving late. Now, they make no payments at all. What do I do now?"

From the Stone Age tribes of New Guinea to the highest social classes in America, parents have shared a common experience: A loan of money to a child, whether the currency is beads, cows, or cash, often becomes a gift.

A parent making a loan to a child always receives an enthusiastic promise to repay. But in a majority of these cases, the child is expressing the ideal rather than the intended reality. Eventually, for both parent and child, repayment becomes a disappearing obligation and a receding memory.

The Cutlers—How a Loan Becomes a Gift

The Cutlers' son and daughter-in-law wanted to buy their dream house. Without financial help, however, it would be an impossible dream.

Mr. and Mrs. Cutler wanted to help their son, but they were the type of persons who believed there was no such thing as a free lunch. They had lived through the Depression of the 1930s and saved every penny to buy their first house. Why should their son be any different?

The Cutlers loaned their son and daughter-in-law $50,000 for the house down payment. Ever so grateful, their son and his wife enthusiastically promised they would "never miss a payment."

In the beginning, all went well. On the first of each month, they found their son's check in their mailbox. In the second year, the checks arrived later and later. Since payments were still coming each month, the Cutlers did not become unduly concerned.

By the third year, payments were, at best, sporadic. In the fourth year, there were no payments at all.

The Cutlers wanted some answers but were reluctant to forcibly press the issue. All they could muster was the standard innocuous inquiry: "By the way, son, did you get a chance to send this month's check?"

Instead of dollars, all the Cutlers ever received was a different excuse:

"The kids need braces."
"We haven't had a vacation in years."
"The car needed fixing again."
"We overcharged on our credit cards again."
"We forgot."

After a few months of these exchanges, the family gatherings and telephone calls were less frequent, leaving the Cutlers little opportunity to see or talk to their grandchildren. When their son and daughter-in-law did visit, awkwardness filled the air. Stress was created from the unspoken discussion about loan repayment.

By continuing to ask for "this month's payment," the Cutlers were pushing their son into lying and had driven the family apart. Afraid of making the wedge permanent, the Cutlers never pressed the issue again.

Their son assumed the silence meant one thing: By not insisting on repayment, Dad and Mom had forgiven the debt.

Solution 1: Let Your Child Know from the Start the Loan Is a Loan

Ann Landers frequently addressed the lament of parents like the Cutlers. The letters basically asked the same question:

> Dear Ann Landers:
> I have loaned money to my daughter but I have not been repaid one penny. I am afraid I will never see that money again. What should I do?

Ms. Landers always gave the same straightforward advice: If you cherish your relationship with your daughter, say good-bye to your money. You will not get your money back without damaging that relationship. Then, Ms. Landers typically added this advice:

> Learn a valuable lesson from this experience. When you loan money to a child, make it known you are serious about getting paid back. Get a promise to repay in writing and charge interest.

Ms. Landers was absolutely correct. If your body language or tone of voice even slightly says you do not expect repayment, you probably will not get repaid. If you want to maximize the likelihood of repayment, don't make the loan a quick-and-easy deal. The greater the formality, the more your child will consider the transaction to be a serious loan commitment.

Of course, there are no guarantees. No matter how formal the written promise and the security, and no matter how sincere the promise to repay, a deadbeat is a deadbeat. But if you undertake the following formalities, you may increase the likelihood of repayment.

First, create a formal Promissory Note that your son (and his wife) will sign. With this note, your son and his wife will forever memorialize the terms of the loan: the amount, interest, payment schedule, due date, late-payment provisions, and all other necessary terms.

Second, your son and his wife should collateralize their loan with a Mortgage or Trust Deed against their home.

Third, insist that your son and his wife confer with an attorney about the loan. The attorney will reemphasize the legal obligations of repayment and the consequences of defaulting on a loan secured by a Mortgage or Trust Deed.

In your heart of hearts, you know you would never sue your son or foreclose. But with these three steps, you may have created an indelible impression—the money *has* to be repaid.

Solution 2: Forgive the Loan and Call It a Gift

What would you do if the loan to your son is not repaid? Would you sue? Would you foreclose on your grandchild's house? Of course not.

If you realize pursuing repayment is driving you and your child apart, perhaps the time has come to call it "a gift."

What About Your Other Children?

Declaring the loan to be a gift will amount to unequal treatment of your other children. But you can easily resolve this side effect. Give each of your children an amount equal to the forgiven loan or leave them this amount in your inheritance plan.

2. "My wife and I loaned my son $25,000 secured by a Promissory Note. I never really pushed for payment and I still have the note. My other children are aware of this situation. What impact will this note have on our other children?"

You may not have pushed for repayment, but your other children may not be so forgiving.

Your forgiven loan may create a potentially volatile situation. Why? Because when you die, the note is an asset to be divided between all your children. Suddenly and without warning, your deadbeat son finds himself pressured by his siblings to pay them off. How will your son react? Will he give in? Will he lash out, telling his siblings his debt "died" when you died?

My point is that if you die with the forgiven loan unresolved, your children's sibling relationship may be seriously hurt. I learned this unintended consequence firsthand with the Donnellys.

The Donnellys—the Loan That Wouldn't Die

The Donnellys wanted the loan to their son, Brett, to be handled like any business loan. If they accepted only an oral promise to repay, they believed Brett would think the obligation to repay was not meaningful.

The Donnellys did what they were supposed to do. They surrounded this loan with formality. The greater the formality, they thought, the greater the likelihood of repayment. So, the Donnellys had Brett (and his wife) sign a Promissory Note. In this note, Brett and his wife promised to repay the loan with interest. Payments would be in monthly installments, and all the loan would be totally repaid in ten years.

For the next two years, Brett made the payments on time.

In the third year, the payments became irregular. In the fourth year, the usual forgiving process began. Skipped payments. Bad excuses. Awkward silences. All pretended the note no longer existed. Ultimately, the Donnellys died, the memory of the loan having long faded into the distant past.

However, though the debt had been conveniently forgotten by Brett and his parents, guess who did not forget? Brett's sister *and* her spouse!

Soon after their parents' deaths, Brett and his sister (and their spouses) gathered in my office to begin the process of carrying out the terms of their parents' Living Trust. One of the first things I did was inquire about their parents' assets, including any unpaid debts anyone owed to their parents.

Surprise, surprise! This is when Brett's sister handed me the note. She had discovered it when rooting through her parents' safety deposit box. It was dusty; it was yellow with age; it was even a bit torn. But to Brett's extreme dismay, there it was.

In my most lawyerlike manner, I read the note aloud and asked if there was any balance due. All eyes turned to Brett and his wife, waiting for their answer.

The Pressure

Brett's sister had not come to the meeting unprepared. When Brett failed to reply to my inquiry, she matter-of-factly removed a sheet of paper from her purse and showed it to me. It was a computer printout. According to her calculations, Brett's original loan at 5 percent interest compounded annually was now in excess of $100,000.

As Brett sat in stunned silence, his sister continued. "Brett, if Dad and Mom had truly forgiven your loan, they would have torn up the note. But the note still exists and your debt remains. I am entitled to one-half of it. Why not be a good guy and pay me off now?"

Brett's silence became deafening. The scene unfolding before us was right out of a daytime television soap. I could only wonder what would happen next.

Brett finally responded to his sister's demand. "You want an answer," he yelled. "I'll give you an answer. Sure, I borrowed the money. Sure, I signed that note. But there is no way you can enforce it against me. I signed that note over twenty years ago, and my lawyer says the Statute of Limitations has run by now."

Brett was right. The Statute of Limitations had run. The passage of time had made the note no longer legally enforceable. Undaunted, Brett's sister gave her brother one last shot: "Even if I can't legally enforce this note," she said, "you are still morally obligated to repay. Why should you receive more money than me? You had the use of that money for twenty years. We should be treated equally. After all, this isn't courtroom justice. It's family."

Brett could not refute his sister's plea about family loyalty. He asked where he would come up with the money. No problem, his sister replied. She would just take an extra share of the inheritance.

Do Not Die with a Child Owing You Money

Before the Donnelly case, I did not appreciate the bitter impact of a forgiven loan on sibling relationships. Today, one of the first questions I ask clients is whether they have made a loan to a child. If they have, I advise them of the Donnelly-like consequences of dying with a child as a debtor.

One client said my interrogation was like facing a courtroom cross-examination. I apologized for my intensity but not for my inquiry. "The Forgiven Loan Syndrome" can be so harmful to the sibling relationship that I pursue this issue with all diligence.

Recognize the Problem

If your loan to your child has become a forgiven loan, you can resolve potential sibling conflicts in one of the following ways:

Solution 1: Call the Note

The preferable solution is not to die being a creditor to a child. Try to collect. If your child pays the loan, the problem disappears.

Solution 2: Cancel the Note and Give an Equal Amount to Your Other Children

If collecting the debt is not a reality, cancel it. I suggest this be done with some theater. Call a family meeting. Gather your children together and acknowledge the outstanding debt. Announce you are canceling the debt and giving a like amount to each of your other children. Then give each nondebtor child a check equal to the unpaid principal plus interest and relish their surprise and delight.

This theatrical approach clears the air and equalizes the money. But more important, you will have maintained (or reestablished) sibling harmony.

Solution 3: Postdeath Equalization

If the debtor child cannot repay (solution 1), and you have insufficient assets to equalize while you are alive (solution 2), then equalize after you die.

In your inheritance plan, provide that the unpaid debt is canceled. (If the loan is secured by a Mortgage or Trust Deed, authorize its removal.) Then leave a like amount of accumulated principal and interest to each of your nondebtor children.

Should your postdeath equalization account for the appreciation of your debtor child's loan? For example, you loaned your son $50,000 twenty years ago to buy a house. Today, that house is worth $300,000. Do you leave each nondebtor child $50,000 or $300,000 to level the playing field? For a more detailed discussion of this issue, see question number 3 in chapter 5.

---

3. "I loaned $100,000 to my son-in-law so he could go into business. I have threatened to sue because he has not made any effort to repay. Now, he won't talk to me, and my daughter says if I sue, I will never see my grandchildren again."

If you have made (or are thinking of making) a loan to a child, keep in mind the lesson I learned from the Fensters: The one with the grandchildren always wins.

Mrs. Fenster cried from the moment my secretary showed her into my office. Before beginning my normal client questions, she was dabbing tears from her eyes. Her husband seemed attentive and repeatedly said to her, "Honey, don't worry about it. Everything will be okay." But these comments only made Mrs. Fenster more despondent.

The problem was the Fensters' CPA son-in-law. And therein lies a tale that is the nightmare of every grandparent.

A year before, Son-in-law found a building he wanted to buy for his accounting practice. The purchase price of the building was $500,000. He had to find a way to obtain the money—even if he had to take in a partner.

Son-in-law approached Mr. Fenster for the money, but Mr. Fenster was not crazy about this idea. He was seventy years old, and his days of wheeling and dealing were through. But for his daughter's sake, Mr. Fenster agreed to put up one-half of the money and be his son-in-law's real estate partner.

A month later, the time to put up the money arrived. Mr. Fenster deposited his $250,000 into escrow . . . but where was the other half? It wasn't there!

Son-in-law was to receive the remaining $250,000 from his

mother. The only glitch was that this money was tied up in certificates of deposit that had not yet become due. His mother promised she would cash out the CDs and have the money available before the close of escrow. But when push came to shove, she just could not stomach the idea of cashing in her CDs before they matured.

Faced with his dream being thrashed to the ground, Son-in-law desperately prevailed upon Mr. Fenster to come up with the additional $250,000, promising that when his mother's CDs matured, the Fensters would be immediately repaid.

Grudgingly accepting this excuse, Mr. Fenster deposited another $250,000 into escrow. But as you can well imagine, Son-in-law's mother changed her mind. She never cashed in her CDs, and Son-in-law's half of the purchase price never materialized.

The Fensters were furious. They felt that Son-in-law had deceived them from the beginning. Mr. Fenster made immediate and angry demands for the money. Son-in-law failed to respond. Finally, Mr. Fenster went to his attorney, who sent Son-in-law a demand letter: "Son-in-law, if you don't repay the Fensters in thirty days, they will file a lawsuit against you."

The Fensters were open to any reasonable offer to settle the matter, including accepting monthly payments. But what they got instead was an angry telephone call from their daughter:

"The pressure you are putting on us is unbearable. It could ruin my marriage. If you sue us or even ask for repayment, you'll never be welcome in my house again . . . and don't expect to see your grandchildren again!"

A brilliant strategy against repayment! What greater threat could there be to a creditor? Immoral, yes, but it certainly got results. And this was the reason for Mrs. Fenster's tears. The very thought of being cut off from her grandchildren was tearing her apart.

Mr. Fenster's initial reaction was, as he said, to "beat the hell" out of Son-in-law. I had no doubt he was capable of carrying out his threat. Notwithstanding his seventy years, he was not the kind of guy you fooled around with. He was over six feet tall, had a square appearance, and looked to be in great shape. During our conversation, he told me that when he walks down the street, he hoped some young thug would attack him so he could "show his stuff."

Fortunately for Son-in-law, there was Mrs. Fenster. Though small in stature, she was big in rational reasoning, and she prevailed upon her husband not to make matters worse.

Playing King Solomon

The Fensters came to my office for Solomon-like advice. Which was the lesser of two evils? If they pursued repayment, their emotional tranquility would be destroyed. If they chose to forgive the loan, it was good-bye to $250,000 they had not planned to invest in Son-in-law's business.

Solution: Bite the Bullet

The Fensters' solution lay in a three-part process.

First, they would have to "bite the bullet." Although their son-in-law had snookered them, they would have to learn to live with the hurt and indignation.

Second, although $250,000 was nothing to sneeze at, they would have to consider the money a gift. Once they could smile through the tears, they would then meet with their daughter and tell her all was forgiven.

Third, the Fensters would treat this gift as an advance on their daughter's inheritance. I redrafted the Fensters' Living Trust to provide that when the last one of them dies, half of the building will be appraised. Whatever the value is, a like amount will go to their other child. For example, if the Fensters' half of the building is appraised at $350,000, their other child will inherit $350,000 off the top, with the remaining assets divided equally between both of the Fensters' children.

The Fensters accepted my advice. They would have preferred to get their money back, but they could live with the idea of treating the money as an early inheritance to their daughter. And more important, this plan gave the Fensters their lives back. The litigation would stop, the grandchildren would not be used as pawns, and harmony with their daughter would be restored.

Part III

Protecting the Inheritance from Your Child's Potential Problems

7

Protecting the Inheritance While It's in the Hands of Your Child

or

After Your Child Inherits—Will It Be There for Your Grandchild?

---

1. "I feel obligated to leave my money to my daughter. But I would like some certainty that when she dies, there will be something left for my grandchild."

Today, more than ever, an *outright* inheritance to a child exposes that inheritance to a greater risk of loss. With half your children's marriages ending in divorce, with multiple marriages and "soap opera" relationships, with economic instability, and with a lawsuit-minded society, your child's inheritance is more susceptible to unexpected loss than ever before.

The result is that the "family money" you leave to your child may never get to your grandchildren.

Parents are increasingly concerned about the fate of the family money when it is inherited by their child. Once in the child's hands, the family money may fall into one of the following risk categories.

Category Number 1: Risk of Losing the Inheritance to a Child's Creditors

"My son is a real estate developer who lost a lot of money in the recent recession. I'm concerned his inheritance may go to his creditors."

"My son is a medical doctor with little malpractice insurance. If he gets sued, there goes everything he inherited from me."

"My son-in-law is on the verge of bankruptcy. If I leave my money to my daughter, will it end up with my son-in-law's creditors?"

"My daughter drives with little auto insurance. If she causes an accident, her inheritance could be eaten up by any judgment against her."

"Can the IRS take my son's inherited money if he and his wife have an income tax liability?"

Category Number 2: Risk of Mismanagement and Squandering

"My son is an addict. Cocaine is his drug of choice. I want him to share in the inheritance. But I'm afraid whatever he inherits could end up with his drug dealer."

"I just know my daughter will drink her inheritance away."

"Does Caesar's Palace need an influx of cash? Just tell them to wait for me to die. The first thing my son will do with his inheritance is hit the craps table."

"My son has has no ability to manage money."

"My daughter belongs to an 'offbeat' religious cult. If I leave her my money, it will end up with her guru."

"My daughter is intelligent but very gullible. She is always doing good work, but her altruism clouds her judgment. If she uses her inheritance for her good work, there will be nothing left for my grandchildren."

"My children are minors."

"My son is mentally disabled and unable to manage money."

Category Number 3: Risk of Loss Through Marriage and Divorce

"My son has been married and divorced twice. If he marries again, I'm afraid any inheritance I leave him may end up in the divorce court."

"If my daughter is married or gets married after she inherits, will her husband have any rights to my money and property?"

"I don't want my daughter to leave her inheritance to her husband. After she dies, my son-in-law could remarry and my money could end up with his second wife."

"My son cannot say no to his assertive wife. After he inherits, I know she will convince him to put the money and property in both their names jointly. If my son dies first, his wife will own it all."

Solution: The "Protection Trust"—Your Voice from the Grave

Your child may be unable to do anything to protect his inheritance from his creditors, marital problems, and other risks he faces in his life. But you have the power to do what your child cannot do. In your Will or Living Trust, you can include a special plan that will protect your child's inheritance from your child's problems.

This plan is called the "Protection Trust." When you die, the Protection Trust will live on, forming a protective wall around your child's inheritance. It may protect the inherited money and property once it is in your child's hands and preserve it for future generations.

If your Will or Living Trust does not contain a Protection Trust, your inheritance plan dies when you die, leaving no voice from the grave to shelter the inheritance from these risks of loss.

How the Protection Trust Works

The Protection Trust is part of the inheritance instructions contained in your Will or Living Trust. These instructions say that when you die, your money and property will not go outright to your child. Instead, it will go to a Trustee of the Protection Trust.

Think of the Protection Trust as a giant bucket. When you die, your child's inheritance—the real estate, stocks, bonds, cash, jewelry—goes into this bucket.

This giant Protection Trust bucket is then handed over to someone called the Trustee. The Trustee is your "out-of-the-grave agent" who will manage and protect the contents of the bucket for the benefit of your child.

In addition to managing the inherited assets, the Trustee must carry out any inheritance instructions you put in the Protection Trust. Typically, these instructions include telling the Trustee if and when he should:

- "Dip" into the bucket and give your child portions of the inheritance from time to time.
- Pay your child any income generated by the assets in the bucket.
- Terminate the Protection Trust and give your child all the assets in the bucket outright.
- Control the inheritance for the rest of your child's life.

You can provide a number of other instructions in the Protection Trust for the Trustee to follow.

Who Should Be the Trustee of the Protection Trust?

The Trustee of your child's Protection Trust could be your child's sibling or other private individual, a bank Trustee or other financial institution, or even the child who is to be protected. The Trustee will hold your child's inheritance and protect it in varying degrees from the risk of loss. Throughout the chapters in this section, I discuss who would best serve as your child's Trustee.

2. "Is the Protection Trust right for my family?"

Attitudes about using the Protection Trust vary from family to family. Whenever I describe this plan and its benefits, I typically receive one of the following five responses:

1. The "Who Cares What Happens After I'm Dead?" Client

"Whatever my child does with the inheritance won't affect me. If it's gone, it's gone!"

This is what I call the "shooting-from-the-hip" response. These clients don't want to be bothered with having to intellectually and emotionally deal with complex after-death issues. All they want is a simple probate-avoidance Living Trust . . . period.

2. The "You Lawyers Are All Alike" Client

"All you want to do is make more money off me!"

These clients come to my office with only a routine Living Trust in mind. When I mention the Protection Trust, they feel that I am making a big deal out of nothing just so I can do more and charge higher fees.

This attitude is understandable, but it stems from ignorance. These clients have little or no lifetime dealings with lawyers and are simply reacting to the negative image that has surrounded lawyers for many years.

Sometimes these clients come around to the Protection Trust after I explain its benefits.

3. The "I Never Thought About It Before" Client

Over 90 percent of my clients have never once considered the need to protect the family money once it is inherited by their child. Why? Because as the typical client says to me: "Mr. Condon, I have no problem children. In fact, my children are perfect. I see no reason why they should not receive their inheritance free and clear when I die."

Years ago, when I was a younger attorney, I readily accepted this opinion without question. Clients, I assumed, knew their children better than I did. And besides, if clients had a reason to protect a child's inheritance, would this not be the foremost fact on their minds when they came to see me?

However, as clients died, I saw the reality of what happens when their "perfect" children received an outright inheritance. With alarming frequency, my clients' money and property ended up in ways they never dreamed. How could they have foreseen their wealth ultimately belonging to their child's creditors, the IRS, the Bankruptcy Court, their daughter-in-law's new husband, or the "crazy cult"?

I no longer assume my clients' children are perfect, no matter what my clients tell me. Today, I automatically assume every client has a child whose inheritance will be exposed to risk of loss. I ask every client several questions about his or her child's life. After I learn about a child's job, business, marriages, divorces, driving habits, and education, I may recognize a potential risk of loss that the client may have never otherwise considered.

Having identified a potential risk to a child's inheritance, I can suggest the Protection Trust as a way to protect the inheritance and assure the family money will ultimately stay in the bloodline.

4. The "Where Do I Sign?" Client

I estimate one out of every five families I see has a child with a self-evident need to have the inheritance protected. Typically, this is a child with a compulsive addiction, a severe emotional or psychological problem, or a permanent mental disability.

These clients do not have to be convinced about the merits of the Protection Trust. They know their child's inheritance must be protected for *and from* that child if they want to guarantee that the family money will end up with their grandchildren.

5. The "I Went Through the Depression" Client

Some clients perceive a need to overcontrol the family money. They perceive a need to protect a child's inheritance when no such need exists. Typically, these are my older clients, who have distorted their children's spending habits because they see the world through a Depression-era mirror:

"My son does not know the value of a dollar. He bought a new car just after getting married. My wife and I didn't get our first car until we were married twenty years."

"My daughter cannot save a dime. I remember spending a quarter to go to the movies. But my daughter thinks nothing about paying $10.00, and that's not including the money she lays out for dinner and a baby-sitter."

If I determine that a child genuinely cannot manage or spend money properly, I will suggest the Protection Trust as a way to protect that child's inheritance. But if it turns out the client sees the world in terms of 1940 dollars, I will attempt to convince that client that the Protection Trust is too much control.

---

3. **"How much protection will the Protection Trust give my child's inheritance?"**

The Protection Trust can give your assets varying degrees of protection. It can guarantee 101 percent that your money and property will be sheltered from your child's problems so it will be around for your grandchildren. On the other hand, it may only give you a hope that the family money will stay in the bloodline.

The amount of protection in your Protection Trust depends on how much protection *you* build into it. And that, in turn, depends on two factors:

You: As you will see in the forthcoming chapters, the more protection you want, the more you control your child's use of the inheritance. Is this acceptable to you, or do you feel uncomfortable tying your child's hands with his own money?

Your Child's Potential Problem: This is a key factor in deciding how much protection you wish to build into your Protection Trust. In the following chapters, you will see that different problems require different degrees of protection, from the highly flexible "Transparent Trust" to the heavy-handed controls of the "Irrevocable Protection Trust."

In sum, you should use the Protection Trust if you want to protect the family money from the risk of loss once it is inherited by your child and if you want greater assurance the family money will be there for the grandchildren and/or other heirs.

The following chapters in this section illustrate the typical circumstances justifying the need for a Protection Trust.

8

Protecting the Money for the Financially Immature Child

or

Will Your Daughter's Inheritance End Up at Nordstrom's or with Her Newfound Friends?

1. "My daughter has a responsible job but cannot save a dime. She spends everything she earns and everything I give her. I'm afraid she will spend her entire inheritance and there will be nothing left for her future (or my grandchildren)."

Is your child on the right track to maturity but has not yet arrived at the final station?

A child's age is not necessarily indicative of maturity. We have all heard someone tell us about their sixteen-year-old daughter who is going on thirty. Just as common is the forty-year-old woman who has the maturity and insight of a teenager.

You look forward to the day in your life when your child reaches emotional and intellectual maturity. But what happens if your child is still immature when you die? If your child receives an outright inheritance, it may be mismanaged or spent foolishly.

Did you work a lifetime to accumulate your wealth just so your immature child could squander it down to nothing?

The Wrong Type of Antisquander Plan

Early in my practice, if a client informed me of a child's immature spending habits, I recommended a special Protection Trust
program called "Interval Allocation." This was, and is today, a
commonly used method to protect the inheritance for *and from*
the immature child.

Interval Allocation is not exactly a Star Wars concept. Instead
of leaving money and property outright to a squandering child,
you leave it to a third-party Trustee. The Trustee holds the inheritance, invests it, collects the income, pays the bills, and uses the
income for your child's "necessities of life." As your child attains
certain ages, the Trustee allocates a portion of the Trust assets
outright to your child.

For example, you trust your son with money as far as you can
throw him. If he receives an outright inheritance, you know there
will be a significant risk of mismanagement and excessive spending. So you leave your money and property to a Trustee, who will
distribute one-third of the Trust assets when your son reaches
forty, one-half of the balance when he turns forty-five, and the
final share at fifty.

The underlying premise of this plan is that it will give your son
the experience of managing money without putting his entire
inheritance at risk. If he squanders the first installment, he learns
the hard way that money must be managed properly and spent
wisely. By the time your son receives the final portion, he has
learned proper money management and will spend his inheritance cautiously in the future.

Good plan? Wrong!

Although Interval Allocation remains popular and is frequently used, I believe it is fatally flawed. Why? Because it simply
does not work! It may do little, if anything, to lead the financially
immature child to maturity.

First, Interval Allocation gives no assurance that your son
will learn anything from the experience of mishandling the first

installment. The plan assumes that with the passage of time, one naturally attains common sense, wisdom, and financial responsibility. However, the only lesson your son may learn is not to "blow the dough" so quickly before the next installment arrives.

Second, the plan may not offer your son the opportunity to make money decisions. If your son's inheritance is a house or apartment building, his first installment will be a deed to a portion of the real estate. What kind of financial moves can your son make with this share, especially with the Trustee as co-owner? None. Until your son receives the entire building, he cannot make decisions without the Trustee's consent.

Third, the underlying premise of Interval Allocation doesn't make sense. Why would you want to risk your son squandering even one installment? You want to prevent risk to all your money and property, not experiment with loss.

The Right Antisquander Plan

I subscribe to a different philosophy about protecting your money and property from your squandering child. If you perceive a risk, allocation should be delayed *until the risk is gone*!

If you want to protect your money for your immature child, why not protect it all? Let a Trustee hold up your child's inheritance until the risk of dissipation is gone, or at least minimized. If the circumstances justify delay until your child is in his thirties, forties, fifties, or even for life, so what? By delaying allocation until then, you have protected the family money for your child *and from* your child.

2. "If I'm going to hold up my son's entire inheritance until the right age, what is that age?"

Sometimes a client says to me, "Mr. Condon, I want my son's inheritance controlled for the rest of his life. He couldn't save a dime if his life depended on it."

Is this opinion justified? Sometimes it is, as some children will never grow up. On the other hand, this opinion could be colored by the client's "I lived through the Depression and walked to school uphill in the driven snow" mentality. In this client's mind, his son is a spendthrift; in reality, the child may be a mature adult whose expenditures are consistent with a reasonable person's needs.

My point is that since you ultimately determine when your child should gain outright control of the inheritance, your decision must be an informed one. You do not want a Trustee to hold up your child's inheritance longer than necessary.

How Not to Make the Wrong Decision

It is extremely important that you do not hold up your child's inheritance longer than necessary. Once you die, the plan is written in cement and cannot be changed. But you can incorporate special programs in your inheritance plan to mitigate against a wrong decision. With these safeguards, your plan can change—if your child changes.

Safeguard Number 1: The "Wait-and-See" Program

The Wait-and-See program gives your inheritance plan the flexibility to change along with your child.

For example, Dad and Mom have a daughter whose credo is, Spend today, for tomorrow you may die. So Dad and Mom's inheritance plan provides that a Trustee will control her inheritance and dole it out incrementally on an as-needed basis until she reaches sixty.

Dad dies first and Mom now holds all the family wealth. As the years go by, their daughter becomes a more responsible and capable person. Gradually, Mom concludes it would be unfair to hold up her daughter's inheritance and that it should go to her outright.

Can Mom change the inheritance plan after Dad's death? Can Mom leave the inheritance to her daughter outright, or at least reduce the age of distribution? Yes. Dad and Mom's inheritance plan can include a special provision that allows the surviving parent (usually Mom) to change the distribution schedule, even after Dad's death. As Mom measures her daughter's progress (or lack thereof), she can change the age her daughter will receive control of her inheritance.

Safeguard Number 2: Make Someone Your Eyes and Ears from the Grave

What happens if an immature child becomes mature after both parents die?

For example, you provide that a Trustee will control your immature son's inheritance until he is sixty-five. After both you and your spouse die, your son turns fifty and finally "wakes up and smells the coffee." He gets a job, gets married, and becomes a responsible person.

But since you and your spouse are not around to witness the miraculous transformation, no one can change the plan so that your son would receive his inheritance at an earlier age. The solution: a Wait-and-See program that operates after the deaths of *both* parents.

In your inheritance plan, provide that after the death of the last parent, a third party can change the age of distribution to your son. I call this third party the "Protector," and he or she will be your eyes and ears from the grave. If the Protector decides your son can properly manage and spend his inherited money before turning age sixty-five, the Protector can instruct the Trustee to give your son all (or part) of his inheritance outright.

What happens if your son turns sixty-five and the Protector determines he *still* cannot properly manage money? The Protector can tell the Trustee to delay the time of distribution. For how long? As long as the Protector deems appropriate.

Who Will Be the Protector?

The Protector ordinarily will be a family member, usually an uncle, aunt, or sibling. Whomever you choose, the Protector will have the sole power to determine if an earlier or later allocation is warranted.

Of course, with power comes the potential for abuse of power. There is always the risk of choosing a hard-nosed and unyielding Protector who may refuse to recommend an earlier distribution, even if your child becomes financially capable. Or the Protector may turn out to be a soft touch who may succumb to your child's demands for an earlier allocation.

In other words, is there protection from the Protector? Yes, with the following provisions:

1. Provide that if the Protector recommends an earlier or later distribution, that decision must be backed up by a psychiatrist. The psychiatrist will render an opinion about your child's competency (or lack thereof) in a written report. When the Trustee receives this report along with the Protector's opinion, the Trustee may accordingly delay or shorten the time for distribution.

2. Provide that if your child believes he can manage and spend the inheritance before the designated age, he can bypass the Protector and show the Trustee proof of financial competency, such as two independent psychiatric reports that both declare that he has attained financial maturity.

3. "I'm convinced my daughter is financially irresponsible. She's twenty-five years old and just paid $30,000 for a new car. I didn't buy a new car until I was forty-five."

Mr. Baldwin thought his daughter spent excessive amounts of money. She was a spendthrift, he told me, and he needed to do something. If she inherited his money outright, he was sure she would spend it irresponsibly.

To protect his daughter from her own folly, Mr. Baldwin wanted to control her inheritance from the grave. He instructed me to hold up his daughter's inheritance in Trust until she attained the age of sixty-five.

However, when Mr. Baldwin died five years later and his irate daughter barged into my office (without an appointment), I learned for the first time that I should have resisted her father's attempt to overcontrol from the grave.

"Condon," she screamed, "I can't believe you let my father do this! Dad probably told you I throw money away, but it's not true! I spend and save like the next person. But Dad was the kind of guy who berated me for spending $7.50 for a movie because he remembered spending only a quarter. And he practically disowned me when I bought a new car because he did not get a new car until he was forty-five.

"My father lived in the past, Condon. He thought in terms of 1940 dollars until the day he died. If you had just called me, I could have told you so. Now I have to wait twenty years to get my money."

Red on My Face

When Mr. Baldwin told me about his "spendthrift" child, I assumed he knew what he was talking about. After all, who was I to contradict his opinion about his own child? Today, when a client tells me about his child who thinks money grows on trees, I dig deeper to determine if that is truly the case.

Certainly, a parent may be correct about a child's immature spending habits. Some children truly have no sense of proportion and need to have their inheritance protected for their own benefit.

Many parents, however, are like Mr. Baldwin. He grew up during the Depression, scrimping and saving religiously for everything he owned. Never forgetting his painful past, he applied the Depression standard of spending to the current world. As a result, Mr. Baldwin grossly misconstrued his daughter's spending habits as carefree and irresponsible.

Are You Like Mr. Baldwin?

According to Mr. Baldwin, his daughter spent more for a night out than he earned in a month. Do you see a little bit of Mr. Baldwin in yourself?

Before you consider your child financially irresponsible, I urge you to stop and think. Are you living with a Depression-era mindset? If you really think about it, you may discover you are looking at your child's spending habits through a distorted lens. And you may conclude that delaying your child's inheritance is not justified.

---

4. "I have no idea what my children will do with their inheritance. They don't have much experience in managing large sums of money."

Inherited money is precious money. It may have taken you and your spouse forty or more years to acquire what you own. You did not work hard to accumulate wealth just so it could slip through your child's fingers. Your child should have a duty to invest the inheritance conservatively, spend it wisely, and preserve it for your grandchildren.

Will your child, however, recognize this obligation? When you die, your child will, most likely, be an adult who has set his own course in life. His attitude about asset management, for bad or good, will have long been established.

If you doubt your child's ability to properly manage the inheritance, now is the time to do something. I strongly suggest you encourage your child to learn the skills of money management while you are alive. The best way to begin your child's financial education is to give him or her hands-on investment experience. Consider introducing your child to your securities broker and opening an account in your child's name. Allocate some money to that account and allow your child to make the investment decisions.

I have seen parents follow this advice with great success. One client told me his twelve-year-old daughter read *The Wall Street Journal* every day before school to see how her investments were doing.

With this plan, you give your child a preinheritance opportunity to manage and earn money. Equally important is the chance to see how your child manages money. From what you observe you may get an indication if your child can be trusted with the family money after you die.

---

5. "I don't care what my son does with his inheritance. If it's gone, it's gone."

If you have a financially immature child who will run through the inheritance like there's no tomorrow, you can ill afford to be so casual about your inheritance plan. When risk is perceived, why not protect against that risk? Leave your money and property to a Trustee to hold for your child until your child reaches a certain age or, if necessary, for life.

On occasion, however, clients tell me they don't care how a child spends the inheritance. Typically, they say, "After I die, it will be their money. If they spend it, they spend it. If it's gone, it's gone. Is there any law that says I have to protect my children's inheritance?"

Parents can leave their money any way they desire. If a client does not care about preserving a child's inheritance, so be it. But I want the client to know that if the inheritance runs out, the loss of money may be more than the mere loss of dollars.

Perhaps you heard about one of Bing Crosby's sons. When this son's inheritance ran out, so did he—the hard way. He committed suicide. In 1992, the following article appeared in the *Los Angeles Times*:

Lindsay Crosby, the youngest son of Bing Crosby from the famed crooner's first marriage, shot himself to death in a Las Virgines apartment after learning that the inheritance he relied on to support his family was gone, a spokeswoman said.

Just 11 days earlier, Crosby and his three brothers had been told by attorneys that the oil investments their late mother, Wilma Wyatt, made for them had gone broke. [The spokeswoman reported Lindsay saying], "My life is one shock after another. I'll find a job as a backup singer, or a gofer on a studio lot."

No one knew the depth of Lindsay's despair—except now in retrospect, [the spokeswoman said].

The Lesson

Not all children who go through their inheritance are going to commit suicide. But the Lindsay Crosby case dramatically points out what can happen when the money runs out and that there may be no place in your inheritance plan for the "if it's gone, it's gone" attitude.

6. "How can I use my inheritance plan to motivate my lazy son into getting a job?"

There is no better incentive than money to motivate your child toward gainful employment. With that in mind, provide as follows in your Will or Living Trust:

1) Leave your child's inheritance to a Trustee to hold until your child reaches a certain age.

2) Provide that while the Trustee is holding your child's inheritance, the Trustee is to match every dollar your child earns.

This "dollar-for-dollar" incentive is the best thing I've found to "coerce" a child into getting a job. After all, even the most irresponsible child will wake up and say, "Hey, here is a chance to double my income."

And who knows? This method may lead your once-irresponsible child to become self-supporting.

9

Protecting the Inheritance from Your Child's Spouse

or

Do You Really Want Your Money to Go to Your Son-in-Law's Second Wife?

It's not inherently bad if your child's spouse receives your child's inheritance. Your son-in-law or daughter-in-law, after all, is the parent of your grandchildren. If he ends up with the family money, he will probably do the right thing and leave it to your grandchildren.

However, today we live in a different world. With multiple marriages and divorces and with intermixed families of children and stepchildren, you cannot be absolutely certain your child's spouse will leave the family money to your grandchildren.

How Your Child's Spouse Will End Up with the Family Money

Your son-in-law or daughter-in-law can end up with your money and property in three ways:

1. By Inheritance

Perhaps your daughter has a Will leaving everything she owns, including her inherited assets, to her husband. If she dies first, your son-in-law will own everything.

2. By Gift

Perhaps your daughter will put her inheritance in her and her husband's joint names with right of survivorship. If your daughter dies first, your son-in-law may own all of the family money. If they divorce, your son-in-law may walk away with half of it.

3. By Law

Even if your daughter does nothing to give or leave her husband a share, her husband may, by law, acquire some rights in her inheritance.

For example, your daughter lives in Hawaii, a state that declares that when one spouse inherits, the other spouse automatically has rights to a portion of the inheritance. Your daughter inherits your money and property and keeps it in her individual name. When she dies, or if she divorces, your son-in-law may receive a portion of her inheritance.

The result would be different if your daughter lived in California, where the law is that the property she inherits is her separate property. If your daughter dies, her surviving husband is not entitled to any portion of what she inherited from you (unless, of course, your daughter left it to him). If your daughter divorces, the judge has no power to award your son-in-law any portion of your daughter's inheritance.

But no matter what state you live in, the following questions will point out a risk that is common everywhere—the risk that your child's spouse will end up with the family money and divert it from your bloodline.

Once you recognize this risk, you can use your inheritance plan to prevent it from becoming a reality.

---

1. "My son has told me if he dies before his wife, he will leave his inherited property to her. My daughter-in-law is a wonderful girl, but how do I know she will leave it to my grandchildren?"

You don't!

If you leave your son an outright inheritance, he has the power to choose who will ultimately receive the family money. And if your son is the typical loving husband, he will probably leave his inherited wealth to his wife. As a result, your daughter-in-law will become the 100 percent owner of your money and property.

Your daughter-in-law may outlive your son for twenty years. What can she do with the family money during that time? Plenty! She is in the driver's seat with no one telling her what to do.

Your daughter-in-law may acquire a new life with a new husband and stepchildren. Will she leave your hard-earned wealth to the children of her second husband's first marriage?

Your daughter-in-law may become physically or mentally incapacitated. Will she leave the family money to her last caretaker or other final friend?

Your daughter-in-law is (or becomes) involved with a church or charity. Will that organization be the ultimate recipient of your money?

Your daughter-in-law may have her own family. She could leave the family money to *her* sisters, *her* brothers, *her* nieces, *her* nephews—anyone she desires. Who, after all, is going to tell her no?

"Not My Daughter-in-Law"

After reading this laundry list of possible fates, you still may believe it can never happen to you. As the typical client says, "Mr. Condon, I don't care what you say. You don't know my daughter-in-law. She loves her children and would never do anything to harm them. No matter what happens in her life, I am certain she will leave our money to our grandchildren."

To that, I say this. On a risk scale of zero to ten, what is the risk that your daughter-in-law will divert the family money from your bloodline? Only God can zero out the risk. If you believe the risk amounts only to a one or two, there is still a risk.

The Doom-and-Gloom Lawyer

Are these potential risks the doom-and-gloom projections of a jaded lawyer who has seen it all? Perhaps they are. But they are also true. I have witnessed these diversion events more often than I can recount.

In all likelihood, your daughter-in-law or son-in-law will not divert the family money from your grandchildren. But my job is to make you aware of the worst-case scenario. It is my business to tell you of potential risks you may not have otherwise considered. Only after you have been enlightened with all the facts can you make an informed decision.

If you believe your daughter-in-law will do the right thing, that is your decision. But if you consider even the slightest risk of diversion unacceptable, and you want to ensure that the family money will end up with your grandchildren, you must plan to prevent the risk rather than let human nature take its course.

In other words, you must do what the Cohens did.

The Cohens Wanted Certainty—Do What They Did

The Cohens took great pride in their daughter, Sarah. She was married to a fine young man, and their two children were the light of the Cohens' lives. According to the Cohens, their daughter had a perfect marriage. And to my surprise, they said that was the problem!

The Cohens felt that when Sarah inherited the family money, she, being a loving and faithful wife, would put the inheritance in both her and her husband's joint names, giving him 50 percent ownership of the real estate, stocks, and other assets. The Cohens were astute enough to realize that if their daughter died first, their son-in-law would own it all.

"Are We Crazy to Worry About It?"

The Cohens felt guilty thinking these paranoid thoughts about a son-in-law whom they adored. But they had seen other "perfect" sons-in-law end up with the family money, remarry, and leave it to their second wives. The Cohens wanted a guarantee that *their* money and property would go to Sarah—and then to Sarah's children.

The Cohens were visibly relieved when I assured them that many of my clients had expressed a similar concern: Why work hard all your life to acquire wealth and then take the risk the family money could end up out of the bloodline? You want it to go to your children and grandchildren, not your son-in-law's second wife.

"We Don't Like Your Solution, Mr. Condon"

The Cohens wanted to make their daughter's inheritance son-in-law-proof. They wanted absolute certainty their money would eventually go to their grandchildren.

I told the Cohens that if they wanted this certainty, they could not leave their daughter an outright inheritance. Instead, Sarah's inheritance would be controlled by a third-party Trustee. (I discuss this solution further in the next question.)

The Cohens were not happy with my advice. While they wanted to control Sarah's inheritance, they didn't want that much control. They didn't want anyone dictating to their daughter what she could or could not do with her money. Besides, they added, they were concerned that by leaving Sarah's inheritance in Trust, she would think her parents had no faith in her.

"We Want It Both Ways"

The Cohens were basically telling me they wanted it both ways. While they wanted to protect Sarah's inheritance, they did not want to completely tie her hands.

I told the Cohens they could compromise by including a special Trust in their inheritance plan. This Trust would give Sarah full access to her inheritance while still providing some after-death controls.

The Cohens liked this idea and described it as a "Transparent Trust," a term that I have since adopted as my own to describe this plan to others.

Solution: The Cohens' Transparent Trust

I use the Transparent Trust for clients like the Cohens who desire to increase the odds of their child's inheritance remaining in the family without imposing heavy-handed controls on the child's use of the inheritance.

This is how the Transparent Trust works:

1) You establish a Living Trust. In your Living Trust, you do not leave your child's inheritance to your child outright. Instead, you leave it to your child "in Trust."

2) The Trustee *and* Beneficiary of this "Transparent Trust" will be your child.

3) As Trustee, your child will have full control of the inheritance with no third-party Trustee looking over your child's shoulder.

4) As Beneficiary, your child will have the sole discretion to spend the Trust assets for *any* purpose.

5) When your child dies, any assets remaining in your child's Trust will pass to your grandchildren.

The Benefits of the Transparent Trust

How does the Transparent Trust guarantee that your child's inheritance will end up with your grandchildren? The answer is that it doesn't give any guarantee!

The Transparent Trust gives your child all the powers over the inheritance an outright owner would have. Your child can spend all the Trust assets, amend or revoke the Trust terms, or terminate the Trust and take the assets out. In fact, your child's spouse can still latch on to the inheritance and divert it from your bloodline.

This is why the Cohens called this Trust "transparent"—it is similar to not having any Trust at all.

So, you may ask, if the Transparent Trust does not protect your child's inheritance from your child's spouse, what good is it? The answer is that it is pretty good nonetheless. The Transparent Trust has four benefits that are so compelling that I recommend this plan to all my clients with married children.

1. The Transparent Trust Gives Your Child the Power to Say No to His Spouse

When your child inherits the family money, your son-in-law or daughter-in-law may pressure your child to put it in their joint names. The result is that your child's spouse becomes a co-owner of the family money.

What kind of pressures am I talking about? It is impossible to know what goes on at your child's house, but:

It could be pillow talk. ("Honey, we own our other assets jointly. Why not your inheritance, too?")

It could be mild coercion. ("Well, honey, I guess you just don't trust me enough.")

It could be an appeal to your child's common sense. ("This will protect us if you die in an accident.")

It could be an everybody-does-it approach. ("All our friends own everything together.")

It could be an outright threat. ("If you don't put me on title, I'll divorce you.")

Can your child resist these pressures? Perhaps, but in my experience, most cannot. More likely, your child will comply because your child is afraid that saying no may offend his spouse, hurt his spouse's feelings, or imply he does not love or trust his spouse.

However, you can help your child resist this pressure if you use the Transparent Trust. By leaving your child's inheritance in this Trust, your child has a valid, justifiable reason to say no to his spouse: "Honey, you know I love you. And if I could, I would . . . but I can't. My parents put it in Trust for their grandchildren."

This is a valid, truthful, and justifiable excuse—and it may work! Chances are that when your child's spouse hears you left your child's inheritance in Trust, your child's spouse will realize the terms of the Trust must be carried out and that the inheritance is off-limits.

2. The Transparent Trust May Eliminate the Need for Your Child to Ask for His Spouse's Signature

This, if for no other reason, may justify your use of the Transparent Trust.

In many states, your child's spouse has no rights to your child's inheritance. So even if your son is married at the time he inherits, the law may say it all belongs to him.

But if your son wishes to sell or refinance his inherited real estate, your son's wife may have to join in on the deed to the buyer. Why would she have to sign? Because that is what the title insurance company will want.

Before the title insurance company will issue a title policy, it must be 100 percent certain your son's wife has no property rights to your son's inherited real estate. And the only way it can get this assurance is by having your son's wife deed away these rights, whether they are real or speculative.

This is easier said than done. Your son's wife, for whatever reason, may not sign. If she refuses to join in on the deed, your son may be prohibited from selling or refinancing his inherited real estate.

The Transparent Trust may eliminate the need for the wife's signature. Why? Because your son does not own his inherited property outright in his individual name. Rather, he owns it only as a Trustee.

3. The Transparent Trust Is Your Voice from the Grave

You want your child to comply with your ultimate goal of keeping family money in the bloodline. The Transparent Trust can help you achieve this goal.

Although there is no guarantee, the Transparent Trust is designed to play upon your child's conscience to follow your wishes. It will serve as a living reminder that you want your money and property to end up with your grandchildren.

But equally important, the Transparent Trust is your voice from the grave, reminding your child there is a duty to preserve for future generations the wealth that took you and your spouse a lifetime to accumulate.

4. The Transparent Trust Saves Your Child the Expense of Arranging His Own Living Trust

You paid your lawyer a fee to prepare your Living Trust that holds your money and property. After you die, your child will have to pay *another* fee to *another* lawyer for *another* Living Trust to hold the same money and property!

I have no objection to making additional fees, but you should hear what my dead clients' children have said. As one child put it: "What a racket, Mr. Condon. My parents paid you a fee to do their

Living Trust. Why should you receive a second fee to do a new Living Trust for the same property?"

"Well . . . why not?" I replied. "If you inherited through a Will, you would still have to do your own Will. If you inherit through a Living Trust, why should it be any different?"

But there is a difference to my clients' children. They wonder why their parents' Living Trust could not become their Living Trust. Good point! So I made it happen, with the Transparent Trust.

After you die, your Living Trust does not "die" with you. Instead, it will dissolve and reappear as a Transparent Trust for each of your children. In effect, the Transparent Trust becomes a Revocable Living Trust for each of your children, with no cost.

---

2. "My son-in-law has cash-register eyes. I just know he will find a way to get his name on my daughter's inheritance."

There are times when the Transparent Trust is not strong enough to protect the family money from your child's spouse. You may need more controls from the grave to prevent your child's spouse from ending up with your money and property.

You can achieve this greater protection by using an irrevocable "Protection Trust" in your inheritance plan.

The Johnsons and Their Lout of a Son-in-Law

The black spot in the Johnsons' lives was their son-in-law, whom they described to me as a "lout." The Johnsons were galled by the son-in-law's cash-register eyes. He was always hinting how he was going to spend the Johnsons' money once they died. And whenever he visited, they could tell he was mentally adding up the value of their estate.

The Johnsons never considered themselves wealthy. But, in fact, they were "real estate rich." In 1946, the Johnsons paid

$20,000 for their Southern California home. Forty years later, inflation boosted their home's value to $900,000. Adding another $350,000 in cash and stocks, the Johnsons were technically millionaires.

The Johnsons had no doubt the son-in-law would someday get their money. He dominated every aspect of their daughter's life. They knew that when they were both dead, the son-in-law would find some way to get his hands on their daughter's inheritance.

The Johnsons ached to express their true feelings to the son-in-law, but they had to refrain. Why? Because he was the father of their grandchildren. The Johnsons were deathly afraid that if a confrontation occurred, the son-in-law would prevent them from seeing their grandchildren.

Making the Inheritance Son-in-Law-Proof

To protect their daughter's inheritance from the son-in-law, I suggested they leave their daughter's inheritance in a "Transparent Trust." (See question 1 of this chapter.) But the Johnsons felt it was too weak to prevent him from gaining access to the family money. They wanted the strongest possible after-death controls of their daughter's inheritance. They knew they had to fight fire with fire. If they didn't, the son-in-law would end up with all their wealth.

When the Johnsons asked me for the "big gun," I brought in the third-party Irrevocable Protection Trust.

Solution: The Irrevocable Protection Trust

The Johnsons' inheritance plan provided that all their money and property would go to a third-party Trustee. This third party would control their daughter's inheritance for as long as they specified. As long as the Trustee was in charge, their daughter could not change or deviate from any of its terms.

The Johnsons selected their longtime bank to be the Trustee. Why? Because the bank would be out of Son-in-law's manipulative reach and would not succumb to any harassment.

After the Johnsons died, the bank took control of the daughter's inheritance. The bank Trustee invested her inheritance and gave her money to pay for her everyday needs. From time to time, the Trustee gave her extra amounts for her recreation, travel, and enjoyment of life.

Did this Irrevocable Protection Trust work? You bet it did! When the son-in-law called the Trustee trying to extort more money, all the Trustee did was politely hang up the phone.

How Long Should the Irrevocable Protection Trust Last?

The Protection Trust should remain for as long as the protection is required. If the problem disappears, your child should gain full access to and control of the inheritance. In the Johnson's case, this would be:

- When the son-in-law dies.
- When their daughter dies.
- When their daughter gets a divorce.
- When their daughter reaches an age and maturity at which she can protect herself.

How will the bank Trustee know if the "son-in-law problem" has disappeared and the Trust is no longer needed? Some person must be the eyes and ears of the bank Trustee. I call this person the Protector. Among the Protector's duties is to advise the Trustee if the risk to the inheritance remains. If the risk is gone, or at least minimized, the Protector can instruct the Trustee to turn over control of the inheritance to the daughter.

Protection from the Son-in-Law Without the Irrevocable Protection Trust

Some clients with this problem cringe at the idea of this solution. They simply cannot get past the idea of any third-party Trustee holding on to the family money.

Are there alternative remedies that will protect a child's inheritance? Yes. You can skip your child and leave that share to your other children or your adult grandchildren. If your grandchildren are minors, a third party must control their share until they reach the age of majority.

Of course, your child will be extremely resentful. With this plan, you have deprived your child of an inheritance. Put another way, you have "penalized" your child because of whom he or she married.

But if you cannot stomach the idea of the family money being deposited with a third-party Trustee, you do not have much choice. Your only other solution to the "son-in-law problem" is to outlive the son-in-law.

---

3. "My married son has no children. My daughter has two children. My children will share their inheritance equally. When my son dies, I don't want 'my money' to go to his wife—I want it to go back to my daughter."

If your childless son dies and leaves his wife everything he owns, everything will include what your son inherited from you.

What will happen to the family money when your daughter-in-law dies? Will she leave it to your daughter or your daughter's children? Probably not. Your money and property, which took you years to accumulate, will probably end up with *your daughter-in-law's family!*

To make certain the family money stays in your family, don't let your son have the power to decide who gets it after he dies.

You must retain this power. You must be the one who decides who gets your childless son's inheritance share after he dies.

You can retain this decision power by using the Irrevocable Protection Trust in your inheritance plan. This Trust will allow your son to use his inheritance. But when your son dies, the Trust requires that whatever is left reverts to your daughter or grand-children.

The Irrevocable Protection Trust works well to keep family money in the family. But even so, many of my clients cannot live with the idea of such heavy-handed controls from the grave.

Mrs. Jones Couldn't Do It—Could You?

Mrs. Jones's daughter had two children, but her son chose to live a childless life. She planned on leaving her money and property to her son and daughter equally. But she was deeply concerned about what would happen to her son's share when he died. As she put it, "Mr. Condon, when my son dies, I want whatever is left of his inheritance to go to my daughter or her children. But I have no confidence in my son. I just know that he will leave his share to his latest girlfriend or short-term wife."

How Much Control Is Necessary?

Arriving at Mrs. Jones's solution was easy. To ensure that her money and property remained in the Jones bloodline, Mrs. Jones had to come up with a plan that would control her son's inher-itance. The hard part was ascertaining how much control was necessary.

"How much" control depended chiefly on the degree to which Mrs. Jones could trust her son to do the right thing. If Mrs. Jones thought her son would leave his inheritance to his sister, she could back up her faith with the flexible Transparent Trust (as the Cohens did in question 1 of this chapter). However, if her son was going to leave it to his next ex-wife, Mrs. Jones could employ the more restrictive Irrevocable Protection Trust (as the Johnsons did in question 2 of this chapter).

Mrs. Jones agonized over this decision. On one hand, she wanted a guarantee that her son would keep the family wealth in the family bloodline. On the other hand, she did not want to tie her son's hands. "The money he inherits, after all," she said, "is his money."

If a client cannot decide, I'll decide. A client is, after all, paying me for my judgment call.

My decision will depend on the nature of the risk to the inheritance once it is in the child's hands. If the family money will be in serious risk of diversion, I will select the Irrevocable Protection Trust, which would forever foreclose that risk. If the risk of diversion is minimal, I would select the Transparent Trust.

In Mrs. Jones's case, I saw only one real choice. Since her son had multiple marriages and divorces, and since Mrs. Jones was grievously concerned her son would divert his inheritance from the bloodline, I selected the Irrevocable Protection Trust.

But after I explained the plan in more detail, Mrs. Jones balked. Why? Because its inflexible restrictions simply went against her grain. She did not wish to dictate what her son could or could not do with his money. All she wanted was to nudge the money in the right direction.

So Mrs. Jones left her son's inheritance in a Transparent Trust. The risk of diversion still existed, but to Mrs. Jones, that risk was preferable to tying her son's hands.

10

Protecting the Inheritance for the Disabled Child

or

"Who Will Take Care of My Disabled Child When I Am No Longer Able To?"

---

1. "My son is an alcoholic." "My daughter is addicted to cocaine." "My son is a compulsive gambler." "My daughter was born with a permanent mental disability." "My son is a schizophrenic and won't stay on his medication." "My daughter suffers from muscular dystrophy."

One out of every four families I deal with has a "disabled" child. Whatever the disability, the parents share one common concern: How should they leave their disabled child an inheritance?

The Irrevocable Protection Trust is the predominant way of protecting the inheritance for your disabled child. With this plan, a third-party Trustee will control and manage your disabled child's money and property until he attains a certain age or, if necessary, for the child's life. In essence, this Trustee will be your disabled child's Money Manager.

Now the question becomes, who will be your disabled child's Money Manager? You may have only two alternatives: your so-called healthy child (your disabled child's sibling) or a corporate Trustee.

Your So-Called Healthy Child as the Money Manager

In some families, the disabled child is fortunate to have a sibling willing to assume this role. The parents welcome this choice because they hope that blood is thicker than cash. Because of the family connection, they think, the healthy child will not fiddle with the disabled child's money.

However, for three compelling reasons, I strongly urge you not to have your healthy child be the Money Manager for your disabled child.

Reason Number 1: There Is No Policeman Looking over the Healthy Child's Shoulder

Say that you have a disabled son and a healthy daughter. You provide in your Living Trust that when you die, your daughter will receive your son's share of the inheritance and be his Money Manager.

According to terms of your plan, your daughter must use your disabled son's share for his benefit. But what will happen to your son's share if:

Your daughter or her husband has creditor problems and needs to find money to pay her bills?

Your daughter or her husband has found a can't-lose investment opportunity and has to come up with money yesterday?

Your daughter or her husband loses her job and must find a way to pay the mortgage?

Your daughter commingles the Trust money with her money, making one indistinguishable from the other?

Your daughter or her husband or their children suffer an illness that adds up to significant medical and hospital bills, and they have insufficient health insurance?

Your daughter or her husband must find a way to pay her children's school tuition?

Your daughter or her husband decides that anything she does for herself is a benefit for your disabled son, including keeping her business afloat, going on vacations, or remodeling her house?

You probably get the point. When the healthy child serves as the Money Manager for the disabled child, that money goes straight into the healthy child's pocket or purse. The bank accounts go into the name of the healthy child. The real estate goes into the name of the healthy child. The stock and securities go into the name of the healthy child. If the healthy child wants to use your disabled child's share for his or her own purposes, no court-imposed restrictions or words on paper can prevent this abuse.

A "normal" child would have some ability to protect himself from the Money Manager's indiscretions. Your disabled child, however, may not understand the financial workings of the Trust, leaving himself vulnerable to his sibling Money Manager. And even if your disabled child senses some mismanagement, will someone listen? Will your disabled child have the ability to seek legal redress?

Your disabled child may be totally at the mercy of the sibling Money Manager, with none of the safeguards that normally protect a beneficiary from a Trustee's abuse.

Reason Number 2: There Is a Conflict of Interest Between the Disabled Child and the Healthy Child

The following two provisions in your Living Trust make for a dangerous mix:

1) When you die, your healthy daughter will be the Money Manager of your disabled son's share of the inheritance; and

2) When your disabled son dies, his share of the inheritance will go to your healthy daughter.

By including these provisions in the same document, you may have inadvertently created two sharp conflicts of interest between your children.

The Spending Conflict

You may not see this conflict, but your daughter will. Sometime after you die, she may realize that she's next in line to her brother's share of the inheritance. The less she spends on him, the more there will be for her when he dies.

For example, if your disabled son requires professional care, will your daughter use his inheritance share to hire the best care possible—or spend just enough to meet his minimal needs?

The Investment Conflict

As Money Manager, your daughter has a legal duty to invest your disabled son's share of the inheritance so that it produces the maximum possible income. But what does your daughter want? Since she is next in line to her brother's money, she wants growth. She wants her brother's inheritance to double in value by the time he dies.

Your daughter cannot have it both ways. There is no investment in America that allows for the highest income and highest growth. Your daughter must choose between income for her brother and growth for herself.

What will your daughter decide?

Reason Number 3: The Death of the Sibling Relationship

When one of your children holds money for another, the money relationship may replace the blood relationship.

For example, your disabled son continually demands more Trust money from his Money Manager sister. She, thinking his demands are unreasonable, refuses, or makes alternative suggestions. He demands a Cadillac, but she suggests a used Chevrolet; he demands a wide-screen television, but she offers to buy a modest twenty-five-inch model; he demands a monthly trip to Las Vegas, but she suggests twice a year.

If this "demand-refusal cycle" persists, your son may no longer see his sister as his sister but as someone who won't give him his money.

Who can predict the actions of your frustrated son to get more money? There could be threats, harassment, or actual violence . . . any of which could hound your daughter into submission or deter her from continuing to act as Money Manager.

The Corporate Trustee: A Safe Choice

I strongly urge you to select a corporate entity to serve as your disabled child's Money Manager. With the corporate Trustee, such as a financial company or bank Trust Department, there are none of the risks that come with the sibling Money Manager. The corporate Trustee has no conflict of interest with your disabled child, will not run away with your disabled child's inheritance, and will not be hounded into submission.

You may be reluctant to use a corporate Trustee because it will charge a fee. Yes, the corporate Trustee charges a fee. But so will the sibling Money Manager—perhaps even more than the corporate Trustee would charge.

There are other advantages of using a corporate Trustee to control a child's inheritance. I discuss these benefits more fully in chapter 16.

A Downside: The Bank Won't Hold Your Disabled Child's Hand

There is one downside to using the corporate Trustee to control your disabled child's inheritance: The corporate Trustee won't be calling or visiting your disabled child every day to ensure that all his financial needs are met.

Ordinarily, a corporate Trustee will only serve your disabled child in one capacity: Money Manager. Its primary function will be limited to measuring your disabled child's financial needs and writing checks to cover those needs.

But if your disabled child is helpless to care for himself, writing the checks may not be be enough. Without assistance, your disabled child may not be able to pay his bills or communicate how much money he requires for his necessities of life and everyday needs.

Since the corporate Trustee may not be equipped to monitor your disabled child's life, you must appoint someone who will be the Trustee's eyes and ears. I call this person the Protector, and he or she will stay abreast of your disabled child's day-to-day needs. The Protector will report his findings to the Trustee, who can then apply the appropriate amount of money to cover those needs.

Whomever you select as the Protector is vital to the overall success of your disabled child's Trust. The Protector may be your disabled child's sibling, another family member, or a trusted family friend. Whomever you choose, this Protector must have a special sensitivity toward your disabled child and take the time and effort to ensure that his everyday financial needs are met.

2. "Shall the Trust be for the lifetime of my disabled son?"

If a child has a lifelong disability, then lifelong protection of the inheritance may be required. But an experience occurred early in my practice that taught me never to discount the ability of the human animal to overcome a disabling condition.

From this maturing episode, I now instinctively rebel against the tyranny of lifetime regulation.

Marvin Kincaid: Miracles Can Happen

Mr. and Mrs. Kincaid's forty-five-year-old son had been an alcohol and drug abuser since he was twenty. All attempts to get their son sober—AA, psychologists, psychotherapy, methadone—failed. I'll never forget what they said to me: "Mr. Condon, our son will die an addict, and there is nothing we can do."

The Kincaids knew Marvin would drink away his inheritance and use it for drugs. To protect the family money from his addiction, they included an Irrevocable Protection Trust in their inheritance plan, using a bank Trust Department as the Trustee. The bank would control Marvin's inheritance for the rest of his life.

A few years later, Mr. Kincaid died, and I met with Mrs. Kincaid to discuss some postdeath matters. Usually when one spouse dies, my meetings with the surviving spouse are fraught with sadness. But this time, Mrs. Kincaid had good news to report. "Mr. Condon, my husband's death was a shock to Marvin, but not as you would think. Instead of climbing into the bottle even more, I think he is starting to reflect on the value of life. He's back at AA and he's taking it day by day."

Mrs. Kincaid called me five years later. She wanted to meet to discuss changing her inheritance plan. When she arrived, she was accompanied by a handsome and well-dressed man who shook my hand vigorously.

This executive-looking guy was Marvin Kincaid! Mrs. Kincaid could hardly contain her joy. In the years since his father's death, Marvin had been sober and had maintained a steady job.

Because of her son's miraculous recovery, Mrs. Kincaid wanted to eliminate Marvin's Protection Trust. Her long-lost son was back, she said, and she no longer felt the need to control Marvin's inheritance. After she died, Marvin should get his inheritance outright.

Happy . . . but Cautious

Naturally, I was extremely happy for Mrs. Kincaid, but I was also cautious. Some semblance of Marvin's Trust should remain in the event of a relapse, and Mrs. Kincaid agreed. Even Marvin said that would be the wise thing to do.

I redrafted Mrs. Kincaid's inheritance plan so that Marvin would get his inheritance outright. But for two years following Mrs. Kincaid's death, his money would remain in Trust. At the end of two years, Marvin could take his money free of Trust *if* the bank Trustee received letters from two doctors indicating Marvin was competent to manage his own money.

Never Say Never

It was fortunate Marvin's metamorphosis occurred while his mother was alive. Had he recovered after both his parents died, his inheritance would have been tied up in Trust for the rest of his life.

Except in the most grievous situations where the disability is unquestionably lifelong, I will include a special provision allowing the Trust to terminate if the disabled child recovers—even if it would take a miracle to make that change. Miracles are possible, even if the miracle takes the form of newly discovered medical or pharmaceutical treatments.

These Trust-terminating provisions vary from case to case. But in every case, they envision a scheme where the disabled child's Protector can instruct the Trustee to distribute the inheritance to the disabled child outright if:

1) That child meets certain medical standards of recovery; and

2) There is convincing proof that the child has met those standards, such as letters from medical doctors or psychiatrists—whoever would be appropriate.

11

Protecting the Inheritance from Your Child's Creditors

or

Whom Would You Prefer to Get Your Money—Your Grandchildren or Your Son's Creditors?

No matter how perfect your child is, when it comes to financial matters, all of those problems that are never supposed to happen can happen. Even the most perfect child can face financial risks beyond his control, such as:

- Lawsuits arising out of your child's professional occupation.
- An economic downturn resulting in the loss of your child's job or business.
- An auto accident resulting in a legal judgment against your child with inadequate insurance.
- A liability to the IRS for income tax obligations.
- An illness or injury to your child or other family member with costly medical and hospital expenses.

In every case, the result is that the money and property that took you a lifetime to acquire may end up with your child's creditors instead of your child and grandchildren.

This was a lesson Brad Wheeler learned firsthand.

99

Brad Wheeler: The Rocket Scientist with Common Sense

In 1975, Brad Wheeler, a Ph.D. in physics, worked at the Rand Corporation, a federal government think tank in Santa Monica. On a whim, Brad and a coworker bought a small house. They made some minor repairs and put it on the market. Within six months, they sold it for a 50 percent profit.

Brad had the smarts of a rocket scientist—but he also had good common sense. That house made him more money in six months than he earned in six months of paychecks. Brad wondered where this opportunity had been all his life.

Brad and his partner rode out the heyday of Southern California real estate inflation, going from one successful investment to the next. From one small house, they built a real estate mini-empire of houses and apartment buildings, all purchased with low down payments and high loans.

You can guess what happened. Brad and his partner, who had flown high and reaped the riches of real estate inflation, eventually crashed.

In the late 1980s, real estate in Southern California, as Brad put it, "went south and did not come back." The Federal Savings and Loan Insurance Corporation inundated Southern California with thousands of foreclosed houses and apartment buildings, supersaturating the real estate market. As a result, the values of Brad's real estate investments dropped precipitously, some even below what Brad still owed on the mortgages.

Brad and his partner were overextended—they could no longer pay the mortgages on their investment properties. Their lenders, though sympathetic, began to call in their secured and unsecured loans. Ultimately, Brad sought the protection of the bankruptcy court.

Why is this story of one man's bankruptcy in this inheritance-planning book? Because one source of money Brad tapped into for his investments was his inheritance.

After his parents died in the late 1970s, Brad pumped his entire inheritance into his real estate investments. When Brad went into bankruptcy, so did his inheritance, plus a small inheritance his wife had received.

Brad conferred with me about saving his inheritance from the bankruptcy court. Unfortunately, there was nothing that could be done. When Brad inherited his parents' money outright, it became *his* money, subject to *his* creditor problems. Brad's creditors became the ultimate inheritors of his parents' wealth.

As Brad poured his heart out, I had a clear picture in my mind's eye of his parents. I was the one who had drafted his parents' Living Trust, and I especially remembered the pride they had in their son's accomplishments. I had the sinking feeling his parents would not, to put it mildly, take too kindly to the ultimate destiny of their money and property.

I felt remorse for Brad's plight—and perhaps a touch of blame. Caught up in the emotion of the spiraling real estate days of the 1970s, I gave little thought to using the Wheelers' Living Trust to protect Brad's inheritance from creditors. The idea of a downturn in the real estate market was, back then, inconceivable.

The Lesson

Brad Wheeler's plight taught me a most valuable lesson: No one has a crystal ball to foresee the future. Your inheritance plan should assume the worst-case scenario and protect your child's inheritance from the unexpected.

It is beyond the scope of this book to discuss creditor rights against inherited assets. These rights vary from state to state. But perhaps one of the following plans may help protect your child's inheritance against a creditor.

Solution 1: The Irrevocable Protection Trust

The Protection Trust is a special plan you include in your Will or Living Trust. Instead of leaving your money and property outright to your child, you leave it to a Trustee. The Trustee will control your child's inheritance until a certain age or, if necessary, for your child's life.

With this plan, you delay your child's outright ownership to an age when his risk of incurring debt is minimal. When your child reaches the designated age, the Trust ends and your child will own his inheritance outright.

There are two types of Protection Trusts: revocable and irrevocable. Warning! Do not use a Revocable Protection Trust to shield your child's inheritance from his creditors. If your child has the power to revoke the Trust, he may be deemed to be an outright owner of the Trust assets. The result is that your child's creditor may look to the Trust assets for payment.

With an *Irrevocable* Protection Trust, you give the inheritance greater protection. Since your child cannot revoke it, he cannot own his inheritance assets until he reaches a certain age. Until then, it's the Trust's money!

Solution 2: A Foreign Country "Protection Trust"

Assume the following scenario: Your child inherits your money. After he inherits, he incurs a substantial business debt that he cannot repay. To prevent his creditors from taking his inherited money, he transfers it to a spouse, a child, a friend, or an overseas bank.

Can your son avoid a debt by making himself poor? No. If your son transfers money to *anyone* to escape a creditor, the creditor can follow that money and recover it from the transferee. In some states, this is considered defrauding a creditor and constitutes a punishable crime.

But you can do what your son cannot do. While you are alive, you can transfer his future inheritance to a foreign country Protection Trust. After you die, his inheritance may not be reachable by his creditors because it is out of the jurisdiction of the United States.

Will your foreign country Protection Trust get your son into trouble? No, because it is *your* property you are transferring out of the country. Are *you* committing a crime? No. Unless you are defrauding your creditors, all you are doing is establishing this Trust as part of your own inheritance plan.

Solution 3: The Family Limited Partnership

In chapter 36, I review the Family Limited Partnership in the context of reducing the federal estate tax. But the Family Limited Partnership may also serve as a way to protect your child's inheritance from creditors.

The Family Limited Partnership is a business entity you establish while you are alive. You transfer your real estate and other assets to the Partnership. In return, you receive the Limited Partnership shares. You own all the Limited Partnership shares, and the Partnership owns the assets. When you die, your child inherits the Limited Partnership shares, and the Partnership continues to own the assets.

Under current law in most states, a child's creditor cannot reach the real estate or other assets owned by the Partnership entity. All that remains for the creditor is the right to go against your child's Limited Partnership shares. However, these shares may have little value if the Partnership makes no distributions.

The Family Limited Partnership is not an absolute guarantee of creditor protection. However, if nothing else, you will have given your child's creditor an uphill climb to reach your child's inheritance. Oftentimes, this added degree of difficulty will give your child more leverage to negotiate a settlement with his creditor.

The creditor-protection benefits of the Family Limited Partnership vary from state to state. It is essential you confer with your own attorney to determine if this is an appropriate plan to protect your child.

Solution 4: Give Your Child the Power to Say, "No, I Don't Want the Inheritance."

A way to prevent your child's inheritance from ending up with his creditors is not to let him inherit. The creditors cannot take what your child does not own.

How can you disinherit your child? One way is not to leave your child anything. But this "cure" may be worse than the disease. If it turns out your child has no creditor problems, you have cut your child out of an inheritance for no reason.

Instead of making the decision to disinherit your child, shift that decision to your child. After you die, your child can say, "I don't want it." Your child writes these words (along with other required language) in a document called a "Disclaimer," which, generally, must be signed within nine months of your death. With a Disclaimer, your child renounces his rights to all, or a part of, his inheritance.

If your child disclaims, who will end up with the inheritance? Whomever you named in your inheritance plan as the alternate heir.

For example, your Will or Living Trust leaves your money and property to your son. It also says that should your son die before you, your money and property will go to his children. If, after you die, your son signs a Disclaimer, the inheritance will skip over him and pass to your grandchildren. By using the Disclaimer, your son never owns the family money. And your son's creditors cannot go after assets your son never owned.

Part IV

Who Says You Owe Your Children an Inheritance?

12

Cutting Out a Child from Your Will or Trust

or

Now Is the Time to Begin to Defend the Lawsuit Your Disinherited Child Will Bring After You Die

---

1. "I want to leave everything to my daughter and cut out my good-for-nothing son."

There is no law preventing you from disinheriting your child. It is your money—you can leave it to whomever you want. You can omit a child, leave more to one child, or disinherit all your children. These are your decisions.

Many times, however, the reason for cutting out a child is not justified. If you want to disinherit because a child will put the family money at risk, disinheritance may not be the answer. The use of a Protection Trust can achieve your goal of preventing your child from "blowing the dough." (Part 3 is devoted entirely to using this method to protect the family money once your child inherits it.)

Although the Protection Trust can save the family money, it cannot heal a family rift.

I never cease to be amazed at how many clients are estranged from a child or have not spoken to a child in many years. It seems

107

that time, distance, geography, and failure to communicate exponentially expand the chasm between parents and their child. The
reasons for these family rifts are many, but the ones I typically
hear are:

"My daughter got married and moved away, and now she
doesn't talk to me anymore."

"My son won't let me talk to my grandchild."

"I keep sending birthday cards or Christmas cards to my
daughter, but she never responds."

"The only time my son calls is when he needs money."

"My daughter did not bother to attend her father's funeral."

"All my life I have helped my self-centered son, and not once
have I even received a thank-you."

Whatever the reason, a client who feels permanently estranged
from a child may tell me to cut out that child from the Will or Living Trust.

My Assessment of the Assessment

I never accept a client's assessment of the rift at face value.
I always probe further to test his motivation and resolve, making
certain he is secure in his convictions. Why? Because disinheriting a child is a drastic remedy that may result in at least two
unintended consequences.

Consequence Number 1: The Lawsuit

As certain as the sun will rise tomorrow, the cutout child will
bring a lawsuit contesting the parents' inheritance plan. This
world is full of attorneys who will take these contest cases on a
contingency basis.

When the lawsuit is brought, the client's other children must hire a lawyer to defend. The attorney fees may run into tens of thousands of dollars. In fact, your other children may find it cheaper to settle the case than pay a lawyer for the defense. The cutout child knows this and often brings the lawsuit for the sole purpose of extorting a settlement.

Consequence Number 2: The Cutout Child Becomes a Burden to His Siblings

A client must always consider the impact that cutting out one child will have on his other children. If the disinherited child has no means of financial support, his siblings may find themselves forced to become his "substitute parents."

---

2. "What can I do to prevent my disinherited child from contesting my Will or Living Trust after I die?"

Begin the Defense Before You Die

If you insist on disinheriting a child, the defense of the lawsuit should begin *before* you sign your Will or Living Trust.

Your cutout child may make several arguments in this lawsuit. The three most common ones are:

1) Your other children forced you to disinherit through duress or coercion;

2) You were incompetent or of "unsound mind" when you signed your Will or Living Trust; or

3) You were mistaken as to the reasons for disinheriting your child in the first place.

Since these are the likely arguments your cutout child will make to the judge, you should address those assertions while you are alive. You should obtain solid proof showing that at the time you signed your Will or Living Trust, you were of sound mind, you were not acting under duress or coercion, and you knew exactly what you were doing.

If you were my client, this is what I would have you do.

1. The proof begins with a visit to your family doctor. I want your physician to show on your medical records that you were thinking clearly on the date of the examination.

2. For stronger evidence, I may require you to meet with a psychiatrist. I want the psychiatrist to prepare a written report stating that in his professional opinion, you are capable, competent, know exactly what you are doing, and are not under any duress or coercion.

3. As additional proof, I require a videotaping of the "ceremony" at which you sign your Will or Living Trust. However, this step involves more than retrieving my camcorder from the closet and setting it up. The videotaping should be done by an independent, professional videographer.

4. When the tape rolls, I will question you in great detail. I want to capture for all the world to see and hear why you are omitting or significantly reducing a gift to a child—and that you appear rational and competent.

5. I also require a handwritten letter from you in which you state your reasons for omitting a child from your inheritance plan.

Using the Proof After You Die

After you die and your disinherited child announces that he is bringing a lawsuit, I may send copies of the medical reports and the videotape to that child's attorney. This proof may be a powerful weapon in dissuading the attorney from proceeding further. No lawyer wants to walk into the mouth of a cannon.

This evidence preparation will cost you additional attorneys' fees, other costs, and inconvenience. But the extra cost and hassle is microscopic compared to the expense and burden your other heirs will bear defending the lawsuit brought by your omitted child after you die.

3. "Should I tell my child that I am leaving him nothing?"

For three reasons, your child should know you are omitting him from your inheritance plan.

First, he may be depending on the inheritance to help him get through life. If you tell him now, he may make other arrangements.

Second, I want *all* your children to know the reasons for the disinheritance. Too often, a child finds himself cut out and is confused as to why.

Third, and most important, telling your child he has been cut out may motivate him to shape up and change his ways. It can even lead to reconciliation.

It can happen. I have seen it happen. Let me tell you about the amazing turnaround of Sam Thomas, the forty-five-year-old flower child.

When my secretary first showed Sam into my office, I could barely keep from bursting out in laughter. Hair down to his waist, wearing flowing robes and thongs, Sam looked like a refugee from the Woodstock generation.

It wasn't just Sam's fashions that were stuck in time. It was Sam. Though forty-five years old, Sam was still a child of the 1960s. He had no wife, no children, and no assets.

Sam came to my office for information. Three years before his visit, I had prepared his parents' Living Trust. He wanted to know how his parents had treated him in their inheritance plan.

Sam could have saved himself the trip. It would have been ethically wrong for me to tell him anything without his parents' permission. Curiosity, however, got the best of me. After he left, I went to my storage room and pulled Sam's parents' file.

A quick glance at the Trust and my notes brought it all back.

Sam's parents had three children. Their two daughters were lovely girls, but Sam was killing them. They would be damned if their money went to support his alternative lifestyle. Since he would not change, they felt no choice but to cut him out of the inheritance.

Later that day, I called Sam's parents and told them of Sam's request for information. Initially, they said this was a private matter but they would think it over. A few minutes later, they called me and asked how I felt about telling Sam the truth. I told them I thought it was a good idea. It was only fair to let Sam know he could not expect any money.

I called Sam and gave him the distressing news. I also volunteered that his parents were disappointed he never married, never held a steady job, and never saw them—except to ask for money.

I also told him another thing his parents said: They were still praying for Sam to change. And I offered my opinion that if he could change, so would they.

Sam—After He Knew

I thought that I had heard the last of Sam. But about three years later, I arrived at my office to discover that Sam and his parents were my first appointment of the day. From the smiles on their faces and their warm expressions, I could tell that there was a lot of love in the room.

Sam was not a rocket scientist, but it was not hard for him to figure out what he had to do to get into his parents' good graces. Since it was his lifestyle that caused him to be cut out, he just changed his lifestyle. Sam got married, got a job, and he and his wife had a baby. He jumped from the unconventional life to a Chamber of Commerce exemplar.

It seemed his parents' prayers were answered. They wanted to change their inheritance plan so the "new Sam" would get his full share.

I congratulated Sam's parents, but I restrained myself from saying what I was really thinking. It wasn't their prayers that brought Sam back into the fold—it was greed! The wonders of money did more than all the psychiatrists could have done to "cure" Sam.

Money as a Motivator

The lesson to be learned from Sam Thomas is never give up hope. Unless your problem child suffers from a permanent disability, he may change if you give him a reason to change, even if the reason is money.

If you plan on cutting out a child, be up-front about it. Tell your "Sam Thomas" that you will cut him out if he does not clean up his act. Or tell him you will arrange to have his inheritance controlled for the rest of his life while his siblings get their money outright to use as they wish. By giving this child advance warning, you have given him the time, the opportunity, and the motivation to rehabilitate himself before you die.

---

4. "My forty-five-year-old son won't work and sponges off his mother and me. I'm afraid if we cut off his inheritance, he will just leech off my other children and make their lives miserable."

If you are considering disinheriting a child, you should factor in the impact of this decision on your other children.

The Holtens and Their "Peter Pan" Son

Many would envy the lifestyle of Waylon Holten. Refusing to be saddled with a conventional lifestyle, Waylon lived for the moment. He planned his day around his own personal plea-sure: skiing, surfing, or tennis. In the evenings, Waylon's pursuits turned to fine dining and hitting the hottest clubs.

Waylon's parents were, to put it mildly, less than pleased with their son. All efforts to get their son to accept some responsibility were for naught. It seemed Waylon's whole life was geared to circumvent the mundane. Eventually, the Holtens became permanently estranged from their son. And when they died, all their money and property went to their two daughters, Collette and Yvette.

Collette and Yvette took special joy that their brother had been cut out. As far as they were concerned, Waylon finally got his comeuppance. While they were raising families and had conventional jobs, their brother was out playing. Getting their brother's share of the inheritance, they thought, was their revenge.

It was not long after their parents died that Collette and Yvette regretted their parents' decision. When their parents dumped Waylon out of their Will, all it did was dump Waylon into their lives. Since Waylon no longer had his parents to lean on for support, he forced himself on his two sisters. He called Collette and Yvette when he needed money. He called them when he had to be bailed out of jail. He called them when his car broke down a hundred miles from home. He called them when he was about to be evicted from his apartment.

Waylon reacted unpredictably when his sisters refused to help. Sometimes he phoned them—up to fifty times a day! Sometimes he showed up at their homes or work. A few times, he slept on their doorsteps. On one occasion, he placed his body under Collette's car.

In hindsight, the Holtens' decision to cut out Waylon was wrong. They believed disinheriting Waylon would force him to get a life. But the only thing it did was shift the burden of parenting Waylon to their two daughters. Because Collette and Yvette had his share of the inheritance, Waylon felt they were morally bound to take care of him and provide for his needs.

The Moral of the Story

When the Holtens cut out Waylon, they did not intend for their son to become a burden on his sisters. Nor did I. It was a totally unforeseen consequence. And because of this lack of foresight, Waylon is making his sisters' lives miserable.

If I was advising the Holtens today, I would steer them toward leaving Waylon an inheritance. Not because of love for him, but to protect their daughters from Waylon's harassment. But any money they would leave to him would go into a Protection Trust. For more on the Protection Trust, see the chapters in part 3.

---

5. "I love my son and two daughters equally. But if my husband outlives me, I know he will cut out our son. Every time they're together, there's fireworks. I want to make certain my son receives an equal share of the family money."

If you and your husband hold your house, money, and other assets jointly with right of survivorship, you own half and your husband owns half. If your husband dies first, you will own it all and you can leave it equally to your children.

But if *you* die first, your husband will own his half *and* your half, and there is nothing you can do to prevent him from cutting your son out of an inheritance.

If you are serious about protecting your son, you have the following alternatives.

Solution 1: The Heirship Agreement

An "Heirship Agreement" will legally bind the last spouse to die to leave the family money to all children equally. But if your husband won't sign it, try this approach:

YOU: Honey, I'm afraid that if I die first, you will cut out our son. I want you to sign an agreement that says if I die first, you will leave everything equally to all our children.

HE: No way! The other kids are fine, but I wouldn't leave him a nickel!

YOU: Fine. Then if I die first, I'll leave my half outright
            to our son. Then you and he will be partners in
            everything.
HE: Where do I sign?

If your husband will not sign an Heirship Agreement, you may
have to consider the following solutions.

Solution 2: Terminate the Right of Survivorship and Leave Your Half Outright to Your Son

You own your half of the jointly held house, cash, stocks, and
other assets. If you die first, your half will automatically go to
your husband. But it doesn't have to be that way. You have the
perfect right to cancel this right of survivorship. Once it is canceled, your husband will not automatically get your half if you die
first. Then you can make your own Will or Living Trust stating that
when you die, all or a portion of your half will go to your son. Or
if you have other children, you can leave your half to all of them.

The Downsides

This solution, however, has two disadvantages:

1. *You Cannot Have Your Cake and Eat It, Too*
If you terminate the right of survivorship, you have given up
the right to automatically get your husband's half if *he* dies first.
Your husband then has the legal right to leave his half to anyone
he wants.

Will your husband leave his half to you? Perhaps . . . perhaps
not. He may have an old Will (or make a new Will) leaving what he
owns to someone other than you.

If losing the right of automatic ownership of your husband's
share (if he dies first) is unacceptable, this is not the alternative
for you.

2. All Your Children May End Up with an Unequal Inheritance

This solution is designed to guarantee that all or a portion of your half will go to your son. However, it may result in your children receiving unequal amounts of the family money.

For example, you and your husband have a net worth of $600,000, each of you owning half. You die first and leave your half ($300,000) to your son. Your husband dies years later, leaving his half ($300,000) to your two daughters in equal shares.

The result is an unequal inheritance: Your son inherits $300,000 while your two daughters inherit only $150,000 each.

Another example: You die first and leave your half ($300,000) equally to your son and two daughters. When your husband dies, he leaves his half ($300,000) to your two daughters. Again, the result is an unequal inheritance. All your son receives is $100,000 from you. On the other hand, your two daughters each receive not only $100,000 from you but $150,000 each from your husband.

Solution 3: Terminate the Right of Survivorship— but Let Your Husband Use Your Half for Life

Provide in your inheritance plan that if you die first, your half of your house, your stocks, and your other assets will go to a Trustee who will hold and control it for the rest of your husband's life. The Trustee can be a third party, your son, your husband, or your husband and son together. Granted, your husband will not own your half outright, but he is not shut out from its benefits:

- Your husband will receive the income from your half of the investment assets.
- Your husband can live in the house for the rest of his life.
- Your husband can sell the house and receive the income generated by your half of the proceeds.
- Your husband can have the right to spend the principal, depending on how generous or strict with your half you want to be.

- Your husband can retain the right to make investment decisions over your half.

This plan serves as an excellent compromise. Your husband receives the benefits of your half, and, at the same time, you are guaranteed that after he dies, your half will go to your child or children (or anyone else you want). However, it still requires you to sever the joint ownership, leaving your husband free to leave his half to anyone he wants if he dies first. If this is an unacceptable risk, consider the next solution, which keeps the right of survivorship intact.

Solution 4: Use a Life Insurance Policy to Guarantee Some Money Goes to Your Child

While you are alive, make your son the beneficiary of a life insurance policy on your life. Following your death, he will receive the insurance money. After that, it doesn't make any difference if your husband cuts out your son—he's already received an earlier inheritance from the insurance proceeds!

---

6. "My thirty-year-old son is a confirmed drug addict. It seems no matter how hard he tries, he can't 'beat the habit.' Although I love my son, I don't want any of my money to end up in his arm, up his nose, or with his drug dealer. To prevent his inheritance going to waste, I'm thinking of leaving all of my assets to my daughter."

Your idea of leaving your son's share to your daughter is a normal reaction to this type of situation. Nobody wants to leave an inheritance to a child that will be improperly used, particularly when a child is an addict. However, following suit may result in the following unintended consequences:

1. If your son has a tendency to violence or uncontrolled anger, your daughter may become a victim of his rage. Even if

your son is not the violent type, he may still harbor ill feelings of jealousy toward his sister because he may, rightly or wrongly, feel that she has "cut him out" of his inheritance.

2. Although your daughter may have no legal responsibility to help your son financially, he may look to his sister for such assistance because, from his point of view, he will think, "my sister took my money." As a result, you will have shifted your son's financial problems to your daughter.

3. You do not want an inheritance to perpetuate your son's drug addiction. However, you also do not want him to become a homeless or street person, which may be the result of cutting him out.

Solution: The Irrevocable Protection Trust

To avoid the unintended consequences of completely disinheriting your drug-addicted son, I believe it is preferable to allocate a portion of your wealth to an Irrevocable Protection Trust, which I discuss in part 3. This method will not allow your son to get his hands on the money. Instead, a third-party Money Manager will use your son's inheritance to pay rent directly to his landlord, and to pay other suppliers for his other fundamental needs, such as food, clothing, and medical bills.

With the Irrevocable Protection Trust, your son's share of the inheritance will be protected for him, and from his addiction.

What If Your Son Overcomes His Addiction?

An addict is an addict for life. Your son may eventually learn not to give in to the overwhelming craving for the next "high." On the other hand, after forty-five years of hearing clients describe the tragic fate of their addicted children—and as crass as it sounds—your son will likely die from his vice.

However, miracles do happen. Your son is in his thirties. He may be a totally different person when he gets into his fifties and sixties. Therefore, I recommend you build some flexibility into the Irrevocable Protection Trust. You should provide that your son will receive his entire portion of the inheritance without controls if he proves to at least two medical doctors (who are not related by blood or marriage to your son, or to each other) that he has overcome or controlled his addiction and is competent to responsibly manage and control his financial affairs.

This provision not only allows your inheritance plan to change if your son changes, it may provide him with an incentive to "kick" his addiction.

13

How Much Inheritance Is Too Much Inheritance?

or

Will Your Child's Inheritance Turn Him into a "Trust-Fund Baby"?

"My wife and I are fortunate to have a significant estate and two well-grounded kids. Each of them is married and has a good job, and everyone gets along with each other. There is no reason why they shouldn't receive our entire estate after we die. But I am concerned about giving my children that kind of wealth. We weren't born with silver spoons in our mouths. Our wealth came as a result of many years of hard work and perseverance. We don't want our children to feel like they don't have to do anything in life."

Since *Beyond the Grave* was first published, this concern has become the "hot" topic in family inheritance planning. Never before have I encountered more people who fear that a large inheritance will lead their responsible children to become classic ne'er-do-wells who hang out at the country club or who will acquire bad habits.

A few years after our book was originally published, my father and I were invited to speak on the chief topic of this book, the human factor in family inheritance planning, at a meeting of a

121

group called the "Captains of Industry." The twenty or so gentlemen who attended comprised some of the wealthiest persons in America. There was the former owner of a National Football League franchise, the owner of a national chain of family-dining restaurants, the owner of a business that manufactures a sailing craft that is a household name in that industry, and others whose services or products you are probably familiar with.

I have given enough inheritance planning talks to have acquired the skill of identifying when an audience is "with me." If I see heads nodding in recognition, unwavering eye contact, and laughter at all my jokes, I know I have an enraptured audience. But as I continued speaking before the captains, I saw none of those signs. They were listening politely, but appeared somewhat detached and disinterested. I remember thinking, these folks probably have inheritance plans drafted by the most high-powered attorneys in the country. I don't blame them for being bored. What could I possibly say that they have not already heard?

As the time mercifully drew nearer for the break, I was speaking on how an inheritance plan can ensure that children are treated equally. At that point, one of the younger Captains interrupted me and asked, quite simply, "Mr. Condon, how much inheritance is too much inheritance?" I was a bit taken aback, because the inquiry had little to do with my present subject. I asked, "What do you mean?" He answered, "I want the money that passes to my children to be a positive. But if they get too much, it could turn into a negative."

After pondering this inquiry for a few moments, I responded with this: "Let me answer your question with a question. Do you have the courage not to leave it all to your children?"

This one remark created a silence, then a buzz of freewheeling discussion. For the remainder of the day, these powerful and wealthy people spoke passionately of this issue and little else. At that moment, the common thread that bound all the Captains was the fear that their vast wealth would turn their children into the image of the old-fashioned "trust-fund babies."

For another dramatic example, Atlanta Braves pitching phenom Tom Glavine discussed in *The Wall Street Journal* his adoption of a "Family Incentive Trust" in his inheritance plan. In essence, this trust states that upon Mr. Glavine's death, all or a portion of his estate will be held by a third-party "Money Manager." The Money Manager will distribute money to his children if they act in accordance with the "instructions" he has set forth in writing. In other words, the manager will pay his children more money if they act the way he wants them to act. As Mr. Glavine stated, "I don't want my kids to feel like they don't have to do anything in life. I want my kids to realize they need to work. They can't just say, 'I feel like a Ferrari today.' "

All Very Nice—but Let Me Tell You What I Think

With the "New Economy" having created more millionaires than ever before in American history, this issue will undoubtedly be considered and addressed more than ever before. But one does not have to be a Captain or a millionaire to share the concern that a significant inheritance can lead a "good kid" down the path of irresponsibility. It is simply a natural feeling to want our children to make the most of their lives.

However, if you were my client and you asked me what I thought of incentive-based planning, I would give you this straightforward response: While I applaud the actions being encouraged by incentive-based planning, I think it's a phony. It's a "carrot-and-stick" approach to inheritance planning that will, for the most part, *not* serve your goal of ensuring that your responsible children will stay well grounded.

Strong opinion? Absolutely. But after having drafted many of these plans and seeing the results after clients died, I believe it is justified. Let me tell you why.

First, I believe that true character cannot be molded by money. You cannot salvage by inheritance what you fear you have not accomplished during your life. If you wish to ensure that your child will not be spoiled by his "inheritance success," the solution is to instill in him *now* the basic underlying concepts of a productive society: character, financial responsibility, family, charity, and contributions to community.

Second, your child will view the plan as your way of continuing to test him, even after you are dead. What reasonable person likes that feeling? The result may not be a hardworking child, but a resentful and bitter one.

Third, you may end up with a child doing the right things for the wrong reason. You intend to foster in your child the genuine feelings of pride and accomplishment that come from hard work and academic achievement. However, what you may get is a child who learns nothing more than how to "play the game" while waiting for the next trust distribution.

Fourth, I typically advise against efforts of parents to control their child too much from the grave. Without proper justification, "dead-hand" control simply goes against my grain.

Fifth, the reality is that when you and your spouse die, your child will be in his mid-sixties and his character and motivation will have long been established. Your child's views about hard work, education, and accomplishment will have already been set and no amount of money will work to "undo" that mindset. The distributions will begin when your child is well past middle age, rendering your "beyond the grave messages" of hard work and academic achievement meaningless.

Sixth, by the time your child inherits, he may be well into his own career and will not necessarily need the distributions for education, housing, professional school, and the like.

Seventh, and finally, these plans often end up with a trip to the courthouse—no matter how well drafted and complete the plan. If the legal battle commences, it will be your child who believes he has met the goals set forth in your incentive-based plan versus the Trustee (or other Money Manager) who believes otherwise. Your child and the psychiatric and psychological experts he hires will testify that he has attained the relevant standards. The Trustee will present experts who will testify to the contrary.

By the time the case settles or goes to trial, tens of thousands of dollars will have been expended in attorneys' fees, court costs, expert witness fees, and other expenses, all of which may be paid by the trust money!

My Version of Incentive-Based Planning

For the aforesaid reasons, I believe that incentive-based plans using the typical "carrot-and-stick" methods simply do not work. I prefer an incentive-based plan not built on reward but on the cold, hard reality of "that's all you get." This is a no-strings-attached plan that states, in essence, as follows: "Child, when we die, your inheritance will be held by a Money Manager who, for the rest of your life, will pay you an amount equal to the monthly support we have given you during our lifetime."

This is more than an incentive-based plan—this is a reality check! Your child will wake up to the fact that if he wants more, he will have to find a way to get more, such as getting or maintaining a job.

A variation of this plan is to take the Money Manager out of the equation. That is, rather than have a Money Manager dole out your child's inheritance in incremental amounts for the rest of his life, simply leave your child a specific lump sum. I describe this approach, and its dramatic effect, more fully in chapter 14 ("Are Your Children Spending Their Inheritance—and You're Not Dead Yet?").

Use Extreme Caution

I do not recommend these alternative incentive-based plans cavalierly. As I have mentioned previously in this book, I instinctively react against a client attempting to exert too much control of his child's inheritance from "beyond the grave."

Therefore, if you asked me to incorporate my seemingly heartless alternatives in your inheritance plan, I have to be convinced that they are justified. Specifically, I need to hear you say—and prove—that your situation matches one or more of the following descriptions:

a. Your child is a ne'er-do-well whose main job in life is waiting for you to die so he can become a trust-fund baby.
b. You have a child who does not march to the same drummer as the rest of conventional society. This child knows what work is: He has seen you go to work, but has decided, "That's not for me."
c. You have spoiled your child throughout his life with all of life's essentials and pleasures, and your permissiveness has led to his inability or unwillingness to make it on his own.
d. You have a total, consuming, and abject fear that your now-responsible child will "shuck" his conventional life once he inherits.

If you truly believe you see yourself or your child in any of these brief descriptions, and if you have the courage to not give your child a normal full share of his inheritance, then my alternative approaches to incentive-based planning may possibly lead your child to attain an educational, employment, or other worthwhile goal he otherwise may never have considered; or they could motivate your already responsible child to maintain his steady and conventional path of work, family, and community contribution.

The Exceptions

Of course, like every hard-and-fast rule, my attitude against traditional reward-based incentive plans has a few exceptions.

a. Minor Children

If my clients have a minor child, I sometimes provide that if they die when that child is still a minor, the child shall receive the inheritance upon attaining certain ascertainable educational and employment goals. This type of provision serves as the parents' "lessons from the grave" to be financially responsible, gainfully employed, and free of harmful dependencies.

b. Disabled/Addicted Children

A child who suffers from an addiction or disability that poses a risk of loss to the inheritance cannot receive that inheritance outright. In those cases, I will provide that the child's share shall be held by a Money Manager who will manage and control the share for the child's benefit. As part of those instructions, the Money Manager will be given the power to terminate this arrangement and distribute that share to that child if he demonstrates he has "kicked" the addiction or has overcome the disability (if possible).

I describe these conditions in more detail in my discussion of protecting inheritances from risks of loss in part 3.

c. Estranged Children

While incentive-based planning is typically used to lead a child to a productive life, I have occasionally used it to try to bring a child back into the family fold.

I will occasionally hear clients state they have not had any meaningful contact with a child for several years. In those cases, I advise the clients to allow me to inform the child that continued estrangement will result in that child being "cut out" of the inheritance.

This is an extreme form of incentive-based planning . . . and it has worked! Greed can do more than all the psychiatrists in the world to bring families together. On the other hand, some reunions are not meant to be and no amount of money can lead to reconciliation. I discuss this issue in greater detail in question 3 of chapter 12.

d. Insistent Clients

While I am secure in my belief that traditional incentive-based plans do not work, I recognize that others believe differently and still want an inheritance plan that ties a child's inheritance to his acceptance of his parents' core values and beliefs. And, certainly, I have drafted my share for clients, which have said, in essence, "Go ahead and take the money . . . as long as you play by my rules."

There are many types of traditional incentive-based plans in existence. The only limitations are the imaginations of you and your attorney, and a few public policies that prohibit certain types of conditions. I address these limitations in chapter 15 ("How to Control Your Child's Life from the Grave").

14

Are Your Children Spending Their Inheritance—and You're Not Dead Yet?

or

"That's My Son—the One Who Is Waiting for Me to Die!"

---

1. "None of my children seem to be making their place in life. They're just waiting for my wife and I to die—so they can live off their inheritance."

The expectation of a substantial inheritance may dilute a child's motivation to pursue educational and occupational goals. Listen to one who knows:

> Inherited wealth . . . is as certain death to ambition as cocaine is to morality.
>
> —*Commodore Vanderbilt's grandson,*
> *heir to some $60 million in 1885*

Vanderbilt's grandson could have been talking about the Perkinses' children.

Mr. and Mrs. Perkins had been enormously successful in real estate development, mostly apartment buildings. Their real estate fortune amounted to approximately $30 million.

The Perkinses were knowledgeable enough to know that more than 50 percent of what they owned would go to the IRS as a death tax when they died. They wanted some ideas on how this tax could be reduced.

After several consultations on ways to reduce the death tax, I asked the Perkinses if they wanted to talk about any other inheritance-planning issues—such as children problems.

Apparently, they did.

"Our Rotten Children"

The Perkinses had three children, two sons and a daughter. Like many parents, they gave their children money to help them get started in life.

The Perkinses, however, took their generosity to the extreme. Their attitude was that their checkbook was their children's checkbook. It started with toys and clothes. Now it was a complete subsidy of their children's lives, from houses and vacations to cars and credit cards.

When their children were growing up, the Perkinses never gave a thought to how this subsidy would affect their children in the future. They believed all they were doing was making their children happy. But when their children were in their late twenties and early thirties, they saw what their money had done.

And the Perkinses did not like what they saw.

"Our wealth," Mr. Perkins said, "started out as a blessing, Mr. Condon, but it became a curse. Our intention was to do good for our children. Instead, we turned them into parasites.

"We wanted our kids to have normal lives. We wanted them to go to college. They keep saying they will enroll 'next year,' but they have been saying that for the last six years. The only one in school now is our daughter, and she's been going to a two-year community college for the past five years." Mr. Perkins wistfully added, "My children wouldn't know a job if it bit them in the backside. The only job my kids are qualified for is finding the best happy-hour bar in town.

"All our kids do is hang around, Mr. Condon. They have built their lives around their expected inheritance. They are just waiting for us to die."

"Mr. Perkins," I said reassuringly, "I'm certain it can't be all that bad." But Mr. Perkins actually had to pause and reflect for a response.

Mr. Perkins finally said he could only think of two good things about his children: They did not do drugs, and they occasionally selected a worthy cause to talk about. Their latest "cause" was helping the homeless. But according to the Perkinses, it was just talk—more camouflage to avoid real employment.

The Damage Is Done

The Perkinses' tale confirms what all us parents know in our hearts: Money not earned is no benefit. When parents give their children a blank check, what motivation do they have to get off the dime? Or, as Ross Perot once said, "If your kids grow up living in fairyland thinking that they're princes and princesses, you're going to curse their lives."

Solution: Do You Have the Courage to Leave No Money to Your Children?

What the Perkinses could not accomplish while alive, they hoped to accomplish after they died. They wanted a way to use the inheritance as an incentive to get their children to do something useful with their lives.

My reply was harsh, but it was the truth: "If your kids are unmotivated now, there is not much I can do to make them good kids after you die.

"However, Mr. and Mrs. Perkins, what law says you owe your

children an inheritance? If you leave them nothing, they may be forced to carve out their own place in this world. Do you have the courage to leave your children nothing and let them know it now?"

The Perkinses sat in stunned silence. Never before had they entertained such a concept. They had always felt duty-bound to pass their wealth to their children and keep it in the bloodline. But now, the lawyer was talking about going against the grain. What I said half in jest had struck a chord.

I thought my suggestion would be rejected out of hand. But when Mr. Perkins finally spoke, he said, "How would this plan work?"

"Leave your kids some money," I suggested, "just enough for them to have a minimal lifestyle. It should be enough to just get by, but not enough for them to feel they can avoid getting a job. Then leave the rest to charity—any charity you want."

The Perkinses said they would think about it. Several weeks later, they called to tell me they did not like this idea . . . they loved it! With this plan, their children would also be forced to "get a life."

In the months that followed, I worked closely with the Perkinses to set up the Perkins Family Foundation. This Foundation would inherit most of the Perkinses' wealth. Its purpose was to give money to charity after the Perkinses died.

What was the charity the Perkinses selected? Their children's latest "favorite" cause: helping the homeless.

The Family Meeting

The Perkinses broke the news to their children at a family meeting held in my conference room, a small office surrounded by shelves of law books with an oblong table in the center. Around this table sat the Perkinses, their two sons, their sons' wives, and their unmarried daughter.

Mr. Perkins allowed me to be bearer of these "good tidings."

"You are so lucky to have such civic-minded parents," I began. "Your parents recognize this community allowed them to become financially successful—and now they want to give something back to this community. And since all of you have a keen interest in helping the homeless, your parents thought they would carry that interest into action.

"When both your parents die, you will each receive $350,000, and the rest of your parents' wealth will go to a charitable foundation. The foundation will be dedicated to providing housing and other services to the homeless. Your parents feel there is no better way to serve the community that has served them so well."

To show the children that their parents were serious, I gave each of them a copy of the voluminous and formidable papers that established the foundation.

The Effect

As I proceeded to talk about the particulars of the foundation, I could see the Perkins children and their spouses struggling to maintain a semblance of composure. But their efforts were for naught. Had they the acting talents of Laurence Olivier, they still could not have disguised the incredulous look on their faces.

As for Mr. and Mrs. Perkins, they, too, tried to keep their composure, with their arms crossed and their eyes fixed on me. Yet every so often, the briefest of smiles would appear on their faces. After years of quiet suffering, they quietly reveled in their children's reactions.

The Perkinses had succeeded in getting their children's attention. In fact, this meeting had proceeded so well that Mr. Perkins told his children something he and I had not rehearsed:

"Kids, we have given you a great start in life. You have things most people struggle for all their lives. A beautiful home, nice cars, wonderful vacations, and an ample allowance.

"In a way, you've been spending your inheritance all along. Why wait for the final installment? We'll give each of you your $350,000 now instead of after your mother and I die. If you can live on that, fine. If you can't, then now is the time to find a way to make more."

The Aftermath

Will the Perkinses' scare strategy work? It remains to be seen. The Perkinses are still alive, so their children have not felt the sting of inheriting nothing.

But as far as each child knows, all they are going to get is $350,000 each. The Perkinses hope this message will motivate their children while they are young enough to do something with the remainder of their lives.

One thing I do know. A few months after this meeting, I heard from the Perkinses that both their daughters-in-law had filed for divorce. It seems that since there would be no inheritance, there was no need for them to hang around.

Is Disinheritance the Answer?

You may not be as rich as the Perkinses, but you don't have to be to have a similar problem. Like the Perkinses, you may have a child whose job in life is waiting to inherit.

Will threatening to disinherit motivate your child to shape up? Perhaps—if your child gets a real sense that you are not fooling around. But you can use your child's inheritance expectations in a more positive way to attain the same goal.

I call this alternative the "Incentive Trust." Why? Because it gives your child an incentive to get a life. This is basically how the plan works:

1) In your inheritance plan, leave the child who has dollar signs in his eyes enough to cover his basic necessities.

2) Leave the rest of this child's share to a third-party Trustee to hold for your child.

3) Instruct the Trustee to pay this child from the Trust one dollar for every dollar he earns.

4) Instruct the Trustee to pay this child substantial portions from the Trust if certain goals are attained, such as graduating college, holding down gainful employment for a certain period of time, or any other goal you deem worthwhile.

2. "I think my son overestimates my wealth and is expecting a large inheritance. Should I give him a better idea of what I own before I die?"

Yes. I believe that giving a child a clearer picture of the future inheritance is a positive thing to do—especially if the child's inheritance expectation is unrealistic.

It is not unreasonable for a child to look at the expected inheritance as a source of retirement money. But will the expected amount really be there when the parents die? Parents may have less money than the child thinks. Or a child forgets to account for the death taxes on the expected inheritance.

It is unfair to allow a child to rely on an inheritance that may be far less than his expectations. Bringing reality to a child's inheritance expectations allows that child to plan his life accordingly.

15

How to Control Your Child's Life from the Grave

or

"If My Children or Grandchildren Want My Money, They'll Do It My Way— or the Highway"

"I'll be damned if my daughter marries out of her faith. Can I control her inheritance to make sure she marries a man of the same faith?"

"How can I use the inheritance to make sure my children and grandchildren follow the Jewish religion?"

"My son has never worked in his life. How can I use his inheritance to make sure he will get and keep a steady job?"

"How can I use my grandchildren's inheritance to get them to go to college and become professionals?"

"I am a die-hard Bruin. What can I do to get my daughter to get her degree from UCLA?"

> "My children won't inherit dime one unless they send my grandchildren to a religious school."

These are the kinds of comments I hear from clients every day. For them, the inheritance plan is not just a way to transfer their wealth when they die. It is a tool to control their child's life from the grave.

Some of these clients have spent a lifetime adhering to certain values and want to impose these values on future generations. Other clients want their children to achieve certain educational, occupational, or professional goals. Whatever their views, clients often feel that setting certain conditions on the inheritance may be the only way to get their children to comply. "If my kids want my money," they say, "they'll have to do it my way."

I am a firm believer in inheritance conditions when they are designed to prevent the inheritance from being squandered due to the problems in your children's lives—addiction, financial immaturity, disability, marriage and divorce problems, creditor problems, and the like. In part 3 of this book, I discuss these conditions and how they are used to protect the inheritance from those risks of loss.

However, if you have read chapter 14, you know that I am somewhat opposed to rewards-based inheritance planning for children whose only addiction is avoiding a conventional lifestyle or whose only disability is not being desirous of attaining education or employment. Not only do I instinctively react against parents attempting to control their children too much from the grave, I believe these plans do not ensure that the goals to be sought will be achieved.

I do not have my head buried in the sand. I am aware that many people, including other attorneys, believe differently. At my seminars, I never fail to hear at least one person describe how effective an incentive-based plan was in getting a child to change his tune. Still, while I applaud the result, I do not agree with the method.

However, I do not want to let my view of rewards-based plans stand in the way of your education and enlightenment. For those who embrace these types of plans, I shall briefly point out four categories of inheritance conditions most often discussed when putting together an inheritance plan.

Conditioning the Inheritance to Control Your Child's Religion

"If my daughter wants my money, she will have to stay in our faith."

"My son will have to raise his children in our faith if he wants my money."

I have heard these same instructions from clients of many religious affiliations. Whatever the religion, these conditions are doomed to failure. Why? Because attempts to force a person to follow a certain religion violate public policy.

Judges and juries throughout the United States have attempted to define what inheritance conditions violate public policy. Basically, if your condition restrains your child from exercising a right that society favors, it is a bad condition and will be voided.

Does society favor freedom of religion? Absolutely. You cannot condition your daughter's inheritance on raising her children in a particular faith. If you do, you have restrained this freedom. The result is that your daughter can disregard your condition and receive her inheritance outright. (Besides, even if the condition was legal, who would be around to enforce it?)

Conditioning the Inheritance on Who Your Child Marries

Like religious conditions, inheritance conditions based on marriage violate public policy. Society, after all, favors the freedom to marry whomever one chooses.

So if you say your son cannot inherit unless he marries a

woman of a certain faith, you have violated public policy. As a result, your condition is void, and your son will inherit without conditions when you die.

Conditioning the Inheritance to Force Your Child to Attend a Certain School

If you want to use conditions in your inheritance plan to coerce your heirs into attending a certain school, go right ahead. Unlike conditions based on marriage and religion, education conditions are, for the most part, valid, and usually take one of the following forms:

1. The Complete Condition

This is the "all-or-nothing" approach. For example, Mr. Mora, an ardent alumnus of Kenyon College in Ohio, said in his Living Trust, "If my sons want to inherit my money, they must first have a degree from Kenyon. If they haven't earned their degree before I die, they get nothing."

2. The Compromise Condition

This approach gives your child a chance to meet your condition even after you die: "My daughter gets my money if she graduates from Pepperdine. If she has not graduated while I'm alive, I leave her share to a Trustee, who will hold on to it for her until she does. If she does not graduate by a certain age, the Trustee will distribute it to my grandchildren."

3. The Education Trust

This condition does not scare your heirs into attending a certain school. It merely tells them that if they comply, you will pay for their education expenses.

For example, Mr. Steinberg, a survivor from a Nazi concentration camp, wanted his grandchildren to receive a Jewish education. In his Living Trust, he provided that upon his death, a Trust would be set up to pay for their education at the University of Judaism in Los Angeles. If they graduated elsewhere, the Trust money would go to the state of Israel.

Conditioning the Inheritance on Your Child Obtaining a Certain Occupational or Professional Goal

"If my son becomes a priest, I'll give his diocese a million dollars."

"When my son becomes a rabbi, he can have his inheritance."

"We've always had a doctor in the family, and I want my only child to become a doctor."

"My daughter can receive her inheritance only if she graduates law school—and I don't care how long it takes."

You have the right to condition the inheritance on your child attaining a certain occupational or professional status. For example, you can establish a Trust that will reward your daughter if she becomes a medical doctor.

On the other hand, your goals may not be so lofty. You may not care whether you have a doctor in the family. All you may want is to motivate your chronically unemployed daughter to find and keep a steady, paying job.

The Incentive Trust can help you achieve this goal. In your inheritance plan, provide that your daughter's inheritance shall go to a Trustee. Then provide that the Trustee shall pay her a certain amount of money for every month she remains employed. Or instruct the Trustee to match her dollar-for-dollar for every legitimate dollar she earns.

With the Incentive Trust, your daughter may realize that even the most menial job will result in her receiving a double salary, which may encourage her to maintain gainful employment.

But before you embark on this Incentive Trust, be mindful that, metaphorically speaking, if the twig is too far bent, no force of money can straighten it out. For whatever reason, your child may not (or cannot) be able to live up to your standards of what a child ought to do.

In some cases, wisdom dictates not to coerce compliance where compliance is unlikely. Rather than use the inheritance to make your child live up to your standards, use the inheritance to make your child's life a happy one—even if it goes against your grain.

Part V

Who Will Hold Your "Problem" Child's Inheritance?

16

Who Should Be Your Child's Trustee?

or

You Can Let Your Sister Hold Your Child's Money—but There Ain't No Policeman Looking over Her Shoulder

---

1. "I'm convinced I cannot leave my son an outright inheritance. If he gets it without controls, it may never end up with my grandchildren. I want to leave his inheritance to a Protection Trust, but who should be the Trustee?"

In chapter 7, I discuss a number of risks the family money may be subject to after your child inherits it. Indeed, once in your child's hands, the family money may be exposed to the problems your child faces in life: addictions, creditors, divorce, bankruptcy, mismanagement, judgments, IRS troubles, and all the other risks of loss.

To protect the family money from your child's problems, I suggest you do not leave the inheritance outright. Instead, leave the inheritance to a Trustee. The Trustee will control, manage, and hold the inheritance for your child's benefit for as long as you specify.

Because this plan protects the family money after you die, I call it the Protection Trust. But the failure or success of this Trust may depend on one crucial element: the Trustee.

145

Who should be the Trustee of the Protection Trust? There are three alternatives:

A private individual;

A banking or other financial institution; or

Your child himself.

Trustee Choice Number 1: The Private Individual

The typical client's first reaction in choosing a Trustee to protect a child's inheritance is to select the brother or sister of that child (the "Sibling Trustee"). The client feels this is the most natural choice because the client believes:

1) The Sibling Trustee will take greater pains to oversee the child's financial needs. "Blood," after all, watches out for blood.

2) Only the Sibling Trustee would assume the burden of helping out the child.

3) The Sibling Trustee is already familiar with the child's needs.

4) The Sibling Trustee can tune in better to the client's thinking as to how the child should be treated.

These are sensible reasons that make it seem right to appoint a child's sibling as Trustee. Early in my practice, I invariably agreed with this choice.

But since then clients have died, and I have seen what happens when one child holds money for another. Inevitably, there will be stress on—or the destruction of—the sibling relationship. Why? Because when one sibling holds money for another, the tie that binds is no longer only blood—it is blood *and* money. When the two are mixed, the sibling relationship becomes adversarial: "You have my money and I want it!"

For example, you have two children, a daughter and a son. Because your son is an alcoholic, you feel he should not get his inheritance outright. Otherwise, you predict, all your hard-earned money will end up at your son's favorite watering hole. When you die, someone must hold your son's inheritance and protect it for him.

In your inheritance plan, you name your daughter as your son's Sibling Trustee. When you die, your daughter will be in charge of your son's inheritance.

In your mind, you have protected your son's inheritance from your son's drinking problem. However, your son is not thinking along those lines. All he knows is that his sister is his Money Manager—anytime he wants money, he must first ask his sister. When your son asks for money, will your daughter give it to him? Since she holds the checkbook, she has the sole power to say no. Or she may give your son less than he requests. Your son wants to buy a Mercedes—your daughter thinks a Ford is sufficient. Your son makes a list of his monthly expenses—your daughter considers the expenses unreasonable and feels he can get by with less.

If your daughter continually refuses your son's requests, your son may harass your daughter to no end. Can your Trustee daughter withstand the pressure from your son? Perhaps she can. On the other hand, she may be unable to handle the stress—and quit the job. One Trustee Sibling put it to me this way: "Who needs it, Mr. Condon? My brother is making my life miserable. He's calling me a hundred times a day saying, 'I want money.' I'm going to give him his money and be done with it. I just can't take his abuse anymore!"

Whether the private individual Trustee is your child's brother, sister, uncle, aunt, nephew, niece, cousin, a close friend, or any individual, the money relationship may ultimately destroy the family connection.

Other Risks of Using a Private Individual as Trustee

Anytime you choose a private individual as your child's Trustee, consider the following:

1) Your child's Trustee does not come into play until both you and your spouse are dead. By that time, the Trustee may be elderly, disabled, incompetent, or deceased.

2) Your designated Trustee may (and probably will) charge as much for his or her services as a bank Trustee would charge—and not do as good a job.

3) Your designated Trustee may not be equipped to fulfill the administrative and investment duties necessary to make the Protection Trust efficient and productive.

4) There is no policeman looking over the Trustee's shoulder. When your choice becomes Trustee, your real estate, bank accounts, stocks, and all other assets go into his or her individual name. The Trustee has unfettered control over the money. If he or she dissipates the Trust assets, the money is gone forever. There may be little recourse for your child because, as a practical matter, lawsuits against a Trustee often turn out to be frustrating and expensive with no beneficial results.

5) Your designated Trustee may not be skillful in investments and may not have the necessary tools to deal with the daily details of managing the Trust assets.

6) You may not want to inflict this burden on whomever you have selected as Trustee. Often, your child may make unreasonable demands on the Trustee and hound the Trustee to the point of frustration and distraction.

7) Your designated Trustee has her own life. She simply may not have time to handle all of the daily details of the Trust estate.

Trustee Choice Number 2: The Financial Institution

I highly recommend using a financial institution as your child's Trustee. With this choice, all the problems inherent with the private individual Trustee do not exist.

The institution I usually recommend to serve as Trustee is the Trust Department of a bank (the bank Trustee). In my thirty-five years of practice, I have found that the overwhelming majority of bank Trustees perform Trust services reasonably, responsibly, and efficiently.

However, I often receive a negative, icy response when I suggest to a client bringing in a bank Trustee to control a child's inheritance. In fact, most clients abhor the idea of any corporate third party running the show with the family money.

Why this reluctance to use the bank Trustee? Most likely, it is because the client has heard:

Banks are poor investors of money. They invest too conservatively for any real gain on principal.

Banks are too impersonal. Whenever your children show up at the bank, someone new will be in charge of your children's Trust.

Banks charge high fees for their Trust services.

Banks are lone guns. They have no one looking over their shoulder to prevent misuse of your children's money.

I have heard these same reasons repeated so often that I sometimes wonder if my clients have read from the same script. Nevertheless, I am personally convinced that the modern bank Trustee is not guilty of these accusations. But for clients without firsthand experience with bank Trustees, overcoming these preconceptions is very difficult.

Of course, there are the occasional exceptions. About once a year, the newspaper services pick up a story about a bank Trustee who is accused of mismanaging Trust money. However, these stories are so rare that when they do occur, they make headlines.

The Advantage of Using a Bank Trustee

If you need a third party to control your child's inheritance, he or she may be better served with a bank Trustee because:

1) Banks treat Trust estates and Trust administration as a full-time job, and an individual may only give your child's Trust part-time treatment.

2) Banks have facilities to manage all your assets, whether real estate, securities, or other assets, but an individual may not be equipped to efficiently and effectively manage the assets.

3) Banks' activities are audited internally as well as by state and federal regulators to ensure that the Trust assets are preserved, but an individual has no such watchdogs.

4) Banks have an unlimited life, but an individual may die, become incompetent, disabled—or disappear.

5) Banks have employees with sophistication and experience in dealing with investment decisions, but an individual may have no such experience.

6) Banks usually have employees willing to help your child, but an individual with his own personal problems may not have the time to deal with your child's concerns.

7) Banks will treat your children impartially, but an individual may not be objective, heightening stress and division between your children.

8) Banks can withstand being hounded and pressured by a problem child, but an individual may throw up his hands in disgust and accede to your problem child's demands.

2. "You convinced me. I have decided to let a bank act as Trustee of my son's Protection Trust. There are several banks in my community to choose from and I would like to interview them. However, I don't know what to ask in order to make a decision."

Whether a particular bank Trustee is for you depends on your set of circumstances. What may be right for you may not be what the next person is looking for. The size and character of your wealth, the nature of your child's problem, the age of your child, and the way you want your money distributed are all factors in your decision.

However, whatever your particular set of circumstances, you want the bank Trustee to give you three assurances:

Assurance Number 1

You want the bank Trustee to know and adhere to your investment philosophy. In this regard, ask the bank's top Trust administrator the following questions:

A) Does this bank see eye-to-eye with me as to how I want my child's money managed?

B) What procedures are made or followed in making investment decisions?

C) Who makes the investment decisions? If a committee, how often does the committee meet?

D) How is the investment mix determined?

E) Will the bank invest the principal entirely in growth assets, entirely in fixed income assets, or a mixture of both?

F) Is the investment analysis done in-house or by an outside investment firm?

G) What is the bank's performance on its Trust funds?

Assurance Number 2

You want to know that the bank Trustee will distribute the Trust income and assets in accordance with your wishes. In this regard, ask the Trust administrator the following:

A) Does this bank deal with Trusts similar to the one you have in mind for your child?

B) Will this bank telephone your child occasionally to determine if everything is all right?

C) How will this bank deal with pressure from your child to be paid more money?

D) How will this bank determine whether it is meeting your child's financial needs?

E) How will this bank discover if your child is receiving more Trust income than he actually needs?

Assurance Number 3

You want the bank Trustee to have a good working relationship with your child. In this regard, ask the Trust administrator:

A) Is the Trust Department so large that it will not have a personal relationship with my child?

B) How does this bank typically handle an estate of my size?

C) Are there frequent personnel changes in the bank's Trust Department?

3. "How much will a bank Trustee charge to be my child's Trustee?"

Bank Trustees schedule their own fees, but they are usually in line with what is ordinary and reasonable. Find out from a bank Trust administrator what his minimum fee is and ask to see his fee schedule.

But do not let fees deter you from using the bank Trustee as your child's Trustee. Chances are, the bank Trustee will save your child more money than would a private individual Trustee because:

1. Banks can better preserve the Trust assets. The fees charged by a bank can be less costly than the mistakes of an inexperienced individual Trustee.

2. Banks may have on-site specialists and may not have to hire outside professionals for investment advice, accounting services,

appraisals, and other administrative needs, but the individual Trustee may incur extra expenses for these support services.

3. Banks may purchase stocks or other securities at discounts that may not be available to the individual Trustee.

4. Banks give you more for your dollar. For their fees, your child gets an experienced team of professionals who have the time and knowledge to administer the Trust, but an individual Trustee may receive a fee even if he lacks the ability to handle the Trust assets.

5. Who says your child's brother, sister, or other individual will not charge a fee? And what's more, this fee could be more than what the bank Trustee will charge.

---

4. "I plan on using the bank to act as my children's Trustee. However, I am concerned about the stability of banks in America. What will happen to the Trust money if the bank goes into bankruptcy or is taken over by the federal government?"

Clients often ask why I recommend bank Trustees so highly, when banks all over America are going belly up. Given the history of bank failures in America, this is a legitimate concern.

Trust assets are not bank assets. Your money and property is owned by the Trust and *not the bank*. Any assets you leave to the bank Trustee to hold for your problem child are not subject to any bank failure or takeover.

However, a note of caution. The bank's misfortunes can still indirectly impact on the Trust assets if:

1) The bank Trustee invests some of the Trust money in the bank's own stock; or

2) The bank Trustee deposits the Trust money in an account at that bank.

To prevent your money from being tied to the bank's misfortunes, instruct the bank Trustee not to invest it in the bank itself or deposit it in the bank itself.

5. "Most of my wealth is tied up in real estate. If the bank acts as Trustee, I don't want my real estate liquidated. I would prefer that the bank Trustee keep the real estate intact for my son's future benefit."

If your child's Trust will contain real estate and you want the bank Trustee to keep it intact, you must first determine the bank Trustee's real estate attitude.

The vast majority of bank Trustees have no problem maintaining real estate as part of the Trust portfolio of assets. However, some bank Trustees are not equipped to manage or deal with real estate. For these bank Trustees, their natural tendency is to sell the real estate and convert the cash proceeds into stocks, bonds, and other securities.

6. "I live in Wisconsin and plan to have a local bank act as Trustee of my children's Trust. I have real estate investments in California. Can a Wisconsin bank act as Trustee over my California property?"

A bank Trustee in your state may not have the authority to act outside that state. For example, if you select a bank Trustee in Wisconsin, it may be powerless to operate and manage your California real estate.

To get your California property under the umbrella of the Trust, you can appoint a "Special Bank Trustee" who does business in California. If you are not familiar with any such entity, you can give the authority to the Trustee bank in Wisconsin to make the designation.

7. "I am remarried, with children from my first marriage. If I die before my wife, my money will go to a bank Trustee that will pay my wife the income for the rest of her life. When she dies, it will distribute the assets to my children from my first marriage. However, this plan could cause a big conflict. My wife will want the bank Trustee to get her as much income as possible. On the other hand, my children will want the bank to invest for growth."

A bank Trustee often finds itself in the middle of this conflict. If he invests solely in high-income assets, the growth-minded "first children" will be extremely upset. On the other hand, investing solely in growth assets will not allow the wife to receive sufficient income.

There is a way you can make life easier for the bank Trustee. In your inheritance plan, instruct the bank Trustee if you want to favor income or growth. If you do not specify your preference, the bank Trustee will not attempt to guess what you had in mind. Instead, he may compromise. He may invest 50 percent of the Trust in high-income assets and 50 percent in growth assets.

At first glance, this apportionment may sound fair. But is this the investment plan you wanted? If you intended to favor your second wife, this compromise will give her less income. If you intended to favor your first children, the appreciation on their inheritance may be less than you anticipated.

8. "After my wife and I are dead, the bank will act as Trustee for my son's inheritance. Our son is financially immature, and this Trust will protect his inheritance from his own folly. However, we are concerned the bank won't know how to determine our son's needs. All the bank will see is a piece of paper saying it should pay our son the amount of money he needs to live."

A primary duty of the bank Trustee is to keep the Trust assets productive. He will invest the assets conservatively for an average market rate of return. The bank Trustee will collect this income and pay it to your son in the manner provided in your inheritance plan.

If your inheritance plan instructs the bank Trustee to use the income for your son's needs, how will the bank Trustee know he is paying your son the right amount? The Trust income may be insufficient for his needs—or more than he actually requires.

One way your son can receive the right amount is to give the bank Trustee the power to pay your son as much income and principal as necessary for his reasonable support and mainte-nance. With this provision, the bank Trustee can exercise dis-cretion to pay more or less in accordance with your son's actual needs.

How Does the Bank Trustee Know What Your Son's Needs Are?

How will the bank Trustee determine what your son requires? He has to investigate.

The degree of this investigation may vary. Some bank Trustees are willing to independently verify your son's expenses. Others may meet with your son and ask, "What do you need?"

You may find it acceptable for the bank Trustee to rely entirely on your son's word. After all, who knows his financial needs bet-ter? On the other hand, the bank Trustee will hear only what your son wants to reveal. Given that your son's money is on the line, is he a reliable source of information?

To give the bank Trustee the most accurate picture of your son's financial needs, appoint a Protector for your son in your inheritance plan. The Protector (usually a sibling or close family member) will be the bank Trustee's eyes and ears monitoring the reality of your son's actual needs and advising the bank Trustee accordingly.

---

9. "Can one of my other children be a Cotrustee with the bank Trustee?"

Absolutely. You can appoint your child's sibling as Cotrustee, giving that sibling the power to veto any investment and manage-ment decisions made by the bank Trustee.

Trustee Choice Number 3: The Child Himself

Can the child who is to receive the benefits of the Protection Trust also serve as the Trustee? The answer depends on the child's problem. Obviously, if the problem is addiction, mental disability, or financial immaturity, the child cannot be his own Trustee. If that were the case, the Protection Trust would not protect the family money from risk of loss.

However, if the problem threatening the family money is less acute, it is possible for the child himself to serve as his own Trustee.

For example, your son has a creditor problem. If he owns his inherited money and property outright, it may be eaten up by his debts. You may be able to keep your son's creditors at bay if you leave him the inheritance by making him the sole Trustee of a Protection Trust. But you must first check your state's creditor laws to ascertain if this shelter can still exist with your son as sole Trustee.

Another example: Your daughter's problem is that she cannot say no to her husband. If you leave her an outright inheritance, you know it will ultimately end up with your son-in-law. But if you leave it to her as Trustee, you have at least minimized the risk of her diverting the family money to her high-pressure husband. This plan is called the Transparent Trust, and I discuss it in detail in chapter 9.

17

Your Underage Child's Guardian

or

Your Children Are Terrific Kids— but Who Will Want Them Full-Time If You Die?

---

1. "My wife and I have a ten-year-old son and an eight-year-old daughter. We cannot agree who will raise them if they are minors when we die. I think my sister would be the best choice—but my wife thinks the same thing about her brother."

I don't see many young married couples in my office. The majority of my clients are from middle age on up. But on occasion, a young married couple will confer with me because they are about to get on a plane and want a Will in the event the worst occurs.

Mr. and Mrs. Tyson were a prime example. They had been married for five years and had two very young children. The Tysons were one week away from their first vacation without their children. I observed Mr. Tyson crossing off the word "lawyer" from his checklist of last-minute things to do.

The Tysons came to my office thinking "Living Trust," but I advised that a simple Will would be sufficient. A Living Trust would keep their children and property out of the probate court.

But at this stage in their lives, the Tysons' young age and few assets did not make probate avoidance a pressing concern.

The Tysons' primary concern was their children. "Mr. Condon," asked Mr. Tyson, "who should take care of our children if the plane crashes?"

The first thing I told the Tysons was not to worry about the plane crashing. The greatest risk to their lives was the drive to the airport.

After this feeble attempt at levity, I explained to Mr. Tyson that when he asked, "Who should take care of the children?" he was really asking:

1) Who should be their children's substitute parent, legally called the "Guardian of the Person" (in some states, "Conservator of the Person"); and

2) Who should be in charge of their children's inheritance, legally called the "Guardian of the Estate"?

The Tysons could select the same person to assume both guardianship responsibilities or separate persons for each duty.

"My Brother Is Better than Your Sister"

Mr. Tyson felt his brother would be the best choice to raise the children and be in charge of their children's money. Mrs. Tyson strongly suggested that her sister would be the far superior choice.

Each tried to gently convince the other of his position, but neither was willing to budge. In frustration, both brought out the big guns. Mrs. Tyson told her husband why she would never allow her children to be raised by his brother. And as long as she was being so honest, Mr. Tyson decided to say what he really thought about his sister-in-law.

A sincere discussion of important family issues was quickly deteriorating—they now needed a referee instead of a lawyer.

To alleviate the tension, I gave the Tysons something else to think about. "Your argument may be much ado about nothing. The Guardians you select must be willing to accept the job. Before you really get into it, I suggest you call your respective siblings to see if they'll volunteer. If either one rejects the job, your dilemma is resolved."

This suggestion seemed to placate the Tysons. At least, they realized they could not continue their argument in the face of this logic.

The following afternoon, I received a call from Mr. Tyson. He said neither his brother nor his wife's sister was willing to volunteer. Both siblings had given a thumbs-down to the idea of becoming responsible for someone else's children.

Much Ado About Almost Nothing

In the real world, a youthful married couple dying simultaneously or within a short time of each other is a rare event. In thirty-five years of lawyering, I recall only one or two occasions where both parents died leaving minor children. However, this statistic should not diminish the importance of making a wise and intelligent guardianship decision. Guardianship issues are deeply felt concerns that young parents should address.

2. "What should we consider when selecting a Guardian for our children?"

In the ideal world, selecting your children's Guardians should come after careful thought and analysis. But in the *real* world, you may not have the opportunity to select from a pool of candidates. Whom you choose may depend on who is available and willing to serve. Usually, the choice comes down to each parent's siblings, which may be a very small group.

If you have a large group from which to choose, you have the luxury of asking questions. I suggest you make your decision based on the following considerations:

1) Does your choice have the necessary maturity, experience, temperament, patience, and stamina to raise your children?

2) Does your choice have a genuine interest in your children's welfare, either through family relationship or personal friendship?

3) Do you and your children have confidence in the prospective Guardian?

4) Is your choice a person of integrity and stability?

5) Is your choice physically able to undertake the care of an additional child or children, and does your choice have the time necessary to devote to this task?

6) Is your choice willing to serve?

7) Does the age of your choice pose any problems?

8) Does your choice have children of an age close to that of your children?

9) Does your choice have a financial lifestyle comparable to your own?

10) Does your choice follow the same religion?

11) Does your choice live in the same geographical area as you? Would your children have to move to a new city or state?

---

3. "My sister and her husband volunteered to be our son's Guardian. They are terrific people and great parents. As Guardian, they will manage our son's money, which is enough to provide him with the best in life. But my sister's financial status is well below ours. If our son has more money available to him than my sister's children, won't there be a conflict?"

Mr. and Mrs. Richardson nominated Mrs. Richardson's sister, Melinda, as their son's Guardian, and they could not have made a better choice. Melinda and her husband loved children and had two of their own. If anything happened to the Richardsons, Melinda would be a most willing and able substitute parent.

The Richardsons were confident Melinda and her husband would do a wonderful job raising their son. Yet despite this assurance, there was one problem that nagged the Richardsons, one they could not get out of their minds.

The Richardsons were financially upscale people. They could afford to provide their son with all the trappings of wealth, from private schools to tennis lessons, from Disneyland vacations to summer camp in the hills of Malibu, California.

On the other hand, Melinda and her husband, although far from destitute, could not afford such luxuries for their own children.

The Richardsons thought this disparity could be a problem. For example, while their son attended private schools, Melinda's children would be bused to public schools. While their son would be at camp during summer recess, Melinda's children would be on the school playground.

Could these separate financial lifestyles peacefully coexist in the same household? Could the Richardsons' son enjoy all these extras without engendering jealously in Melinda's family?

Solution: Share the Wealth

The Richardsons were absolutely correct. A plan was needed to adjust this financial difference.

In the Richardsons' inheritance plan, they provided that their son's Trust money could be used to provide an equal financial lifestyle for Melinda's children. For example, if the Richardsons' son went to private schools, the Trust would pay for private schooling for Melinda's children. Or if the Richardsons' son went to summer camp, the Trust would pay for Melinda's children to go as well.

The result: Melinda's children and the Richardsons' son would be on equal financial footing while living in the same household.

---

4. "We have no choice other than my brother to be our daughter's Guardian. We trust him, but he is an agnostic. We don't want him to cause our daughter to abandon her faith and everything we have taught her."

You and your brother differ in an area that is key to you. Perhaps you and he follow different religions—or he has no religion. Perhaps you feel his moral code is not up to par with yours. Or perhaps you are not thrilled with his social attitudes. But by default you are forced to nominate your brother as your daughter's Guardian. If your brother becomes Guardian, you are concerned your daughter will forget her life's lessons and adopt those of your brother.

Solution: Money Talks

Motivating your brother to raise your daughter your way is easy enough. All you need to do is make it worth his while.

First, in your inheritance plan, you must list in detail how you want your brother to raise your daughter. If you want to ensure she follows a certain faith, or if you want her to graduate from a certain school, write it down.

Second, provide that your daughter's inheritance shall go to a third-party Trustee, preferably a bank Trustee or other financial institution.

Third, provide that a private individual other than your brother will be your daughter's Protector. This Protector will serve as the eyes and ears of the bank Trustee. The Protector will monitor your daughter's life to determine if your brother is following your instructions and report his or her findings to the bank Trustee.

Fourth, instruct the bank Trustee to financially reward your brother for following your instructions. If your brother is faithful to your wishes, the bank Trustee will periodically pay him a designated amount of money.

You may think this solution is crass and tasteless. But if your brother is your only choice, there is no better incentive than cash to get him to follow your instructions on how you want him to raise your daughter.

5. "My wife and I agreed my sister will be our children's Guardian. If we die simultaneously, is my sister automatically considered their Guardian?"

No. Your sister won't become the official Guardian until a judge officially appoints her.

Whom will the judge appoint as your children's Guardians? Usually, whomever you nominate in your Will. But the judge may not appoint your nominee for one of the following reasons:

1) The judge must first be satisfied your nominee is qualified to act as a substitute parent. Your nominee may not pass that judicial scrutiny.

2) Your nominee may be ill, incapacitated, or dead.

3) Your nominee, who once enthusiastically said yes, may no longer want the job.

4) Another person, thinking he or she could do a better job than your nominee, may oppose the judge's appointment of your nominee.

If you don't make any nominations in your Will, you create a free-for-all. Anyone who is interested can ask the probate judge to be your children's Guardian. The judge then has the job of ferreting out the best candidate. The winner will be the one the judge believes would best serve your children's personal and financial needs.

6. "My sister volunteered to be the Guardian for my minor children. I trust her to raise my children. However, she is somewhat casual in money matters. How can I be certain she won't dissipate my children's inherited money?"

You can't. That is why I recommend separating the guardianship duties. Let a bank Trustee or other financial institution preserve your children's inheritance (the "Estate" Guardian) while your sister preserves your children (the "Person" Guardian).

This separation of duties has two distinct advantages. One, each Guardian would be free to carry out its functions more effectively. Two, the safety of your children's inheritance is greatly enhanced. Most losses in guardianship estates are caused by honest but inexperienced or unbusinesslike persons acting as Estate Guardians.

Ask yourself: If your sister became Guardian of your children's inheritance, would she do what she is supposed to with your children's money?

Would she keep your children's inheritance in a separate account?

Would she use your children's inheritance only for your children's benefit?

Would she invest your children's inheritance prudently and without risk?

Would she have an all-around business ability and a past record of success in managing the affairs of others?

Would she be familiar with good accounting practices?

Would she keep accurate and adequate records?

Would she be able to anticipate problems with your children's inheritance?

Would she know when to seek legal advice and other professional help?

Minimal Protections from Abuse

Of course, there are exceptions. Your sister may have specialized knowledge in managing money. Or perhaps the inheritance is so small that it is not worth the trouble to have someone else manage it. But whatever the reason, if you allow your sister to hold your minor children's inheritance, be aware there are three minimal safeguards to prevent her from inadvertently (or intentionally) mismanaging it.

1. The Guardian Reports

Typically, about once a year, the probate court requires the "Estate" Guardian to present a detailed account that reports every transaction taken with the children's inheritance. The probate judge will review this report before he places it in the court's guardianship file. However, because most courts lack adequate resources, the report is not usually scrutinized unless a specific problem is brought to the judge's attention.

2. Public File

Guardianship files are public records, meaning that any person can get information about the affairs of the guardianship. Thus, if a person is so inclined, he can look through the file to determine if the Guardian is "above board." However, who do you know who will take the time and trouble to intervene? To determine if the money is being mismanaged, someone must drive to the courthouse, find a parking space, find the right department, locate the file, and review all of the reports.

3. Bond

Guardians are generally required to post a bond. The amount of the bond depends upon the size of your children's inheritance. If a Guardian misappropriates money from your children, the bonding company will reimburse your children, but only to the extent of the bond.

If there is no bond, action must be taken directly against the Guardian.

Part VI

How Will Your Children Divide Your Noncash Assets?

18

How to Leave Your Valuables and Household Contents to Your Children

or

"The First One to Mom's House After Her Funeral Wins"

---

1. "It's been fifteen years since my mother died and I'm still mad at my brothers. After Mom died, they went into her house and took everything, including the necklace Mom promised me. I didn't get anything—not even pictures. When I'm gone, I don't want the same thing to happen between my children."

It's often the least important part of the inheritance that causes the longest-lasting emotional reaction. When it comes to dividing up the jewelry, silverware, and household contents, people never forget it if they did not get what they thought was coming to them.

I'll never forget what Sharon Pearl told me. When her mother died, she and her sister, Wendy, attended the funeral. After the ceremony, Sharon stayed at the gravesite to meet and greet her fellow mourners, but Wendy mysteriously disappeared.

Sharon thought Wendy left early to prepare the reception at their mother's home. When Sharon arrived at the reception, she discovered that the china hutch and the jewelry were no longer there. And fifteen years later, this incident is still a sore point in Sharon's life.

Dr. Rice had a similar experience. As he recounted how his sisters treated him when his parents died, I could see his face becoming flushed with anger.

After Dr. Rice's mother died, his two sisters cleaned out their mother's home, taking with them a doll collection that had been promised to Dr. Rice's daughters. When Dr. Rice asked his sisters to return them, they stonewalled him.

Eventually, Dr. Rice no longer bothered to press the issue. But twenty years later, recalling the incident still left a bad taste in his mouth.

Will It Happen to Your Children?

Perhaps you have had a similar experience or read about one in "Ann Landers." But in the real world, most children cooperate with each other in the division of their parents' personal items and household contents. The stories about back-stabbing make for interesting reading, but they are the exception and not the norm.

Since most children will get along, I suggest you leave your personal items and household contents to your children equally as they shall agree. This general instruction will leave your children free to decide among themselves what each of their shares will be.

However, this general instruction to divide things equally may not apply because:

1) You may have promised a certain item to a certain child; for example, your engagement ring to your daughter, your Steinway piano to your musically inclined son, and so forth.

2) There is an understanding—spoken or silent—that one child is to receive a certain item.

3) One child may have staked out a certain item and feels entitled to it.

4) You know your children, and they will never be able to work it out without a referee.

If you cannot use a general instruction, you may have to resort to leaving each child specific items, using one or more of the following methods:

1. Use Your Inheritance Plan

In your Will or Living Trust, simply list which items you want to leave to which children. But if you cherish keeping your personal items private, you may feel uneasy about this method. Why? Because after you die, your inheritance plan may be subject to public disclosure. And if the "whole world" can see your Will or Living Trust, it will also see what personal items you owned.

However, I developed a method that allows you to "dispose" of your personal property in a way that allows for a greater level of privacy.

In every Living Trust that I draft, I include a provision that authorizes you to make a list of instructions—separate and "outside" your Living Trust document—for distribution of your personal items. This list of instructions is called a "Personal Property Memorandum" (PPM). You can change the instructions in the PPM whenever you wish—without an attorney. And in your own handwriting.

If you change your mind as to the disposition of a certain item, you can cross out that entry and write a new one. Or eliminate that entry altogether. Whatever your heart tells you to do.

As casual as the PPM seems—and as "outside" your Living Trust that it appears—its instructions are part and parcel of your Living Trust that must be carried out after your death.

I discuss the PPM in greater detail—and with a much more haughty attitude—in question 6 of this chapter.

2. Use a "Side Letter"

Instead of using your Will or Living Trust to tell your children who gets what, tell them in a Side Letter. The Side Letter will not be part of your official Will or Living Trust, so its contents will, most likely, remain private.

Now for the downside. Because this Side Letter is separate from your inheritance plan, your children will not be legally bound by it. But if your Side Letter clearly states your wishes and instructions, your children will, in all probability, feel morally obligated to comply.

The Side Letter requires you to do the following:

- Provide in your Will or Living Trust that your children shall receive your personal effects equally.
- Write a letter to your children. In this letter, let your children know what your actual wishes are. For example, tell your children who you would like to get the grandfather clock or the rosewood table.
- Keep this Side Letter separate from your Will or Trust. Otherwise, it may be considered part of your inheritance plan and its contents may be published for all to see. (However, tell one or all of your children where the Side Letter can be found after your death.)

3. "Tagging"
On the underside of each article you wish to specifically designate, mark the intended child's name.

4. Photo Journal
Take photographs of each item and write the intended child's name on the back of the photograph. You may keep these pictures where you keep your Side Letter.

5. Auction Sale
If you do not care about leaving your children particular items, your inheritance plan can provide that all your personal possessions will be sold after your death and the proceeds divided equally.

When faced with children who just cannot get along when

dividing your personal property, this alternative, more than any other, may prevent conflict.

I remember that when Mrs. Gilbert died, her two daughters brought a lot of negative and irrelevant family "baggage" to the property-division process. They argued and fought over everything, from the diamond ring to the salt shaker. Finally, with the attorneys' fees having well exceeded the items' lowly value, and with my patience at its end, I said (yelled, actually) "Enough!" and coerced them into contracting with a nearby auction house. The very next day, representatives from the auction house came to Mrs. Gilbert's house, inventoried the items, trucked them to their warehouse, and scheduled a silent auction to be held two weeks later.

Though bitterly opposed to each other, both daughters were united in their complaint that they did not want some items to end up with strangers. No problem, I said. Just show up at the auction and make the appropriate bids.

And that is exactly what happened. At the auction, each daughter who desired an item simply placed a bid and spent the appropriate funds from their own pockets. When all items were sold, the daughters split the money and went their separate ways.

2. "Without a referee, I don't think they will be able to divide my things equally. But I don't want to take the trouble to make a detailed list of who gets what. Is there another alternative?"

Yes. It is called the "rotating choice" division method.

Remember when you were a child and you and your friend would split a Hershey bar? To divide the chocolate as equally as possible one of you would cut it and the other would get first choice.

This is the principle behind the rotating choice. In your inheritance plan, provide that your children will cut cards. Whoever gets the highest card gets first "dibs" on any item. The child with the next highest card gets the next choice, and so on.

3. "What happens if I leave a certain asset to a certain child and I no longer have that asset when I die?"

When you leave a specific item to a specific child (whether in your inheritance plan or Side Letter), you assume you will still own that item when you die. But before you die, you may have sold or gifted this item away.

Solution: The "Backup" Provision

You can include in your inheritance plan one or more of the following backup alternatives:

1) If the intended item is no longer there, the child gets nothing in lieu of that item; or

2) Instead of the intended item, the child gets the cash equivalent; or

3) The child gets to choose another item with a value equal to that of the intended gift.

4. "I have some valuable jewelry stored in my safe-deposit box. I never use it and it just sits there. Should I give my jewelry to my children now?"

If you are rich enough when you die, the IRS will want to know how much jewelry you own. This includes any jewelry you have in your home, safe-deposit box, or elsewhere.

The IRS may impose a death tax on this jewelry when you die. This tax could be as much as 40 percent of the value of each piece of jewelry. Your children cannot pay this "jewelry death tax" with jewelry. The IRS wants cold, hard cash.

Solution: Give It Away While You're Alive

Reduce this jewelry death tax by gifting it to your children before you die. You cannot be taxed on what you don't own when you die.

You may make these gifts tax-free under the annual exclusion law. Under this law, you can make gifts of up to $14,000 of value each year to each child, grandchild, son-in-law, daughter-in-law, or any other person. There is no gift tax to you, and there is no income tax to the recipient. For more information on the annual exclusion law, see chapter 36.

However, can you handle the idea of parting with control of your jewelry? Some clients won't give up their jewelry for anything, even if it means their children will pay a jewelry death tax to the IRS.

One client had $40,000 worth of jewelry sitting in her safe-deposit box. I warned her that that would cost her children about $12,000 in death taxes. But if she gave her jewelry to her children while she was alive, the IRS would get nothing.

She did nothing. These jewels were part of her, and she just could not let them go. Years later, she died and her children paid the death tax.

Most clients, however, eventually come around to the idea of saving money for their children. I remember Mrs. Zuckerman, a matronly lady who had $100,000 worth of jewelry sitting in her safe-deposit box. When I advised her to gift these items to her children, she abruptly told me, "Not on your life. I attend many society functions and I use my jewelry quite often." Knowing the cost to her children, I would not let Mrs. Zuckerman off so easy. "Mrs. Zuckerman," I asked, "isn't it a hassle to go to your safe-deposit box every time you need your jewelry? If you give your jewelry to your children now, you could always borrow it back to use on a particular occasion."

After much persuasion, Mrs. Zuckerman finally gifted the jewelry to her children. She died three years later and her children saved about $20,000 in death taxes.

I met with Mrs. Zuckerman's children shortly after her death. They told me that their mother never asked to use her jewelry. Why? Because she had no need for it. Their mother never went out. The lavish society functions were only wishful thinking.

---

5. "I live alone and have no children. I have some valuable paintings, antiques, and jewelry. I'm leaving everything to my church. But I'm afraid the first one into my apartment after I die will just help himself."

If you have seen the movie *Zorba the Greek*, you will remember the deathbed scene of a woman in a small Greek village. Surrounding her house and looking through the windows and doors were her neighbors. As long as she was breathing, they were deterred from entering the room. As she gulped her last breath, the neighbors converged and removed her meager possessions.

Elderly clients often recount the image of this scene to me when they describe their fears of being similarly violated. Their worst nightmare is that immediately after they die, strangers will pick their home bare, leaving nothing for their intended heirs.

Sometimes there is truth in paranoia. This scenario my elderly clients envision is not without a kernel of reality. Before the coroner arrives, it is not unusual for neighbors, final friends, the last caretaker, or whoever is first on the death scene to help themselves to what is available. Unless children, loved ones, or close friends take immediate control, the jackals may have the advantage.

What may be needed is an arrangement for jackal protection.

Solution: "Jackal Protection"

Frankly, there is no real protection from this threat. If someone gains entry to your home after you die, little can be done to prevent the theft of your possessions. And if they're gone, they're gone!

But do not let this dismal reality stop you from trying. To make your home as jackal-proof as possible, consider the following:

1. If you have a Living Trust, your Successor Trustee should be on red alert to take immediate control following your death. If your last days are spent in a hospital or convalescent facility, your Successor Trustee can take control prior to your death.

2. Compile a photo journal and/or a written inventory of all your valuables. Deposit these records with the Successor Trustee of your Living Trust or the Executor of your Will. After you die, they can use these records as a checklist as they secure your belongings. If they notice a missing item, they can attempt to discover the responsible party and seek recovery. (Good luck!)

3. Give a friend or neighbor whom you trust written authority to take immediate control of your home after you die—or earlier if you are in a hospital or convalescent facility.

4. Instruct a trusted neighbor to call your county's public administrator or other appropriate authority when you die. Once notified of your death, that authority is to secure your assets against theft and seal your home.

---

6. I change my mind all the time about who gets my personal property after I'm dead. But I'm sick of coming to you and paying a fee every time I want to make those changes in my Living Trust. What can I do to cut you out of the loop?

You are not the only one who is tired of making those types of changes to your Living Trust. I'm not crazy about them myself.

One of the more simple services I render is amending Living Trusts to accommodate changes in the disposition of personal property. Rings, antiques, cars, computers, clothes, dogs, cats, pictures, art . . . all the stuff that you have in your home, storage facility or safe-deposit box.

But, do not equate simplicity with lack of effort. Like any amendment to a Living Trust, a Personal Property Amendment still involves intake, attorney time, drafting, review, secretary time, and client time. While I don't charge for Living Trust consultations on the phone or in person, I do charge for work that, of course, includes the preparation of the simple Personal Property Amendment. As my father said, "Jeff, you can be the greatest estate planning attorney that ever lived, which you are not, but if you're not being paid for your work, you might as well be at the beach."

Still, I don't like drafting Personal Property Amendments. The client resents me because he feels the work is not enough to justify a charge. I resent the client because he resents me, and because the Personal Property Amendment takes me away from more pressing matters, more intellectually challenging pursuits, and, yes, more work that can result in higher billing.

So, to remove myself and the client from this vicious Circle of Resentment, I now craft a standard provision in all of my Living Trusts called the "Personal Property Memorandum" ("PPM"). This provision states that the client instructs that all of his personal property will be distributed by the Successor Trustee in accordance with the wishes of the client as expressed in a separate Personal Property Memorandum ("PPM"). In this PPM, which I supply to the client, he simply makes his own instructions on who receives what. The PPM does not have to be on the form that I provide. It can be on any piece of paper the client entitles "PPM."

The beauty of the PPM is that if the client changes his mind, he simply erases or crosses out one instruction and fills in a new instruction—all without having to involve the lawyer! It does not matter if there are endless revisions to the PPM. It's still valid, and the instructions on the PPM are still valid. This isn't grade school where you get your grade marked down for neatness issues.

What if the client does not include instructions in the PPM for the disposition of all his personal property items? For example, perhaps the client only used the PPM to distribute his jewelry, piano, and gun collection, but did not mention who gets his clothes, furniture, or automobile. Or even more compelling, perhaps the client did not complete any portion of the PPM. Who gets his personal property in that case?

To both concerns, fear not. In the PPM provision in the Living Trust, there is a "back-up" plan that says what happens to items not described in the separate PPM, or in the event that the separate PPM does not exist at all. The back-up plan can be whatever the client wants it to be. Perhaps it leaves the personal property to the client's children "as they so shall agree." Or perhaps it gives the Successor Trustee full discretion in selecting the recipients. Or, perhaps it says that all personal property shall be sold with the sale proceeds distributed in equal shares. When it comes to the "back-up" plan, the possibilities are only limited by imagination.

19

Planning for the Succession of the Family Business

or

When You Die, Will Your Business Die with You?

Two Out of Three Don't Make It

Statistically, two out of three family businesses do not survive the death of the founding parents. The federal estate tax, the death of a key man, a lack of management skills, no child with a desire to take over and carry on—all these problems work against the family business surviving into the next generation.

Volumes have been written on these obstacles to the succession of the family business. This chapter, however, is limited to the most common concerns children have when the family business is a major asset in a parent's estate.

1. "My son and I have worked side by side in the family business, and he has been a dynamo. He has doubled the business's value. This business is my major asset, and I plan on leaving it to all my children equally. But my son tells me if I don't change my mind, he will leave and become a competitor. He says he does not plan to spend his life building up the business's value for the benefit of his two sisters."

Leaving the business to your children equally will create a severe inheritance conflict if its equity is your major asset *and* one child helped to create that equity. The child who helped develop your business (the "business child") may see his years of labor and effort unjustifiably going to benefit his nonbusiness siblings.

That is what Hayley Rose thought, and it almost destroyed the family business.

Hayley Rose: From "Flower Child" to "Flower Lady"

Hayley Rose was known as the flower child. In junior high, she began working in her parents' flower stand and continued through high school. She went to college and focused on a business administration degree. After graduation, she poured her knowledge and zeal into the family floral business.

Hayley became active in community affairs, joining the Jaycees, community chest, Rotary, and helping in local charities. After two years of making personal connections, orders for flowers came from everywhere. No matter what affair you went to—weddings, Bar Mitzvahs, business conferences—the cards on the flowers said, "Flowers by Hayley."

No longer was Hayley the flower child—she was the flower *business*! Its value and earnings increased exponentially because of her efforts. Within five years, her parents' flower stand had turned into several florist shops throughout the community.

I met Hayley and her husband after they had their first child and decided to prepare their Wills. As part of my standard client interview, I asked Hayley what assets she owned.

According to Hayley, this seemingly simple question became the pivotal moment in her business life.

For the first time, Hayley stopped to think about her relationship to the business. She had single-handedly increased the business's value. For her efforts, she drew a good salary, but her parents remained the 100 percent owners. It dawned on her that when they died, she would have to share this increased equity value with her brother.

This was not an attractive prospect. She asked, "Why should I stay and continue to build up my parents' business if one-half of my effort will go to my brother? If I'm going to sell flowers, I could just as well sell for my own business."

I advised Hayley not to make a hasty decision. There were things her parents could do to be fair to everybody. I invited Hayley to bring her parents to our next meeting to discuss these options. She agreed.

Several weeks later, she and her parents were in my office, and her parents did not look happy. In a grumbling voice, her father said they really did not want to be there. Even though Hayley was the key employee, it was still their business, and they could leave it any way they wanted.

How did Hayley get her parents to come? She threatened to quit and go into business for herself unless they showed up.

With these combatants in the ring, and with me as the referee, I advised them of the following alternative solutions.

Solution 1: Leave the Business to the Business Child

Hayley's parents would continue to own the business until they died. Hayley would then inherit the business from her parents, and their son would inherit assets of equal value. Unfortunately, this solution would not work for two reasons:

1) The flower business was the parents' only major asset, and they had few other assets to leave to their son.

2) Even if her parents had sufficient assets to equalize, leaving the business to Hayley would still cause trouble . . . IRS trouble. When Hayley inherits the business, she may have to pay the IRS a death tax on its value—perhaps up to 40 percent. The more she increases the business's value before her parents die, the more she will pay in death taxes.

Building up the business's value just to pay a bigger tax to the IRS was not Hayley's idea of sound business judgment. It would be like pulling the lever on her own guillotine.

Solution 2: After the Parents Die, the Business Child Buys Out the Share of the Nonbusiness Child

When Hayley's parents die, they would leave the business to both their children equally. But they would also provide Hayley with an option to purchase her brother's half. If Hayley exercised the option, she would own the business, and her brother would receive cash or, if agreed, an Installment Note.

However, as quickly as this solution was brought up, it was dismissed because of the following downsides:

1) If Hayley did her usual good work and increased the business's value, she would also increase the purchase price for her brother's half of the business.

2) Again, the IRS loomed overhead. As the value of the business increases, so does the death tax.

Solution 3: The Business Child Buys the Business from the Parents Now

There would be three benefits to Hayley buying the business from her parents while they are alive (with an Installment Note at a modest interest rate):

1) The IRS is the loser because it will not receive a death tax on the value of the business's equity when the parents die, even if Hayley quadruples its value. Why? Because when they die, the parents won't own it! All the parents would own is the Note.

2) In return for the business, the parents would receive an Installment Note requiring Hayley to pay them interest. The inter-

est would be calculated to be roughly equal to the salary the parents were drawing from the business.

3) While the business may increase in value, the Note will not. With the value of the Note frozen, there will be no value increase for the IRS to tax when the parents die.

The Disadvantages of Buying the Business Now

Along with the advantages come the disadvantages. Every time Hayley makes a principal payment on the Note, her parents will have to pay a capital gains tax. And when her parents die, the balance of the Note may be subject to a death tax.

But to Hayley and her parents, this was the ultimate solution. Hayley liked the idea of owing the business and not having to share the fruits of her efforts with her brother. Her parents loved the idea of receiving their usual amount of income without the usual amount of work. And when Hayley's parents die, the Note would go to Hayley and her brother, leaving each of them with an equal inheritance.

How Much?

The next step was to work out a purchase price. Hayley's father suggested that the business was worth about $500,000. Hayley thought that was too high. "Dad," she said, "why should I buy a 'value' that I myself created? When I first started, the business was worth no more than $50,000. Everything after that was due to my effort!"

Good point, I thought—even her parents said so. So Hayley and her parents reached a compromise. Hayley would buy half of the business for $250,000 and her parents would make a gift of the other half.

How to Make the Gift Tax-Free

Hayley's parents gifted half of their business under the annual exclusion law. Every year, each parent gave $10,000 shares of the business to Hayley, her husband, and their child. This gifting went on every year until Hayley and her family received the entire half. With this process, the entire gift would not come off the parents' lifetime exemption from the death tax.

In chapter 36, I discuss these tax-free gifts in more detail. But for purposes of completing this story, this is how this gift was structured in Hayley's case:

1) Hayley's parents established a Limited Partnership. Hayley's parents were the owners of 100 percent of the Limited Partnership shares.

2) Hayley purchased one-half of her parents' shares for $250,000.

3) Each year, Hayley's father and mother each gifted $14,000 worth of Limited Partnership shares to Hayley, her husband, and their infant grandchild. With two donors giving $14,000 to three recipients, the parents could give $84,000 worth of shares each year tax-free.

4) Within four to five years, all the Limited Partnership shares would be in the hands of Hayley and her family.

---

2. "I plan to leave the business to my son and daughter, but I don't want them to be equal owners. If someone is not boss, no business decision can ever be reached. So I plan on leaving my son a controlling share."

Your attempt has merit. By making your son the "boss," you will have made it impossible for your son and daughter to deadlock over any business decision. But you have also laid the foundation for two other problems:

1. You May Have Made Your Daughter's Share Worthless

If your son is boss, your daughter may never receive any business profits. As the major shareholder or equity owner, your son can regulate his salary and business expenses so little or no profit is available for distribution to the other shareholders.

2. You May Not Have Eliminated Any Business Conflicts

Making your son the boss may not eliminate any business conflicts. Though you leave your daughter with a minority interest, she can attempt to equalize the power by threatening to litigate every business move your son makes. She can sue to compel liquidation, sue to demand and receive dividends, and can ultimately devastate the business through countless lawsuits challenging your son's every business decision.

In fact, making your son boss in and of itself can lead to the breakup of the business. Your daughter, despising even the idea of being shut out, may combat her brother just for the sake of conflict.

Solution 1: Leave the Business to One Child

You can eliminate the deadlock entirely by leaving the business to one child and the other assets of similar value to your other child. If you have insufficient assets to equalize, consider buying an insurance policy on your life to be owned by the child who will not receive the business. When you die, that child will receive cash death benefits roughly equal to the value of the business.

If this plan is not feasible, you may have to resort to the following alternative solution.

Solution 2: Leave the Business Equally, Subject to a Dispute-Resolution Plan

If you feel you must leave the business to all your children, leave it to them equally. When the power is shared between all your children, no out-of-power child can gum up the works.

Of course, this plan puts you right where you started. With

both children as boss, there could be conflict and deadlock over every business decision. This is why you must provide a detailed and articulate formula for dispute resolution in your inheritance plan. It may be arbitration, mediation, majority rule, or decision by a private third party who has a concern for the family and the business.

If you are the "gung-ho" type and you want an extreme method to prevent sibling conflict over the family business, provide that the business should be managed and operated by an independent Board of Directors, none of whom are your children. You could further provide that the Board's decisions cannot be challenged or overturned by any child no matter what that child's shareholder or equity position is.

Whatever the formula, leaving precise inheritance instructions on how to resolve deadlock is often the salvation of the business when it gets into the hands of your children. If your inheritance plan has no such instructions, the family business may face the ultimate resolution: dissolution.

3. "I own a parcel of real estate on which my son has a successful business. I wanted his business to succeed, so I gave him a sweetheart lease—his rent is about 50 percent of what I could get from someone else. If I leave this property to my son and daughter equally, won't she bump up the rent to market rates?"

Your son's sweetheart lease certainly helps your son's business. The less rent he pays to you, the more profits he makes. But if you leave the land to all your children equally, your nonbusiness daughter will become your son's landlord.

After you die, will your daughter raise your son's rent to fair rental value? It depends. If your son's lease is in writing, she is stuck with the low rent until the lease expires. However, if the lease was a handshake deal, your daughter will, most likely, raise the rent. She may love her brother, but not to the point where it costs her money.

Your son, accustomed to his below-market rent, will naturally resent the increase. If you include one of the following solutions in your inheritance plan, you can minimize your son's future headache.

Solution 1: Leave the Business Property to the Business Child and Other Assets to the Nonbusiness Child

You can solve this problem by leaving the business property to your business son and assets of equal value to your daughter. If you have no other assets equal to the value of the business land, you would be leaving your children an unequal inheritance.

In this case, consider Solution Number 2.

Solution 2: Leave the Business Property to the Business Child and a Life Insurance Policy to the Nonbusiness Child

If the business property is your most valuable asset, you can leave your children an equal inheritance by purchasing a life insurance policy with your daughter as owner and beneficiary. When you die, your son gets the land, and your daughter gets an equal amount in death benefits.

This solution presumes you have ready cash to pay the premiums or have assets you can liquidate to get the cash. If insurance is not the answer for you, consider the following alternative solutions.

Solution 3: Sell the Business Property to the Business Child

During your life, sell the land to your son for its fair market value. In return, your son can pay you with cash, an Installment Note, or both. When you die, your son already owns the land, eliminating any potential landlord problem.

Looming over this solution, however, may be a large capital gains tax. For example, say you purchased this land in the 1950s for $100,000. If you sell it to your son for its current $2 million fair market value, you would face a capital gains tax on the $1.9 million dollar profit.

Solution 4: Give the Business Child the Option to Buy the Business Property After You Die

When you die, leave the land to your son and daughter equally and give your son an option to purchase his sister's half at fair market value. If your son exercises the option, he will be sole owner of the land and your daughter is cashed out at the same amount as though the property were sold to a third party.

Your son may find it difficult to accept this plan because he's got to come up with the money to buy his sister's half. If he gives his sister an Installment Note, he may struggle just to pay her the interest.

But your son should realize that this plan makes good business sense. Better he should give his sister a few thousand dollars each month in interest payments than an unacceptable increase in rent.

---

4. "Our family business is a real family business. It includes my wife and our two sons. Our two sons will inherit it after we die. But what will happen when they become partners and one of them dies? We don't want the surviving son to be partners with his sister-in-law."

The Romanos' two sons grew up in their parents' restaurant. When they were young, they started out sweeping floors and taking out the garbage. As adults, the business became their careers. They did everything—from keeping the books to waiting on tables.

Mr. and Mrs. Romano wanted to leave the restaurant to their two sons and conferred with me to put this plan into writing. They knew their business would be safe in their sons' hands. But they were concerned what would happen if one of their sons died. As Mr. Romano said:

"Mr. Condon, when the first son dies, he will probably leave his share of the restaurant to his wife. I am not so sure our other son will get along working with her. Or instead of working, she may ride on the other son's coattails, collecting half the profits without lifting a finger to help out."

Solution: The Business Succession Plan

I drafted a special inheritance plan that allowed the Romanos to guarantee their restaurant's family succession from the grave. This plan was designed to achieve four goals:

1) To keep the restaurant in the sons' control while both sons are alive;

2) To keep the restaurant in the surviving son's control if one son dies;

3) To provide some financial benefit to the wife and children of the first son to die; and,

4) To keep the restaurant in the bloodline after both sons are dead.

This plan was structured as follows:

A) Mr. and Mrs. Romano established their Living Trust.
B) The Romanos transferred their equity ownership of the restaurant into their Living Trust.
C) The Romanos were Cotrustees of their Living Trust. Instead of them owning the restaurant as individuals, they owned it as Cotrustees of their Living Trust.
D) When the first spouse died, the surviving spouse would be the sole Trustee (owner) of the restaurant.
E) When the last spouse died, the Living Trust provided that the restaurant would continue to remain in the Living Trust.
F) The Romanos' two sons would take over the restaurant as Successor Cotrustees (co-owners).
G) When one son died, the other would continue as the sole Trustee (owner). As sole Trustee, the surviving son

would control the restaurant with no interference from the wife and children of his deceased brother. However, his deceased brother's wife and children would receive the economic benefits from a one-half share of the restaurant.

H) When both sons died, the restaurant would go to the Romanos' grandchildren—if they wanted to continue the business. If not, then it would be sold, with the proceeds divided among the grandchildren equally.

20

The Family Residence

or

Be It Ever So Humble, There's No Place Like Home—Until Your Children Fight over It After You Die

---

1. "Our home has always been the center of family activities for ourselves, our children, and our grandchildren. We always thought our home would be there for the family after we die, but our lawyer tells us it's doubtful."

Your lawyer is correct. It is doubtful that the family home will stay in the family after you die.

To some people, this news is no big deal. Their attitude is, it's only bricks and mortar and if it's sold, it's sold. On the other hand, many people want to preserve the family home for future generations and are distressed by the prospect of it being sold after they die.

The Packers: The West Coast Version of the Kennedys (but Without the Money)

In the 1950s, Mr. and Mrs. Packer bought their home on the beach in Malibu, California. Back then, the area was considered to be semirural. If you lived there, you were considered to have been a trailblazer. But twenty-five years later Malibu had evolved into a celebrity-filled enclave with the lowest-price house costing $600,000.

The Packers considered their beach house as their small version of the Kennedys' Hyannis Port home—it was always full of family. They raised three children, who all enjoyed the sun, surf, and the "Malibu lifestyle." These children grew up, married, and brought their spouses and grandchildren home whenever they could. Holidays, birthdays, reunions, anniversaries—whatever the occasion, it was time for a day at the beach.

When the Packers conferred with me, the first thing they told me was how much they enjoyed their home being the focal point of Packer family gatherings—and hoped this tradition would continue after they died.

However, the Packers were taken aback by my response. I told them that it was doubtful their house would remain in the family.

Like the majority of Americans, the Packers' home was their most valuable asset. And when they die, their home will be the major asset of their estate. When their Living Trust states that "everything" is to go to their three children equally, everything, for the most part, means their beach home.

How do three children divide one house? It depends on what each child wants to do with his or her one-third share. Usually, the possibilities are:

1) The children could keep the house and continue to use it for family vacations.

2) The three children could sell the house and divide the proceeds.

3) The child (or children) who wants to keep the house could buy out the interests of the child (or children) who wants to sell.

I suggested to the Packers that they get their children's thoughts on this matter. A week later, Mr. Packer reported his findings.

One son said he was counting on selling the house and using

his share to retire. The other son said he would use his share of the sale proceeds to go into business. The daughter desired to keep the home for her family but would be unable to buy out her siblings.

The Impossible Dream? Not Quite!

There was a way for the Packers to force their children to keep the beach home in the family. When they both die, the home would not go outright to their children but would remain in their Living Trust. Whoever they selected as Successor Trustee would be instructed not to sell the home until the death of their last child or grandchild, or if appropriate, earlier.

The Packers considered this option but quickly dismissed it. Knowing that their children counted on selling the home to enhance their personal lives, the Packers could not bring themselves to force their feelings on their children.

The Packers could not believe there was no practical way of keeping their precious home in the family. They had lived there for thirty-seven years and raised their children on the beach. They had seen its value go from $75,000 to over $1 million. And the value could only go up because, as Mr. Packer said, "There is only so much beach frontage to go around."

Nevertheless, because of their children's different desires, keeping the home in the family after they died was an impossible dream.

---

2. "My son lives in his own home—my daughter lives in an apartment. I'd like to leave my house to my daughter so that both of my children will have their own home."

You may perceive the need to allocate the family home to one child. Though well-meaning, this plan may eliminate your other children from their share of the inheritance.

The Ransoms: "Our Daughter Needs It More than Our Son"

The Ransoms' major asset was their Southern California home. They purchased it in 1952 for $20,000. Forty years later, it could have easily sold for $400,000.

The Ransoms had two children. Their son owned his own home. Their daughter was another story. Unable to hold any job for more than six months, all she could afford was a small, dingy apartment.

The Ransoms did not have the means to help their daughter get a better place. But they came up with a way to assist her in the future. As Mrs. Ransom said:

"Mr. Condon, when we're dead, we want our house to go to our daughter. That's the only way we know she won't wind up in the gutter."

The Ransoms' story of their stuggling daughter was sad, but I worried that their plan would make things worse.

"Mr. and Mrs. Ransom, in your mind, you are doing economic justice between your children. Your daughter needs your home more than your son. But look at this plan from your son's point of view. Because your only asset is your home, your son will inherit nothing. In effect, you are cutting him and his children out of an inheritance."

The Ransoms thought they were doing the right thing, but they had not considered how their son would see it. Eventually, they reconsidered and decided to leave their home to their son and daughter equally.

Did the Ransoms' daughter wind up on the street because she did not receive the "home alone"? Just the opposite.

When both the Ransoms were gone, their two children sold the house and divided the proceeds. Their daughter used her share to turn her life around. She paid off her debts, made a house down payment, and got a steady job.

The Ransoms felt that leaving their daughter the home was the only way they could give her a leg up in life. It turned out she did just fine with half the sale proceeds.

Compromise Solution: Allow the "Needier" Child to Live in Your Home for a Specified Period of Time After You Die

Like the Ransoms, you may be torn between satisfying one child's need for a home and being fair to all your children. But there is a middle ground—a plan that compromises between giving your poor child a place to live while giving all your children their fair share.

In your inheritance plan, provide that your needier child may remain in the house after you die for a specified period of time, say five years. Thereafter, the house is to be sold and the proceeds divided equally among all your children. (Or instead of having the house sold at the end of the rent-free term, you can provide that your needier child can stay in the house *as long as* your successful child is paid fair market rent on his share.)

This compromise plan will benefit both your children. Your successful child benefits from five years of additional appreciation (hopefully). Your needier child gets the right to live in your home rent-free for five years—and the opportunity to get it together without the additional burden of paying rent looming overhead.

---

3. "Because my son suffers from severe emotional problems, he never left home. After I die, I want him to live in the house for the rest of his life. However, my other children think this plan is unfair."

A more difficult situation exists if you have a child who resides with you. This child may desperately need to remain in your home after you die. But if you leave it equally to all your children, your "at home" child may literally be forced out on the street.

The McNallys' Son: Back Home Again

The McNallys' son, who suffered from severe emotional problems, was not capable of living on his own. His psychiatrist advised him to live somewhere where he felt secure and comfortable. And, of course, there was no place that fit the bill like his old room at his parents' house.

The McNallys were in their retirement years and had looked forward to, as Mrs. McNally said, finally being able to move on. Having their son move back was not exactly their idea of freedom. Yet the McNallys loved their son and welcomed him back. If living at home was essential to his well-being, they felt he should continue to live at home as long as necessary—even for the rest of his life.

When the McNallys conferred with me, they said that because of their son's condition, they felt compelled to leave him their house. I pointed out how unfair this would be to their other children, but the McNallys were not deterred. "It's our home," Mr. McNally stated, "and we can leave it any way we want. There is no law saying we have to leave all our children something. Our son needs help, and we're going to make sure he gets it."

I offered to meet with them and all their children to discuss this issue further, but they refused. I truly wish they had accepted my offer, for it might have saved me some grief later on.

About ten years later, shortly after the funeral of Mrs. McNally (the last spouse to die), their daughter charged into my office and shrieked, "You idiot! I was a good daughter! I never did anything wrong! Why the ——— did you let my parents leave everything to my brother?" After a few minutes of more ranting and raving (which included a threat to sue for malpractice), she stormed out the door.

It was easy to see that the McNallys never clued their daughter in to their inheritance plan. My guess is that the McNallys knew their daughter would explode if she learned the truth, and they just did not want to deal with her reaction.

Solution: Compromise—Let Your At-Home Child Live at Home While Allowing Your Home to Revert to Your Other Child

If, for whatever reason, you are adamant about leaving the family home to the child who lives at home, you do not have to completely cut out your other child. You can strike a compromise that at least gives your out-of-the-house child a hope of an inheritance.

In your inheritance plan, provide that your at-home child can live in the house for the rest of his life. When he no longer uses it as his main residence, or when he dies, the house will revert to all your children equally.

Of course, your out-of-the-house children may still think this plan is unfair—and they would be correct. Even with this compromise, they will be deprived from using and enjoying the benefits of their inheritance until the at-home child dies or moves out. This could be a long, long wait.

But in the face of your absolute insistence that your at-home child live in your house after you die, this solution is preferable to entirely cutting your other children out of their inheritance.

---

4. "My house is my most valuable asset. I planned on leaving it equally to my three children. One child recently told me he would like to own the home by himself."

If your home is your major asset, your children will most likely sell it after you die and divide the proceeds. But if you have a child who prefers to own the home, there are ways you can help him in your inheritance plan.

Solution 1: If You're Rich Enough, Leave Your Home to One Child and Other Assets to Your Other Children

You can leave your home to the child who wants it and assets of equal value to your other child.

This solution plan presupposes you have other substantial assets. If you have cash, securities, or other assets worth as much as or more than your home, this is an easy solution that works very well.

For example, you have two children, a daughter and a son. When you die, your home is worth $350,000 and you own $800,000 in cash, stocks, and other assets. To equalize, you leave your $350,000 home to your son and $350,000 in cash and securities to your daughter. Everything else is shared between them equally.

Solution 2: If You're Not Rich Enough, Leave Your Home to One Child and a Life Insurance Policy to Your Other Child

You want to leave your $350,000 home to your son, but you do not have the financial ability to equalize with your daughter.

Consider equalizing with an insurance policy. While you are alive, give $14,000 each year to your daughter. The money will be used for premiums on a $350,000 life insurance policy on your life owned by your daughter. When you die, your son will receive your $350,000 home; your daughter will receive $350,000 in tax-free cash from the insurance company.

Solution 3: Give One Child an Option to Buy Your Home from Your Other Child

If you are not rich enough to equalize with other assets, give your child who wants the house an option to buy out his sibling's share.

In your inheritance plan, structure this as a purchase option, setting forth such terms as:

1) The purchase price. If you do not set a price, provide a formula by which the fair market value of the home can be determined and a plan to resolve any difference of opinion over what that value is.

2) The time period within which the option can be exercised. You should limit this option to six months after your death. Otherwise, your other child's receipt of the inheritance may be unreasonably delayed.

3) The amount of the down payment, and what the down payment can consist of (e.g., cash, Installment Note, Mortgage, Deed of Trust, or other form).

4) What happens if the option is not exercised. (Most likely, the house is left to all children equally.)

5) All other provisions commonly associated with the purchase and sale of residential real estate.

5. "I moved my second wife into my house, and my children from my first marriage are already worried about who gets the house when I die."

You are remarried and have brought your second spouse to live in your home. Your second spouse may tell you that if you die first, he or she wants to live in your home for life. On the other hand, you have children from your first marriage (whom I call the "first children") who are adults, who are out of your home, and who have no stepparent relationship with your second spouse. They tell you *they* want to inherit your home immediately after you die.

You have a dilemma that is not easily resolved. If you abide by one's desires, the other will be the loser.

Mr. Franklin

Five years after his wife died, Mr. Franklin, age sixty-eight, met and married a sixty-year-old widow. They resumed their marital life in the house Mr. Franklin owned with his first wife. Their second time around was loving, quiet, and carefree—until they conferred with me and I pointed out the dilemma to Mr. Franklin.

Mr. Franklin said that if he died first, he wanted to leave the home to his children from his first marriage. But his second wife felt she had the right to live there for the rest of her life. Eventually, they arrived at a compromise, but at the cost of the tranquillity of the marriage.

Mr. Kanter

Mr. Kanter, age seventy, hired a live-in nurse to tend to his ill wife. During Mrs. Kanter's illness, this fifty-five-year-old lady assumed the role of homemaker as well as caretaker. After Mrs. Kanter died, her husband thought it convenient for the nurse to continue that role—so he married her!

Underlying this marriage was an unspoken understanding: If the nurse took care of Mr. Kanter for the rest of his life, the nurse could remain in Mr. Kanter's beautiful home for her life.

Mr. Kanter died six years later, and his son was outraged to find that he would not inherit his mother and father's house until "this stranger" died. That could be a long wait. When Mr. Kanter died, the son was fifty, and the nurse was sixty-five. If the nurse lived twenty more years, the son would be seventy—a little late to enjoy the benefits of his parents' home.

Mrs. Gold

Mrs. Gold was a widow after fifty years of marriage. She remarried a man of about the same age, and they lived in Mrs. Gold's house. Six months later, her new husband let her know the deal straight out: In return for his company, he wanted to live in Mrs. Gold's home for the rest of his life.

Afraid she would once again be alone, Mrs. Gold caved in to her new husband's demand. She changed her inheritance plan to allow her new husband to live there for life should she die before him.

Do You Have Such a Dilemma?

If you are on your second marriage and your house is your major asset, you may someday experience this emotion-packed dilemma. Later, I will give you three solutions you can use to resolve this dilemma. But first, you should determine if you even need these solutions. If you look at what your first children and second spouse think, you may discover you have no dilemma at all.

Your Second Spouse's Attitude

Your second spouse may have moved into your home knowing it would not last forever. Recognizing that you would never divert your home from your first children, she may expect to move out and reestablish her old life after you die. Perhaps your second spouse even kept his or her old apartment.

If your second spouse does not expect to inherit your home, you have no dilemma, allowing you to leave your home to your first children immediately after you die—guilt-free.

However, you may have a second spouse who feels absolutely entitled to live in your home for life because:

1) Your second spouse believes she has earned it after taking care of you in your old age (when no one else would).

2) Your second spouse gave up her life to marry and live with you and feels you have a duty to provide her with a house.

3) Your second spouse will have no place to live after you die.

Your First Children's Attitude

Your first children may not mind if your second spouse remains in your home if you die first. Perhaps they like your second spouse and want her to be comfortable for the rest of her life. Perhaps your first children are grateful to your second spouse for shouldering the burden of tending to your needs. Or perhaps your children are financially independent and don't need your home immediately after you die.

On the other hand, your first children may not be so magnanimous. They may think you are treating them unfairly because:

1) Your first children believe it rightly belongs to them after their last parent dies, not to some stranger.

2) Your second spouse may outlive you for many years. If your second spouse dies in her eighties, your first children may be past the age when they could have meaningful use of your home.

If You Have a Dilemma, What Should You Do?

You can resolve the dilemma with one of the following alternative solutions.

Solution 1: Don't Let Your First Children Wait Too Long

In your inheritance plan, provide that your second spouse can live in your home for a short time after you die, for as little as a year, but not for more than five years. At the end of that time, the house shall be sold, with a portion of the sale proceeds going to your second spouse and the balance to your first children.

Both your first children and second spouse would find this plan workable. Your second wife will have some money (in addition to any assets she owns from her first marriage) that may provide for her well-being. Meanwhile, your first children will get their inheritance sooner.

Granted, this solution may result in your children receiving a smaller inheritance. If they wait until your second spouse dies and sell it then, the home may sell for more. But better a dollar today than $1.50 untold years later.

One time I suggested this solution and it nearly caused a divorce. The husband was seventy-two years old and recently remarried; she was his fifty-five-year-old second wife. They lived in his $1 million home. After I discussed this plan with them, he gave me a look of approval, but she gave him a fierce look of disdain. The next thing I knew, the second wife rose from her seat, took her husband's hand, and said, "We'll think about it and get back to you."

A few days later, the husband called me, saying he was caught in a trap with no escape. He definitely did not want his children to wait until his second wife died to inherit the home. But his second wife said that if she could not live there for life—there would be no second wife.

I'm uncertain what the husband chose, but I did find out one thing: The second wife found a lawyer more to her liking.

Solution 2: Leave Your House to Your Second Spouse for Life and Leave Your First Children the Rest

If you're rich enough, I suggest that you leave your home to your second spouse for life and all your other assets to your first children.

This alternative somewhat ameliorates the conflict. Granted, your first children still have to wait for your second spouse to die before they inherit your home. But immediately receiving some portion of their inheritance may go a long way to satisfying their inheritance expectations. Feeling less deprived, the "sharp edge" may be removed on the ensuing relationship they have with your second spouse.

Solution 3: Leave Your House to Your Second Spouse for Life and Give Your Children a Life Insurance Policy

If you want to placate your first children with an immediate inheritance, but you have insufficient assets to leave them, you can leave them a substitute inheritance with a life insurance policy.

While you are alive, you can give your first children enough money to pay the premiums on a life insurance policy on your life. When you die, the insurance company will pay the death benefits tax-free to your first children.

(For more on using life insurance to give children a tax-free inheritance, see chapter 37.)

If No Solution . . .

If you cannot use any of the above solutions, and you still want to leave your home to your second spouse . . . don't come to me!

After you die, all that may remain is bitterness between your first children and second wife. And inevitably, the lawyer who drafts a conflict-ridden Will or Trust always somehow manages to get sucked into the conflict following the client's death. Sometimes the risk is worth the fee. But when it comes to conflicts between first children and second spouses over the family home, my gut feeling is that no fee is worth it.

If you want to know what I'm talking about, read the next question.

6. "I'm sorry my husband let me live in his house—now that he's gone, his children from his first marriage are driving me crazy!"

If you leave your home to your second spouse for life, the only connection between your second spouse and your first children will be your home. Your first children know that before they can inherit the home, your second spouse has to die.

Your children may not want to wait. If your second spouse outlives you for many years, how old will they be? They may be in their sixties, seventies, eighties, or maybe they have died. What good will the home do them then?

What may your first children do? They may find ways to hasten the time they inherit. They may make threatening phone calls to your second spouse. They may hire attorneys to write letters to your second spouse, complaining that their future inheritance is being mismanaged. They may file lawsuits, telling the judge that your second spouse is letting the home fall apart.

In this crazy world of ours, God only knows what else your children may do. I remember one client who left his home to his second wife for the rest of her life. The client's first children harassed this second wife to no end. They made her life so miserable that she abandoned the home just to have some peace of mind.

At least that second wife stayed alive to tell the tale. On another occasion, a client's first children were extremely irate to discover she left the family home for life to her second husband. About a year later, I read in the newspaper that the second husband was dead. He had been killed in a car accident.

Although no foul play was proved, many think that it was no accident.

Solution: Terminate the Connection

If the only thing connecting your first children and your second spouse is your home, I strongly suggest this connection be terminated after you die so your first children and second spouse go their separate ways.

How do you terminate this connection? You can use the John Wayne approach to inheritance planning—leave your home outright to one party and simply cut out the other. Or you can try to bring fairness to both and employ one of the compromise solutions I discuss in question 5 of this chapter.

21

Dividing Your Real Estate Investments

or

Your Investment Properties—Your "Pyramid" to Future Generations?

---

1. "We don't want our children to sell our apartment building after we're gone. We want it to remain in the family."

I hear this from my investment-property-owning clients time and time again. They have spent years of effort in managing and maintaining their properties. And after all the sweat and sacrifice, they want to die knowing their properties will remain intact for their children.

The children, however, may have different ideas.

The Mitchells and Their Pyramid to the Future

In the 1950s, Mr. and Mrs. Mitchell purchased a ten-unit apartment building for $100,000. Thirty years later, after managing the building, doing all the maintenance, dealing with crazy tenants, and paying all the bills, they had accumulated (thanks to inflation) $1 million in income-producing debt-free equity.

The Mitchells came to see me with a specific goal in mind:

After they died, they did not want their children to sell their apartment building. They wanted it to be, they said, their pyramid to future generations, their way to provide their children with a source of income.

To achieve this goal, the Mitchells provided in their inheritance plan that their building would be held in Trust for the rest of their children's lives. I recommended that the Mitchells allow a Trust Department of a bank to serve as the Trustee. But the Mitchells did not trust banks, so they decided to let their three children serve as Cotrustees.

The Aftermath

The Mitchells died years later thinking they had established an indelible plan. However, their pyramid to future generations didn't last one year.

After the Mitchells died, their children simply got together and, contrary to the Trust's terms, sold the property. Why? Because the children thought that a three-way division of income made for meager benefits. They would rather sell the building and divide the proceeds equally.

How could this happen? How could the Mitchells' children get together and so casually disregard their parents' "no-sale" instruction? Because there was no policeman looking over their shoulders. With all three in control as Trustees, nobody was around to say no. Had the Mitchells put a corporate third party in charge, their no-sale instruction would have been followed to the letter.

Rotten Kids?

Are the Mitchells' children "rotten kids" because they went against their parents' wishes? Not really. They did not go hog wild with spending sprees, new cars, or trips around the world. One child used his share to buy a house. One child invested in the stock market. The remaining child used her share to pay for her children's college education.

The Point Is . . .

In most cases, it is best not to make your children's choices from the grave. Do not tie their hands by prohibiting the post-death sale of your investment property. Let your children make the economic decisions following your death.

Indeed, perhaps one child would like to buy out your other children's share of the building. Perhaps your children would rather sell it, refinance, or exchange. Perhaps they would like to cash out and invest elsewhere—or pump the cash proceeds into their business. Or perhaps your children simply need the cash, not bricks and mortar.

If left to their own devices, your children may even discover the merits of owning rental properties and decide to keep the building. But whatever your children choose to do, they will inevitably find a way to serve their own best interest.

And whatever they do, the consequences of those decisions are with them and not with you.

---

2. "We want our children to sell our apartment building after we're gone and divide the proceeds equally."

The Kleins: Sell and Divide

Unlike the Mitchells, Mr. and Mrs. Klein did not identify their apartment building as their life achievement. They were more practical. To them, it was simply a business investment.

The Kleins told me that after their deaths, they wanted their building sold, with the proceeds divided between their two children. I applauded the Kleins for their good sense. With the building sold, both children would be economically independent from each other and could do whatever they wished with their shares.

The Kleins' daughter readily agreed with this plan. Living in Idaho, far away from her parents' building in Los Angeles, she had no reason or desire to keep the building in the family.

The Kleins' son, on the other hand, was adamantly opposed to cashing out. He wanted his parents to leave the building intact. With the investment benefits and future growth potential of real estate in Los Angeles, he thought it ill-advised for his parents to order the sale of their building after their deaths.

Solution: Consider What Your Children Want

The Kleins had a serious potential inheritance conflict on their hands. Selling the building would upset their son—retaining it would incur the wrath of their daughter. If they did not address this potential inheritance conflict, they might leave a legacy of bitterness and litigation between their children.

(Some parents would not have cared one whit about this potential inheritance conflict. In their minds, their children are lucky to get anything. But most of my clients are like the Kleins, who thought it important that their children always maintain a warm and loving family relationship.)

After much discussion, the Kleins and I finally decided on a plan. This plan appeared a reasonable compromise between their children's competing desires. However, we all realized it was theory and experiment. None of us knew if this plan would succeed until after the deaths of Mr. and Mrs. Klein.

The Plan

For five years after their deaths, the Kleins' building would be kept intact. This five-year plan would accomplish two goals.

First, the five years would give the son sufficient time to raise the money to buy out his sister. If the son could not come up with the money at the end of five years, the property would be sold and the proceeds distributed equally.

Second, the five years gave the son and daughter ample time to change their minds. Indeed, after getting accustomed to receiving income checks for five years, perhaps the daughter would adapt to the son's view. On the flip side, perhaps the son, after experiencing the headaches and hassles of managing investment real estate, would come around to the daughter's point of view.

The Aftermath

Eventually, the Kleins died. The plan worked. Within the five-year period, the daughter changed her mind and decided to keep the property. The passage of time allowed her to see the benefits of retaining investment real estate.

Ultimately, the Kleins' son and daughter were satisfied with the outcome.

Part VII

Protecting Your Surviving Spouse's Ownership and Control of the "Family Money"

22

The Three Issues You Must Address to Protect Your Surviving Spouse

In the conventional family, you have Dad, Mom, and the children. While Dad and Mom are alive, they usually own everything in some form of joint ownership. Whatever they have—real estate, bank accounts, stocks, bonds, cars, jewelry—one-half belongs to Dad and one-half belongs to Mom, with right of survivorship.

When Dad dies (usually, the first spouse to die), his half of the family wealth will pass to Mom. Mom will then become the 100 percent owner of all the family money. If Mom is the beneficiary of Dad's life insurance policies, IRA accounts, or qualified pension plans, she will own all of those assets.

Mom will retain control and sole ownership over all the family wealth for the rest of her life. The children do not inherit the family money until Mom dies. But while Mom is alive and owns it all, three issues should be considered.

1) Who will assume control and management if Mom becomes incapacitated or incompetent to the extent she can no longer control and manage the family wealth?

2) Who will protect Mom's ownership and control of the family money from children who are intent on an "early inheritance"?

3) Who will preserve the family money for Mom if Mom does not have the motivation, skill, or temperament to make investment and business decisions?

Are These Your Concerns?

If you are like most of my clients, these issues are not of major concern to you. You probably assume that the transition of wealth after you die will be smooth and automatic, with the survivor capably and competently controlling the family wealth until he or she dies and the children take over.

In the vast majority of cases, that is how it works out. But today, people are living longer, and the time between Dad's death and Mom's death is expanding—and it is not unusual for that interval to be ten to fifteen years. The longer Mom survives Dad, the greater the risk she may lose ownership and control of the family money prior to her death.

I strongly believe that protecting the surviving spouse's ownership and control of the family money from risk is a major goal of inheritance planning. Most clients agree with me, but usually not until I bring these risks to their attention. Therefore, the chapters in this section will focus on the need to protect and preserve the family money while the last spouse owns it all.

Chapter 23 deals with protecting the surviving spouse from efforts by children to obtain premature ownership and control of the family money.

Chapter 24 discusses protecting the family money when the surviving spouse becomes incapacitated or incompetent and who will take over the money and property if the incapacitated or incompetent surviving spouse has no children.

Chapter 25 discusses the advantage of having a third-party Trustee assist the surviving spouse in managing the family wealth.

23

Protecting the Surviving Parent from "Grasping Children"

or

"When Mom Dies—I'll Be Too Old to Enjoy My Inheritance"

In the vast majority of families, Dad will die first, leaving Mom with ownership and control of the family money. When Mom dies, everything will go to the children.

Most children wait patiently for their inheritance . . . no matter how old Mom may get. However, I will occasionally hear children tell me without any sense of embarrassment that Mom is taking too long to die. As one child said, "Mom is eighty-five and just keeps on going. I'm sixty-two. If Mom dies at ninety-five, I'll be too damn old to enjoy my inheritance."

If a child is intent on an early inheritance, that child may be very persuasive when trying to convince Mom to part with ownership and control of her home and other assets. This chapter deals with the most common scenarios in which a child attempts to advance the time he or she can grasp all or part of the family money.

Scenario Number 1: The "Promise"

"My daughter says she will take care of me for the rest of my life if I put her name on the deed to my house now."

Once 60 *Minutes* addressed this very issue. This segment depicted an endemic situation in our country: Husbands die before their wives, wives outlive their husbands for several years, and wives become vulnerable to their children who want their inheritance sooner rather than later.

In the 60 *Minutes* segment, a surviving mom spoke of her wish to live in her home for the rest of her life. But Mom needed some help in taking care of herself and her home. If she could not find a part-time caretaker whom she could afford, she would be forced to sell her house and move to an "old folks home."

Mom's daughter came up with a solution to this plight. The daughter promised to come to Mom's home and take care of her for the rest of her life. In exchange, the daughter insisted on receiving title to Mom's home immediately instead of waiting until after Mom's death.

Mom felt this was a reasonable solution to her problem. And after all, if she could not trust her daughter, whom could she trust? So Mom signed a deed transferring the title of her home to her daughter.

A few months later, Mom received a letter that said that her house had been sold—and she had to leave! Extremely distraught and confused, Mom telephoned her daughter to find out what was going on. Mom nearly fainted when she heard the news: Her daughter had "deeded" the house to *her* son, and he then sold it to a buyer for well below its fair market value.

In other words, Mom's grandson sold the house right out from under her.

Why did the daughter and grandson do what they did? Reporters from 60 *Minutes* tried to talk to them, but they refused to be interviewed. However, I can surmise that perhaps the daughter believed Mom belonged in a nursing facility. Or perhaps the daughter felt that she and her son were at a time in life when they could best use their inheritance.

Mom refused to give up her home for as long as she could. But, ultimately, she had to leave. Her grandson brought eviction proceedings and the court forced her to vacate.

Solution: Require That a "Special Trustee" Join In on a Transfer of Assets Mom Makes to a Child

Mom could have protected herself and her home from her daughter as follows:

1) Mom could have established a Living Trust with herself as sole Trustee;

2) Mom could have then transferred title of her home to her Living Trust. (After the transfer, Mom would have owned 100 percent of her home as Trustee of her Living Trust);

3) Mom's Living Trust could have included a special provision that said that any deed transferring the home to the daughter would require the signature of a third party whom I call a "Special Trustee";

4) The "Special Trustee" could have been the Trust Department of Mom's local bank or any private individual in whom Mom had complete trust and faith. Whomever Mom chose, this Special Trustee could have been Mom's "backstop"—the one to protect Mom from making unwise or emotional decisions in transferring her home to her daughter.

Scenario Number 2: The "Pressure"

"My son says I should give him my power of attorney." "I don't know who to turn to for advice. Everything my children tell me turns out to be for their own benefit." "Before my husband died, he told me to watch out for the children. I didn't know what he meant at the time. But I sure know now."

After the 60 Minutes episode aired, I received a deluge of phone calls from worried viewers who feared similar abuses from their children. Of all the new clients I spoke with that Monday morning, Mrs. Housman is the one who stands out in my mind.

Mrs. Housman, like many people that day, was immensely disturbed by the case of the mom on 60 Minutes who lost her house to her daughter and grandson. But the show also prompted her to remember her husband's deathbed statement. She told me that in the moment before he died, Mrs. Housman's husband whispered in her ear, "Watch out for the children."

Mrs. Housman did not understand her husband's final words until a few years after her husband died. It started with jokes from her children about all the money they stood to inherit. Later, her children seemed to begin almost every sentence with "When my ship comes in . . ." Eventually, these hints and jests turned into outright pressures for an early inheritance.

So, heeding her late husband's words and prompted by the 60 Minutes report, Mrs. Housman sought my advice to protect herself and her money from her children.

Solution: Using the Special Trustee

Mrs. Housman protected herself by establishing a Living Trust and incorporating the Special Trustee provisions I discussed above in Scenario Number 1.

Mrs. Housman was the sole Trustee of her Living Trust. But she also provided that a bank Trustee would serve as Special

Trustee whenever a transfer between parent and child occurred. Unless the Special Trustee consented *in writing* to transfers of Trust assets between Mrs. Housman and her children, the transfers could not take place. (However, the plan did provide that Mrs. Housman could make annual tax-free gifts to each child without the bank Trustee's approval.)

At first, Mrs. Housman did not like this solution. It unnerved her to think of a bank Trustee telling her what she could or could not do with the family money.

Before she adopted this plan, I arranged for Mrs. Housman to meet with her bank's senior Trust officer. After this meeting, Mrs. Housman was rarin' to go. She was convinced the bank Trustee would protect her wealth *from* her "grasping children," and she would still have ownership and control over her money.

Once her children saw they had to go through the bank Trustee to get her money, they did not bother to drop any more hints of an early inheritance.

Scenario Number 3: The "Avoiding Probate" Approach

"My son says that giving him my home now will keep him out of probate when I die."

Your son is correct. If you give him your house now, or even if you give him a 50 percent interest with right of survivorship, your son will own 100 percent after you die without a costly and time-consuming probate.

But you have to be "this side of insanity" to give in to this reasoning. Why? Because if you give all or part of your home to your son, you are also making him an owner of record. From then on, your house will be subject to your son's problems.

If your son declares bankruptcy, his ownership interest in your home could be taken over by the Bankruptcy Court and sold to pay off his creditors.

If your son gets a divorce, your house could become one of the assets to be divided by the divorce judge.

If your son gets into an accident, and he has insufficient insurance to satisfy a judgment, the accident victim could force a sale of your son's ownership interest in your house to satisfy the claim.

If your son has business creditors or gets in trouble with the IRS, the first thing they may look to as a source of payment is your son's interest in your house.

Solution: The Living Trust

The Living Trust is the perfect answer to the child who wants the house now for probate-avoidance reasons. It accomplishes exactly what this child wants while retaining your ownership and control of your home and other assets during your life.

You establish a Living Trust, into which you transfer your home and other assets. With this Trust, you continue to control and own these assets as Trustee.

While you are alive and your Living Trust exists, your child has no right to any of the Living Trust assets, and these assets will not become subject to any of your child's problems. After you die, any assets remaining in your Living Trust pass to your child—probate-free.

Scenario Number 4: The "Avoiding Death-Tax" Approach

"My daughter says that if I give her my home and other assets now, she will save money in death taxes after I die."

If you transfer title of your home to your daughter before you die just to save death taxes, you will have gone to a lot of trouble for nothing. Gifting the home now will not save one penny of death tax for two reasons:

1. There Is No Death Tax

As I discuss in the completely revised Chapter 33 ("The Repeal of the Death Tax"), the death tax was virtually wiped out in 2013. Unless you own more than $5,340,000 on your death, your home will go to your daughter without being subject to any death tax. Do you have own more than $5,340,000? Are you planning on winning the lottery? If your answers to both these questions are "no," then don't be suckered by this approach to get your house before your death.

2. You Can't Escape the Death Tax by Impoverishing Yourself

If the death tax applies to you because you own more than $5,340,000, you cannot escape the death tax just by giving away what you own before you die. If that were the case, everyone would give away their assets before death and the IRS would never get its share.

Therefore, if you gift your home to your daughter before you die, she will be legally required to report this gift to the IRS after you die, even if you made this gift fifty years before your death.

The value reported is the value of your home at the time you gifted it to your daughter. If your daughter does not know this value, she will have to hire a real estate appraiser who will find out for her.

3. You Can't Give Away That Which You Keep

If you continue to live in the home after you give it to your daughter, the IRS will say it was not a real gift. After all, how can you have "really and truly" made a gift if you control the thing you gave away?

Therefore, when you die, the IRS will say 100 percent of the home belongs to you, even if title is in your daughter's name, and it will impose a death tax on its full value.

Solution: Don't Buy It

Once you are forewarned, you are forearmed. When your daughter tells you that gifting your home "now" will save money in death taxes, you are in a position to tell her otherwise.

Scenario Number 5: The "Anti-Medicaid" Approach

"If I ever have to resort to Medicaid, the Medicaid authorities may sell my home after I die to replace all the money spent on my convalescent care. But my son says that if I don't own my home when I die, Medicaid cannot touch it. So he says I should give him my home now."

There may come a time in your life when you desperately need Medicaid benefits to pay for convalescent care. However, after you die, Medicaid may want to recoup the money it spent on you.

How will Medicaid get its money back? It may impose a lien on your house after you die and force a sale of it. Medicaid will then reimburse itself from the sale proceeds.

Your son, however, does not like the prospect of most or all of his inheritance going to pay your convalescent care. So your son urges you to protect the house from Medicaid by giving him your house now! If your house is not in your name when you die, Medicaid cannot use your house as a source of repayment.

Is this a powerful argument for you to give your son your home now? It depends on the state in which you reside. Some states are extremely aggressive in pursuing reimbursement for monies they expended on a recipient's convalescent care, and others are more passive.

But whatever your state's recoupment policy is, be forewarned.

There are two major disadvantages to gifting your home to your son now.

1) As I mentioned in Scenario Number 3, you will have lost ownership of your house, subjecting it to your son's financial risks and other problems.

2) If your son sells your home after you gift it to him, he may discover that the capital gains taxes are greater than the amount Medicaid would have received.

Scenario Number 6: The "Blackmail" Approach

"My wife is dead and I can no longer take care of myself. Since my son hardly ever comes around, my daughter has to provide for my needs. But my daughter threatens to stop caring for me unless I leave her all of my money when I die."

In almost every family, it is inevitable that children must care for their surviving parent if that parent can no longer care for himself. However, bringing all the children together to act as a team may be difficult if not impossible. And without teamwork, one child invariably winds up shouldering most or all of the burden of being the unwell parent's caretaker.

Caring for the aged and unwell parent is a very time-consuming and stressful job for the caretaker child. Suddenly, this child's life is put on hold so she can attend to her parent's needs. But what makes it worse is that while the caretaker child is driving Dad to the doctor, doing Dad's errands, and going to Dad's house five times a day, Dad's other children may be going about their daily lives.

Is it any wonder that Dad may be pressured into leaving the caretaker child a greater share of Dad's money when Dad dies?

The Caretaker Child Syndrome

If a parent needs his child's help to get into my office, the warning signs and flashing lights go off in my head that say: DANGER AHEAD!! THE ONE PUSHING THE WHEELCHAIR WANTS MORE OF AN INHERITANCE FROM THE ONE IN THE WHEELCHAIR!!

I remember Mr. Newman's daughter, who immediately confirmed this suspicion. After struggling to wheel her father through my small doorway, she loudly berated her absent brother for not lifting a finger to help her take care of her father. "While I'm slaving away helping my father, my brother is having the time of his life."

After telling me all about her "rotten" brother, she eventually got down to the bottom line. Since she was shouldering the burden of taking care of Dad, and since it appeared her brother did not care about Dad's well-being, she should be entitled to more of the inheritance than her brother when her father dies.

(How generous of her, I thought. Most caretaker children want it all. And to get it all, they persuade incapacitated Dad that his other children don't care about him and he should not hesitate to cut them out.)

Did Mr. Newman have anything to say about all this? Not really. When I asked him directly what he wanted to do, he meekly said he agreed with his daughter and would do whatever she wanted. And later, with his daughter cooling off in my waiting room, I asked him again—and his response was the same.

However, having seen this caretaker situation many times before, I knew this was not a choice from the heart.

"Driving" Mr. Newman

Sometimes, for the lawyer to do what's best for a client, the lawyer has to steer the client in a direction the client does not want to go. For the next hour, I steered Mr. Newman and pressed him on this issue.

Finally, Mr. Newman said what was really on his mind.

"I have a problem, Mr. Condon. I don't want to change my Will. Like it says, I want my son and daughter to inherit my money equally. But I am convinced I have no choice but to go along with what my daughter wants. If I don't, she will abandon me. Then who will take care of me?"

I knew I could talk Mr. Newman into leaving his Will as it stood. However, that would not solve the problem. His daughter would simply take him to another lawyer, who would have little compunction about changing his Will.

Solution: Convince the Caretaker Child That Changing Dad's Will Is More Trouble Than It's Worth

The only way I could solve this problem was to work on the daughter. I had to convince her it was in her best interest to leave things alone and not try to get a greater share of her father's money and property.

This is what I said to Mr. Newman's daughter. And what I told her is what I tell all caretaker children who come into my office.

Tactic Number 1: The Human Cost

I told Mr. Newman's daughter about the conflict that would arise between her and her brother. If her father left her more, it would create a chasm in the family that would never be bridged.

Had this daughter cherished her sibling relationship, this point would have been all she needed to hear to forgo her scheme. However, not everyone loves his brothers and sisters. For Mr. Newman's daughter, money was far superior than the loss of her brother's affection.

So, since she lived for money, I simply hit her where she lived.

Tactic Number 2: The Money Cost

I told the daughter about the financial fallout of her scheme. If she pressured her father into changing his Will, her brother would file a lawsuit against her as soon as her father died. In this law-suit, her brother would claim that she pressured her father into decreasing his inheritance.

The daughter responded with a laugh. "It will never happen," she said.

"You are wrong," I admonished her. "When your brother finds out that he got less, he will sue you. As sure as the sun will rise tomorrow, he will claim that you unduly influenced your father into changing his Will. And you know something? Your brother won't have to lay out a dime for it. There are a hundred lawyers who will take his case on a contingency basis.

"You, on the other hand, are going to wind up spending a lot of money to defend your brother's lawsuit. What will it cost you? Who knows? It may be $25,000. It may be $100,000. What's more, your inheritance will be held up for as long as the suit lasts. And these suits can drag on forever."

In many cases, the prospect of a Will contest following the parent's death convinces the caretaker child to drop the demand. Did this point convince Mr. Newman's daughter? Yes and no. Yes, because she shuddered to think of the potential cost of a lawsuit. No, because she remained adamant about being entitled to more of an inheritance than her brother.

Tactic Number 3: The Salary

Later in our meeting, I offered Mr. Newman's daughter another perspective on her situation.

"I can imagine what you are going through," I began. "I've seen it many times before. Since you've had to take care of your father, you've had no life of your own. It's like a full-time job. And like any job, you feel you should be compensated. Certainly, if your father hired a nurse, he would be paying for services rendered.

"Daughter, you are looking for this compensation in the form of an extra inheritance. But as I've mentioned to you before, there are problems with that. So instead of being paid after your father dies, be paid now. Let your father pay you a salary, and let him keep his Will the way it is."

Most caretaker children believe this to be a pretty good solution. After all, they think, getting money now feels better than getting money later. And besides, the compensation after death will be eaten away by lawyers and held up indefinitely by litigation.

Mr. Newman's daughter, however, was not like most caretaker children. Whatever salary she received, she said, it would never be enough to relieve her indignation. "I'm doing everything while he does nothing," she repeated, "and no salary can take that hurt away. The only way I can achieve satisfaction is if my father leaves me 75 percent of the inheritance."

The Final Tactic

Since the daughter resisted all my powers of persuasion, I resorted to my final tactic.

On my desk sat Mr. Newman's files. These files had been in my office for twenty-five years. I gathered up these files, got out of my chair, thrust them in the daughter's hands, and opened up my office door. As I stood by the door, I said to her, "There are a hundred attorneys out there who would be more than happy to change your father's Will. Find one. If your new lawyer has any questions, I'll be glad to accommodate him."

This was the strategy that convinced the daughter. You should have seen her mouth go agape. The shock of hearing my words finally drove home the seriousness of changing her father's Will to increase her inheritance.

24

Who Controls the Money and Property for the Incapacitated or Incompetent Surviving Spouse?

You May Not Want a Stranger to Control Your Surviving Spouse's Money—but Are Your Children a Better Choice?

---

1. "I expect my wife to outlive me and be the sole owner of all our money and property. What happens if she becomes incompetent or incapacitated before she dies?"

Look in a convalescent home and you'll see it is filled with more women than men. This is a sign of our times, for the likelihood is that Mom will outlive Dad by many years. And at some point before Mom dies, she may become incompetent or incapacitated and not be able to manage her financial affairs. (Of course, dads experience the same problem, but since women have a longer life expectancy, Mom is usually the surviving spouse.)

Who will take over management and control of the family money on behalf of Mom? Who will make Mom's financial decisions? If there is no plan in place, it may be Mom's conservator.

230

The Conservatorship Process

If Mom is medically unable to manage her money and property, someone must go into court and ask to be appointed Mom's conservator—the one who can legally make all investment, management, and spending decisions on Mom's behalf.

Usually, one of Mom's children asks to be appointed her conservator. This child will hire a lawyer, who will prepare endless forms and make several court appearances to show the judge two things:

1) Mom is incapacitated or incompetent to the extent that she can no longer manage her financial affairs. Usually, this is proved by securing the testimony of Mom's attending physicians.

2) The child seeking to be the conservator has good character and can effectively do the job. Typically, this means that the child must convince the judge that he will not run off with Mom's money.

If Mom has more than one child, they may agree among themselves who will act as her conservator. If they disagree, the process becomes more expensive and cumbersome, with each child trying to prove to the judge that he, and not any of his siblings, is the best one for the job.

After Mom's child (or children) has been appointed conservator, that child will probably be required to prepare and file an "accounting" with the court. Basically, this is a report that lists every money transaction the child has made with Mom's money: every bill paid, every penny spent, every investment made, and all income or interest collected.

This accounting must be filed periodically, typically once a year. And on each occasion, the child will probably hire an accountant and a lawyer to prepare the accounting and put it in proper legal form so it can be filed with the court.

Alternatives to Conservatorship

There are two documents you can use to avoid the expensive and cumbersome conservatorship process.

The Power of Attorney

A "Power of Attorney" is a document one signs authorizing someone else to act on the signer's behalf. In the business world, an employer may sign a Power of Attorney giving a trusted employee the power to sign contracts on the employer's behalf. In the real estate arena, an owner may sign a Power of Attorney giving someone the right to sign the owner's name to deeds or other title documents.

When it comes to protecting Mom's money if she becomes incapacitated or incompetent, there is the "Durable Power of Attorney." With this document (which Mom must sign while she is competent), Mom gives her child the power to sign her name to financial papers (checks, deposit slips, withdrawal slips, investment orders, and so on) in the event Mom is medically unable to manage her own financial affairs.

Every state has its own laws about the Durable Power of Attorney, and generally, they are very easy and inexpensive to prepare. But be forewarned—you get what you pay for, and the Durable Power of Attorney is no exception to that rule.

I have found the Durable Power of Attorney to be very ineffective in allowing Mom's child to gain access to Mom's money. The powers that be, usually the banks and brokerage houses that hold Mom's savings and stock accounts, are reluctant to recognize the authority it grants to Mom's child. Why? Because they usually have one or more of the following doubts:

1) The Durable Power of Attorney kicks in only if Mom becomes incapacitated or incompetent, and she may not yet be incapacitated or incompetent.

2) Mom's signature on the Durable Power of Attorney may not really be Mom's signature.

3) Mom can only legally sign the Durable Power of Attorney while capable and competent, and she may not have been competent at the time she signed it.

It does not matter if Mom's child has the most legitimate Durable Power of Attorney in the world. In today's litigious climate, the account holders are extremely cautious, and nothing your child says or does may resolve their doubts. If Mom's child tries to use a legal Durable Power of Attorney to gain access to Mom's accounts, access will probably be denied.

What happens then? Mom's child will have to get a document that the financial institutions will recognize as a court order that says that he is Mom's officially appointed conservator who can legally act on behalf of Mom.

(Not all Durable Power of Attorney documents are so uncertain and unreliable. In question 3 of this chapter, I discuss the Durable Power of Attorney for Health Care in which Mom empowers a child or third party to make *medical decisions* on her behalf. This document is universally recognized and declares who has the authority to decide Mom's medical treatment if Mom cannot make such decisions for herself.)

The Living Trust: The Least Costly and Most Effective Alternative to the Conservatorship

The Living Trust is the most efficient and least costly means for a child to acquire control over Mom's assets if Mom becomes incapacitated or incompetent.

Mom can establish a Living Trust and transfer into the Trust all of her money and property. Thereafter, Mom will continue to own her assets as Trustee of her Living Trust. Mom can include a special provision stating that if she becomes incompetent or incapacitated, a child (or children) can take over as Trustee, empowering that child to manage, control, and spend Mom's assets for Mom's benefit.

Leave No Room for Abuse: Require Certification of Mom's Incapacity

There is a concern that empowering a child to take over may open the door for abuse. If a child is intent on an early inheritance, he may attempt to come into power as Trustee of Mom's money *before* Mom becomes incapacitated or incompetent.

To combat this problem, Mom can include a special provision in her Living Trust that allows her child to take over *only if* no fewer than two medical doctors certify in writing on their letterheads that Mom is incompetent or incapacitated to the degree she can no longer manage and control her financial affairs. If Mom wants this certification to be made by a specific doctor in whom she has faith and confidence, she can specifically designate that doctor's name.

Usually, the child will have no trouble getting these letters. If Mom is truly incapacitated or incompetent, Mom's family doctor and/or the doctors who have been attending to Mom throughout her illness will be happy to immediately oblige.

When the child obtains the doctors' letters, he becomes the Trustee of Mom's Living Trust and has the power to deal with all the assets contained in the Trust. When the child presents these letters to the bank or brokerage firm that holds Mom's accounts (along with a copy of Mom's Living Trust), there will be little delay in gaining access to the money or securities in those accounts.

2. "I like the idea of the Living Trust designating our children to take over control if the survivor of my wife and me becomes incapacitated. But I'm not so sure I want them making the investment and spending decisions."

In the vast majority of cases where Mom becomes incapacitated or incompetent, the children who take over do a reasonable and honest job managing Mom's money for her benefit. However, in three circumstances it is preferable not to let a child have control of the family money:

1) When the child is geographically distant from Mom, making the logistics of taking over impracticable;

2) If Mom expresses discomfort about a child taking control of her money prior to her death;

3) If Mom feels a child will not be capable of managing the family money or cannot make proper spending decisions.

In these circumstances, it may be preferable to use the services of a bank Trustee or other institutional Trustee to take over the management, control, and spending decisions if Mom becomes incapacited or incompetent.

Solution: Use the Living Trust to Bring in the Bank If Mom Becomes Incapacitated or Incompetent

In Mom's Living Trust, she can state that if she becomes incapacitated or incompetent, a bank Trustee can step in as Trustee and manage the assets contained in Mom's Living Trust. (Or, Mom can allow a child to act as a Cotrustee with the bank.) The bank Trustee will safeguard Mom's assets for her use, and all its investment and spending decisions will be made competently and independently.

When Mom dies, the bank Trustee is already in place to transfer the assets in accordance with Mom's wishes as she has set forth in her Living Trust.

Bringing in the Bank Before Mom's Incapacity or Incompetency

Mom may wish to lean on the shoulder of the bank Trustee, *even if she is not incapacitated or incompetent!*

If Mom wishes, she can turn over to the bank Trustee any responsibility she sees fit, and she retains any duty that she does not specifically give away. For example, if Mom is tired of making the investment decisions, she can let the bank do it. If Mom does not want to be bothered with the burden of collecting income and paying bills, she can let the bank act on her behalf.

If, thereafter, Mom becomes incapacitated or incompetent, the bank Trustee is already in place to take over full management and control. When Mom dies, the bank Trustee can distribute the Trust assets in accordance with the dispository provisions of Mom's Living Trust.

3. "My wife will probably survive me for many years. If she becomes incapacitated and our son takes over control of the family money, won't he be tempted to spend less on my wife's care so there will be more for him when she dies?"

Occasionally, an elderly client will discuss this concern with me. She has seen her contemporaries "warehoused" in the least costly convalescent facilities, where they are waiting to die. As one surviving Mom said, "My kids won't care if they put me in the cheapest place around. And my mind will probably be so gone, I may not have much to say about it."

In the vast majority of cases in which the surviving spouse (usually Mom) becomes incapacitated or incompetent, the children will do the right thing and give her the best care possible. But this fact is of little comfort to the client with a gnawing concern that she will be "railroaded" if her child takes over control of her money.

Certainly, this is a legitimate concern, as there is a potential conflict of interest between Mom and her child if the child is in control of Mom's money. If the child spends less on Mom's health care, he will end up with more of an inheritance when Mom dies.

There is little I can do for the surviving Mom who is tortured by this prospect. If her children believe that what is best for them supersedes what is best for Mom, they may indeed put Mom in the most minimal of facilities.

But if Mom wants some protection from this abuse, she can sign a special document that leaves the decision of Mom's care in the hands of someone other than her children.

Solution: The "Durable Power of Attorney for Health Care"

Mom can sign a Durable Power of Attorney for Health Care, a document in which she appoints someone to make medical decisions on her behalf if she becomes incapacitated or incompetent.

On most occasions, Mom will give her child (or children) the power to make her medical decisions. But if Mom is concerned her child may abuse this power, she can name a third party to decide:

1) Should Mom remain at home with the appropriate nursing care?
2) Should Mom be placed in a convalescent care facility?
3) If Mom needs care at a convalescent facility, which one?

This third party can be Mom's friend, sibling, or any other person whom Mom can trust to do the right thing. However, I recommend that Mom choose a third party who has two characteristics:

1) The third party should have no axe to grind. That is, he or she should have no stake in Mom's financial affairs and should not be a beneficiary of Mom's Will or Living Trust. This assures Mom that the third party can make medical decisions independent of any money considerations.
2) The third party should be roughly the same age as Mom. Why? Because of the "there but for the grace of God go I" attitude. A third party who sees himself as being one step away from

Mom's plight will probably be more sympathetic and sensitive to Mom's needs and will see to it that Mom gets the best care possible.

Once the third party decides where Mom will be cared for, the one who has the authority to spend Mom's money can make the appropriate medical payments. This spending authority may be vested in Mom's child (see question number 1 above) or the Trust Department of a bank (see question number 2 above).

---

4. "My wife and I have no children. If I die first, she will be alone. I don't want some stranger to be put in charge of our money if she becomes ill or incapacitated. I remember that happened to Groucho Marx."

The prior questions in this chapter dealt with the common scenario of Dad dying first and Mom becoming the sole owner of the family money. Before Mom dies, Mom becomes incapacitated or incompetent, and her child takes over managing, controlling, and spending the money for Mom's benefit.

But if Dad and Mom have no children, what will happen to the family money after Dad dies and Mom becomes ill? Who will be the one to manage and control the money for Mom? Most likely, it will be a stranger whom I call the "caretaker." This is how it may happen.

The "Caretaker Syndrome"

When Dad dies, Mom may live for another twelve to twenty years. At some point, Mom may, as most elderly women do, find herself in a declining state of health. Eventually, Mom realizes she needs help to take care of everyday business. So, she hires a caretaker. Most likely, this caretaker will be a nice young lady from another country whom Mom has heard of through the grapevine or newspaper ad.

The caretaker may become Mom's only way of maintaining any

semblance of a normal life. The caretaker is the one who buys the food; prepares the meals; does the laundry; and drives Mom to the doctor, to the market, or wherever Mom has to go.

After spending much time together in a relatively short period, the caretaker wins Mom's trust. This caretaker may become Mom's friend and confidante—perhaps the only one Mom will have.

As Mom's mental acuity gradually diminishes, her dependency on her caretaker will increase. Mom may ask for her help in paying bills, depositing checks, balancing the checkbook, and keeping her up to date on financial statements. And in order for the caretaker to accomplish these tasks more readily, Mom may place the caretaker's name on her checking account. Or Mom may just tell the caretaker to "go ahead and sign my name."

Eventually, Mom's physical and mental abilities may diminish to the point where she is completely dependent on her caretaker. And the greater the dependency, the greater the control and power the caretaker can have over Mom.

How will the caretaker exercise this power? In the majority of cases, the caretaker will discharge her duties honestly and faithfully. But occasionally, a caretaker will abuse her power to her financial advantage. The caretaker may threaten to leave Mom, physically abuse Mom, or steal money behind her back.

If the caretaker's power grab is successful, Mom may do things she would never otherwise do:

Mom may sign a deed transferring title of her home to the caretaker.

Mom may put the caretaker's name on all the bank and brokerage assets.

Mom may sign a document giving the caretaker Power of Attorney.

Mom may change her Will or Trust to include her caretaker as a beneficiary.

There is nothing anyone can do to protect Mom from the caretaker's abuse. After all, who is around to stop it? Mom has no children, and no court or caring agency will involve itself in Mom's affairs unless the abuse is brought to their attention. Even then, with minimal government support and diminished resources, the caring agency will simply lack the time to get involved.

If It Can Happen to the Benders, It Can Happen to Anyone

Are you unconvinced this process will never happen to your spouse if you die first? Mr. Bender did not believe it, and what happened to his wife was a tragedy—a tragedy that could have been prevented.

Mr. Bender told me straight off that he and his wife did not want a Living Trust. He did not care if their money would go through probate. They had no children, and their only family consisted of a few nephews on the East Coast he barely knew. "Let them pay the probate," Mr. Bender said. "Let it be their problem."

Mr. Bender's attitude is shared by many people who have no children, and I agree with them. Why pay more for a probate-avoidance Living Trust if you don't have children and don't really care if your heirs inherit less? In fact, the heirs should consider themselves lucky to get anything at all.

However, the Benders needed the Living Trust for another reason. The Living Trust can defeat the "Last Caretaker Syndrome." If Mr. Bender dies first, the Living Trust can assure his widow that someone trustworthy will be around to care for her needs if she becomes too ill or incapacitated to care for herself.

I explained how a Living Trust could be used to protect Mrs. Bender in the event of illness or incapacity. (See solution below.) But Mr. Bender scoffed at this advice: "Mr. Condon, my wife's mother lived to be a hundred and five. She was healthy and alert to the day she died, and my wife is going to do likewise. The idea of paying you good money to protect my wife is downright silly."

I am not the type of attorney who has a lot of patience with parsimonious clients. In exasperation, I turned to Mrs. Bender, who had been silent thus far, and said in a semiangry tone:

"Mrs. Bender, you and your husband are right about not wanting a Living Trust just to save your nephews the expenses of probate. But if your husband had any concern for you, he would want to protect you and your money if he died first and you became incapacitated. If your husband doesn't do something now, no one will be around to care for you and protect your money!"

I provided Mrs. Bender with example after example of pitiful situations in which the widow was physically abused or "ripped off" by the last caretaker. After I ended this parade of horribles, I said:

"Mrs. Bender, this abuse can occur if you have no one around to protect you. Where there is a vacuum, someone may move to fill that vacuum, usually, the last care provider. You may become so dependent on that person, you and your money will be an easy target."

Her Mouth Said "No" but Her Eyes Said "Yes"

Mrs. Bender's eyes told me she understood the need for protection after her husband's death. However, being unable to fight off her husband, she remained silent.

The Benders slipped into my memory until two years later when my secretary interrupted a meeting with an emergency call from Mrs. Bender's physician. He received word that "something was going on" at Mrs. Bender's apartment. When he arrived, Mrs. Bender appeared beaten up and needed immediate treatment.

The doctor went through Mrs. Bender's purse to find someone to contact. The only number he found was the one on my card. The doctor asked me to come over, and I left my office right away.

I hardly recognized Mrs. Bender. With her head down, her hands in her lap, bruises on her arms, and no sign of recognition in her eyes, I had to be convinced that this was the same lady who had appeared in my office only two years before. As the doctor and I waited for the ambulance to arrive, the neighbor who called the doctor told us how Mrs. Bender arrived at such a sorry state. Of course, it was the same old unfortunate story.

After Mr. Bender died, Mrs. Bender hired "some girl" to help her get along. After a few months of employment, Mrs. Bender grew completely dependent on her caretaker. Whenever the neighbor saw Mrs. Bender, the hired help was with her.

About a year later, Mrs. Bender signed a Power of Attorney that gave this caretaker the power to sign Mrs. Bender's name. With this document, the caretaker had unlimited access to Mrs. Bender's checking accounts and certificates of deposit. Mrs. Bender told the neighbor that she knew her caretaker was stealing her blind. But, afraid she would be left alone, Mrs. Bender did not confront her caretaker.

Being used was bad enough, but being beaten was even worse. By the look of the bruises on her arms, the doctor surmised that Mrs. Bender was being "manhandled." Thinking I was Mrs. Bender's attorney, the doctor asked why I did not do something to prevent Mrs. Bender from ending up in this sorry state.

After Mrs. Bender was taken to the hospital, I received a phone call from her nephew. He told me he lived on the East Coast and did not know his aunt from Eve. But since he was the closest thing she had to a living relative, he felt morally obligated to find out what had to be done next.

I told him that since his aunt did not have the capacity to make decisions for herself, someone had to make those decisions for her. The only person who had this power would be her court-appointed conservator. So the nephew went to court to establish a conservatorship over his aunt, giving him the legal power to make decisions over her personal, medical, and financial affairs.

The nephew's involvement in his aunt's life was minimal. All he did was deliver her to the nearby Golden Sunset Retirement Home and write the monthly check for room and board. Mrs. Bender lived there until she died.

The Moral of the Story

If you have no children (or even if you have children who are not around), and you are the surviving spouse, you may experience this story firsthand. Who will take care of you if you are no longer able to care for yourself? What assurances do you have you won't be controlled by the last caretaker? Who will be there to protect you?

If you do nothing to protect yourself (or your spouse, if you die first), you may have no protection at all. Unable to control the last friend or hired hand, you may end up in a plight as pitiful as Mrs. Bender's.

Therefore, the last kindest thing you can do for yourself and your spouse is to establish a three-part plan that will protect the last spouse to die. Since women typically live longer than men, I will explain this plan using the wife as the surviving spouse.

Part 1: Use a Living Trust to Protect Your Wife's Money

Establish a Living Trust while both you and your wife are alive and transfer to the Trust all your money and property. After the transfer, you and your wife will continue to own your assets as Trustees of your Living Trust.

Then provide that if your surviving wife becomes incapacitated or incompetent, a bank Trustee will take over as Trustee of the Living Trust. As Trustee, the bank Trustee will have the power to manage and control the Trust assets and perform such financial responsibilities as paying the bills, collecting the income, and investing the Trust assets.

When your wife dies, the bank Trustee can distribute the remaining Trust assets in accordance with the inheritance instructions contained in your Living Trust.

The Bank Trustee Can Act Even If Your Wife Is Not Incapacitated or Incompetent

You can provide in your Living Trust that the surviving spouse can authorize the bank to take over certain duties, even if the surviving spouse is not incapacitated or incompetent!

With this provision, your wife can request that the bank Trustee handle functions that may become too burdensome for her, such as paying bills, collecting income, managing income-producing real estate, or investing the Trust assets. Your wife retains any financial duty that she has not specifically delegated to the bank Trustee.

Later, if your wife becomes completely ill or incapacitated, the bank Trustee can immediately step in and control all the Living Trust assets.

Part 2: Use a Power of Attorney So Someone Can Make Health-Care Decisions for Your Wife

While the bank Trustee manages and controls your surviving wife's money, someone has to take care of your wife's physical well-being if she can no longer care for herself.

In question number 3 of this chapter, I described the Durable Power of Attorney for Health Care as a way to give a third party the power to make health-care decisions on your wife's behalf. Typically, this third party is one or more of the children. For the childless widow, the choice may become more difficult.

Who should be appointed to make medical decisions for your surviving wife? Perhaps your wife has a sibling, nephew, niece, or other family member who may be willing to serve. If no such person exists, perhaps a trusted friend or neighbor will take the job.

Part 3: Arrange in Advance for Someone to Take Care of Your Wife's Personal Needs and Comfort

If your surviving wife cannot attend to her own everyday needs, someone else must! A third party will have to do what your wife cannot do for herself, from grocery shopping to meal preparation, from cleaning to doing laundry, from driving her to the doctor to taking her to the movies.

Tending to your wife's day-to-day needs may be a full-time job. Therefore, you should arrange in advance of your wife's incapacity for someone to fill that job. Ask the bank Trustee for a recommendation, as any bank Trustee knows of several bonded and/or licensed individuals or companies that specialize in tending to the everyday personal needs of widows and widowers.

25

Does Your Wife Want to Manage the Family Money?

or

"My Wife Says She Wants to Die First—So She Won't Be Left with the Bookkeeping"

---

1. "During our forty-five years of marriage, I have always taken care of our financial affairs. My wife does not know the family lawyer or CPA. I'm afraid that if she outlives me, there is no way she will be able to manage our money and property."

Mr. and Mrs. Wagner embody the typical couple that comes to my office for inheritance planning. When I met them, he was in his early seventies, and she was in her late sixties. Married for forty-five years, Mr. Wagner created the family fortune while Mrs. Wagner ran the household.

Mrs. Wagner was a delightful lady who acknowledged she never did a thing to make or manage the family money. When I asked her if she knew what she and her husband owned, she said cheerfully, "Are you kidding? All I know is how to write the checks. My husband has always taken care of everything." At this point, Mr. Wagner chimed in. "She's right, Mr. Condon. I made it my business to keep my wife from worrying about money."

Mr. Wagner felt a special satisfaction in keeping his wife from the money side of family life. His attitude was that if he took care of the family financial matters, his wife would be free to focus on the children and the house. And with a limited financial background, Mrs. Wagner was more than willing to subscribe to her husband's point of view.

But now, Mr. Wagner was faced with the reality that maybe he did not do his wife any favors.

Mr. Wagner invested the family money in over fifty different stocks, mortgages, and mutual funds. If he died first, Mrs. Wagner would have to step into her husband's shoes and manage these investments. But with no knowledge or participation in family money matters, she would be unable to make investment decisions, collect the income, pay the bills, or deal with the family attorney and accountant.

It seemed the Wagners never sat down and talked about this issue, but it was apparent Mrs. Wagner had given it some thought. During our meeting, she said to me in jest, "I sure hope I die first so I won't be left with the bookkeeping."

Truth in Humor?

The more I talked to Mr. Wagner, the more he realized that there was some truth in his wife's humor. Since his wife was younger than him, and since wives statistically outlive their husbands, he would probably die first and leave his wife with the burden of managing the family money—a burden that she was ill-equipped to handle.

What could happen to the family money in his surviving wife's hands? Having counseled dozens of financially ill-equipped widows, I envisioned several possibilities:

- If Mrs. Wagner becomes incapacitated or incompetent, it could all end up with the last caretaker or final friend.
- If Mrs. Wagner listens to advice from friends or relatives, it could be lost in bad investments and poor management.

- If Mrs. Wagner has an aggressive child, he could pressure her into receiving an early inheritance.
- If Mrs. Wagner puts her trust, faith, and confidence in a third party, she may authorize this person to make financial decisions for her—not a good idea if this third party is not so trustworthy.

Three Choices—Each One Better than the One Before

I advised the Wagners to establish a Living Trust and transfer all their money and property to it. While alive, they would both continue to own their assets as Trustees of their Living Trust. But the Wagners had a decision to make: If Mr. Wagner dies first, would someone step in as a Cotrustee to help Mrs. Wagner manage and control the family money? If so, who would serve as the Cotrustee?

The Wagners had three alternatives:

Alternative 1: Let Mrs. Wagner Serve as Sole Trustee

The first thing I suggested was to let Mrs. Wagner be the sole Trustee and hope for the best.

I thought that this alternative would be quickly dismissed. But to my surprise, Mr. Wagner actually considered it! "Mr. Condon, people can do extraordinary things if they have to. If my wife is the sole Trustee, I bet she can rise to the task of managing the money."

Mrs. Wagner, however, was not as confident as her husband. She knew her limits and admitted that she was not a quick study. If she was the sole Trustee, she would be overwhelmed by even the most simple of management duties.

Alternative 2: Let the Wagners' Son Serve as Cotrustee

I suggested that the Wagners' son could serve alongside Mrs. Wagner as a Cotrustee, allowing him to assume all the management duties. But the Wagners felt uncomfortable giving their son such power over the family money.

Alternative 3: Let a Bank Trustee Serve as Cotrustee

In their Living Trust, the Wagners could appoint the Trust Department of a bank (bank Trustee) or other corporate entity to act as Mrs. Wagner's Cotrustee. As Cotrustee, it would make the investment decisions, collect the income, pay the bills, see to the preparation of income tax returns, and put all the income into the wife's personal account.

The Wagners liked this alternative because with the bank Trustee as Cotrustee, Mrs. Wagner would have her own personal financial manager. Being removed from the burden of management, Mrs. Wagner would be free to carry on with her daily life. The only money job she would have is to write the checks for her personal needs.

Other than releasing Mrs. Wagner from management duties, using the bank Trustee as a Cotrustee will have four additional benefits:

1) The bank Trustee can protect Mrs. Wagner's money from third parties if she becomes incapacitated or incompetent.

2) The bank Trustee can protect Mrs. Wagner should her son be intent on receiving an early inheritance.

3) If Mrs. Wagner becomes ill, the bank Trustee will be there to keep the investments going and to pay all medical bills.

4) When she dies, the bank Trustee is in place to assemble the family money for distribution to her son.

Ignorance Is Not Bliss

Bringing in the bank Trustee does not mean Mrs. Wagner should remain blissfully ignorant. If her husband dies first, Mrs. Wagner should have some ability to read and understand the bank Trustee's periodic statements. Why? To protect herself from the bank Trustee.

Granted, the vast majority of bank Trustees perform their duties honestly, efficiently, and responsibly, but Mrs. Wagner should not remain at the total mercy of the bank's investment and management discretion. If Mrs. Wagner became financially "aware," she could stay abreast of the investments and see what is generally going on with her money.

Mrs. Wagner, however, was not interested in becoming financially educated—all she wanted to do was write checks. Fortunately, Mr. Wagner knew what I was getting at. To protect his wife, someone had to pay attention to what the bank Trustee was doing with the family money.

Therefore, the Wagners provided in their Living Trust that their accountant could make reasonable and periodic requests from the bank Trustee for reports, statements, and other information. With this provision, the bank Trustee would know that someone out there with financial know-how has the power to look over its shoulder.

---

2. "I understand that appointing a bank Trustee to serve as my wife's Cotrustee can make life a lot easier for her if I die before her. But I'm still uneasy about the idea of my money being in the hands of the bank after I die."

Placing the family financial affairs in the hands of the bank Trustee may be one of the most loving gifts you can bestow on your wife. By appointing the bank Trustee as your wife's Cotrustee if you die first, you free her from the burden of bookkeeping, income tax preparation, and making management and investment decisions.

But if you are like many people, you may feel uneasy about allowing a bank Trustee to manage the family money. In chapter 16, I list the reasons people typically cite when they reject the use of a bank Trustee.

I have dealt with many bank Trustees during my practice, and I have found that they do not deserve their negative reputations. But my point here is that your reluctance about "the bank" serving as your wife's Cotrustee is not only unjustified but should not stand in the way of the benefits the bank Trustee would provide your wife if you die first.

3. "My wife and I will select a bank Trustee to serve as my wife's Cotrustee if I die first. But what if the bank Trustee turns out to do a lousy job? Is my wife stuck with the choice we made in our Living Trust?"

If you and your wife select a bank Trustee as your wife's Cotrustee, and it turns out that the choice was a bad one, you do not have to be stuck. Simply provide in your Living Trust that your wife has the power to substitute a new Trustee for your first choice for any reason. For additional protection against a bad choice, you should provide that your wife has the power to veto any of the bank Trustee's management or investment decisions.

Will Your Surviving Spouse Divert the Family Money from Your Children?

Part VIII

Will Your Surviving Spouse Divert the Family Money from Your Children?

26

You May Leave Everything to Your Spouse—but Will Your Spouse Leave Everything to Your Children?

or

Preventing Your Money from Ending Up with Your Spouse's Bowling Instructor

---

1. "My husband is the type of person who cannot find his way to the kitchen. If I die first, I know he would remarry just to have someone to take care of him. I'm afraid that a new wife could end up with some or all of our money and property."

In the vast majority of long-term marriages, Dad and Mom own everything jointly. Whatever they have—real estate, bank accounts, stocks, bonds, cars, or jewelry—one-half belongs to Dad and one-half belongs to Mom.

When Dad dies (statistically, the first spouse to die), his half of the family wealth will pass to Mom. Mom then becomes the 100 percent owner of all the family wealth. Later, when Mom dies, usually all the family wealth will be distributed to their children. (If Dad and Mom have no children, then to whomever they choose to be their heirs.)

Dad and Mom may expect that the surviving parent will leave

255

it all to the children. But there is always the risk of that expectation not becoming a reality.

Mr. Randall's New Wife

My meeting with Mr. Randall lasted only a few minutes. That's all it took for him to become irate, tell me to "go to hell," and storm out of my office.

It was Mr. Randall's three children who scheduled this meeting. They, too, were in attendance—and stunned by their father's sudden departure. In the awkward moment that followed, one child said to his siblings, "I never thought Dad would make good on his threat. Now, I'm not so sure."

The Randall children then told me their story. And what they related to me is a scenario I see more and more often.

Their mother died after forty-five years of marriage to their father. Unfortunately, Mrs. Randall was not lucky enough to die suddenly. She had a painful, protracted, and debilitating illness.

Mr. Randall knew little about caring for his sick wife and less about the daily household requirements. He was the "breadwinner," not the "breadmaker." Without his ailing wife's help, there was no one to cook, clean, do laundry, or do any of the things to keep the house going.

After a referral from a friend, Mr. Randall hired Mrs. Bronson to be his wife's part-time nurse and part-time housekeeper.

Mrs. Bronson was fifty-five years old, divorced, and had grown children of her own. And according to Mr. Randall's children, she was attractive and somewhat youthful in appearance.

Mrs. Bronson took care of Mrs. Randall's needs until she died. Apparently, Mrs. Bronson was more to Mr. Randall than his wife's nurse. Barely six months after Mrs. Randall's death, Mr. Randall and Mrs. Bronson announced they were going to marry.

The Randalls' children could not believe it. What could this dynamic lady possibly see in their seventy-two-year-old father? If it was his money, then she was marrying him for the wrong reason. They felt secure their father would never divert their inheritance to a new wife.

Confident their inheritance was secure, Mr. Randall's children welcomed their future stepmother with open arms. They were truly happy for their father. And secretly, they were more happy for themselves. Their stepmother would provide their father with a permanent nurse and housekeeper, relieving them of the burden of taking care of Dad.

However, as the wedding date drew nearer, the children began having second thoughts. They realized this marriage was motivated not by love but by a mutual understanding: Dad would have a "built-in" nurse and housekeeper, and Mrs. Bronson would ultimately get some of Dad's wealth when he died.

The children expressed concern to their father, but his response made them more nervous: "Tell you what I'll do. I'll leave half of the family assets to you and half to my new wife. But if you're not nice to her, I'll cut you out entirely. Now don't ever talk to me about this again."

Money not only talks, it controls. Shortly after this encounter, his children made it their business to shower their future stepmother with affection. But it appalled them to think of this stranger getting half of the family money. And the possibility she could get it all gnawed at them to no end.

They raised their concern again with their father. But this time, they raised it within (what they thought to be) the safety of my office.

I don't know how they got their father to see me, but it must have been under false pretenses. After we exchanged the usual pleasantries, Mr. Randall began talking about death taxes and probate. A few minutes later, Mr. Randall's son interrupted and let his father have it.

"Dad, let's forget the death tax for right now and let's talk about something that's more pressing. You're getting married in a few days and we only wish you the best of life with her.

"But, Dad, before you get married; don't you think you ought to do something to protect your money from her? Don't you think it best to plan now to prevent her from ending up with your money if you die?"

The children thought discussing their concern with their father in my presence would make their father more sensitive to this issue. They hoped he would listen to an attorney point out the need to protect his children's inheritance from the second wife and, ultimately, make him realize he had to do something about it before he remarried.

True to his word, Mr. Randall refused to listen and promptly stormed out of the office, with the threat that it was his money and he could leave it to whomever he pleased.

No Solution for the Randalls' Children

The Randalls' children realized they had no power to prevent their father's remarriage. So they asked me if there was anything they could do to prevent their father from leaving some of the family wealth to his new wife.

The only solution was to become their father's conservator. As conservator, they would have the power to revoke any inheritance plan their father made and substitute one of their own liking.

However, a judge would not appoint them conservator just because they might lose their inheritance. They would have to prove to the judge their father was so mentally incapacitated and irrational that he did not know what he was doing. But Mr. Randall knew exactly what he was doing and showed no signs of being incapacitated or incompetent.

For all practical purposes, they were powerless. There was nothing they could do to constrict what their father could do with the family money. I advised them to go along with their father's wishes and hope for the best.

Variations on a Theme

The Randall case is a variation of an age-old concern: "When I die, how do I know my spouse will leave everything to our children?" Throughout my practice, clients have expressed this concern to me, usually in one of the following ways:

- "My husband and I have been married for fifty years. If I die first, I know he will leave everything to the children. He is starting to show signs of forgetfulness and early senility. Now I am not so sure what he will do with our money if I die first."
- "My wife loves our children and would do nothing to harm them. If I die first, I know she will leave everything to our children. However, I have a gnawing concern that she could remarry after I die and our wealth could end up with her new husband."
- "I have very expensive jewelry and furs that I am giving to my children while I am alive so that when I die, my husband's second wife won't get to enjoy them."
- "My wife thinks that if I outlive her, I will leave our house and money to a new girlfriend. She wants to die knowing that her half of our wealth will go to our children instead of my 'new wife.' So my wife plans on leaving her half to our children instead of me."

What these clients are asking is, "Can we be certain that our surviving spouses will not divert our halves of the family money away from our children?" The answer is: Yes! You can get this assurance if you employ one (or all) of the following alternatives in your inheritance plan.

Solution 1: Bypass Your Spouse

In your Will or Living Trust, provide that if you die first, your half will immediately go to your children, not your surviving spouse.

The upside of this arrangement is that you have guaranteed that your half has made it to your children.

There are three downsides, however, to this arrangement.

First, your surviving spouse and your children are partners in the real estate and other indivisible assets. Now your surviving spouse must negotiate with her children on any business decisions that relate to those assets.

Second, when parents and children become partners in indivisible assets, it may be difficult to separate family and business. Eventually, the family's affairs may spill over into the partnership.

Third, your surviving spouse may need your half to live on. But if you bypass your spouse and leave your half to your children, your spouse loses the income from that share.

Solution 2: Leave Your Half to Your Surviving Spouse in a "Surviving Spouse Life Estate Trust"

In your Will or Living Trust, provide that if you die first, your half will not go outright to your spouse but to a Surviving Spouse Life Estate Trust. During your spouse's life, she will be the Trustee over your half. She can invest it, receive the income it generates, and even dip into it for necessities (food, housing, medical needs, clothes, and so forth).

In essence, this is like giving your surviving spouse a "life estate" in your half of the family wealth.

If your surviving spouse has limited financial experience, consider making a Trust Department of a bank as Cotrustee. This institution will assist your surviving spouse in making investment, management, and spending decisions.

When your surviving spouse dies, your half will then revert to your children (or other heirs).

The Disadvantages

The Surviving Spouse Life Estate Trust can accomplish your goal of maximizing the likelihood that your half will pass to your children if you die first. But there are some disadvantages.

1. The Investment Conflict

As Trustee of the Surviving Spouse Life Estate Trust, your surviving spouse will have the power to decide how to invest your half. Since she is entitled to the income, she may invest it in assets that will give her maximum immediate income, such as T-bills and certificates of deposit.

But what will your children want? As the ultimate beneficiaries of the Trust, they will want your surviving spouse to invest your half in growth assets and other products that will keep pace with inflation. Their attitude is that when your surviving spouse dies, and your half reverts to them, a dollar from your half must still be worth a dollar, maybe even two dollars . . . but not fifty cents!

If your children perceive that your surviving spouse is only investing for her sake, they can petition the court to remove her as Trustee or change investments.

2. The Inconvenience

If your half of the money and property is a business or income-producing assets, your surviving spouse must do double record keeping: a set for her half and one for your half contained in the Surviving Spouse Life Estate Trust.

In addition, your surviving spouse must file separate income tax returns for income generated by your half, incurring additional accounting and bookkeeping fees.

3. The Hassle

As the ultimate beneficiaries of the Surviving Spouse Life Estate Trust, your children will have the legal right to look over your surviving spouse's shoulder and judge every managerial and investment decision she makes as Trustee. Will your children let your surviving spouse know if they disapprove of her actions? You bet they will! They realize that everything she does with the Trust assets will directly impact on the amount they will receive from the Trust after she dies.

Solution 3: "Back Up" Your Children's Inheritance

If you leave your half of the family wealth outright to your surviving spouse, you are, in effect, betting that she will leave it to your children when she dies. You, however, can hedge this bet by making sure your children receive a backup inheritance.

This backup can be in the form of a life insurance policy on your life.

The way insurance works as a backup inheritance is very simple. You make tax-free gifts to your children, who will use the money to buy a life insurance policy on your life. When you die, the insurance company will pay a tax-free death benefit to your children.

So if you die first and your surviving spouse leaves your half to a new friend, your children need not be completely disheartened. They will already have received an inheritance from you in the form of life insurance.

---

2. "I plan to leave all my money to my wife. But it kills me to think that she could use my money to support a new husband."

You may not want your surviving spouse to remarry after your death. Jealousy? Perhaps. But more likely, you simply cannot stomach the idea of your money supporting your spouse's new spouse or newfound friend.

You can prevent this from arising by leaving your half of the money and property to your wife in such a way that it would make remarriage unprofitable!

Solution 1: Make Remarriage Unprofitable with a "Support Trust"

Leave your half of the family money not outright to your spouse but to a "Support Trust." In this Trust, you name a third-party Trustee, who will receive your half when you die.

You instruct the trustee to pay support to your surviving spouse from the Trust assets. This support can last as long as you want. You can instruct the Trustee to pay support for a period of years or for the rest of your surviving spouse's life.

You may also impose certain conditions for the support to continue. For example, you can provide that if your wife remarries, the Support Trust shall end and the Trustee will distribute the remaining Trust assets to your children.

Will your wife be upset with her loss of support if she remarries? Probably. But if she thinks about it, it makes sense. Her new husband's obligation to support her replaces the support obligation of the Support Trust.

Conditioning the Amount of Support

You can also condition the amount of support your surviving spouse receives from the Support Trust. For example, you can provide that before the Trustee decides how much to pay your surviving spouse, the Trustee can consider other income and assets available to her. So if your wife becomes involved with a new boyfriend after you die, and the boyfriend uses his money to wine, dine, and support her, the Trustee can adjust your wife's support stream accordingly.

Solution 2: Give Your Surviving Spouse a Lump Sum

Leave your surviving spouse an outright share of your half of the family assets and the balance to your children or to whomever you choose.

This does not solve the problem of your surviving spouse using your money to support a new spouse or newfound friend. But it does limit the amount your surviving spouse can use for that purpose.

27

The Potential Battle Between Children of Your First Marriage and Your Second Wife

or

How Your Children Can Make a Difficult Life for Your Second Wife

"I dearly love my second wife, to whom I've been married for fifteen years. If she outlives me, I want her to spend the rest of her life in my home and receive support from my other assets. After she dies, my house and assets will revert to my children from my first marriage."

You and your wife come to my office and tell me that both of you are on your second marriage. You have just celebrated your fifth wedding anniversary and both of you describe a very happy marital relationship.

You are ten years older than your second wife, and you know you are likely to be the "first one to go." You love your second wife, and you have a profound concern that after you die, you want her to be "well provided for."

You tell me of your plan. After you die, you want your second wife to have the right to live in your home rent-free for life and receive all the income from your investment assets. When she

265

dies, everything will pass to your children from your first marriage.

When I was a young lawyer, I thought this was an excellent plan—your loving second wife is protected and your first children get your money and property after you die. What could be more natural? It is just like your first children inheriting after the death of their natural mother had she still been married to you.

But what makes perfect sense in the abstract does not work in reality. In the older-person second marriage, there is, typically, no stepparent relationship between the first children and the second spouse. You are the only connection between them. And after having seen what happens between first children and second wives when death occurs and that connection is severed, I am left with one conclusion:

If you hate your second wife and you want to punish her, leave her in a situation where your first children cannot get their inheritance until *she* dies. This plan will leave your second wife with several battles on her hands, the consequences of which may be unfathomable to you but are assuredly horrendous to her.

Battle Number 1: High Income versus High Growth

Your second wife wants as much income as she can get for the rest of her life. This motivates her to invest your assets in high-yielding income investments. The more the income, the more money for her support.

However, your first children have different investment desires. They want to know that a thousand dollars at the end of ten years will not be reduced by inflation. They can achieve this goal if your second wife invests in growth assets. But if she sticks with high-income-yielding investments, your assets will not keep pace with inflation.

The issue is drawn. The gladiators are at the opposite ends of the ring. Your children want capital growth so that your assets will have appreciated when your second wife dies. Your second wife, however, couldn't care less about what your property is worth then—all she wants is high interest.

There is no compromise. What do your children do? They may go to a lawyer who will send a letter to your second wife, demanding that she invest your wealth in capital growth. If your second wife refuses, the battle is on, and the lawsuits may commence.

Battle Number 2: "You're Spending Our Money"

Your first children warn your second wife about what she spends. If she buys a car, some furniture, or even a dress, she may get a telephone call from your children, who say, "Why are you spending our money on frivolous things?"

Your first children warn your second wife that they are looking over her shoulder. "Hey, the house is falling apart. Why don't you spend some of the income you are getting from Dad's assets and fix the roof?"

Whatever your second wife does (or does not) do with the money, she knows she may get a call from your first children or a letter from their lawyer. With all these warnings, a cloud looms over your second wife's head. It is not a comfortable world for her, because she lives with the bothersome knowledge that someone is out there watching her every financial move.

Battle Number 3: "We Don't Want to Wait for You to Die to Get Dad's Money"

Typically, second wives are several years younger than their husbands. For example, when Mr. Rasmusson died, he was seventy-six, and his second wife was sixty-six. When she dies, Mr. Rasmusson's children may be in their late sixties or early seventies. They may even be dead.

When children are confronted with an unacceptable delay in receiving their inheritance, they may attempt to reduce that delay. I'm not talking about killing their stepmother (although not a far-fetched scenario in today's world). But I have seen a number of situations in which the first children badgered and harassed the second wife so much that she agreed to turn over some of the money before she died.

What kind of harassment? Incessant telephone calls. Endless lawyer's letters. Threats of physical harm. Hints that there are people out there who just can't wait for your second wife to die.

Battle Number 4: "Get Out of Our House"

If you give your second wife the right to live in your house for the rest of her life, the battle may become even more visible and pronounced.

Your first children can see the house. They can touch it and feel it. They realize that one day it will be their house. After they get it, they can sell it and split the money.

But they also realize one other thing. If your second wife lives an additional twenty years, they may be in their late sixties and seventies. What good will the house do them then?

Your first children may do all they can to motivate your second wife to move out of your home so they can sell it and divide the proceeds. This is an extremely distressing prospect to your second wife, especially if she was planning a quiet life there for the rest of her days.

Solution: Eliminate the Money Connection

When you leave your wealth to your second wife for life, you have created a money relationship between her and your first children. In this world of extremes, who can predict what actions children will take when it comes to getting their money, especially from someone who is not their "real" mother and with whom they have no stepparent bond?

What I do now is not what I did years ago. I will not allow my clients to create a situation in which the first children have to wait for the second wife to die before they inherit. Instead, I prefer a plan in which you leave your second wife a specific amount and the rest to your children (or vice versa, depending on how you feel about your first children).

Whatever division is made, this plan terminates any economic union between your second wife and first children after you die, and each can go their separate ways.

Alternative Solutions

If, for whatever reason, you cannot make this cut-and-dried division, here are three alternatives you may be able to employ.

Alternative Number 1

Allow your second wife to live in your home rent-free for a period of time (e.g., two to five years). At the end of the period, the house can revert to your first children. Or the house can be sold, and a portion of the proceeds can go to your second wife for her support.

Alternative Number 2

Provide that when you die, your house and other assets will go to a Surviving Spouse Life Estate Trust with your second wife as Trustee. For the rest of her life, this Trust will entitle your second wife to live in your home rent-free and receive the income from your other assets. When she dies, everything will revert to your first children. (I discuss this special Trust in more detail in chapter 26.) Then buy a life insurance policy on your life with your first children as the beneficiaries. With this policy, your first children will be placated with an immediate inheritance and, hopefully, may be more amenable to having to wait for your second wife to die before they get the rest.

Alternative Number 3

Leave your home and other assets to your second wife outright, and buy an insurance policy that will pay death benefits to your first children that are roughly equal to the value of your entire estate. The result is that after you die, your children will receive the full value of their inheritance without any delay.

Benefits to Both Sides

If you can incorporate any of these alternatives into your inheritance plan, both sides will benefit.

Your first children's benefit is economic. They get an inheritance to use and enjoy at a time when they could most use your money. And giving them a dollar when you die is more valuable than three dollars following the death of your second wife, which could be many years later.

Your second wife also benefits, because she is assured all or some of your money and property for her support. But she also receives another benefit that I believe is more important than money: peace of mind in her remaining years.

The last thing your second wife wants to experience is what one second wife related to me.

She finally finagled an invitation to her stepchildren's house for the holidays. When she arrived, she was greeted by one of her stepgrandchildren, who unabashedly said, "Gramma, Gramma! We're all going on a vacation to Hawaii." The second wife enthusiastically stated, "Oh, that's marvelous. When are you going?"

The stepgrandchild replied in all innocence, "As soon as you die."

28

If You Are on Your Second Marriage, Who Will Get Your Half If You Die First—Your Children or the Children of Your Second Spouse?

or

"I Know My Second Spouse Will Do the Right Thing If I Die First, But . . ."

When husbands and wives enter second marriages, they typically bring with them assets they acquired during their first marriages. Most of the time, this property remains the separate property of the spouse who brought it in. But sometimes they merge these assets together and hold them jointly, each owning one-half of the merged assets.

The result is, when the husband dies (as noted, typically the first spouse to die), the surviving wife may end up with 100 percent of all the merged assets.

Will the surviving wife leave her husband's half of the merged assets to his children from his first marriage? Perhaps. But, then again, she has the power to leave his half to *her* children from *her* first marriage, to *her* next spouse or boyfriend, to *her* brothers and sisters, or to anyone she sees fit.

The result is, the last spouse to die could cut out the children of the first spouse to die.

1. "My wife and I both have children from our first marriages. We own our house and bank accounts as joint tenants. I love my wife, but I am worried. If I die first, she may cut out my children and leave everything to her children."

If both the husband and wife have children from prior marriages, the children of the last spouse to die may wind up with it all.

Ask yourself: Is your second wife hoping you die first so she can leave everything to her children? For good reason, this is what Mr. Caronna thought.

The "Scheming" Mrs. Caronna

Mr. Caronna dragged his wife to two family inheritance-planning attorneys. She did not like their advice, and she wasn't about to see a third. So Mr. Caronna came to my office alone.

"My wife and I are on our second time around," Mr. Caronna began. "We've been married for ten years and we both have children from prior marriages. After we married, we took all our assets and placed them in both our names jointly. When the first one of us dies, the survivor will own it all.

"Putting both our names on everything seemed like the thing to do. It's what all our friends did. Now I think it was the worst thing I could have done. I'm ten years older than my wife, so I know I will die before her. When I'm dead, she will be in control of everything. And what I'm afraid of is that she'll leave it all to *her* children.

"Mr. Condon, I don't want my kids to be left in the cold. I want to establish a plan where my half will go to my children and her half will go to her children. But she won't do it, and nothing the other lawyers said could convince her. She says I should just trust her to do the right thing. She seems sincere, but I just don't know."

Was Mrs. Caronna the schemer her husband imagined her to be? No one could say for certain. But had she been the loving and reasonable spouse, she would have accepted her husband's commonsense proposal. After all, she was in the same boat. If she was the one to die first, Mr. Caronna would control who inherits and who does not.

Severing the Tie That Binds

I suggested a way the Caronnas could ensure that their respective halves wound up with their respective children. This solution is called the Surviving Spouse Life Estate Trust. (I discuss it more fully below.) However, without Mrs. Caronna's participation (and her signature), this solution could not be implemented.

Mr. Caronna was down, but not out. There was one thing he could do *without* his wife's participation that would guarantee his children would inherit his half.

I told Mr. Caronna to sever the joint tenancy. This would "erase" the joint tenancy *and* the right of survivorship. From then on, Mr. Caronna would be free to bypass his wife and leave his half to his children.

Mr. Caronna could sever the joint tenancy by signing some special legal documents, with those involving real estate being recorded at the county recorder's office. Once these documents were correctly processed, Mrs. Caronna would be completely deprived of her right of survivorship.

(Mr. Caronna recognized that severing the joint tenancy was a two-way street. After the severance, his wife could leave her half to anyone she wanted. But since Mr. Caronna was nine years older than his wife, he assumed he would die first and was not concerned with this risk.)

Too Extreme?

At first, this news rejuvenated Mr. Caronna. None of the other lawyers had discussed this option. Hearing about something he could do unilaterally seemed to perk him up.

However, the more Mr. Caronna thought about it, the less

enthused he became, saying the plan was somewhat extreme. He did not wish to deprive his wife of his half if he died first. He just wanted to be certain that if he died first, his wife would leave his half to his children.

Mr. Caronna thanked me for my advice and said he would "let it stew" in his mind. I, however, interpreted this to mean he would not be back. A few months later, I discovered Mr. and Mrs. Caronna in my waiting room. Guess which one looked defeated and which one looked elated!

Apparently, my advice took hold. Armed with this information, Mr. Caronna told his wife that he wanted her to join him in signing a mutually beneficial inheritance plan. If she refused, he threatened to sever the joint tenancy and leave his half outright to his children, shutting her out from the benefits of his half if he died first.

Mrs. Caronna caved in to her husband's demand. We then proceeded to draft the appropriate inheritance plan.

Solution: The Surviving Spouse Life Estate Trust

When Mr. Caronna died, his half would not go to Mrs. Caronna outright. Instead, it would pass to a special Surviving Spouse Life Estate Trust. The Trustee of this Trust would hold this half and pay Mrs. Caronna any income it generated. Later, when Mr. Caronna died, the Trust would dissolve, and Mr. Caronna's half would revert to his children.

This special Trust guarantees that Mr. Caronna's children will inherit his half. However, before it could be drafted, three wrinkles needed to be ironed out.

Wrinkle Number 1: Who Would Be the Trustee?

As sole Trustee of the Trust, Mrs. Caronna would have the right to dip into the Trust and take out portions of Mr. Caronna's half for her support and maintenance. But with no other Trustee looking over Mrs. Caronna's shoulder, she could dip into the Trust for any purpose. She could use the Trust assets for a trip around the world, a wildly expensive new car—she could even give it to her children and grandchildren. It would be illegal, but no one would be around to say no.

With Mrs. Caronna as sole Trustee, Mr. Caronna's children may be in for a big surprise when she dies. They may discover that nothing is left in the Trust for them to inherit.

Smoothing Out the Wrinkle: Appoint a Cotrustee

To meet this concern, the Caronnas' plan provided that when Mr. Caronna died, Mrs. Caronna would serve as a Cotrustee along with a child of Mr. Caronna (and vice versa if Mrs. Caronna died first). If Mr. Caronna died first, one of his children could safeguard the Trust assets from embezzlement or other risk of loss.

Wrinkle Number 2: The Investment Conflict

As the income beneficiary of the Trust, Mrs. Caronna would naturally want the Trust assets to generate as much earnings as possible. So she would like the Trustee to invest solely in income-producing assets.

Mr. Caronna's children, however, would not exactly be thrilled with that investment plan. As the ultimate beneficiaries, they would like their father's half to double or triple in value. This growth could occur if the Trustee invested in growth assets. But if the Trustee stuck with only high-yield assets, the growth would be minimal, if any!

Smoothing Out the Wrinkle: Instruct the Trustee to Make Investment Decisions That Do Not Favor One over the Other

Not every conflict can be resolved to the satisfaction of all. The only thing the Caronnas could do was compromise. They provided that regardless of which spouse died first, the Trustee would invest the Trust assets equally in income and growth assets. Granted, this strategy will not be a cure-all. Mrs. Caronna will not get the highest possible Trust income, and Mr. Caronna's children will not see the Trust assets appreciate as much as they would like.

However, this plan may minimize the investment conflict between both parties.

Wrinkle Number 3: Waiting for Mrs. Caronna to Die

If Mr. Caronna lives to the statistical life expectancy of the average American male, he will die at age seventy-six, at which time Mrs. Caronna, nine years younger than her husband, would be sixty-seven. Since women are living longer today, Mrs. Caronna may outlive her husband for many years.

By the time she dies, Mr. Caronna's children may be in their late sixties or early seventies. They may even be dead.

Mr. Caronna's children may be very distressed knowing they may have to wait twenty years for their father's half. As for Mrs. Caronna, the last thing she needs is the stress of knowing someone is out there who just cannot wait for her to die.

Smoothing Out the Wrinkle: Arrange for Children of the First Spouse to Die to Receive an Immediate Inheritance

Mr. Caronna could smooth out this wrinkle by arranging for his children to receive an inheritance immediately after he dies. How? With life insurance.

While he is alive, Mr. Caronna could give money to his first children to buy a life insurance policy on his life. When he dies, his first children would get the death benefits from the policy while Mrs. Caronna would have the use and benefit of the assets in the Surviving Spouse Life Estate Trust.

With this plan, Mr. Caronna's first children could receive an immediate inheritance without having to wait for their step-mother to die.

2. "I have children from my first marriage and my second marriage. When I die, I want all my children to share in my wealth equally. My second wife tells me not to worry. She promises that if she outlives me, she will take care of it. I love and trust my wife, but . . ."

If you have children from your first and second marriages, will your two sets of children be at each other's throats over who gets your money?

Mrs. Brown: The Exception to the Rule

Mr. Brown was married two times. When he was twenty-two, he married his first wife and had two children with her (whom I shall refer to as Mr. Brown's "first children"). Several years later, they divorced.

Mr. Brown married a second time at the age of thirty-four. This marriage was like most first marriages. He and the second Mrs. Brown had two children and were married for forty years. During this time, Mr. Brown and his second wife amassed their family fortune and held it jointly with right of survivorship.

Mrs. Brown's Deathbed Promise

Mrs. Brown told me her husband loved his first children very much. However, he rarely saw them. A year after his divorce, his first wife remarried and took the first children to live in another state.

Though out of sight, his first children were never out of mind. Mr. Brown took great pains to see they were not cut out of his life, and he wanted certainty that they would not be cut out after his death. He wanted a plan that would leave his half of the family wealth to his first children and second children in equal shares. But as is so often the case, he never got around to setting up an inheritance plan that would achieve his goal. Mr. Brown suddenly took ill, and his plan came in the form of a deathbed conversation with his second wife at the hospital:

"You've got to carry the ball for me. Promise me that you'll make sure that my half of everything goes to all four of my children."

Mr. Brown died, and the second Mrs. Brown became the

100 percent owner of all their money and property. A few years later, Mrs. Brown sat in my office and related the deathbed promise she made to her husband.

No Legal Obligation

Mrs. Brown recognized she did not have to follow through on her deathbed promise. She realized that when Mr. Brown died, she owned 100 percent of their house and all their other jointly owned assets. She knew she had the legal right to leave everything to her two children (Mr. Brown's "second children") if she wanted, and nothing to his first children.

Mrs. Brown, however, said she felt a moral obligation to carry out her husband's last wish. So she established the appropriate inheritance plan: a Living Trust that left one-half of her husband's first children and second children equally, and the remaining half to her two children (Mr. Brown's second children).

When Mrs. Brown died several years later, Mr. Brown's half was divided accordingly, and there was satisfaction all around. All of Mr. Brown's children recognized their stepmother did the right thing by allowing them to share equally in their father's share of the money and property.

Your First Children Should Be So Lucky

Mr. Brown's first children were extremely lucky. They had a stepmother willing to carry out her lifetime promise. Such promises by second wives are often made but just as often disregarded for the following reasons.

1. She Feels No Moral Obligation

The surviving second wife may feel no moral obligation to leave anything to her husband's first children. To her, it is her money. She and her husband worked for it during their married lives. Now that her husband is dead, it all belongs to her and she can leave it as she pleases.

2. She Has No Loyalty to the First Children

The surviving second wife may feel no emotional bond with her husband's first children. Perhaps she did not raise them. Perhaps they did not come around while their father was alive. Or perhaps she had little contact with them. Whatever the reason, the second wife may feel no compulsion to leave anything to people she barely knows.

3. When Circumstances Changed . . . She Forgot the Promise

When the surviving second wife made the promise, she may have truly believed she would faithfully execute. But as the years passed and time went by, she and her "world" may have changed. If her husband's first children have been out of the picture, they may be strangers to her, leaving her to focus on her children and grandchildren.

4. Her Children Pressured Her to Change Her Mind

The surviving second wife's own children may pressure her into leaving everything to them. If she is vulnerable to this pressure, it may be almost impossible to resist, especially if her husband's first children have not become or remained a part of her life.

Solution: Don't Rely on Your Spouse's Promise

Forewarned is forearmed.

Do not gamble on your surviving spouse's promise to do the right thing. You may love and trust your second spouse. But a lot can happen in the span between both your deaths.

If you want your first and second children to share your wealth equally if you die first, you must reduce this desire to writing. Arrange in your inheritance plan, whether a Will or Living Trust, that half of the wealth you accumulated during your second marriage will be shared by all your children.

To make this a certainty, you should leave your half to a Surviving Spouse Life Estate Trust, providing that after your surviving second spouse dies, your half will be equally divided between your first children and second children. I discuss this special Trust more fully under question 1 of this chapter and in chapters 26 and 27.

Part IX

Your Grandchildren

29

Grandparents to the Rescue!

or

"If I Don't Help My Grandchildren While I'm Alive—Help May Never Come"

This chapter deals with the main issues you may wish to consider if you are a grandparent who wants to gift money or property to your grandchildren during your lifetime. The next chapter deals with leaving money to grandchildren after the deaths of Grandpa and Grandma.

When making lifetime gifts to grandchildren, the primary issues you should consider are:

1) Equalizing lifetime gifts among the grandchildren;

2) Losing control over the assets you gift to your grandchildren; and

3) The possibility that your grandchild may mismanage or inappropriately spend the gifts you made to him or her.

---

1. "We have a son with one child and a daughter with four children. We plan to give each grandchild $14,000 a year. Our son feels this plan is unfair to him because his sister's side will get $56,000 while his side only gets $14,000 . . . and he complains that with each gift we make to our daughter's children, we reduce his expected inheritance."

As grandparents, we view our grandchildren as a collective group. When we make lifetime gifts to them, we are concerned about treating all of them equally. Giving each the same amount, we feel secure in the knowledge we have done the right thing.

Our children, however, may see it much differently.

The Hudsons and Their Son Who Thought Too Much

Annual Exclusion Gifts are discussed more fully in chapter 36. But in a nutshell, it means:

1) You can give away up to $14,000 of money or property each year to as many recipients as you want.

2) If you have a spouse, your spouse can also give $14,000 to each recipient.

3) You do not pay a gift tax.

4) The gifts do not come off your Lifetime Exemption.

Why is making these gifts beneficial? Because the less you own when you die, the less the death taxes will be. The general rule is, for each $14,000 Annual Exclusion Gift you make, you save your children up to $5,000 in death taxes. The only loser is the IRS!

The Hudsons' Attitude Is the Right Attitude

I told Mr. and Mrs. Hudson that when the last one of them dies, the IRS would get $400,000 of their money in death taxes. I advised them of several death-tax-savings opportunities, and they decided on the simplest thing to do: gift money to their grandchildren every year using the Annual Exclusion Gifts.

Most clients are reluctant to give away portions of their wealth while they are alive, even if it means that more of it will go to the IRS when they die. The Hudsons, however, were a remarkable exception. They were enthusiastic about the idea that with each gift, less would go to the IRS and more to their children and grandchildren when they were both gone.

So, motivated by the death-tax savings, the Hudsons did what most of my clients find so difficult to do: move to action!

The Hudsons' Plan "in Action"

As I explain in chapter 36, in 2014, the Annual Exclusion Gift was raised from $10,000 to $14,000, and the Lifetime Exemption is now $5,340,000. These are changes that effectively wiped out the death tax in America . . . except for those with estates over $5,340,000 for single persons and $10.68 million for married couples. However, the Hudsons' plan arose in the 1990s, when the death tax was alive and well. With their estate of $4 million, they (or rather, their children) were going to be hit with a $900,000 death tax when both spouses were dead.

But if the Hudsons walked into my office today, I would say to them they would require zero Annual Exclusion Gifts or any other plan of action. Their combined $4 million estate falls substantially under their combined $10.68 million Lifetime Exemption. Still . . . this story serves as a great example of Annual Exclusion Gifts to grandchildren in action to reduce estates and prevent estate taxes.

The Hudsons had five grandchildren. Their son, Tony, had one child and their daughter, Tami, had four children.

In December 1989, they gave $20,000 ($10,000 each) worth of securities to each grandchild. These gifts removed $100,000 from their estate, saving approximately $50,000 in death taxes.

In 1990, 1991, and 1992, the Hudsons gave an additional $100,000 to their grandchildren. Over the course of four years, the Hudsons reduced their estate by $400,000. Because they will not own that amount when they die, there will be no death tax on that amount, saving roughly $200,000 for their children.

I gently urged the Hudsons to include their daughter and son as annual gift recipients, but they rejected this idea. As Mr. Hudson said, "Our children will get plenty of money when we're dead. Right now, we want to help our grandchildren get a leg up in life."

Another Unhappy Camper

A few days before the Hudsons were to make their $100,000 gift in 1993, my secretary informed me that their son was on the phone, and he sounded quite upset.

"Mr. Condon, I think I'm being cheated. Since 1989, my parents have been giving money each year to their grandchildren. But look at what's happening! They are taking part of my inheritance and giving it to my sister's four children. And it's not fair that my sister's side of the family gets more money just because she had more children."

Tony was correct. Of the $80,000 annually received by his sister's four children, a portion was coming from Tony's share of his expected inheritance. It was as if the Hudsons were using their son's money to subsidize their daughter's children.

And what's more, Tony was being, in effect, penalized for having one child. While his sister's side received $80,000 every year, Tony's side received only $20,000.

Resolving the Unfairness

Many of my clients would disregard the issue of inequality of gifts between family sides. The typical attitude I hear is: "As long as I treat each of my grandchildren equally, my children have no right to complain."

Fortunately for Tony, his parents were not of that mind. They cherished family harmony between their children and grandchildren and were very receptive to resolving the unfairness to preserve family peace.

One day, the entire Hudson family arrived at my office so we could arrive at a workable resolution. These were the alternatives from which they could select:

Alternative Number 1: Give Each Side the Same Amount Each Year

Since the Hudsons gave Tami's side $80,000 each year, they would also give Tony's side $80,000 a year. This would mean the Hudsons would give away a total of $160,000 to their grandchildren each year.

The Hudsons did not like this idea. Although they wanted to help their grandchildren, they did not want to give away more than a total of $100,000 each year.

Alternative Number 2: Divide the Total Amount of the Annual Gift Between Both Children

Since the Hudsons did not want to give away more than $100,000 each year, I advised them they could gift $50,000 each year to both their children. Their son and daughter could then divide their respective shares among themselves, their spouses, and their grandchildren as they saw fit.

The Hudsons recognized that this division could resolve the unfairness in its entirety. But they wanted these gifts to benefit their grandchildren—not their children, son-in-law, or daughter-in-law. The Hudsons did not accept this alternative.

Alternative Number 3: Give Each Grandchild an Annual Gift and Make Up the Difference Later

The Hudsons decided to keep the gifts as they were: $20,000 each year to each of their daughter's four children and $20,000 to their son's one child. The yearly total would continue to be $20,000 for the son's side and $80,000 for the daughter's side.

The Hudsons wanted to equalize with their son by giving him an extra $60,000 each year, but they did not want to give more than a total of $100,000 annually. The Hudsons resolved this difficulty by choosing to equalize with their son *after they die*!

In the Hudsons' Living Trust, they provided that when they both die, their son will receive off the top $60,000 for each year the Hudsons made the gifts. After the son receives this extra share of the family money, both their son and daughter will divide the balance equally.

2. "I would like to give my grandson a large amount of stock. Does this have any advantages or disadvantages?"

Making large lifetime gifts to your grandson has two distinct advantages.

1. Your Grandson Will Have Money When He Can Best Use It

If your grandson is reasonable and responsible, he may eventually want to buy a home, begin a family, perhaps even start a business. But before he can embark on these hallmark events, he must have money.

It could take your grandson many years to accumulate enough money to get this start in life. Will your child help your grandson? Probably not! Your child and his spouse may still be trying to eke out a living and may not have the money to spare. And don't count on your child being generous when he inherits your money and property. Chances are, your child may be unwilling to part with portions of his inheritance.

You, however, can give your grandson a leg up in life. If you have assets you can spare, consider giving your grandson money now, so he can benefit from your money when he needs the most financial help.

2. You Prevent the IRS from Taxing Your Wealth Twice

When you die and your wealth passes to your child, the IRS will impose a death tax on it. That's bad enough. But when your child dies and your money finds its way to your grandson, the IRS may tax it again—two bites of the same apple!

The less you leave your child, the less your child will own to be taxed a second time when he dies. For an in-depth discussion of how to avoid this second bite, see chapter 38.

The Downsides

There are three distinct disadvantages to giving your grandson a substantial amount of money and property before you die.

1. No "Stepped-up" Tax Basis

If you give your grandson "low-basis" property (meaning that its value was low at the time you bought or inherited it), your grandson will take the property at that basis. The result is that if your grandson sells the property, he may end up paying a large capital gains tax.

If your grandson *inherited* the same property from you, he may not pay one penny in capital gains tax.

2. *Your Grandson versus Your Child*

If your child is like most children, his attitude about your lifetime gifts to your grandson is:"Dad and Mom, your gifts are great, but don't give him too much. Leave your money to me and I will take care of my child." If you don't follow this thinking, your child may resent that you gave away some of *his* inheritance. The result is that you may have created enmity between your child and your grandson.

Before you make an appreciable gift to your grandson, I urge you to be sensitive to this possibility. If there is doubt as to how your child would react, you may wish to arrange a family discussion to get a true measure of your child's feelings.

The last thing you may want to do is make your child feel as if he was robbed of his inheritance and that his own child was the bandit.

3. *The Risk of Your Grandson Mismanaging the Gifts You Make*

Are you concerned that your grandson will mismanage or inappropriately spend the money you give him? You are not alone. See question 5 of this chapter, where I discuss this issue more fully.

---

3. "Our daughter does not have enough money to pay for our grandchild's education. My wife and I will probably have to pay these educational expenses ourselves."

Your daughter may have her hands full trying to maintain her current lifestyle. More often than not, as caring and hardworking as she may be, she may not be able to afford her child's private school or college tuition.

Invariably, it's Grandpa and Grandma to the rescue.

Many of my clients willingly assume the financial burden of providing for their grandchildren's education. Years ago, this meant putting grandchildren through college and graduate school. Today, the process starts long before that, with Grandpa and Grandma paying for their grandchildren's preschool!

In planning for your grandchild's education, consider the following alternatives.

Alternative Number 1: Write a Check

If you are rich enough, you do not need a plan. Simply write a check to pay your grandchild's school tuition and related expenses.

Important note: When the time comes to pay the education costs, *do not make the check payable to your grandchild*. Instead, make the checks out to the school for tuition, the bookstore for books and supplies, and to whomever for other related costs and expenses.

I'm not worried about your grandchild absconding with the money. I want you to be entitled to an additional tax break. Like the Annual Exclusion Gifts I discussed earlier in this chapter, education expenses can be made tax-free. If you pay your grandchild's education expenses directly, you will not owe a gift tax, your grandchild will not owe an income tax, and the amount you pay will not come off your Lifetime Exemption.

Alternative Number 2: Insurance

Insurance companies provide products that can help put your grandchild through school.

One, for example, is the investment life insurance policy, a policy on your grandchild's life and owned by your grandchild.

The insurance company will take your premiums and invest them. Ordinarily, the investment return will not be taxable and may be greater than what you could get from bonds, stocks, or certificates of deposit.

When your grandchild gets to college age, he can get the money he needs by borrowing against the policy's equity. By borrowing the money (as opposed to cashing in the policy), your grandchild will not have to pay an income tax, and the insurance policy remains in effect to be a valuable postcollege asset for your grandchild.

Alternative Number 3: The Education Trust

If you cannot provide for your grandchild's education while you are alive, you can do so after you die.

In your Will or Living Trust, specify that a portion of your wealth is to be held "in Trust" for your grandchild for educational purposes. When you die, a Trustee will hold these funds for your grandchild and will use them to pay for tuition, room, board, books, and other related expenses.

If you wish, you can specify the levels of education you wish your grandchild to attain (high school, college, postgraduate) and instruct the Trustee to apply the money at each level.

When your grandchild finishes the education level you specified, any money left over in the Education Trust can revert to your child. However, my preference is that surplus funds be distributed to your grandchild on arriving at age twenty-five—or any other age you deem appropriate.

4. "I want to make gifts to my grandchild. But I feel uneasy about losing ownership and control of my money."

You may have more than enough money for your daily needs. With your grown children living on their own and your mortgage paid off, your annual expenses may be far less than your annual income. If that's the case, perhaps you can spare enough money to make gifts to your grandchild.

At this point, you may either laugh in my face or look at me as if I had just descended from another planet.

Like many, you may have grown up in the Depression and worked very hard to accumulate your money. After going through those troubled times, giving anything away is anathema to you—even if you won't miss the money, and even if it means denying financial help to your precious grandchild.

Or perhaps you simply cannot bear the thought of losing control of your money. Indeed, you may feel secure knowing your money is around if you need it. Gifting it away may reduce that comfort level, even if you have money to spare.

Solution? I Have No Solution!

If parting with money goes against your grain or makes you uncomfortable, forget the gifts to the grandchildren! I have no magic words or tricks up my sleeve to help you feel at ease with giving up ownership and control of your wealth.

Besides, I am not in the business of making clients do something they don't want to do.

5. "If I give money to my granddaughter, I'm afraid she will 'blow the dough.'"

Sometimes this concern is justified. On occasion, a client sadly tells me about a grandchild who is addicted to drugs, alcohol, gambling, or another negative habit. Needless to say, I advise this client to refrain from giving money to that grandchild. Why fuel that grandchild's destruction?

However, for the most part, this concern is not justified. Why? Because grandparents often blow their grandchildren's spending habits out of proportion. I have many clients who still see the world in terms of ten-cent haircuts, twenty-five-cent movies, and a sandwich for a buck. That their grandchildren spend more on the same items today is solid proof they cannot manage money or spend it wisely.

One client put it this way: "Mr. Condon, we'd love to help out our granddaughter, but we are not going to give her a penny! She runs through money like it grows on trees. She and her husband haven't been married a year and they already have a new car. Hell, my wife and I didn't get a new car until our twentieth wedding anniversary."

This thinking is understandable, for we are all products of our experience. Nevertheless, this reluctance can be overcome if a client can be assured that a grandchild cannot blow the dough.

The following are alternatives that can minimize the risk of a grandchild mismanaging or inappropriately spending the gifted money.

Alternative Number 1: Make Gifts to an Irrevocable Trust for Your Grandchild's Benefit

Instead of giving money to your grandchild outright, set up an Irrevocable Trust (meaning that once you set it up you cannot revoke it) and give the money to the Trustee. The Trustee will hold the money and distribute it to your grandchild when he or she reaches an age you deem appropriate. Until your grandchild attains that age, he or she will not have direct access to the money. You can select any third party you wish to serve as Trustee. The typical choice is the parent (or parents) of your grandchild.

Alternative Number 2: Make Gifts to Your Grandchild's Custodian

If your grandchild is a minor, most states allow you to give money to a Custodian who will hold it for your grandchild's benefit. The Custodian will allocate the money to your grandchild when he or she reaches the age of majority. This is just like appointing a Trustee of your grandchild's money, but without the formality of setting up a Trust.

Ordinarily, the Custodian you choose will be the parent (or parents) of your grandchild.

Alternative Number 3: Use a Family Limited Partnership to Make Gifts to Your Grandchild

If you want to give property to your grandchild, such as securities, bonds, or real estate, you can make these gifts by using the Family Limited Partnership. With this method, you can give your grandchild a valuable asset that he or she cannot do anything with . . . except retain!

Using the Family Limited Partnership to make gifts of property to your grandchild requires that you do the following:

1) Establish the documents that create and breathe life into the Family Limited Partnership.

2) Select the asset you wish to eventually give to your grandchild and transfer it to the Family Limited Partnership. Once the transfer is made, the asset becomes Partnership property.

3) Provide in the documents that you are the General Partner of the Family Limited Partnership. As General Partner, you continue to own and control the Partnership property.

4) Give your grandchild some or all of the Partnership property. You make this gift in the form of Limited Partnership shares that, according to the terms of the Partnership documents, your grandchild is prohibited from selling, transferring, or encumbering.

5) You retain ownership and control of any Limited Partnership shares in the Partnership property you have not given away.

Alternative Number 4: Make Your Grandchild Account for the Gifts You Made

The most informal way to ascertain if your grandchild is misusing your gifted money is to ask. As you present your gift, tell your grandchild you want to meet at the same time next year so he or she can inform you how every dollar was used and where each dollar went.

Then tell your grandchild one more thing: If you believe your grandchild's accounting has not been truthful, or if you perceive that your gift was not used or spent properly, there will be no future gifts!

30

Including Your Grandchildren
in Your Inheritance Plan

or

"I Like My Children—but I Really Love My Grandchildren"

---

1. **"My wife and I have grandchildren whom we love very much. To help them get started in life, we want to leave them a good portion of our wealth when we die, with our children getting the rest."**

I used to advise clients against leaving a substantial inheritance to their grandchildren. My philosophy for the most part was: Leave your money to your children, and let your children worry about their children.

However, there is a saying in life: If you live long enough, you get smarter. And when you get smarter, you are entitled to change your mind, and I have changed mine.

When I was a younger attorney, grandchildren were not even a gleam in my eye. Today, I have five adorable grandchildren, and they are the ultimate dividends of my life. The personal experience of having grandchildren has significantly changed my advice to clients on leaving portions of their money and property to their grandchildren.

We Like Our Children, but We Love Our Grandchildren

When our children became adults with lives of their own, our connection with them may also have changed. Over time, the emotionally driven bond we feel with our children may have flattened and shifted to our grandchildren.

We want the security of knowing that our grandchildren will have a good start in life. For most of us grandparents, a good start means graduating college, buying a home, supporting a family, getting a responsible job, starting a business, or entering a profession.

But we also know that in today's world, it is very difficult for young people to get started without help.

If we don't help our grandchildren, who will? Our own children, caught up in their own economic struggles, may not have sufficient finances to assist our grandchildren. If our grandchildren have to borrow money for their education, home, or business, they begin that part of their lives with an already crushing financial burden.

In order for our grandchildren to get a leg up in life, we, their grandparents, may be the only ones to give them the helping hand at a time when they can best use our money.

Sooner Is Better than Later

If you adhere to my old philosophy of leaving nothing to your grandchildren when you die, your grandchildren may not receive your wealth at a time when they could put it to its best use.

In the conventional situation, Grandpa will die first. Grandma will live for another twelve to twenty years and die in her late eighties or early nineties.

When Grandma dies, her grandchild may be in his late thirties, the time when the benefits of Grandma's money would serve him best. But the grandchild cannot count on Grandma's money to help out. Why? Because Grandma will probably do what most Grandmas do: She will leave it to *her* child (the grandchild's parent). The grandchild will not see Grandma's money until *his* parent dies.

This could be a long wait. If Grandma's child dies in her seventies or eighties, the grandchild won't see any of Grandma's money until he is in his fifties or sixties.

The Solutions

Clients who want a portion of their wealth to benefit their grandchildren in a more timely way can incorporate that wish as part of their inheritance plan with one of the following three solutions.

Solution Number 1: Leave It to Your Child and Hope for the Best

Grandma and Grandpa can leave their wealth entirely to their child and hope their child will be generous in using the inheritance to help their grandchild.

There are two downsides to this plan.

First, this expectation often does not meet the test of reality. Your child may not necessarily be inclined to part with substantial dollars to buy his child a home, get his child started in business, or upgrade his child's economic lifestyle.

Second, when you leave wealth to your child, you incur a risk it will never reach your grandchild. Throughout the chapters in part 3, I discuss a number of ways the family money can be lost once it is inherited by your child.

If you want certainty that your wealth will enhance your grandchildren's lives, consider the following alternatives.

Solution Number 2: Give the Grandchild a Share When Grandpa Dies

On the death of Grandpa (usually, the first spouse to die) a portion of Grandpa's half of the family wealth can go to a grandchild. Grandma will receive the rest.

The benefit to the grandchild is timeliness. If Grandpa dies in his mid-seventies, his grandchild will be in his or her thirties, a time when he could use Grandpa's money the most.

There is another benefit to this plan. The more that goes to the grandchild after Grandpa dies, the less that goes to Grandma. And the less Grandma owns when she dies, the less the IRS may get in death taxes.

However, I will not allow my clients to make any plan that impoverishes the surviving spouse. If Grandma requires all of Grandpa's wealth to survive, she gets it, period.

Solution Number 3: Allocate Your Wealth Between Your Children and Grandchildren After Both Spouses Die

When Grandpa dies, everything will go to Grandma. Then, when Grandma dies, her wealth may be shared between child and grandchild.

But before Grandma and Grandpa put this plan into their Will or Living Trust, consideration must be given to the wishes of their child. The last thing Grandma and Grandpa want is to drive a wedge between their child and grandchild.

I recall one occasion when a father and son inherited portions of Grandma and Grandpa's apartment building. They were partners, but they could not get along. They were in constant conflict over how to manage the building, and this stress spilled over into other aspects of their lives.

They are still partners today, but they no longer consider themselves father and son.

2. "I would like my son and grandson to inherit my money equally. However, I don't know what my son will think about this. I don't want my son to think he was 'robbed' by my grandson."

When an inheritance is divided between parent and child, I am very sensitive to how that division will impact on that relationship.

On one occasion, Grandpa left his $1 million stock portfolio to his son and granddaughter equally. After Grandpa died, his son stormed into my office screaming, "My father had no business giving away one-half of my inheritance." Years later, the son met with me to establish his own inheritance plan. Even though time had passed by, he had not been able to shake off the feeling his daughter had, as he put it, "robbed" him of half of his inheritance.

Solution: Be Sensitive to How Your Child Feels About Your Leaving Money to Your Grandchild

If you want to leave your money and property to your child and grandchild, I recommend a full and frank discussion of your wish with your child. Take into consideration his feelings prior to making your final decision.

Do you believe your child will happily go along with your decision? Unfortunately, I have found that most children are *shocked* by the idea of sharing the inheritance with their children. As one child said to his father, "Dad, what did I ever do to you? I've been a good son! So how could you even think about taking what is mine and leaving it to my stupid kid?"

If Your Child Objects . . .

What do you do if your child objects to you leaving a portion of his inheritance to his child? If you are sensitive to your child's needs, and you wish to preserve family harmony, leave it all to your child. On the other hand, you may be like some of my clients, whose steadfast attitude is: "It's our money and we'll leave it any way we want, and damn the consequences."

Of course, these clients are correct. It is their money, and they can dispose of it as they see fit. Their decision may drive a wedge between their child and grandchild, but at least they are aware of this consequence.

Don't Forget About Your Child's Spouse

If your child *does not* voice an objection, you are still not out of the woods. Remember, when it comes to money, you are not just dealing with your child—you may also have to contend with *your child's spouse*.

For example, you plan on leaving your money to your son and grandson equally. It is all right with your son, but not with your daughter-in-law. She counted on her husband inheriting all your money and using it to enhance the quality of their lives. But, she thinks, 50 percent will only go so far.

What does your daughter-in-law do? She whispers in your son's ear about all the opportunities they will lose because of your proposed plan. Ultimately, he demands that you reconsider your decision and leave him everything.

This isn't a scenario out of the movies. This is real life, and I have seen it play out time and time again.

---

3. "My son has one child and my daughter has four children. I plan to divide my $1 million estate equally between my son and my daughter. My daughter bitterly complains this is unfair. She says that when she dies, her four children will divide her $500,000, but when my son dies, his one child will get $500,000."

Your daughter has a point. When your son dies, his one child will get $500,000 all to himself. But when your daughter dies, her four children will receive only $125,000 apiece.

But . . . do you care?

Most parents are willing to equalize to prevent problems between their children. However, equalizing among grandchildren is a bit too much for most people to wrestle with. In fact, most of my clients simply dismiss this issue when I put it on the table for discussion.

On occasion I meet a client who insists on treating grandchildren equally. Typically, this client is elderly, affluent, and has a child approaching his seventies. Because of the client's advanced years *and* the advanced years of the child, the client can foresee the grandchildren inheriting the family money within one decade of the client's death. Feeling this sense of immediacy, the client desires to ensure that the grandchildren are treated equally.

Are You Sure You're Sure?

If you insist on ultimate parity among all your grandchildren, there is a solution that can guarantee they will be treated equally. Once implemented, no jealousies or conflicts will come between your grandchildren when they inherit your wealth.

However, this is a most difficult and extreme plan. After I explain this plan and what it entails, even the most motivated clients will throw up their hands and give up their goal of equalizing.

But if you want to give it the proverbial shot, the solution is noted below.

Solution: The Irrevocable Trust

Say you have a son with one child, a daughter with three children, and an estate worth $1 million. By using an Irrevocable Trust, each of your grandchildren will ultimately inherit $250,000. The plan works as follows.

1) When you die, your son and daughter will not inherit your $1 million estate outright. Instead, your wealth will be delivered to a third-party Trustee.

2) The Trustee will hold this $1 million of wealth in an Irrevocable Trust for the rest of your children's lives.

3) The Irrevocable Trust is for your children's benefit. The Trustee will invest the $1 million and pay your children the income it generates. In addition, the Trustee can dip into the $1 million for your children's support, maintenance, and medical needs.

4) When your son dies, the Trustee will take his half ($500,000) and divide it equally between all your grandchildren, regardless of the family unit from which they came. So your son's one child and your daughter's three children will each receive $125,000 from the Trust.

5) When your daughter dies, the Trustee will distribute her half ($500,000) to all your grandchildren, each one receiving an additional $125,000, for a grand total of $250,000 each.

The "Ups and Downs" of the Irrevocable Trust

The "Down"

The downside of this plan is, of course, that you have denied your son and daughter outright ownership of their inheritance. How will they feel about not having direct access to their money?

The "Up"

With this plan, you will have treated your grandchildren equally. But there is also a tax upside: You keep more of your wealth in the family with less going to the IRS.

If you left the $1 million to your children outright, they would own it, and the IRS will impose a death tax on what your children own when they die. But by leaving the $1 million to the Irrevocable Trust, your children don't own it outright. And your children cannot be taxed on what they don't own.

This advantage is discussed more fully in chapter 36.

4. "I want to leave some money to my grandson, who is fifteen years old. If my grandson is still a minor when I die, my son will be Custodian of the money until my grandson becomes an adult. However, I'm afraid that my son will squander my grandson's money."

I was surprised when my secretary said John Cole had made an appointment to see me. John swam with my son in college and was probably in his mid-twenties. Why would someone that young want to talk about an inheritance plan?

John had come to discuss his grandfather's Will. It said that John would inherit $100,000 *if* he was twenty-five years old when his grandfather died. If John was not twenty-five at that time, the $100,000 would be held in Trust, with John's father as the Trustee.

John was seventeen when his grandfather died and his father took control of John's inheritance. As Trustee, John's father was legally obligated to preserve the $100,000 so it would be there when John turned twenty-five. But, as John found out, the plan had a "weak link"—his father!

When John turned twenty-five he approached his father to claim the $100,000. John was stunned to learn his father no longer had the money.

John related his father's excuse. John's father never established a formal Trust for the $100,000. Instead, he just took the money and put it in his own checking account.

John's father did not steal the money. He fully intended to give it to John when John turned twenty-five. However, times got tough and he used it for family and business expenses. As the years went by, so did the money. By John's twenty-fifth birthday, all the money had been spent—but not on John.

John understood his father's reasoning, but he was visibly disappointed. His expectation of a relatively large amount of money had been thrashed into the ground.

What to Do?

John sought my advice on what to do. Of course, he could bring a lawsuit against his father, but that was pointless. You can't, after all, get blood from a stone. And even if he could, John was not going to sue his father.

I told John of other possible ways in which his father could make it up. Perhaps he could repay John in installments over a period of time. Perhaps John could get his father to sign a Promissory Note. Or perhaps John could inherit an extra $100,000.

The more ideas I threw out to John, the more dejected he became. How could he ask his parents to repay when they were in a daily financial struggle? And how could he tell his parents what to put in their Will or Trust? He did not even know if they had an inheritance plan.

A Gift to Your Grandchild May Turn Out to Be a Gift to Your Child

You may want to leave your grandchild an inheritance to give him or her a leg up in life. But if you let your child hold your grandchild's money, all you may have done is make an extra gift to your child. Like John Cole's father, your child may take the attitude that it's all family money.

The result is that when your grandchild reaches the age of inheritance you have selected, the money may not be there. Instead, all your grandchild gets is an explanation: "Your money's not here because you've been receiving it all along in the form of food, clothing, and shelter."

How can this happen? It's easy. If you give your child money to hold for your grandchild, whether as Custodian, Guardian, or Trustee, your child has complete power over that money. It does not matter what the words of your Will or Trust say. It does not matter what the law says. Your child has power and access over the money and can do what he pleases. No one, after all, is looking over your child's shoulder to say no.

If you want to maximize the likelihood that the money you leave to your child will end up with your grandchild, bypass your child. With the following alternatives, your grandchild can receive outright and immediate access to the money without any intervening control from your child.

Alternative Number 1: The Joint Bank Account

Allocate money to a bank account held jointly by you and your adult grandchild. When you die, your grandchild will simply take the money.

Alternative Number 2: The "Pay Over on Death" Account

This is an account that you open in your name with your grandchild as beneficiary. While you are alive, your grandchild has no access to the money in this account. After you die and your bank is shown your death certificate, the bank will "pay over" the money to your grandchild.

However, there is a one distinct downside to establishing these accounts. If your grandchild is a minor when you die, the bank may release the funds only to your grandchild's parents or Guardian.

Alternative Number 3: Use a Bank Trustee to Hold Your Grandchild's Inheritance

You can protect your grandchild's funds until he or she becomes an adult (or reaches an age you deem appropriate) by not allowing a private individual to hold your grandchild's inheritance. Instead, provide in your Will or Living Trust that an institutional third party, such as a bank Trust Department, will be the Trustee of your grandchild's inheritance.

With this method, you can die knowing that when your grandchild reaches the appointed age, the money will be around.

However, you may find this alternative is not available to you. If your grandchild's inheritance is not of sufficient size, a bank Trustee or other Trust company may decline to serve as Trustee. If that is the case, a private individual may be your only choice.

5. "I own an apartment building and I want to leave it to my daughter and granddaughter equally. When they inherit, they will be business partners. However, I am concerned they will not be able to get along."

It's easy when you leave cash or other liquid assets to your child and grandchild equally. When you die, they divide the money and go their own ways, with no ongoing entanglements. But when your child and grandchild inherit portions of a nondivisible asset such as real estate, it's a much different story. You have done more than leave them wealth—you have made them partners.

Can your child and grandchild get along owning and managing the same property? Look at what happened when Michelle Williams and her daughter shared an inheritance.

It seems Michelle got along with everyone in town except her own daughter, with whom she was always at odds. It did not get any better when they became partners in the same apartment building. When Michelle's father died, he left it to Michelle and her daughter in equal shares. And no business decision could be reached without a shouting match.

What is surprising about this story is the fact that Michelle's father *knew* about this conflict. With his daughter and granddaughter arguing constantly, he could foresee nothing but trouble ahead if they shared the inheritance.

So why did Michelle's father leave his building to them equally? Because he made his Will when his granddaughter was nine years old, and the light of his life. So precious was his granddaughter to him that he insisted on making her an equal beneficiary of his estate.

Michelle's father made his Will with a mythical image of his granddaughter, and not the reality that existed years later. He should have taken her out of his Will so that his daughter could own and manage the apartment building alone. But for reasons unknown, he did not change his Will, making his daughter and granddaughter unsuitable business partners.

You Can't Predict the Future, But . . .

Leaving your child and grandchild equal shares in the same non-divisible asset may be a great idea. Then again, you never know. A child and grandchild can have a wonderful family relationship and turn out to be lousy partners.

The point is that it is impossible to predict with certainty how your child and grandchild will get along. When they inherit an asset that cannot be physically divided, there is an ongoing business relationship between them. As in any business, conflicts and disputes may arise.

Solution: Plan Ahead for Conflicts

In your Will or Living Trust, provide your child and grandchild with a way to resolve their disputes. For example, you can instruct that in the event of a deadlock, they are to submit the matter to a neutral third party, such as an arbitrator or mediator, or even a family friend. Or, if applicable, you can provide that the voting power is to be held by someone other than your child and grandchild.

There are many other dispute-resolution methods, and I strongly urge you to incorporate one in your inheritance plan. If you do not give your child and grandchild a vehicle to resolve their deadlocks, the conflict may spill over into their family relationship, perhaps leading to their permament estrangement and liquidation of the property you left them.

Part X
Pets and Charities

31

How You Can Die "Knowing" Your Pet Will Live Comfortably for the Rest of His Life

or

What to Tell "Fido" About His Inheritance

---

1. "I want to make certain my dog, Fido, is well cared for after I die. Is this a crazy idea?"

No. If you are like me, your pets are part of your family and you care for them as such. Pictures of my dog, Dixie, sit prominently on my desk alongside those of my children and grandchildren.

Providing for your pet in your Will or Trust is not an unusual or unnatural plan. I have drafted pet provisions for many elderly clients who would be all alone in the world but for their dog or cat. For them, their pet is the last love of their lives, and they want to be sure that their pet is protected.

---

2. "Who will take care of Fido and make sure he is comfortable after I die?"

You can use your inheritance plan to assure your pet is comfortable and cared for after you die. In your Will or Trust, simply leave your pet to a reliable person who genuinely wants the pet.

This plan is really an act of faith. Your pet's comfort and care is completely at the whim of his new owner. Fido cannot speak for himself and cannot seek legal protection if he is not being cared for or is mistreated.

Before you select your pet's new owner, first review the following criteria.

Compatibility

Be sure your pet's new owner will be compatible with your pet. You do not want to create a situation in which your pet cramps the new owner's lifestyle.

For example, your dog is an "inside" dog that has always roamed in your house as much as it pleased. Will the new owner allow this to occur? Or perhaps your cat sheds every summer, leaving fur everywhere. Does your cat's new owner cringe at the mere thought of finding furballs all over the house?

Capability

A promise to take care of your pet after you die is most likely a well-meaning one. Unfortunately, the reality often becomes that the person making the promise may not have the ability to follow through.

One client left her German shepherd, Bear, to her brother. The brother promised that he would faithfully care for Bear for the rest of Bear's life. But one month after the client died, the brother boarded Bear at a kennel. Why? Because the brother discovered that Bear was too big and cumbersome to handle.

Another client left her cat, Bruno, to her sister. After this client died, the sister moved to a place that did not allow pets. The sister had no choice but to give the cat away, and God only knows where Bruno wound up.

Solution: Do Your Homework

People who love their animals usually know others who feel the same way. I strongly suggest you choose someone, friend or relative, who talks about his or her pets in the same way that you do. Whomever you choose, you must feel in your gut that he or she will be truly good to your pet. If you do, you can rest assured that your wishes will be followed.

3. "Should I give money to my pet's new owner to take care of my pet?"

Yes. Do not depend on the new owner to support your pet's existence. Leave the new owner supporting funds to take care of your pet for the rest of its life.

There are many ways you can allocate funds to support your pet after your death. One possibility is to simply leave the money outright to your pet's new owner. Of course, there is always the risk this fund could be used to provide the new owner with a great time in Las Vegas. Another way is to leave money to a trusted third party who will use it to reimburse your pet's new owner for all pet-related expenses.

Then there is the Pet Trust, which most states have created by statutes in the last five years. Yes, your state legislature has seen fit to create laws designed to protect and preserve funds that you want applied for your pet's care and comfort after your death. If you are an animal lover, you will consider those legislative efforts to be time well spent by your state government. And of course, if you deem pets to be, as one of my clients said, "one step above hamburger," you will think that any law related to pet care after pet owners die is a sign of the Apocalypse.

How does the Pet Trust work? These are provisions in your Living Trust that create a "sub-trust" for the care of your pet. You state the amount of money you want to allocate to the Pet Trust, how long the Pet Trust should last, the person whom you select as the Pet Trust "manager," and how that manager should apply those funds. And this is a legally binding arrangement that must be carried out.

Here are some essential specifics about how the Pet Trust works. Because the Pet Trust laws vary from state to state, consider these to be sweeping generalizations until you look up your state's Pet Trust statutes:

The Pet Trust can be for as many pets as you have.

The Pet Trust ends when the surviving pet dies. You can't set up a Pet Trust to continue indefinitely. Therefore, you must provide for the distribution of the funds in the Pet Trust if any remain after your pet's death. This is your choice. Family. Friends. Charities. Anyone.

The Pet Trust needs a "manager," someone who will be in charge of your pet's care and the money you leave to the Pet Trust. Select a "manager" of the Pet Trust whom you believe capable to do the job and who is compatible with your pet. I discuss in more detail in question 2 of this chapter.

The Pet Trust needs money for the care of your pet. How much? Estimate how much the caretaker of your pet will need to take care of your pet. The amount will vary widely depending on your pet's age and condition. Be careful about selecting too high an amount because your other beneficiaries may attack that amount in court as being an "unreasonable amount." Remember when Leona Helmsley left a $12 million trust fund for her dog? A judge reduced that to $2 million and ruled that the rest should go to Helmsley's charitable foundation.

The Pet Trust needs specific care instructions. Since your pet is a nonspeaking sentient being, you need to be very detailed when it comes to the caregiver's instructions. What kind of food to buy? What kind of toy does your pet love? Put it all in the Pet Trust's instructions.

The Pet Trust needs proper oversight. You need to appoint a person who makes sure that the manager of the Pet Trust is spending the funds appropriately on your pet . . . and not for any other purpose.

Which method should you choose? The answer depends on

how you feel about your pet's new owner. If you are absolutely assured that the new owner is reliable, I suggest the outright method. If you harbor any concerns the new owner will dissipate the supporting funds, choose the Pet Trust.

However, you must realize that even the third-party method is not fail-safe. I learned this from my brush with *Chauncy, the Wonder Dog.*

Mrs. Green wanted to die knowing that Chauncy, her black Lab, would be happy and comfortable for the rest of his days. I suggested several ways she could accomplish this goal, but Mrs. Green dismissed them all. For her, there was only one solution: When Mrs. Green died, Chauncy had to live in her home.

For Mrs. Green's solution to work, she had to find someone who was willing to live in her home and baby-sit Chauncy for the rest of the dog's life. This someone turned out to be Mr. McSorley, a sixty-five-year-old widower who rented the house next door to Mrs. Green.

After Mrs. Green died, Mr. McSorley moved into Chauncy's home and took good care of Chauncy. In return, Mr. McSorley got a free place to live and a $1,000 monthly salary! This is how I set up the arrangement in Mrs. Green's Will:

- When Mrs. Green died, the Trust Department of her local bank (the "bank Trustee") would control her cash assets for the rest of Chauncy's life.
- From the cash, the bank Trustee would pay Mr. McSorley his monthly salary.
- About two times a year, the Trust officer in charge of the "Chauncy Trust" would make field trips to Chauncy's home. Why? To see if Chauncy was still alive. Once Chauncy was no more, the bank Trustee would stop Mr. McSorley's salary, sell the home, and deliver the proceeds and other assets to several pet charities.

This seemed to be a terrific way to accomplish Mrs. Green's goal. In fact, it worked too well.

Chauncy was nine years old when Mrs. Green died. About a year later, the Trust officer in charge of the Chauncy Trust left the bank. The Chauncy Trust was then assigned to a new Trust officer. Like his predecessor, this new Trust officer paid Mr. McSorley his monthly salary and checked on Chauncy twice a year to see if he was still alive.

This Trust officer "cycle" repeated itself, with Trust officers coming and going. During the next twelve years, six different Trust officers had been assigned to the Chauncy Trust, all of them paying Mr. McSorley's salary, and all of them checking up on Chauncy's health.

Wait a minute! How could this be? Chauncy was nine years old when Mrs. Green died. Twelve years later, Chauncy would have been twenty-one years old. Was Chauncy a miracle dog, still kicking around that many years after my client's death?

Of course not. Chauncy died of natural causes at the age of fourteen, but Mr. McSorley did not tell anyone. Instead, he bought another black Labrador and named him Chauncy. When *that* dog died, Mr. McSorley bought yet another black Lab and named him Chauncy.

Whenever a new Trust officer dropped by, Chauncy was there and Mr. McSorley still got his salary, and a free place to live.

---

4. "What should I do if I can't find anyone I trust to look after Fido when I'm gone?"

If you cannot find a person whom you trust, consider leaving your pet (and sufficient supporting funds) to a charity whose purpose is to find good homes for orphaned pets. There are several excellent pet charities around the country that will find the right home for pets.

Be aware, however, that not all pet charities have an orphaned pet policy. You do not want a charity that will dump your pet on the first willing person it finds. You also do not want your pet to live in the charity's kennel for the rest of his days. What you want is for the charity to go through fire to find the right owner for your beloved pet.

Solution: Your Pet Cannot Talk, but Money Sure Can

It may sound crass, but there is no better incentive than money to ensure that a pet charity will find a happy home for your pet when you die. So, in accordance with this philosophy, do the following:

1) Find a pet charity that specializes in finding good homes for orphaned pets.

2) Visit the pet charity you select at its corporate headquarters *and* its kennel. Even better, join the charity and get involved. Whatever you do, you must be able to see its orphaned pet policy firsthand.

3) Leave money to a trusted friend in Trust and provide that it is to be handed over to the charity *only after* your friend is assured that your pet has been placed in a satisfactory home. Also provide that if your friend and the pet charity disagree, a neutral third party can decide if the charity has "earned its money."

4) If you implicitly trust the charity to find your pet a comfortable home, include it as an outright beneficiary in your Will or Living Trust.

If you still harbor doubt that this four-step process will work to assure your pet's proper care and comfort, then employ the Pet Trust that I discuss in question 3 of this chapter.

32

Leaving Your Money and Property to a Charity

or

Do You Really Want to Leave Everything to a Charity That Clothes Naked Horses?

The "Off-Brand" Charity

Many years ago, a man went on *The Tonight Show* and announced to the national television audience that he wanted to clothe nude horses.

You may remember him. This young man, who appeared most sincere and presented an executive-type appearance, sat with Johnny Carson and talked about the offensiveness of nude horses. To protect the public from this "abomination," he founded an organization that provided clothes to cover horses' private parts.

If you saw this guest, you probably reacted the way I did. This had to be a joke. Who, I asked myself, would buy into this?

As it turned out, he sold a lot of people. Yes, the majority of Americans thought him to be an eccentric young man who had too much time on his hands. But he also stimulated a voluminous response in the form of checks and pledges from those who agreed with his concept.

Sometime later, he confessed he had put on America. His charity was a hoax. His explanation? It was an experiment to measure the gullibility of the American contributing public. He was offered and had received about $100,000 to support this nonexistent charity.

We can only hope that he returned the contributions, but this experiment served a significant purpose. It pointed out that serious individuals will contribute to support even the most ludicrous purposes and will contribute without any prior investigation of an organization's qualifications.

Sometimes, it falls on the lawyer to protect the donor from his or her own gullibility. And the only way the lawyer can prevent the donor from being taken is to step in between the susceptible donor and the bogus charity.

However, even a lawyer coming to the rescue may never be enough.

Mrs. Delcy—the Cat Lady

Mrs. Delcy, a widow with no children, had a great fondness for cats. After her husband died, she became an active member in a small organization, the Cat Ladies, whose purpose was to provide homes for orphaned or homeless cats.

Years before she died, Mrs. Delcy sought my advice on whether it was wise to leave her wealth to the Cat Ladies. The only way I could assist her in making this decision was to grill the Board of Directors. So the following week, I accompanied Mrs. Delcy to one of the monthly Board meetings of the Cat Ladies.

I was suspicious right off the bat. Ordinarily, the Board of even the most off-brand charity consists of professional-looking people meeting in a hotel conference room or the back room of a nice restaurant. The Cat Ladies, however, crowded around a regular-size table at a local delicatessen. Around this table sat six ladies, all widows, all over the age of seventy.

Mrs. Delcy had called the club's president in advance, so they were expecting her. However, they were not expecting her lawyer in tow. When Mrs. Delcy introduced me, I could see the dismay on their faces. They realized that in order to get to Mrs. Delcy's money, they would first have to go through me.

Not to appear nonplussed by my appearance, they welcomed me to lunch. From there, they told me about their devotion to saving the lives of cats in their community. They regaled me with stories about the hundreds of cats they had saved from sure destruction.

They also told me about their funding. Their source of contributions was childless, cat-loving people like Mrs. Delcy. The members would befriend a Mrs. Delcy and offer to provide her cat with a happy home after that person died. Of course, along with the cat would come some financial contribution as well.

To try to win me over, the Cat Ladies offered to show me their Cat House, a rented single-family residence they used as a way station for homeless cats. Reluctantly, I accepted, and the president volunteered to drive.

I still remember this short drive. I equate it to my battle experiences during the Korean War. This eighty-seven-year-old lady, who somehow still managed to keep her driver's license, hardly looked through the windshield. For practically the entire drive, her eyes and voice were focused on me as she tried to overwhelm me with the virtues of the Cat Ladies.

The president did not have to tell me when we arrived. I could smell the Cat House from the car window. Inside, the house was overrun with cats, cat litter, cat toys, cat cages, cat food, and cat runs. Only one human was in this house, an elderly lady watching television with cats covering her entire body.

Thirty seconds after I arrived, I was gone. I didn't even want to know how they managed to violate the zoning laws and keep a thousand cats in a family neighborhood. I walked back to the restaurant, pulled Mrs. Delcy aside, and said she had to be nuts to even consider leaving her wealth to the Cat Ladies.

Mrs. Delcy, however, would not reconsider. She rebuffed me.

When she died, the Cat Ladies received Mrs. Delcy's $800,000 estate.

Out of curiosity, I met with the Cat Ladies a few months after Mrs. Delcy's death to find out what they were doing with her money. Do you know what I discovered? Each Board member was driving a brand-new Cadillac.

Solution: Get Involved in the Charity

The Delcy experience reinforces plain old common sense. If you leave your money to an off-brand charity, there is the significant risk the beneficiary will be the principals.

The best way to ensure that your intended charity will properly use your money is to involve yourself in that organization before you die. Your involvement should be more than attending a luncheon or the annual dinner. Preferably, you should get involved as a member of the Board. Get a hands-on feeling about how that charity really functions and what really happens to the donations. If a client has not personally participated in the internal affairs of an off-brand organization, I will insist that he or she does. Most clients see the wisdom of my insistence and join up. Many have come away from the charities with their minds changed.

Others, however, tell me they don't want my unsolicited advice. It is their money, they say, and they will do with it whatever they see fit.

In that case, I refuse to do that client's inheritance plan—not out of moral outrage, but out of fear. If the charity turns out to be a bunch of phonies, there may be a rebound effect on me personally. Somehow, the lawyer who drafts the Will or Trust is darkened by the shadow created by the bad guys.

---

1. "My wife and I have no children, so we want to leave our money to charity. But which one?"

Like many of my charity-minded clients, you probably have a definite idea which organization you will benefit with an inheritance. On the other hand, you may be undecided. You may like the idea of leaving money to charity but do not know which one to choose.

Helpful Hints If You Are Undecided

1. Get Involved

If you are looking for a charity with which you can find that special connection, there is no better way than to get involved. Find a charity in your area that deals with your specific concerns, whether it is children, AIDS, church, hospitals, the homeless, veterans, or any other worthwhile cause.

However, you may have little time or energy for community involvement. In fact, the only connection you may have had with a charity is from having been a patient at a hospital. If you lack the time to get involved, consider the next alternative.

2. Do the Research

Log on the Internet and go to www.charityfinder.com, which I have found to be a very user-friendly provider of information about charities. (And no, I'm not a paid shill for that site or affiliated with it in any manner.) On this site, you can search for charities based on your preferred purpose. If you want a charity that benefits children with AIDS, you can input "children and AIDS" in the search box. Like magic, up will pop listings of dozens of youth Aids charities and information about their specific purposes, financials, websites, and contacts.

If you haven't become part of the "wired generation," you can get the same information at your local library. Go to the reference desk and ask for the books that list all the qualified charities in the United States. They will be voluminous, so take care not to strain a muscle as you carry them to a nearby desk.

Once you have accessed the charity navigation system of your choice, review the qualifications of each charity from your category of preference. Select one or more charities from each of your preferred categories. But do not select some off-brand charity. The charity you want should be mainline, long-lived, and well-respected.

Once you pick your finalists, send a small contribution to each of them to see what kind of response they give you. Many on-the-ball charities will fuss over you, the "New Donor." They may tell you more about their organization and invite you to visit their facilities. They may even ask you to attend a Board meeting or the annual dinner dance. From the acknowledgment you receive or don't receive, you can tell if that charity is the one for you and for your inheritance plan.

2. "Mr. Condon, you decide. Which charity should we leave some money to?"

On occasion, a client will ask me to select one or many worthy charities to receive some of that client's money. This request is not like throwing money in the street, but it's close. How can anyone who has worked years to accumulate wealth be so cavalier about who gets their money?

Nonetheless, if I can do my clients a service by using their money to fund some worthy educational, scientific, or medical research purpose, then I will do so. And besides, who am I to turn down an opportunity to funnel money to a favorite charity?

Room for abuse? Of course, especially from attorneys who believe charity begins at home. I have heard of several attorneys who have advised charity-minded clients to leave money to an organization in which the attorney is a member of the Board of Directors.

I, however, go out of my way to avoid even the mere appearance of impropriety. The last thing I want to do is give people one more crooked-lawyer story to discuss over morning coffee. Therefore, I never advise clients to leave money to any charity in which I have any active involvement.

I will, however, confess to one act of selfishness.

On one occasion, a client instructed me to divide her estate among six charities. Since the client was a native of the area, I selected five local entities: a hospital, two elementary schools, the high school, and the junior college.

For the sixth charity, I selected St. Jude's Hospital. Not because it was in the area, because it wasn't. Not because I had ties to the place, because I didn't.

The reason? I just wanted to meet Danny Thomas, the late actor and primary benefactor of St. Jude's Hospital.

In this client's Will, I literally incorporated an instruction that St. Jude's would get the money only if Danny Thomas came to my office and picked up the check. And after my client died, there he was in my office library, posing with me for the community newspaper, with a check for $300,000 in his hands.

Danny Thomas took this condition with the good humor I intended. I can still recall the jokes he told that had my office staff in hysterics for a half hour.

From this one meeting with Mr. Thomas, I became a big fan and a semiregular contributor to St. Jude's.

---

3. "I plan to leave my money to provide scholarships for underprivileged kids to go to school."

It is not as simple as you would think to leave money to provide scholarships for a specific purpose.

Several years ago, I spoke with the scholarship chairman of a local college. He told me he receives many annual contributions for his staff to award as scholarships. But he added that it is rare that the money actually goes to someone for whom it was intended, namely, underprivileged college-bound kids.

The scholarship chairman was not pocketing the money. But like many small colleges, this school lacked the resources to effectively administer the scholarship program. It takes a great deal of money, time, effort, and manpower to solicit scholarship applications and investigate and review requests. These were things the scholarship committee just did not have.

Just who was getting the college's scholarship money? People on the inside: children of faculty members as well as aggressive scholarship hunters who target such scholarships but who are not the persons originally intended by the donor.

Investigate the Scholarship Program

Before you leave your money to a scholarship program, learn more about its allocation procedures. Determine if your intended program has the tools to do the job right. If it does, you will feel more comfortable knowing the money will go for your intended purpose.

4. "I was recently a patient at my local hospital where I was taken care of very well. I want to return the favor by leaving some money to the hospital after my death. But I am concerned about them using my money for frivolous purposes. I want my money to help support their pediatrics program. How can I be sure that my wishes *will be followed after my death?*"

The good people who budget and administer for the charities are not mind readers. If you want your money to be used for a specific purpose, you have to let them know in your inheritance plan what that purpose is.

However, be forewarned. Informing the charity of your purpose is one thing; enforcement of that purpose is another. Who will be around to police the charity? Will your Trustee, Executor, or other "after-death agent" know if the hospital uses your money for its annual holiday party in the Bahamas? And even if your agent discovers that the charity has run afoul of your instructions, will he be on the scene to get the charity back on track?

For all practical purposes, the hospital will use your funds the way you want. Hospitals, like most major charities, rely heavily on contributed dollars and they do not want to do anything to jeopardize future donations.

There are, however, no guarantees, and there is always room for abuse. If the hospital decides that buying Cadillacs for its Board of Directors is indirectly beneficial for its pediatrics program, then that will be its decision.

But if you engage in the following steps, you will increase the likelihood that the hospital will use your money as you wish it to be used:

1. Provide in your Will or Living Trust that you wish for your money to be used for the hospital's pediatrics program. For example, one client's Will, which I recently prepared, states: "I specifically direct that my estate be used solely for medical or research purposes that are vital to the support of the hospital's pediatrics program, and that my estate not be used for non-medical or administrative purposes that are mildly related or not related to such support."

2. Provide that before the hospital receives the money, it must enter into a written contract with your agent (i.e., the Successor Trustee of your Living Trust or the Executor of your Will) that it will use your money for the purposes you intend.

3. Let people in the hospital administration know of your intended purpose while you are alive. Attend the Board meetings. Write an open letter and make the charity publish it in its newsletter. The more people who know of your purpose now, the more scrutiny the charity will receive once it inherits your money.

By the way, if you are rich enough, forget using your Will to leave money to the hospital. Instead, you can set up your own private foundation to fund your specific charitable purpose. Or if you wish to save the expenses of establishing the private foundation, you may wish to leave some money to a Community Foundation already in existence in cities throughout America. You and your Community Foundation enter into an agreement, which states that you promise to leave the foundation some money, and the foundation promises it will allocate your money for the specific charitable purpose you have in mind.

5. "I am property rich and cash poor. So I will just leave my real estate to charity."

Charities don't want your house. They want your cash.

Once a charity becomes the title owner to your real estate, it assumes all the liabilities of an owner. It could be sued by buyers of the property for any title defects, hazardous substances, health and safety issues, or any other problems that then exist or subsequently arise.

In today's litigious climate, those are risks charities may not be willing to take. Though charities are not going to look a gift horse in the mouth, they will be reluctant to take your real estate. Rather, they would prefer you to instruct your Trustee (or Executor) to sell the real estate after your death and distribute the cash.

6. "I keep getting letters from charities telling me I can sell my investment real estate and get an income for the rest of my life. What are they talking about?"

They are talking about the Charitable Remainder Trust (CRT).

You get three benefits from the CRT, which are:

1) You get investment real estate out of your name, so there will be less death taxes when you die;

2) You get more income than you are presently receiving from your investment real estate; and

3) You sell your property without incurring a capital gains tax.

The CRT is not for everyone. But if you see yourself in the following scenario, you may do well to consider it.

The CRT Scenario

You are in your fifties or sixties. You have a house and a ten-unit apartment building (or other investment property). You bought your apartment building years ago for $10,000 a unit. Now, it's worth $100,000 per unit.

After you figure out rental income versus expenses, you find you are getting 4 percent from your million-dollar equity. This is certainly not putting equity to productive use.

In addition, you are getting tired of upkeep, tenants, rent control, and knocking your brains out for the IRS, which will get half of the value of the building in death taxes when you die.

You want to take the equity out of your building so you can at least get money market rates. So what can you do?

1) You can sell the building. But commissions, expenses, and capital gains will eat up approximately one-half. The remaining proceeds will be additionally eaten up in death taxes. Out of the $1 million you create, taxes will be levied on $400,000 while you are alive. The rest will be taxed after you die.

2) You can swap the building for another, but all you would be doing is switching one problem for another.

3) You can sell and carry back installment financing. This way, you would not have to pay an immediate capital gains tax. But you still have problems. There is a risk of your buyer going into default or bankruptcy. You still have to pay capital gains taxes eventually. And when you die, there will be a death tax on the cash you received and on the remaining balance of the Note.

Is there any way you can get a large return on your million-dollar equity? Yes. You sell your property. However, the escrow will not be writing the check to you. It will write the check to a charity. The charity can be any charity you desire or a combination of charities.

But before this check is written, you and the charity have

already met and entered into a special agreement. This is an annuity agreement. Every year for the rest of your life (and the life of your spouse) the charity will pay you, say, 10 percent on the $1 million, which is $100,000 a year, or $8,333 per month. All you have to do is go to your mailbox each month and pick up the check.

Where will the charity get this money? From dipping into the $1 million? No. The charity will take the $1 million and invest it. All the income will go to you. The charity cannot touch the $1 million until after you are dead.

This is a win-win situation. You win because you get $100,000 a year for doing nothing. The charity wins because it has a future right to $1 million. When you (and your spouse) are gone, the charity will take it all.

This annuity from a charity has proved to be a welcome relief for many of my clients. Here are the most common questions I receive on the CRT.

Q. *How is the CRT set up?*
A. Basically, it works like this. You take your real estate and transfer it to a charity. The charity will put your real estate in a special "Charity Trust." The Trustee of the Charity Trust will be the charity.

The Charity Trust will sell your real estate and invest the proceeds. For the rest of your life, the Charity Trust will collect the income, administer the Trust, and pay you an annual amount.

Q. *How much will the charity pay me each year?*
A. Whatever amount you and the charity agree on before you give them your real estate.

Q. *Is there a risk to the sale proceeds that the charity is holding?*
A. Yes. If anything bad happens to the sale proceeds, there goes your annuity, and you will have sold your investment real estate for nothing.

You can ensure the sale proceeds are protected by keeping the charity out of the loop. That is, you can sell your real estate and give the sale proceeds not to the charity, but to the corporate Trustee of your choice, such as a bank or Trust company. The corporate Trustee will not only keep the sale proceeds safe, but its financial counselors may get, on the average, a 10 percent return.

Q. *Can I get the charity to guarantee the amount of the annuity we agree upon?*
A. Yes. You can structure your agreement so the charity guarantees it will pay you the agreed-upon amount. For example, if you are supposed to get 10 percent and the charity is only earning 7 percent, so what? You still get the whole 10 percent annuity, even if it means the charity has to dip into the principal to come up with it all.

Q. *Do I pay income tax on the annuity I receive?*
A. Yes. This is the same as receiving interest income on your bank deposits. However, you get an income tax deduction because you transferred property to charity.

The IRS will let you make a deduction against your income based on the value of the property going to charity less the value of your retained income rights. If you do not write it off all in one year, you can carry it forward for up to five years.

How do you know how much you can write off? If the charity you select is on the ball, it will have annuity tables that can tell you.

Q. *What happens when I (and my wife) die?*
A. The annuity stops, and the Charity Trust turns the proceeds over to the charity.

Q. *If a bank is Trustee of the Charity Trust, what happens if the bank fails? Are the proceeds lost?*
A. Unequivocally no. The proceeds are not bank assets. The bank is only holding on to the money for the charity. And to pay off its creditors, the bank cannot use someone else's money.

Q. *Is there anyone who loses with the CRT?*
A. Yes. Your children will lose. They will not receive the building you sold or the proceeds from the sale.

However, this may not be a concern to you because you may not have children. Or you do have children but:

- You don't care what your children think;
- You are more concerned with your own lifestyle than you are with what your children will get after you die; or
- You have other assets to leave your children.

If you are concerned about your million-dollar apartment building not going to your children, consider this: If you are rich enough, your death tax may be 40 percent of what you own. The result is that your children would not be getting the full million anyway because the IRS may eat up 40 percent of its value in death taxes.

Q. *I don't like the idea of my children missing out on the building, but I like the idea of the* CRT. *Is there a compromise?*
A. Yes. In fact, there are two compromises.
- Sell your building, set up the Charity Trust, invest the proceeds, and get your annuity. But give a portion of your monthly check to your children. Your children will then buy a life insurance policy on your lives for $1 million. When you die, the insurance company will write your children a tax-free check for a million dollars.
- Sell your building, set up the Charity Trust, and invest the proceeds. But instead of you getting the monthly payments of interest and income, let them go to the charity. Then, after you die, the sale proceeds will revert to your children.

Q. Do I *have to use real estate for the* CRT?
A. No. You can contribute anything of value you own: cars, paintings, stocks, bonds, vacant lots you haven't seen for years, and the like.

The charity will take your assets, sell them, and pool the proceeds in a special "Pooled Trust." In this Trust are the proceeds of other assets other people have contributed.

You will get a share of interest in the Pooled Trust that entitles you to receive a lifetime income from that fund. If you donated $50,000 of assets, and the income from the Pooled Trust is 8 percent, you will receive $4,000 a year for the rest of your life. If you don't need the money, assign the right to receive this income to your children or grandchildren.

Q. *If the CRT is so great, why doesn't everybody do it?*
A. Using the CRT means you have to give up ownership of assets, and not everyone is willing to do that.

Q. *Will the CRT always be around, or is this something Congress will axe to reduce the deficit?*
A. It is possible that Congress may eliminate this opportunity to reduce the death tax, but I seriously doubt it. If we don't give to charity, Congress would have to through our tax dollars.

Part XI

The Final Triangle: You, Your Children, and the IRS

33

The Permanent Repeal
of the Death Tax

or

Well . . . That's Kind of a Vicious Lie.
There's Still a Death Tax . . . But
Only If You're Really Rich

As I previously mentioned in the Preface, the estate tax is a tax on the transfer of assets after the death of the owner of those assets. Because this tax takes place after death, some folks call it the "death tax." It's a completely misleading label, as it gives the impression that there is a tax on death, only a tax on the transfer of wealth after death. Nonetheless, since most of my clients use that term, I use it as well when communicating about this concept.

In this chapter, I'll start by telling you how the 2013 change in the death tax law made me look like an idiot to all of those who ever asked me, "So, Mr. Expert Attorney, what do you think is going to happen to the death tax?"

A few years after the first edition of *Beyond the Grave* was published, I was invited to appear on John McLaughlin's *One on One* to discuss the repeal of the death tax. At the time, the death tax was imposed on estates exceeding $675,000 and the political discussion to have the death tax fully repealed was in its embryonic stage.

As I waited in the studio's greenroom before the taping, I had the occasion to meet and converse with my copanelist, Republican congressman Christopher Cox of California, a staunch supporter and spearhead of the repeal movement. Congressman Cox said to me, "I presume you are against repeal because it will affect your business." Without missing a beat, I replied, "I'm here today because my father and I wrote a book on inheritance planning. The section on reducing death taxes comprises maybe 5 percent of it. If the death tax repeal is good for our clients, then we're in favor of it. We'll simply continue focusing on the human side of inheritance planning, which is covered by the remaining 95 percent." A bit taken aback, Congressman Cox said, "Well, Mr. Condon, you are certainly an anomaly among estate lawyers I've met on this issue. All of them want to stop the repeal effort to save their jobs."

I was really proud of myself for momentariliy holding my own with a renowned politico with degrees from both Harvard *and* Yale. And it seemed he was impressed with my confident assertion that my inheritance planning practice will survive without the fees I have come to count on from tax planning services.

Sure, I was confident. I could afford to be. Because at that moment, I believed that the death tax would never go away. While Congressman Cox saw my mouth moving, he didn't hear my brain saying, "Jeff, you're going to take a big hit if those death tax planning fees go away. But the death tax is so ingrained in our tax structure, it will never go away. And all this noble stuff you're saying to the congressman sounds really convincing. Keep it up!"

Well, I was right in that I put on a very good show for the congressman, but my prognostication turned out to be dead wrong. In 2013, the death tax's long and circuitous political trail concluded when President Obama signed a law proclaiming that it will not be imposed on individuals who die with $5 million or less, and on spouses who die with a combined $10 million or less. (I will refer to that exemption throughout this chapter as the "Lifetime Exemption".)

Because only .1 percent of Americans possess that kind of wealth, the death tax—a staple in the United States Tax Code since 1913—was essentially wiped out.

In 2013, the Lifetime Exemption was a generous $5 million. But those of us in industries that deal with the Death Tax World—estate planning professionals, accountants, trust departments, charitable entities, insurance companies, real estate brokerages—knew that changes were afoot. We perused the same dozen online and print articles that mulled over the myriad proposals that had been proffered as compromises between the Republican-led House of Representative's mission of death tax repeal and the Obama administration's advocacy of maintaining a tax originally enacted in 1931 to prevent great concentrations of wealth in relatively few wealthy hands.

These proposals were all over the map. Keep the Lifetime Exemption at $1 million but increase the death tax rates. Raise the Lifetime Exemption to $3.5 million. Maintain the Lifetime Exemption at $1 million but make up for the lost tax dollars by eliminating stepped-up capital gains tax basis on death. And a whole bunch more.

There was only one certainty: If Congress and Obama could not come up with a compromise, the death tax would stay and the $5 million Lifetime Exemption would be reduced to $1 million. Forever. Remember: the smaller the Lifetime Exemption, the more estates that get caught up in the Death Tax World. And a $1 million Lifetime Exemption would certainly catch a whole bunch more estates.

So, while Washington, D.C., fiddled in 2012, we inheritance planning attorneys were hamstrung. We had nothing but guesswork and conjecture upon which to base our tax planning advice. For every client with an estate of $1 million or more who asked me if they should hire me to do some planning to eliminate or minimize their death tax, I could only respond, "I have no idea. I don't know whether we'll still have the death tax. And if we still have it, I have no idea what the Lifetime Exemption will be. The only thing I know for certain is that if you want to lock in your $5 million Lifetime Exemption, you have to die this year!"

Fortunately no one took seriously my facetious remark to commit suicide just to preserve their 2012 $5 million Lifetime Exemption. However, what a lot of folks *did* do was make substantial gifts of their assets to their children and grandchildren in 2012. Why? Because the Lifetime Exemption can be used during, well, during your life. While you are alive, you can transfer your assets equal to your Lifetime Exemption without one penny of gift tax. If you don't use the Lifetime Exemption while you are alive, you don't lose it after you die. What's left of your Lifetime Exemption can be applied by your beneficiaries to the assets they inherit from you. Hence the term *Lifetime Exemption*.

So, with about two months left on the 2012 clock, I became uber-busy with clients who hired me to draft and implement plans that gifted their assets—houses, stocks, limited liability company membership interests, businesses—to their succeeding generations before the year's end. These were not, to say the least, casual endeavors. These were transfers of lifetimes of accumulations, all made under the assumption of the worst; that at 12:01 a.m. on January 1, 2013, their $5 million Lifetime Exemption would be significantly reduced to $1 million.

Would you voluntarily give up ownership and control of your assets on the chance that such an effort might save your family from entering the Death Tax World? It depends on what kind of taxpayer you are (see chapter 36, "Pay the Death Tax or Fight Back—Which One Sounds Like You?"). But all of you would most likely agree that giving away nearly all of your net worth to capitalize on what you assume to be a dwindling opportunity to make tax-free gifts is truly the tax tail wagging the dog.

And then there was this important consideration: What if Congress and President Obama actually kept the Lifetime Exemption at $5 million? Although I thought that highly unlikely, that was one of the proposals bandied around in the legislative branch–executive branch compromise discussions. If that turned out to be the case, then my clients' last-minute plans to reduce their estates with irrevocable gift transactions would accomplish absolutely nothing. Indeed, if your Lifetime Exemption is $5 million and you own less than $5 million of assets, there is no need to lessen your estate.

Believe me, my CYA (Cover Your Ass) letter covered this contingency. Any client who wanted to engage in this last-minute gift planning in 2012 was given a written warning that essentially said, "You are giving up ownership and control of your assets to your children because you want to strike while the iron is hot. Meaning, you want to give away up to $5 million of your assets while you still have a $5 million Lifetime Exemption. But, if January 1, 2013, rolls around with the $5 million Lifetime Exemption intact, you will have paid me oodles of dollars to perform meaningless work. So please sign at the bottom of this warning letter. And if the Lifetime Exemptions somehow stays at $5 million in 2013, I can prove that I told you so when you try to haul me into court to you sue me for malpractice."

Well, 2013 did roll around, and the unthinkable happened. Congress and the Obama administration compromised at keeping the death tax, but with a Lifetime Exemption of $5 million. (Actually, the Lifetime Exemption is now $5,340,000, which will be adusted annually based on the percentage change in the Consumer Price Index, but I will continue to round the Lifetime Exemption down to $5 million in this chapter just to keep the math simple.)

Truly, I did not see that one coming. But to be fair, neither did a lot of my colleagues. Whenever I had the occasion to meet with people for whom the death tax matters, I always brought up the subject and asked what they thought. I must have asked that question to fifty different people in professions that are part of the Death Tax World, and I listened to commentators and pundits who supposedly have their ears to the political ground so they can prognosticate and report tax changes. All of us were wrong. Not one of us predicted the rise of the Lifetime Exemption to a level that can be be likened to a repeal.

Still, the death tax is part of our nation's tax fabric, and here are the hot and juicy scenarios of the death tax law that you need to know right now.

If You Are Unmarried and Die with Less Than $5 Million

If you are an unmarried person and your net estate is less than $5 million on your death, the beneficiaries of your estate *will not* pay a death tax when your estate is transferred to them. There is nothing that you need to do during your lifetime to make sure that your beneficiaries can claim that $5 million Lifetime Exemption after you die. No fancy tax planning is needed. You get that Lifetime Exemption without doing anything.

If You Are Unmarried and Die with More Than $5 Million

If you are an unmarried person and your net estate is more than $5 million, on your death the beneficiaries of your estate *will* pay a death tax when your estate is transferred to them. If you see yourself in this scenario, proceed to chapter 34, "How Does the IRS Know How Much I'm Worth When I Die?" and chapter 36, "How to Leave More to Your Children and Grandchildren and Less to the IRS."

If You and Your Spouse's Combined Worth Is Less Than $5 Million When the First Spouse Dies

This scenario is simple, but still best explained by way of example.

You and your spouse have a combined estate of $4 million—

which is $2 million each. Your spouse dies and you inherit your spouse's half. There is no death tax when your estate passes to your spouse.

You now have an estate of $4 million. When you die, your beneficiaries will receive your $4 million estate without paying a penny in death tax. Why? Because after your spouse died, you became an unmarried person. And as I explained previously, an unmarried person possesses a $5 million Lifetime Exemption without doing anything.

If You and Your Spouse's Combined Worth Is More Than $5 Million When the First Spouse Dies

This is the only scenario where you have to do something to make certain that your beneficiaries will not pay any, or minimal, death tax when both you and your spouse have died and your estate is transferred to your children or other heirs.

You and your spouse are alive. Your combined net worth is $8 million. That's $4 milllion for each of you. Your spouse dies and her $4 million goes to you. Now you, the surviving spouse, own the entire $8 million. If you die with an $8 million estate, your $5 million Lifetime Exemption will shelter the first $5 million from death tax. But there will be a death tax on the remaining "unsheltered" $3 million at a top estate tax rate of 40 percent, which would be $1.2 million.

However, that $1.2 million could have been avoided if you had gone to your inheritance attorney *within nine months after your spouse's death* and said to him or her the following:

> *"Hi there! Long time no see. My spouse died and I would like you to prepare whatever documents are necessary to transfer her $5 million Lifetime Exemption to me."*

Those three sentences (well, just the last one if you want to skip the perfunctory pleasantries) will have saved your family a death tax of $1.2 million. Because with that marching order to your attorney, you will have picked up your deceased spouse's Lifetime Exemption (which is $4 million in this case because your spouse only had $4 million of assets) and added it to your own $5 million Lifetime Exemption. Which gives you a total $9 million Lifetime Exemption! And with your $8 million estate being less than your full $9 million Lifetime Exemption, your total $8 million estate will transfer to your beneficiaries without a single penny of death tax.

So what is this form that you instructed your inheritance attorney to draft? It's your deceased spouse's federal estate tax return. Otherwise known as "IRS Form 706."

Before the 2013 death tax changes, this return had only one function: to serve as your inventory of your deceased spouse's assets, which the IRS scrutinizes for all its worth so it can assess a death tax on your beneficiaries based on the net value of the inventories assets.

But in today's Death Tax World, that Form 706 now has another purpose: to tell the IRS that you want to pick up whatever remains of your deceased spouse's Lifetime Exemption and combine it with whatever remains of your Lifetime Exemption.

Is it just that simple? Well, did you forget we are talking about our government tax law? In other words, it ain't easy. There are a lot of rules that have to be followed in order to capitalize on picking up your deceased spouse's Lifetime Exemption. Here are the Greatest Hits:

1. You must file your deceased spouse's estate tax return within 9 months after your spouse's death. If you need more time, you can get a 6-month extension.

2. In chapter 35, I point out that an estate tax return has to be filed if the inventory of assets exceeds the Lifetime Exemption. So if your deceased spouse's assets total, say, $3 million, you would not have to file that return.

But, if you want to pick up your deceased spouse's Lifetime Exemption, you have to do all the work to complete and file the return. Even if your deceased spouse's assets do not rise above her $5 million Lifetime Exemption. So legal work is now required where it was not required before. You still have to hire the real estate appraisers, pester your stockbroker representative to get a list of stocks as of the date of your spouse's death, inventory every asset you and your deceased spouse owned together, and fork over a few thousand dollars to the attorney to prepare the return.

3. It is common knowledge that the IRS has, in general, a three-year limit to examine an income tax return. Well, that does not apply to an estate tax return where you elect to pick up your deceased spouse's Lifetime Exemption. Why? So the IRS can change that return to adjust to any changes in the death tax law, including a reduction in the $5 million Lifetime Exemption!

So, say you and your wife own a combined $6 million—$3 million each. Your wife dies and you inherit her half. You now own $6 million.

You file your deceased wife's estate tax return to pick up the maximum amount of her $5 million Lifetime Exemption, which is $3 million because her half is only $3 million. You now have your $5 million Lifetime Exemption and her $3 million Lifetime Exemption for your grand total $8 million Lifetime Exemption. When you die, your estate of $6 million will fall under your $8 million Lifetime Exemption. So your children escape all death taxes. Everyone wins!

However, while you are still alive, the death tax becomes, once again, a political football. The legislative and executive branches reduce the $5 million Lifetime Exemption to $2 million. You may not believe this but the new death tax rules say that no matter how many years pass after your wife's death, the IRS can then go back to your deceased spouse's return and retroactively adjust your $3 million Lifetime Exemption pick-up to $2 million.

Can they do that? Yes. And I can hear your screams of obscenities from here, but stay with me to finish this example.

This reduction in the Lifetime Exemption from $5 million to $2 million thrusts your beneficiaries into the Death Tax World.

Specifically, you would be left with a $4 million combined Lifetime Exemption that would subject your $6 million estate to an $800,000 death tax. Using the only math equation you will find in this book because it was my inability to do math that drove me to law school, that's your $6 million estate minus $4 million combined Lifetime Exemption = $2 million net taxable estate x 40% tax rate = $800,000.

4. There is a serial remarriage prevention clause in the new death tax law. Say you file your deceased spouse's estate tax return to pick up her $5 million Lifetime Exemption. Subsequently, you marry again and then your second spouse dies. In such a case, the IRS will cancel your pick-up of your first spouse's Lifetime Exemption even though you timely filed her estate tax return.

But, don't go full-blown yet with your anti-IRS tirade. Even though you lost your pick-up of your first spouse's Lifetime Exemption, the IRS will permit you to pick up your second spouse's Lifetime Exemption, assuming she has not used up her Lifetime Exemption by making gifts before she met you. And in the midst of your mourning your second spouse's death and lamenting your fate of having two spouses die on you, you have to engage in yet another inventorying process for yet another estate tax return to pick up that Lifetime Exemption.

34

"How Does the IRS Know How Much I'm Worth When I Die?"

or

If Your Children Don't Tell— They May Go to Jail!

---

1. "Dad just died and Mom is alive. What do we do now?"

When a parent dies, nine times out of ten it is Dad who dies first, leaving Mom as the sole owner of the family home, the apartment building, the stocks, the bonds—anything that was jointly owned between them.

When Dad dies and his wealth share goes to Mom, the IRS does not impose a death tax if Mom is a citizen of the United States. If Mom is not a citizen, a death tax may be due when Dad dies.

If the value of Dad's wealth share exceeds a certain amount (called the "Lifetime Exemption," which is discussed in question 5 below), the IRS wants to know about it in the form of a "Death Inventory," which is a detailed list of everything Dad owned when he died. (I discuss this inventory in questions 3 and 4 below.) If Dad's wealth share is valued at less than the Lifetime Exemption, no Death Inventory is required.

2. "Dad died ten years ago and Mom just passed away. What happens now with us and the IRS?"

When Mom dies, the children (or other heirs) must deal with the IRS because:

1) If the value of Mom's assets exceeds the Lifetime Exemption (discussed in question 5 below), the IRS must be advised of what Mom owned when she died; and

2) If the value of Mom's assets exceeds the Lifetime Exemption, the IRS will receive a share of those assets in the form of a death tax.

3. "What do we do if Mom died with assets exceeding the Lifetime Exemption?"

Within nine months after Mom dies (and a possible extension), the IRS requires that someone (typically, one of Mom's children) file an Estate Tax Return. In English, this is a Death Inventory, a list of everything Mom owned when she died. From this Death Inventory, the IRS assesses the death tax that is due.

4. "What information goes in this Death Inventory?"

Literally everything Mom owned or had an interest in when she died. And to the IRS, everything means *everything*:

Mom's "Bank Assests"
Mom's children must list on this Death Inventory the date-of-death value of all Mom's bank assets. This typically includes bank accounts, certificates of deposit, checking accounts, and cash.

Mom's Securities
On this Death Inventory, there is a separate schedule for the children to list Mom's stocks, bonds, Mutual Funds, Treasury Bills, and other security assets.

Mom's Personal Property

Mom's children must list the appraised value of Mom's personal property, such as cars, jewelry, fur coats, pictures, paintings, and any other tangible personal assets.

Mom's "Death Benefit" Accounts

If Mom owned any life insurance policies, annuities, IRA accounts, pension plans, 410(k) plans, and any other asset that pays a death benefit, the value of these assets and/or the death benefits are listed.

Mom's Real Estate

Mom's children must list the fair market value of all the real estate that Mom owned or had a share in when she died. How will the children know what Mom's real estate was worth? They hire and pay an appraiser who makes an appraisal report, which the children will send to the IRS.

It's ironic. Mom's children have to pay an appraiser to appraise Mom's real estate so they can determine the amount of death tax they have to pay on it. It's as if the children are pulling the lever on their own guillotine.

This appraisal report may not be the final word as to the value of Mom's real estate. If the IRS believes that the real property was worth more, they will hire their own appraiser, who will invariably appraise at a higher value. And the higher the appraised value, the more the death tax. To avoid "appraisal wars" with the IRS, the appraisal report should be a reasonably accurate reflection of the value of Mom's real estate at the time of her death.

Mom's Miscellaneous Assets

In the Death Inventory, Mom's children must list any of Mom's business interests, limited partnership interests, the contents of safe deposit boxes, coin and stamp collections, unusual works of art, and any other asset Mom owned or in which Mom had an interest.

Anything Mom Owned Jointly with Someone Else

Mom's children must list any asset Mom owned jointly with anyone else. Why? Because the IRS presumes that Mom owned 100 percent of any jointly owned asset.

For example, if Mom had a joint bank account with a child, the IRS says the account all belongs to Mom. If the child wants to fight the IRS on this presumption, the child has the burden of proof. It is up to the child to show that Mom was on the account for convenience only or that Mom made no contribution to the account.

This presumption can produce cruel results, especially with real estate. A common example is when Mom goes on title to her child's house (with her child) so her child could qualify for a home loan. If Mom dies with her name still on the Deed, guess what? *The IRS will presume that 100 percent of the house equity belongs to Mom!* The IRS will then attempt to list the house in Mom's Death Inventory and impose a death tax on its value.

This presumption can be rebutted, but who wants to fight the IRS? It's best to clear up this title problem before Mom dies.

5. "After the IRS receives the Death Inventory, then what happens?"

Ultimately, the IRS taxes the combined value of all the assets (less deductions) listed in Mom's Death Inventory. Whatever the total is, a certain amount will go to Mom's children tax-free. This amount is called the Lifetime Exemption, and it is the maximum amount Mom can leave to the children without a death tax.

As it stands in 2014, the year of the publication of this revised edition, Mom's Lifetime Exemption is at least $5,340,000, which will adjust annually. Thus, Mom's children will pay a death tax on the value of assets over the Lifetime Exemption. For example, if Mom dies in 2014 and her Death Inventory shows a value of $6 million, there is no tax on the first $5,340,000. The tax on the remaining $660,000 is approximately $264,000.

The richer Mom is, the more the death tax. If her Death Inventory shows $7 million, the death tax will be approximately $664,000.00. If it shows $8 million, the death tax will be $1,064,000. If the Death Inventory shows Mom owned $9 million when she died, the death tax will be $1,464,000.

6. "I know how I'll beat the IRS. I'll give away my property to my children while I'm alive. When I die, I won't own anything."

Great idea! But it just won't work!

If you thought you could beat the death tax trap by gifting what you own while you are alive, think again. If this were the case, then everyone would make lifetime gifts and the IRS would never get its share.

So when you die and your children prepare your Death Inventory, your children must list the value of any gifts you and your spouse ever made to anyone while you were alive (except for the Annual Exclusion Gifts, which I discuss in detail in chapter 36).

For example, if you and your spouse gifted $100,000 to your son for the down payment of a house twenty years ago, the IRS will require this amount to be in the Death Inventory. This $100,000 becomes a value upon which the death tax applies.

7. "Ten years ago, my wife and I gave $50,000 to my daughter so she could start a business. How will the IRS find out about that?"

Clients invariably ask how the IRS will find out about a substantial gift they made to their children or grandchildren so long ago. The answer is that unless someone tells, the IRS may never know.

Unquestionably, children will conveniently forget what their parents gave them twenty years ago, until I tell them the consequences of forgetting. Whoever signs the Death Inventory signs it under "penalty of perjury." If the IRS discovers any large gifts you made that your children did not list on the Death Inventory, they could be subject to IRS penalties, interest, criminal fines, and even jail.

How will the IRS discover these unreported gifts? Consider the following scenarios:

1) A Child Divorces

If your son and his wife divorce, the first thing she will say to her divorce lawyer is that your son didn't report the $50,000 you gave him so he could start up a business. She will either report your son to the IRS or use this tasty bit of information to extort a better divorce settlement.

2) A Child's Revenge

When it comes to blood wars between siblings, all bets are off—even if it means a child turns himself in to the IRS.

On one occasion, my client died and a major fallout developed between his children after they inherited the family business. The sister was so irate at her brother that she told on him to the IRS. She reported that she and her brother did not list on the Death Inventory the $250,000 they each received from my client years before.

Certainly, this sister was cutting off her nose to spite her face. However, she felt her fury had no other outlet but to bring the IRS down on her brother.

The sister tried to minimize the damage to herself by cutting a deal. In exchange for telling the IRS what she knew, she wanted to avoid criminal prosecution. Did the IRS go along with her proposal? You bet it did! The IRS believes that something is better than nothing.

3) A Child's Income Tax Audit

Assume that before you died, you gave your child an apartment building or other income-producing asset. After you die, your child forgets to report this gift on the Death Inventory.

The statistical average is small that your son's income tax return will be audited by the IRS. But if your son is among the lucky few, this will be the scene when the IRS agent interviews him:

IRS Agent: It looks like you saw some income from an apartment building. But I don't see that building on

your previous tax returns. How did you get that
building anyway?

Your Son: Help!

8. "Where will my children get the money to pay the death tax?"

The death tax usually comes directly out of what you own at the
time of your death. The more you own, the happier the IRS. If your
children do not have the cash to pay the death taxes when you
die, they may have to sell your real estate or other noncash assets
to raise the tax money. If this occurs, your children will pay commissions and/or sales costs *on top of* the death tax.

When I told this to one client, he said, "Mr. Condon, it seems
all I'm doing is managing one-half of my apartment building for
the IRS. I collect the rents, pay the property taxes, manage the
building, deal with crazy tenants, handle the evictions, and maintain the place. And not only will the IRS get half, they don't even
pay me a manager's fee."

My client is absolutely correct. His silent partner is the IRS.

9. "What can I do to fight back so that more of my money and property goes to my children and less to the IRS?"

The inevitable question my clients ask is whether there is anything that can be done to reduce this tax. This topic is explored
in chapter 36.

35

Pay the Death Tax or Fight Back—
Which One Sounds Like You?

<u>or</u>

"I'm Not Crazy About My Kids—
but I Hate the IRS Even More"

---

1. "I knew there was a death tax on my children's inheritance, but I never thought much about it until I talked with my lawyer. It seems I spent my life working just so the IRS can end up with one-half of what I own when I die."

During the last four presidential campaigns, the death tax became a much-discussed topic in the media and among the electorate. But prior to that time, I believe that relatively few people were aware of its existence. How do I know this? Because during the first twenty years of my inheritance-planning practice, many of my clients told me they first learned about the death tax when I told them about it.

You probably know from this book and recent media that the death tax is a tax on what you own when you die. Beyond that basic knowledge, the concept of the death tax probably has little current reality in your life. Like most of my clients, you may treat it as something to learn about and deal with in the distant future.

Let me tell you something. Until the president puts pen on

paper and completely repeals the death tax, the future is now! If you own more than $5,340,000 and you don't do something before you die, you may have voluntarily allowed the IRS to take a portion of your wealth in death taxes.

The death tax is not fun and games. It is paid in real dollars that come from what you have acquired and earned throughout your life. The IRS wants these dollars nine months after you die. Your children can always apply for an extension, but they pay interest on the amount of the tax owed. And what's more, if you are rich enough, your wealth may be taxed again when your child dies.

Extremist Attitudes

After reading chapter 34, you will have some idea of what your death tax will be when you die. Whatever you estimate the tax to be, are you going to do something about it?

It all depends on your attitude . . . and how you feel about lawyers. After forty years of practice, I have found there are four types of taxpayers. Which one sounds like you?

The "Do-Nothing" Taxpayer

I have known dozens of clients who do absolutely nothing to reduce the death tax, even with their knowledge that it will be substantial. Although I am a bit jaded after practicing in this field for so many years, I continue to be astounded by this attitude. Why would people willingly give more than necessary to the IRS when they die?

The most common reason is hatred of paying money to lawyers. For example, I had one client who would let $250,000 in death taxes go to the IRS rather than pay me a fee to come up with a plan to reduce it. As he stated, "I'm not crazy, Condon. I hate paying the death tax. But that won't kick in until after I die. What hurts during my life is throwing money at you to create a plan that's expensive to create, expensive to maintain, and will cause me more bookkeeping hassles than it's worth. I swear, I think you lawyers dreamed up this tax just to fill your pockets."

It's not always about the perception of greedy lawyers. Here are a few more reasons I have heard why people do nothing to reduce the death tax:

"I dislike the IRS, but I hate my kids even more."

"I don't give a damn how much the IRS takes when I die. If I can die knowing that my wife is cared for, I'll be happy. My children will just take less, and be thankful they get anything."

"America has been good to me. I have no objection to giving something back to America when I die."

"It's not my problem. It's my kids' problem. If they want a plan to reduce the tax, let *them* deal with it."

The Passive Taxpayer

Most of my clients fall into this category. They do simple things to reduce the death tax, such as setting up a Living Trust with provisions that preserve the Lifetime Exemption of the first spouse to die. But beyond that, they have willingly accepted that the IRS will get a portion of their wealth when they die.

Why this passive attitude? Some clients are apathetic about the death tax. Some clients don't want to deal with death issues. And some clients do not like the death-tax-reducing strategies, which mostly involve giving up control of some of their wealth before they die.

The Fight-Back Taxpayer

These clients look at the death tax as the final "bully" of their lives, and are not going to allow themselves to be beaten without a fight. As more than a few clients have told me, "Jerry, it's just so unfair to tax the same money twice. I've paid income taxes on money I've earned. I've paid capital gains taxes on assets I've sold. Why should I pay again after I die?"

These clients welcome aggressive planning techniques to reduce their death taxes. Although many of these plans require giving up control of wealth during their lives, they do so willingly so that most of their wealth will end up with their children and grandchildren, with the IRS being the ultimate loser.

The "Do-Anything" Taxpayer

These clients come into my office and boldly pronounce that they want their death taxes eliminated by any means necessary. They don't care what kind of plan I come up with, its ramifications, or even whether or not it is legal. All they want to know is where to sign.

I remember one client who came into my office with an almost tangible air of desperation. Before he sat down, he signed a blank check, ripped it from his checkbook, threw it on my desk, and shouted, "Condon, I don't care what it costs. Give me 'Star Wars'! Just tell me when and where to sign. I want every conceivable plan so that not one more dollar than necessary will go to the IRS when I die."

From a financial standpoint, I love these types of clients. But from a planning perspective, I prefer a more mature, deliberate, and informed process.

2. "I don't want my children to think I was an old fool by not doing something to reduce the death tax. I know I should do something. But if the solution involves losing control of my money, I'm not so sure I want to do anything."

In chapter 36, I offer a checklist of planning opportunities you can incorporate in your inheritance plan to reduce the death tax. Many of these require you to give up immediate control of some of your wealth to your children and grandchildren before you die.

If you are the fight-back taxpayer, this is no big deal. Better, you think, that your children get the money than the IRS. However, for many of you, the idea of giving up some of your wealth before you die is unthinkable, even if it means more will go to the IRS than to your children and grandchildren.

Certainly, this reasoning is understandable. As we age, we lose control of many things precious to us: our sight, hearing, ability to drive, mental faculties, and even our children. However, no matter what happens to us, we know there is one thing we can control: our money.

And to some people, losing control of their money is the death knell of their lives.

Fighting Back Is Good, But . . .

To reduce the death tax, you must develop an attitude to fight back. The clients who save the most for their children are those who do not willingly accept the IRS getting a share of what they own.

However, I do not suggest you do anything you feel uncomfortable with, nor should you gift yourself into poverty. If you simply don't want to part with your money, that is the end of it. It is my hope, however, that you will find among the ideas in chapter 37 a workable solution to your death-tax problem.

If you cannot do it for your sake, perhaps you will do it for your children's. The most regrettable refrain I hear from my clients' children comes up when both Dad and Mom have died, and they write that long-dreaded check to the IRS. As they tear it from their checkbook and place it on my desk, they look at me and ask, "Why couldn't our parents have done something?"

36

How to Leave More to Your Children and Less to the IRS

or

Patriotism Does Not Require That You Pay More in Death Taxes

Throughout this book, I have addressed the human conflicts, problems, and realities you should consider before preparing your Will or Living Trust. But now it is time to focus on the money side. A vital component in the right way of leaving money to children is to ensure that more of what you own goes to your children, and less to the IRS.

In this chapter, I discuss eleven planning opportunities you can use individually or in combination to reduce or eliminate the death tax. They are:

1) Not banking money for the IRS.

2) Using annual tax-free gifts to your children, grandchildren, and others.

3) Using up your Lifetime Exemption while you are alive or preserving it so it can be used after you die.

4) The House Trust.

5) The Family Real Estate Limited Partnership.

6) The Charitable Remainder Trust and other charitable giving techniques.

7) Using life insurance to provide the money to pay the death tax.

8) The "Deathbed Power of Attorney."

9) Retained Income Trusts.

10) The Generation-Skipping Exemption Trust.

11) Sales to children and the Self-canceling Installment Note.

Before I discuss these methods in detail, I feel it is vital to make four brief points:

- The only purpose of this chapter is to identify and briefly summarize the concept of these tax-reducing opportunities so that you can discuss them in detail with your own inheritance-planning attorney.

- This is not an exclusive list. Numerous other death-tax-planning opportunities may be available to you. The methods in this chapter are the ones I most commonly advise for my clients.

- It is imperative you consult with an experienced inheritance-planning attorney before you embark on any of these methods. He or she will review these methods with you and focus on the ones that will be the most comfortable for you and compatible with your particular situation.

- For purposes of this chapter, I shall assume that you and all the people in my examples are in the 40 percent death-tax bracket.

Planning Opportunity Number 1: Don't Bank Money for the IRS—Try Harder to Spend Money

ATTORNEY CONDON: So, Mrs. Green, are you taking my advice and spending more of your money? Remember, the less you own, the less the death tax will be.

CLIENT: Jerry, I'm really trying, but it's just so hard. I never learned to spend money.

ATTORNEY CONDON: Try harder!!

This is a conversation I had with eighty-year-old Mrs. Green. Almost every dollar she received from Social Security, her late husband's retirement fund, and her investment income went straight to her bank and brokerage accounts.

Why did I advise Mrs. Green to spend? Because for each dollar she did not spend, the IRS would get fifty cents when she died.

"Mrs. Green," I told her, "when you deposit your income in the bank, all you are doing is banking money for the IRS. So start spending more. Forget the early-bird dinner. Put your children and grandchildren on a plane and take everyone first class to Hawaii. Buy a new car. Go on a cruise. Pay your grandchildren's college expenses. You're only spending the IRS's money."

Mrs. Green, however, just could not follow my advice. She is far from being alone. Many people are prisoners of their past and simply cannot shed their old spending habits. If they've always gone for the early-bird dinner, they will not spend $100 for the same meal.

Some of my clients tell me, "Mr. Condon, I really want to spend more. But I want to know I have my money for a rainy day." And some clients tell me, "I want to be sure I have money for my doctors if I become ill."

To that, I say this: The rainy day is long behind you, and let your doctors worry about getting paid. When you get to the time in your life when the death horizon years can be measured in single digits, continuing to accumulate savings you don't need serves no purpose (other than some deep psychological need to accumulate).

Unless you need your income for support, why save for the IRS? Better you spend your money on yourself, your children, and your grandchildren.

Planning Opportunity Number 2: Give Your Money or Property Tax-Free to Your Children (and/or Grandchildren) While You Are Alive

The death tax is based on what you own when you die. The less you own, the less the tax. One way to own less is to give away some of your money and property while you are alive.

As noted previously, there is a law I call the Annual Exclusion Gift law. Basically, it says that in each calendar year, you can give up to $14,000 to as many individuals as you wish tax-free. For most of us, this means a child, grandchild, son-in-law, or daughter-in-law.

For each $14,000 gift you make, that is $14,000 you won't own when you die, saving $5,600 from the IRS in death taxes.

This is how to play the Annual Exclusion Gift game. But first, my locker-room pep talk: This method is a simple plan that can significantly reduce what you own when you die. Why not take advantage of this opportunity? After all, your children and grandchildren will get it when you die. Why not give some of it to them now—tax-free?!

The Rules of the Game

A) Every calendar year, you can transfer $14,000 of value to any recipient you desire.
B) You can gift to as many recipients as you wish. However, rare is the person who will make these gifts to anyone other than children and grandchildren.
C) If you are married, you and your spouse can together transfer $28,000 to each recipient.

The Benefits of Playing

A) You pay no gift tax.
B) Your recipients pay no income tax.
C) Each Annual Exclusion Gift does not come off your Lifetime Exemption.

D) Neither you nor your recipient has to report the gift to the IRS.

E) For each $14,000 gift you make, you prevent $5,600 from going to the IRS in death taxes.

How to Play the Game

- The Annual Exclusion Gift can be as simple as writing a check once a year for $14,000 and handing it to the recipient. The gift does not have to be cash. You can give each recipient up to $14,000 worth of stocks, jewelry, cars, partial interests in real estate, insurance policies, or anything else of economic value.

- If your children or grandchildren are minors, you can still make Annual Exclusion Gifts to them, but under the Custodian laws of your state or in an Irrevocable Gift Trust.

How You Win the Game

For each $14,000 Annual Exclusion Gift you make, you deny the IRS $5,600 in death taxes when you die.

How You Lose the Game

- You gift your way into poverty.

- If you expect your children will give it back to you if you need it, don't hold your breath. It is better you keep your money and let your children pay the death tax than have to face the possibility of relying on your children for support.

- If you give your child a partial interest of real estate or other nondivisible assets, you increase the risk of loss of that share because of your child's creditors, divorces, bankruptcies, judgments, and income tax liabilities.

You Are Eligible to Play If . . .

You have surplus income property that you don't need, won't need, and won't miss.

Another Way to Play

In addition to the Annual Exclusion Gifts, you can give away money tax-free by paying *directly* your children's and grand-children's medical and education expenses. This means that when the payments become due, you must make the checks payable to the hospital or school.

Planning Opportunity Number 3: Use Your Lifetime Exemption While You Are Alive—Preserve It So It Can Be Used After You Die

While you are alive, you can transfer money or property equal to your $5,340,000 Lifetime Exemption without one penny of gift tax. This method is commonly known as using up your Lifetime Exemption (I introduce and discuss the Lifetime Exemption in question 5 of chapter 34).

Think of this method as $5,340,000 of money or property in a barrel. While you are alive, you can dip into this barrel and give away some or all of the $5,340,000 to anyone you want and whenever you want, tax-free. However, this barrel is not renewable. Once the barrel is empty, it's empty forever. Once the $5,340,000 exemption is gone, it's gone.

If you are married, you and your spouse each have a barrel of $5,340,000. Each of you can give away during your lives $5,340,000 apiece (a total of $10,680,000) tax-free.

The Advantage

The primary advantage of gifting $5,340,000 in money or property while you are alive is that the income and appreciation on the gifted asset is not part of what you own when you die.

For example, suppose that right now you have an estate of $5 million, which includes a $1 million apartment building. If you die ten years from now with the building appreciated to $2 million, the IRS will impose a death tax on that $1 million appreciation. But if you give away the building now, when it is worth $1 million, the $1 million appreciation will not be taxed when you die because you don't own the building.

The result is that you save your children approximately $400,000 in death taxes.

Using the Lifetime Exemption After You Die

If you are an unmarried person and you don't use all of your $5,340,000 Lifetime Exemption while you are alive, you don't lose it after you die. What's left of the $5,340,000 in your barrel at your death will automatically pass to your heirs tax-free.

If you are married, you and your spouse both have your respective $5,340,000 Lifetime Exemptions. But, do not make the incorrect assumption that you and your spouse automatically can pass a combined $10,680,000 to your children without any death tax.

Like most married couples in America, you and your spouse probably hold title to the family assets jointly. If you die first, your spouse will inherit your half of the family money. And the second your spouse inherits your half of the family money, you will have lost your ability to leave up to $5,340,000 to your children tax-free. Since your Lifetime Exemption doesn't automatically "live on" after you die, only your surviving spouse's $5,340,000 remains, and she can leave up to $5,340,000 of the family money to the children tax-free. If your surviving spouse owns less than $5,340,000 on her death, this is not a big deal. But if she owns more, there will be a death tax on the excess.

Your goal is to preserve BOTH you and your spouse's Lifetime Exemptions so that up to $10,680,000 will pass to your children without any death tax.

How is this goal achieved? After the first spouse dies, something must be done by the surviving spouse to ensure the survival of the deceased spouse's Lifetime Exemption. And wouldn't you know it? The new death tax law enacted in 2013 talks about that "something."

The "Something": Your Surviving Spouse Picks Up Your $5,340,000 Lifetime Exemption and Adds It to Her $5,340,000 Lifetime Exemption

Assume you and your spouse own a combined $10,680,000 or less. You die first. Within 9 months of your death, your surviving spouse shall file your federal estate tax return (which I refer to in chapter 34 as your "Death Inventory").

Beginning in 2013, this Death Inventory comes with special section called "Election of Portability".

This new section in your federal estate tax return has a box for your surviving spouse to check off that states, in essence, "Yes, in fact, I WOULD like to take my poor deceased spouse's $5,250,00 Lifetime Exemption, or whatever amount of it that remained at his death." After your surviving spouse timely (meaning, within 9 months after your death) sends that return to the IRS, she will have magically picked up your Lifetime Exemption and added it to her Lifetime Exemption of $5,340,000. That's all there is to it. No fuss, no muss. As a result, your wife can leave all of the family assets (up to the full amount of those now-combined Lifetime Exemptions) to your children without one penny of death tax.

I discuss this in more detail in chapter 33 when describing

how the 2013 increase in the Lifetime Exemption to $5,340,000 effectively wiped out the death tax in America.

But . . . What About the A-B Trust?

For as long as there has been the death tax, there has been this method that is designed to preserve the Lifetime Exemption of the first spouse to die (which, for purposes of following this discussion, is you). You have heard this referred to as the A-B Trust or the Exemption Trust, or the Credit Shelter Trust, or the Credit Trust, or something of similar nature.

Whatever the name, you likely have these provisions in your Living Trust that provide that on your death, your half of the trust estate will be allocated to a separate "account." During your surviving spouse's life, she gets to use and manage the assets in this separate account for the rest of her life. And upon your surviving spouse's death, the assets in this separate account will be distributed to your children with no death tax. Why? Because your surviving spouse is NOT considered the owner of the assets in this separate account. And if she doesn't own them, the IRS cannot impose a death tax on them when she dies.

However, to implement this plan correctly, your surviving spouse must jump through some burdensome hoops for the rest of her life (which are discussed below) in order to achieve the goal of preventing the assets in that account from being subject to death taxes. With those hassles and limitations, and in light of your surviving spouse having the newly enacted ability to pick up your Lifetime Exemption after your death by simply signing and filing a form, why resort to this seemingly archaic method?

I must admit, I did not initially have a good response to this inquiry, and was about to eliminate this entire section about the A-B Trust. After all, why confuse you with ancient history when grasping the new stuff is difficult enough? But as I was about to redline these paragraphs out of existence, I thought of two decent reasons to keep this stuff in.

The first is, say you and your spouse have a combined $15 million estate. (Hey, if that's the case, you're not reading this book because you have your own hot-shot inheritance attorney on retainer to handle this stuff for you. But humor me!)

So, an estate of a combined $15 million. Your half is $7.5 million. You die first and your wife completes and files your estate tax return to preserve your $5,340,000 Lifetime Exemption. Your spouse then allocates the remaining portion of your half (which is $2,160,000) to the separate account. Because your spouse has picked up your entire $5,340,000 Lifetime Exemption by filing that return, this excess of your half ($2,160,000) will be part of your spouse's taxable estate on her death—even though it's in that separate account. But any appreciation on that excess between your death and your spouse's death will not be included in your spouse's taxable estate when she dies.

That method is what we inheritance lawyers call "freezing" your assets. Meaning, we make it so your assets do not have appreciation that would otherwise be subject to a death tax on your spouse's death.

Two, a law is only permanent until Congress decides to change it. As the struggle in Washington, D.C., continues to keep incoming revenues up to speed with the insane amount of government spending, Congress may very well be forced to once again lower the Lifetime Exemption. If that occurs, then the A-B Trust becomes VERY relevant yet again.

So . . . with those two justifications in mind, take a look at the instructions in your husband-and-wife Living Trust that establish this separate account when the first spouse dies. Since women statistically outlive their husbands, and in order to convey this concept simply and with real-world perspective, I will assume that you, the reader, are the husband, and that you've died with your wife surviving you. And I will refer to this separate account that contains all or a portion of your share of the family wealth as "Dad's Tax-Free Account."

Basically, those instructions state three functions of the account after your death and during your surviving wife's life:

1. Your wife receives the income from the account, which she keeps, invests, and spends on anything and everything she desires.

2. Your wife gets to spend the principal from the account for her health and support, which is usually defined as the amount of assets necessary and reasonable to provide her with a comfortable standard of living..

3. Your wife gets to wheel and deal with the assets in the account (buy, sell, trade, refinance, invest, borrow against—whatever) in any way she wishes.

With all of your wife's power and control over the assets in Dad's Tax-Free Account, it appears that she owns those assets. However, she is NOT the owner of the assets in that account. Yes, she gets the income and the ability to "dip" into the principal, and the managerial power over the assets, just like any owner of property. But the real owner is still YOU, the deceased spouse.

In other words, you are the owner of the assets in the account, and your wife is merely the authorized user of those assets for the rest of her life. And if your wife doesn't own them the IRS cannot impose a death tax on them when she dies.

So how can this be the case? Because when your wife allocated your half of the Living Trust assets to Dad's Tax-Free Account, she transferred assets that were "painted" with your Lifetime Exemption amount. The effect of that paint job is the assets in Dad's Tax-Free Account do not belong to your wife. Instead, those assets stay in Dad's Tax-Free Account for the rest of your wife's life. And when your wife dies, the assets in Dad's Tax-Free Account will pass to your children (or other beneficiaries) with no death tax. In effect, Dad's Tax-Free Account has preserved your Lifetime Exemption.

What's more, any appreciation or growth in the assets in Dad's Tax-Free Account will also go to your Living Trust beneficiaries tax-free. In other words, if the "root of the tree" is tax-free, the "fruit of the tree" is tax-free.

This is a pretty nifty trick, ay? Dad's Tax-Free Account will, like magic, prevent your share of the Living Trust assets, and the appreciation on those assets, from being death taxed when your wife dies. But, like any magical illusion, there is some effort the magician must make in order for it to work. If the "trick" doesn't work, then the IRS will deem your wife to be the owner of the assets in Dad's Tax-Free Account—and this account will not work as a death tax prevention mechanism. Here is a brief sketch of those required steps:

1. Your wife will need to file a separate income tax return each year for Dad's Tax-Free Account if those assets generate income. Like any corporate or business entity, Dad's Tax-Free Account is considered a separate person for income tax purposes. And like any person, it files its own income tax returns—for the rest of your wife's life.

2. All assets in Dad's Tax-Free Account must be vested in the name of Dad's Tax-Free Account. This means that your wife has to retitle the bank assets and brokerage assets that she allocates to Dad's Tax-Free Account. If she is transferring all or a portion of real estate to Dad's Tax-Free Account, the deed to that property must reflect the new ownership.

3. All income generated by Dad's Tax-Free Account cannot be allowed to sit and accumulate in Dad's Tax-Free Account. The income must, instead, be taken out and transferred to your wife's accounts. So . . . your wife has to arrange with your property manager, bank representative, and brokerage officer to have all income (dividends, rent, interest, etc.) automatically transferred to her accounts.

4. Your wife has to keep the assets in the name of Dad's Tax-Free Account at all times, no matter what form those assets subsequently take. This means she has to trace assets in Dad's Tax-Free Account from one form to the next. For example, say your wife allocates your share of the family home to Dad's Tax-Free Account. Your wife later sells the house for $500,000 and puts those sale proceeds in the bank. She has to open up two accounts: one for $250,000 in her name as "trustee" of Dad's Tax-

Free Account, and the other in her name (or in the name of your Living Trust).

5. Your wife cannot give away assets in Dad's Tax-Free Account. Sure, she can wheel and deal with them as often as she wants, and she can use them for her health and support, but she cannot make gifts of them.

6. Your wife cannot use the assets in Dad's Tax-Free Account for anything other than her health or support. This is huge. If she is caught using these assets for any purpose other than her support or health, or if her support expenditures go beyond what is reasonably necessary for her support, the IRS will take away the tax-free status of Dad's Tax-Free Account. If that occurs, the IRS will include the assets in Dad's Tax-Free Account as part of the assets your wife owns on her death—and subject them to death taxes. (Your wife may also be sued by your children—the beneficiaries of Dad's Tax-Free Account after her death—for making "dips" into the principal for unpermitted purposes; but that's a whole different issue.)

What is considered a "violation" of the support standard? The IRS gives no guidance. It decides these matters based on the circumstances of each case. But there are some obvious universal truths. Is it reasonable to use principal for food? Of course! Food would be considered a reasonable support expenditure in any context. But . . . would it be reasonable to travel to England on a monthly basis for some incredible fish-and-chips at the Bull & Dungeon Pub? Hardly.

I suppose the only guideline I could give your wife on recognizing whether a support expenditure is reasonable is this bit of existentialism. As your wife contemplates making an expenditure, she should step outside herself and see it from a third-party vantage point. What does she see? An expenditure that appears aboveboard—or one that just doesn't pass the smell test? If she harbors any doubt on the answer to that question, then her proposed expenditure probably constitutes an unreasonable invasion of principal in Dad's Tax-Free Account for support.

7. While your assets are in Dad's Tax-Free Account, your wife's share of the Living Trust assets are contained in another account called the "Survivor's Trust." And until your wife exhausts her Survivor's Trust assets, she cannot use the principal of Dad's Tax-Free Account for her support or health.

Harsh, but true! For as long as there are assets in your wife's Survivor's Trust, she cannot touch the principal of Dad's Tax-Free Account for her needs. And since it is likely that your wife may never spend down her Survivor's Trust assets, she may never be able to resort to the principal of Dad's Tax-Free Account for any purpose. As a result, the principal of Dad's Tax-Free Account will literally just sit there until your wife dies and it's distributed to your children.

Wow! Those seven steps to make this arrangement valid and effective are a lot of work. Well, no one said this trick would be easy. But, as I say to my clients, once it's done, it's done. And if you have done the job right, you will save your family perhaps tens of thousands, maybe hundreds of thousands of dollars in death taxes when both you and your wife have died.

Planning Opportunity Number 4: The House Trust

Congress has passed a special law designed to reduce the death tax on the family home. We lawyers implement this law in a special trust known as the "House Trust."

This is how the House Trust comes into play.

You are a widow or widower and live in a $500,000 house, which you expect to appreciate in value before you die. If you live long enough, you may see your house appreciate to $800,000. But when you die, the IRS will take up to 40 percent of the house's full value in death taxes.

There is a way to lessen the death-tax bite on your home. It is a magical pill that allows you to give away *now* your home's future appreciation. This pill is called the House Trust, and here is how it works.

You transfer title of your $500,000 home to the House Trust. The House Trust will own your home for the next ten years (or other term). Since the House Trust owns your house, any appreciation on your home will be attributed to the House Trust and not to you.

If your $500,000 home is worth $800,000 when you die, the entire $300,000 growth remains tax-free, saving your children up to $120,000 in death taxes.

Another Advantage of the House Trust

This House Trust provides you with another death-tax savings opportunity. Not only does it remove the growth from your house, it discounts the present market value of your house for gift-tax purposes.

When you give away a $500,000 house but retain the right to live there, you have devalued the amount of the gift. After all, a house in which the occupant has the right to live for ten years (or other term) is certainly less valuable than a vacant house you could move into tomorrow.

The Catches

There are two catches to the use of the House Trust:

1. You Cannot Die Before the House Trust Ends

For the House Trust to work, you must be alive at the end of ten years (or other term). If you die before the term expires, the IRS will consider your house as part of your estate and, thus, will impose a death tax on its value as of your date of death.

2. Your Children Get the House When the House Trust Ends

At the end of ten years (or other term), the House Trust will dissolve and your children will assume the title to your house. If you want to remain in your house for the rest of your life, you must pay your children the fair rental value. If you stay but do not pay rent, the IRS may tax the house in your estate when you die.

Paying your children rent is not as bad as it sounds. By paying rent, you remove dollars from your possession. And the more you spend, the less your children will have to pay in death taxes when you die.

Planning Opportunity Number 5: The Family Real Estate Limited Partnership

I refer to this as a real estate partnership because most of my clients are real estate oriented. However, the subject of the partnership can be any type of investment asset, alone or in conjunction with real estate.

The Family Real Estate Limited Partnership is a popular way of reducing the death tax. If you combine the Living Trust and the Family Real Estate Limited Partnership, you will have attained a high level of family inheritance planning.

The most dramatic way I can explain how the Family Real Estate Limited Partnership can reduce your death tax is to tell you how Mrs. Ortiz implemented it in her inheritance plan. Since I established this plan when the Lifetime Exemption was $1 million and the Annual Exclusion Gift was $10,000 I will explain it using those numbers.

Over four generations, the Ortiz family had acquired various pieces of commercial and residential real estate in Los Angeles. Eventually, all of it came to rest with Mrs. Ortiz. When she first met with me, her real estate wealth came to approximately $7 million. If she did not do something, the IRS would take 50 percent of the value less her $1 million Lifetime Exemption when she died.

I explained that this tax could be reduced if she owned less real estate. She could own less by giving portions of it away to her children, grandchildren, and great-grandchildren using the tax-free Annual Exclusion Gifts I discuss in Planning Opportunity #2.

Mrs. Ortiz had eight children, twenty grandchildren, and six great-grandchildren—thirty-four potential recipients. If she gave a $10,000 share of real estate every year to each one, she could annually shift $340,000 worth of real estate wealth from her name tax-free, saving $170,000 in death taxes.

A Few Doubts

Notwithstanding the death-tax-reducing benefits, Mrs. Ortiz had a few nagging doubts about making these gifts.

Primarily, Mrs. Ortiz was concerned about losing control of her real estate. She asked me, "Mr. Condon, what could happen to my properties once I give away some of them to my family?"

The answer I gave was not encouraging. Once she made the gifts, her family would own portions of her property. This could be disadvantageous to Mrs. Ortiz because:

1) With thirty-four children, grandchildren, and great-grandchildren also on title, Mrs. Ortiz could not sell, refinance, or exchange her real estate without everyone's (and their spouses') signatures.

2) Once Mrs. Ortiz made the gifts to her family, each of the thirty-four recipients would be her co-owners, thereby subjecting her real estate to her co-owners' problems, such as creditors, divorces, income tax troubles, and other risks of loss.

Mrs. Ortiz was not going to give away portions of her real estate with these doubts looming in her head. But I told her how she could make these annual gifts with all these potential problems resolved.

The answer is in the Family Real Estate Limited Partnership.

The Ortiz Family Limited Partnership

Two meetings later, I had drafted "The Ortiz Family Limited Partnership." This document named Mrs. Ortiz as the sole General Partner. The next step was to give the Partnership some assets, so Mrs. Ortiz signed Deeds transferring most of her real estate into this Partnership.

Mrs. Ortiz started out as the 100 percent Limited Partner. She then gifted each of her children, grandchildren, and great-grandchildren a $10,000 Limited Partnership share. Instead of each of the thirty-four recipients receiving an outright ownership share of real estate, they were Limited Partners of a combined $340,000 share of the Ortiz Family Limited Partnership.

(For Mrs. Ortiz's grandchildren and great-grandchildren who were minors, their Limited Partnership shares went to their parents as Custodians under the Uniform Transfers to Minors Act.)

In January of the following year, Mrs. Ortiz transferred another $340,000 worth of Limited Partnership shares to each of her children, grandchildren, and great-grandchildren. Thereafter, Mrs. Ortiz repeated this gift annually, including the year she died with the help of the "Deathbed Power of Attorney" (which I discuss in Planning Opportunity #8).

Other Benefits of Mrs. Ortiz's Partnership

In addition to reducing the death tax, five other benefits were achieved with the Ortiz Family Real Estate Limited Partnership:

1) Mrs. Ortiz remained in sole control of the real estate because she retained 51 percent of the Limited Partnership shares.

2) As sole General Partner, only Mrs. Ortiz's signature was necessary if she wanted to sell, refinance, or exchange the Partnership property.

3) The Partnership documents prohibited her thirty-four recipients from cashing out or transferring their Limited Partnership shares. And even if there were no such restrictions, what could her recipients do with a piece of paper?

4) Mrs. Ortiz built up a tax-free fund of real estate for her children, grandchildren, and great-grandchildren.

5) When Mrs. Ortiz died, the IRS discounted the value of the Limited Partnership shares that she did not give away. Why? Because a Limited Partnership share of real estate is less valu-

able than a direct ownership in real estate. And the less the date-of-death value, the less the death tax.

(The amount of the IRS discount always depends on the astuteness of the appraiser and the persuasiveness of the attorney dealing with the IRS. But there should always be a discount of the ungifted Limited Partnership shares. I strongly urge you to consult with your accountant or inheritance-planning attorney about valuation discounts due to owning real estate in the form of a Limited Partnership.)

Planning Opportunity Number 6: Give Real Estate or Other Assets to Charity in Return for a Lifetime Income Stream—the Charitable Remainder Trust

When you die, the IRS will get a share of what you own. But if you leave part of what you own to a charity, that part goes without a death tax.

You can gift wealth to a charity while alive or after death in numerous ways. These range from outright gifts and bequests to complex arrangements that create lots of business for your lawyer and the charity's lawyers.

One method gaining notoriety is called the "Charitable Remainder Trust" (CRT). This relatively popular arrangement allows you to leave wealth to charity while converting your unproductive (or low profit) equity into a higher income stream *while also* avoiding a capital gains tax.

For further discussion of the CRT, see question 6 in chapter 32.

Planning Opportunity Number 7: Let the Insurance Company Pay the Death Tax—Pay the Death Tax Wholesale

Chapter 37 is devoted entirely to using life insurance as a way to provide your children with dollars to pay the death tax.

Planning Opportunity Number 8: The "Deathbed Power of Attorney"—the Last-Minute Planning Opportunity

This solution could have saved a lot of money for Mrs. Sweetzer's son. Again, I shall explain this method using the tax "numbers" in existence at the time it was employed, which are a $1 million Lifetime Exemption and a $10,000 Annual Exclusion Gift.

Mrs. Sweetzer owned about $1.5 million worth of real estate and cash. I told her if she did not take action, the IRS would take about 50 percent of it in death taxes when she died. But her response was, "I have to run, Mr. Condon. I'll call you and we'll discuss this later."

"Later" never came. Two years later, I got a call from Mrs. Sweetzer's son, who said that his mother only had a short time to live. He took his mother home from the hospital to die.

This call really surprised me. Mrs. Sweetzer was one of the most healthy and vibrant sixty-six-year-old ladies I had ever met. Unfortunately, the ravages of cancer had rapidly taken their toll. Now her son wanted to discuss what I had already tried to discuss with his mother—what to do about reducing the death tax.

Unfortunately, it was too late.

With his mother near death, not much could be done. But one way to reduce that tax was the Annual Exclusion Gift. I told the son that, as mercenary as it seemed, he should get his mother to sign a check for $10,000 to each child, grandchild, son-in-law, and daughter-in-law. The less she owned when she died, the less the death tax would be.

The son said that his mother was fading rapidly. She could barely move, let alone sign checks. A few days later, Mrs. Sweetzer died. Had she been able to make these gifts, her son could have saved $5,000 in death taxes for every $10,000 gift made.

It Doesn't Have to Be That Way

With increasing frequency, I receive these kinds of calls. Almost each time, Mom is usually too far gone to make last-minute Annual Exclusion Gifts to save death taxes.

But if you plan ahead, there is a way to give a child the authority to make last-minute Annual Exclusion Gifts *on your behalf*. To take advantage of this last-minute death-tax-savings opportunity, the following steps must be taken.

Step 1

While you are alive and competent, you must sign a Power of Attorney that specifically authorizes someone (usually one or more of your children) to make Annual Exclusion Gifts on your behalf. This someone is called your Attorney-in-Fact.

Warning! A Power of Attorney you buy at a stationery store will be insufficient because it will not contain a specific authorization to make these Annual Exclusion Gifts. Therefore, you should have your inheritance-planning lawyer prepare a Power of Attorney that includes the authority to make Annual Exclusion Gifts on your behalf.

In my office, this document is called the "Deathbed Power of Attorney." This document is not limited to deathbed giving, but that's when most of my clients don't mind parting with their wealth.

Step 2

In this Deathbed Power of Attorney, list all the people you want to receive $14,000 Annual Exclusion Gifts. Most likely, these will be your children and grandchildren, and perhaps their spouses.

Step 3

You must add your Attorney-in-Fact's name to a checking account, savings account, brokerage account, certificate of deposit, or other asset that has sufficient assets to make these

Annual Exclusion Gifts. Your Attorney-in-Fact can then withdraw the money from these accounts to make full use of the Annual Exclusion Gifts.

There are two important things to remember about this step:

- If your Attorney-in-Fact is not on the account, the bank or brokerage house may not allow the withdrawal.
- Your Attorney-in-Fact may not be able to withdraw money from the bank or brokerage account if that account is contained in your Living Trust and you are still the Trustee. Therefore, keep sufficient bank or brokerage assets in the joint names of you and your Attorney-in-Fact for purposes of making these last-minute Annual Exclusion Gifts.

Step 4

Each gift your Attorney-in-Fact makes from the joint bank or brokerage should be completed *before you die*! If the gift is too late, the IRS may claim that the amount of the gift is still in your name and subject to a death tax. (If death is imminent, your Attorney-in-Fact should make the withdrawal in cash, money order, or cashier's check.)

This plan can save your children a significant amount of death taxes. On one occasion, a client made last-minute gifts of $10,000 to each of her six children, fifteen grandchildren, and five great-grandchildren—a total of twenty-six gifts! With $260,000 removed from her name, her children prevented $130,000 from going to the IRS.

Planning Opportunity Number 9: Retained Income Trust—Give Away Your Income-Producing Asset but Keep the Right to Receive the Income

A client will tell me, "I don't mind giving away my apartment building [or other income-producing asset], but is there any way I can still get the income?"

Yes, there is. This type of gift is commonly referred to as a "Retained Income Trust." With this method, you retain the right to the income for a period of years.

The benefit is that you get to enjoy the income for a period of time after you give away the building. And when you die, the asset that produced that income is not part of your estate and, therefore, is not subject to a death tax.

If this idea is appealing to you, ask your inheritance-planning attorney about "GRITS," "GRATS," and "GRUTS." These are the "code words" for the three main types of Retained Income Trusts: the "Grantor Retained Income Trust," the "Grantor Retained Annuity Trust," and the "Grantor Retained Unitrust."

Planning Opportunity Number 10: The "Skip" Trust

Your wealth is taxed twice—once when you die and again when your child dies. But there is a way to prevent the IRS from getting a second bite of the apple with what I call the "Skip Trust."

I discuss the Skip Trust in more detail in chapter 38.

Planning Opportunity Number 11: Sales to Children and the Self-canceling Installment Note

Assume you sell your apartment building (or other asset) to your daughter for $500,000. In return, your daughter gives you an Installment Note. This note is her promise to pay you $500,000 in monthly installments along with a certain interest rate. The note also provides that your daughter is to pay off the note in full in fifteen years.

Your daughter pays you faithfully every month. But before the note is paid off you die. What happens then?

What happens is that instead of dying owning an apartment building, you die owning that note. And to the IRS, that note is an asset in your estate subject to a death tax. If your daughter owed you $400,000 on the note at your death, that $400,000 is an asset to which the death tax applies, costing her $200,000 in death taxes.

But you can prevent that note from being an asset in your estate if it is a Self-canceling Note, which, in effect, means that when you die, there is no note, saving your daughter $200,000 in death taxes.

I tend to use this technique following the death of the first spouse so that there will be a 100 percent step-up in basis for the property sold to the child. But whenever used, take note: The Self-canceling Note is not firmly established in the law. It may or may not work to reduce your death tax. But it is worthy enough to justify discussing it with your inheritance-planning attorney.

37

I Can Get Your Death Tax Wholesale

or

You Never Paid Retail During Your Life—Why Start After You Die?

---

1. "My wife and I have $15 million in real estate, including our house and several apartment buildings. Our lawyer tells us the death tax could be $2 million. This will force our children to sell the real estate to raise this money."

If you are rich enough, the death tax when you die will be significant. In fact, the check your child writes to the IRS for the death tax may be the largest cash payment anyone in your family will ever make.

Where will the money come from to pay the death tax? Most likely, from the assets your child inherits. If you leave sufficient cash, your child can simply write a check to the IRS. But if most of your wealth is real estate or securities, your child may have to sell and incur commissions and other sales costs *on top of* the death tax.

However, you can arrange for your child to use someone else's money to pay the death tax. You can make this arrangement with life insurance.

381

2. "What does life insurance have to do with paying the death tax?"

Think of it this way. The death tax is the biggest purchase your child may ever make. And what's worse, your child will probably pay it retail, paying the IRS one hundred cents on the dollar for every dollar owed.

Most of us take some pride in purchasing our big-ticket items at their lowest cost—why not the death tax? You can arrange for your child to pay the death tax at a wholesale cost—perhaps for as little as ten to twenty cents on the dollar!

How can the death tax be purchased wholesale? With life insurance! When you buy life insurance, you are buying dollars at a significant discount. These dollars will be delivered to your child tax-free after you die. Your child can use these dollars to pay the death tax.

The result is that you have provided the dollars when they are needed to pay the death tax, and your child does not have to invade the inheritance to pay off the IRS.

For example, you estimate your death tax will be $1 million (the retail cost). If your child uses the family money to pay this tax, that is $1 million that will not be around for your child and grandchild. But if a $1 million life insurance policy is purchased on your life, the only cost is the premiums.

What will the premium payments be to acquire $1 million of life insurance? It depends on your age, health, and whether the insurance policy will be on just your life or on the joint lives of you and your spouse. But whatever the premiums are, they will amount to substantially less than $1 million.

3. "Are there any special requirements for using life insurance to pay the death tax?"

Using life insurance to pay the death tax is a specialized and technical area of inheritance planning. If you want the nuts and bolts of this death-tax-planning opportunity, I suggest you consult with an experienced inheritance-planning attorney or insurance specialist.

But one requirement is so vital that it is worth mentioning here: For this plan to work, you cannot own the policy in your individual name. If you own it, the death benefits will be taxed in your estate when you die.

Instead, let your children be the owners of the policy. Give money to your children, either using the $14,000 Annual Exclusion Gift or using a portion of your Lifetime Exemption so they can make the premium payments. When you die, the insurance proceeds will not be taxed in your estate because your children, and not you, own the policy.

If a child is a minor (or you are concerned your child will blow the dough), consider setting up and transferring sufficient money to an "Irrevocable Insurance Trust" with your child as the named beneficiary. With this method, the Trust will own the policy and pay the premiums. When you die, the death benefits will go to your child tax-free.

4. "I am seventy-two and my wife is sixty-eight. We are both reasonably healthy and don't smoke. Our lawyer has asked us to consider life insurance as a way to raise money to pay the $1 million death tax."

Your lawyer's advice is excellent. You can arrange for your child to own a $1 million life insurance policy on your joint lives. Since insuring two lives is cheaper than insuring one life, this policy may be bought for as little as 30 percent (or $300,000). You may even get it for less if you make this payment in one shot. When both of you die, the insurance company will write your child a tax-free check for $1 million. Your child can then turn over this check to the IRS to pay the death tax.

5. "Twenty-five years ago, I took out a $1 million life insurance policy on my life to protect my wife if I died prematurely. My wife will still get the proceeds if I die, but now she doesn't need the money. The proceeds will just sit in some bank account collecting interest. If the money is still there when she dies, it will be subject to a death tax."

You are correct. If your wife gets the insurance money, she owns it. And if she still owns it when she dies, it will be subject to a death tax.

To prevent the IRS from taking a bite of the proceeds when your wife dies, don't let your wife get the proceeds. She cannot be taxed on what she doesn't own. Instead, gift the policy to your child and make your child the beneficiary. With these changes, your wife will not own the $1 million death benefit, thereby escaping the death tax on the proceeds.

Here's the catch: Because of a peculiar IRS rule, you must live at least three years after you have gifted the policy to your child. Otherwise, the death benefits will be taxed when your wife dies.

---

6. "I am forty-two and my husband is forty-three. We are thinking about getting a $2 million life insurance policy on both our lives, which my insurance agent says will only cost one payment of $250,000."

A great idea. At your relatively young ages, the policy you buy will be fairly inexpensive. And for your $250,000 investment, your children will receive $2 million after both of you die, which will not cost them one penny in death tax (assuming you do not own the policy, a factor I discuss in question 3 of this chapter).

Of course, the older you are, the higher the price for the $2 million policy. However, whatever your age and whatever the price, you will still save a significant amount in death taxes. I had one seventy-five-year-old client whose estimated death tax was $2 million. To pay this tax, she bought a $2 million insurance policy for $1 million. When she died, the insurance company wrote her children a tax-free check for $2 million and they wrote on the back of it: "Pay to the Order of the IRS."

Granted, the price of the policy was high, but my client still bought the death tax wholesale. Instead of the death tax being paid dollar for dollar, it was paid for fifty cents on the dollar—the cost of the life insurance policy.

7. "I estimate my death tax will be around $350,000. I would like to arrange for $350,000 worth of insurance so my daughter can use it to pay the death tax. Can my IRA money be used to buy the policy?"

It not only can—it should!

Say you have $750,000 in your IRA account. When you draw down on this account, the IRS may take up to 40 percent in income taxes, leaving you with $450,000. Now, if you happen to own more than the $5,340,000 Lifetime Exemption at your death, the IRS will take a portion of that $450,000 as a death tax. The result is that only $270,000 of your IRA account may end up in the hands of your child.

But there is a way to get around this death tax and provide your child with a substantial amount of tax-free money.

Liquidate the $750,000 IRA account and pay the IRS its 40 percent share of income taxes. But instead of keeping the remaining $450,000, give it to your child to buy a life insurance policy on your life. Depending on your age and health, your child may be able to purchase a $1 million policy, which, in this example, is your estimated death tax.

Which would your child rather receive? A whittled-down IRA of $270,000 or a tax-free check from the insurance company for $1 million, which your child can use to pay the death tax in its entirety?

The choice is yours.

38

Your Money Is Taxed a Second Time When Your Child Dies

or

How to Prevent the IRS from Taking Two Bites of the Inheritance Apple

The IRS taxes wealth at every generation. This means that if you are rich enough, the IRS will not only impose a death tax on your wealth when you die but will take a second bite of the same wealth when your child dies.

Not planning to avoid this second bite is like getting only two strikes in baseball or three downs in football. No plan to reduce the death tax is complete without at least a discussion of ways to reduce the second bite.

---

1. "I can't believe it! My tax lawyer says when my wife and I are both dead, the death tax will be half of everything we own. The other half will go to our son, and when he dies, the IRS will get another tax on that share. After both these hits, the IRS will end up with three-quarters of our wealth, and only one-quarter will be left for our grandchildren."

The death tax is outrageous and confiscatory, but never more so than when the IRS gets a second bite of the same wealth. Like

Bart Lapkin, you may have never before thought about this second bite, until the lawyer makes you aware of it.

Bart Lapkin's Surprise Party

Bart Lapkin was a bit perplexed when I asked him if he was expecting an inheritance from anyone. "Mr. Condon, I'm here for *my* Living Trust. Why are you asking that question?"

This information is highly important, if not critical, in establishing an inheritance plan.

Bart informed me that his father had died some years before and his mother became the sole owner of roughly $8 million in real estate and bank assets. Since Bart was an only child, he expected to inherit it all.

Bart, however, forgot about the IRS. Before Bart inherited the $8 million, the IRS would take about $1,064,000 in death taxes, leaving him with an inheritance of $6,936,000. And if Bart had to sell some of his inherited real estate to pay the death tax, he would wind up losing more money in broker's commissions and escrow fees.

Bart vaguely knew there would be a death tax after his mother's death, but this was the first time some reality was brought to it. I could see he was mildly upset, but what I told him next did not make him feel any better.

"Bart, assume that after death taxes and sales expenses, you net a $6 million inheritance. Now, add that $6 million to what you own now [which was about $1 million in real estate and stocks] and you will own about $7 million. Well, Bart, when you die, this combined $7 million will be taxed before it goes to your children. In effect, the $6 million you inherit from your mother will again generate close to 40 percent in death taxes."

It's a good thing Bart did not have a heart condition. Like most people, he had absolutely no awareness of this second bite. He was outraged to learn that between both tax bites, the IRS would end up with 75 percent of his mother's wealth, with only 25 percent going to Bart's children.

This second bite was not some vague event in the distant future. Bart's mother was in her late eighties. If she dies in her early nineties (when the first bite takes place), Bart will be in his late sixties. Then if Bart lives to the average life expectancy of the American male, he will die in his late seventies (when the second bite takes place).

Within one decade, the IRS will have taken two bites of the family wealth.

Fortunately, it was not necessary for me to resuscitate Bart, because I promptly told him there were several ways to avoid the second bite of the apple.

Alternative Number 1: Tax-Free Gifts to Grandchildren

Bart's mother could make $14,000 Annual Exclusion Gifts to each of her grandchildren and pay for her grandchildren's education and medical expenses. Why should Bart's mother make these gifts? So Bart will inherit less. And the less Bart inherits, the less the second death tax will be when he dies.

I discuss tax-free gifts in more detail in chapter 36.

Alternative Number 2: Life Insurance

Bart's mother could give money to Bart's children to buy an insurance policy on Bart's life. When Bart dies, the insurance company will pay death benefits to Bart's children without one penny of death tax. The children could then use this check to offset the death tax.

I discuss using insurance as a method to reduce the death tax in chapter 37.

Alternative Number 3: The "Skip Trust"

When Bart dies, the IRS will tax what he owns, including what he inherits from his mother. But if he does not own his inherited wealth, the IRS cannot impose a death tax on it.

How can Bart not own his inherited wealth but still have the benefits of it? There is a special plan the IRS allows that I call the "Skip Trust." With this plan, Bart's mother can leave Bart a maximum amount called the "Generation Skip Amount" that will skip the second death tax when Bart dies. The Generation Skip Amount is presently $5,340,000.

The concept of the plan is simple. In her Living Trust, Bart's mother leaves $5,340,000 to the Skip Trust, in which Bart is the Trustee and beneficiary. As Trustee, Bart can control all the investment decisions. In addition, Bart is entitled to all of the income and can spend the $5,340,000 principal should he need it for his support, medical bills, household expenses, and other necessities of life.

When Bart dies, the assets remaining in this Skip Trust will go to his children without being bitten by the second tax. And what's more, if Bart invested the $5,340,000 principal wisely and increased its value, that appreciation will also pass to Bart's children tax-free (assuming the appreciation remains in the Skip Trust when Bart dies).

(Had Bart's father been alive, he, too, could have set up a Skip Trust to leave Bart an amount equal to the Skip Amount that would also escape the second death tax when Bart dies.)

This was the solution Bart liked the most. And when he mentioned it to his mother, she had her attorney incorporate the $5,340,000 Skip Trust as part of her inheritance plan.

2. "My only asset is my house, which has a current value of $350,000. There will be no death tax when I die because my assets do not exceed my Lifetime Exemption of $5,340,000. However, won't this property be added to my son's wealth and be taxed when he dies?"

If your house is worth $350,000 when you die, and your combined assets do not exceed your Lifetime Exemption of $5,340,000, there will be no death tax on your house when your son inherits it.

Certainly your son will be happy to inherit your house. But here is a bit of sobering news. When your son gets your house, it is added to his existing assets and gives him a bigger "pie" of wealth. And when your son dies, the IRS may get a very large slice.

How big will the IRS's slice be when your son dies? It depends. If your son's inherited house becomes his only significant asset, and the house is still worth less than your Lifetime Exemption when he dies, the IRS will not get a penny of death tax. However, if your house kicks your son's net worth over your Lifetime Exemption the IRS will tax the overage.

Solution: Don't Mix Your House in Your Son's Pie of Assets

Your son can only be taxed on what he owns at his death. But he cannot be taxed on what he does not own.

How can your son not own his inherited house but still have the benefits of ownership? You set up a special arrangement in your inheritance plan, leaving your house to your son in a Skip Trust, which I discuss in question 1 of this chapter. Your son will be Trustee of the Trust. As Trustee, he can do everything with the house that he could as the outright owner. He can live in the house or rent it and keep the rental income. He can even sell the house, invest the sale proceeds, and receive the interest or other income produced by the proceeds.

When your son dies, the Skip Trust will dissolve and the house (or sale proceeds) will pass to your grandchildren without one penny of death tax. Why? Because the Skip Trust owned the house, not your son. And because your house was not owned by your son, it never became a part of his taxable pie of assets.

Part XII

Avoiding Probate

39

Using the Living Trust to Keep Your Children and Property Out of the Probate Court

or

Why Provide for Your Lawyer's Retirement Fund?

I am always surprised when people tell me they do not understand their Living Trust, because, I assume, the lawyer who prepared it explained it to them. Nevertheless, at every inheritance-planning seminar, at least three people will come up to me privately and ask in a hushed tone, "Mr. Condon, could I show you my Living Trust so you can tell me what I've got?"

If people who have a Living Trust are confused about it, imagine what those without one must think. I have heard a lot of misinformation from seminar attendees who are shopping around for a Living Trust attorney. "Mr. Condon, my friend says the Living Trust avoids death taxes." Wrong! "Mr. Condon, my brother-in-law tells me I won't own the property I put in my Living Trust." Wrong again!

Tell You What I'm Gonna Do . . .

If you feel you know everything about the Living Trust, skip this chapter. But if you never again want to be confused or misinformed as to what the Living Trust does or does not accomplish, read on.

I would like you to forget everything you have ever heard about the Living Trust, even if you have one. I want you to erase form your mind whatever your friend, neighbor, child, or acquaintance told you about it. Forget the Living Trust's long length and complex words. If you focus on my explanation, you will understand the concept of the Living Trust.

The best place to begin is at the beginning.

---

1. "My wife and I own our real estate, stocks, and bank accounts in joint tenancy. I know if I die first, she will own my half automatically. But when she dies, we want title to pass to our children. How does title get from her to our children?"

Dad and Mom hold all their real estate and other assets jointly. If Dad dies first, Mom owns it all. When Mom dies, she goes to the grave with title to all the family assets.

Before Mom died, she established a Will, which leaves everything to her children. However, that last wish is not self-executing. The Will itself does not transfer ownership or title. It is only a blueprint of who gets what. The only way title can be transferred from Mom to her children is if Mom signs a deed and other title-transferring documents.

However, there is a significant problem. Mom cannot sign after she has died. The solution: Someone must act as Mom's "out-of-the-grave agent" who can sign on Mom's behalf.

Who will be Mom's out-of-the-grave agent? It's the probate judge! When Mom dies, the probate judge becomes Mom's out-of-the-grave agent to sign the deed and other title documents transferring title from dead Mom to her live children.

So how do Mom's children go about getting the probate judge to sign the title-transferring documents? Do Mom's children just go to the courthouse on their lunch hour and flag down a judge in the hallway? Of course not, to get a judge to do anything, you must bring a lawsuit. If you want a judge to grant a divorce, you bring a divorce lawsuit. If you want a judge to order someone to pay you money, you must bring a civil lawsuit.

To get the judge to sign the deed and other title-transferring papers, your children must bring a probate lawsuit. The ultimate goal of probate is to get the probate judge to sign documents that transfer title from dead Mom to live children.

---

2. "Will my children need an attorney to go through this probate procedure? If so, how much will it cost?"

Probate is like any other lawsuit. It involves time and money.

If probate runs its natural course without any hitches, the entire transferring process could take as little as five months. However, for innumerable reasons, many probates run for years.

You may know firsthand of what I speak. After going through a probate yourself, all you may remember is that it went on interminably and that the lawyer had you sign countless documents that you did not understand.

The cost of probate includes attorney fees, executor fees, filing fees, appraiser fees, publication fees, and other charges. As a rule of thumb, the total cost approximates 4 to 6 percent of the value of the assets that are being probated. If Mom died with title to a house worth $300,000, the approximate cost to probate the house is $15,000.

---

3. "Couldn't my child avoid all this probate stuff by putting her name on the title to my assets now? When I die, everything will go to her outright without hassles."

These goals of avoiding probate's costs and expenses can be achieved through many methods. One common method is holding property jointly with your children, which is discussed at greater length in chapter 41.

However, it is dangerous to put your child's name on title to your assets. If you have done so, understand that your property is now subject to your child's (and your child's spouse's) financial problems.

---

4. "Is there a hassle-free and risk-free way of transferring my property to my children after I die?"

Yes. You have the perfect right to appoint your own out-of-the-grave agent. You can sign a special document that gives your children the power to do what the probate judge does—transfer title of your money and property from dead you to your live children.

This document is commonly known as the Living Trust. It is also referred to as the Family Trust, the Inter Vivos Trust, the "AB Trust," the Probate-Avoidance Trust, and a host of other names.

But whatever its name and no matter how long it is, don't be confused. *The Living Trust is only a document in which you make your children your out-of-the-grave agents who can sign your name to the title-transferring documents after you die.*

---

5. "If all the Living Trust does is give my children the right to sign my name after I die, why call it the Living Trust?"

I agree it's confusing, because the Living Trust is not a true Trust.

A true Trust occurs if you transfer your assets to a third party. But when you establish a Living Trust, you keep your property, and you continue to own it. The only transfer taking place is when you retitle your assets so you own them as Trustee. Instead of your owning your assets in your individual name, you own them as Trustee.

So why call it a Living Trust? Perhaps this explanation will help.

When you authorize your children to sign your name after you die, you are, in a sense, giving them an "After-Death Power of Attorney." But the laws of every state say that no such document exists. Any Power of Attorney you sign expires when you die, canceling your children's authority to sign your name.

Well, we lawyers, not to be daunted, came up with an expensive and lengthy document that does the same thing as this fictional After-Death Power of Attorney—the Living Trust.

The Living Trust says that you and your spouse own your assets as Cotrustees. When you die, your spouse will own all the assets as sole Trustee. When your spouse dies, your children take over the assets as your after-death Trustees, who typically have only one duty: to sign the deed and other title-transferring documents.

The Living Trust looks like a Trust, smells like a Trust, and uses the words of a Trust. But the only purpose of this document is to give your children an After-Death Power of Attorney so they will have the authority to sign your name after you die.

---

6. "I heard that the Living Trust will keep my children and property out of the probate court. Will it also reduce the death tax?"

Notwithstanding what you may have heard, the Living Trust does not, in and of itself, save one penny in death tax. This is the biggest misconception the general public has about the Living Trust.

The Living Trust does not suddenly and magically confer on you the power to save death taxes. With or without the Living Trust, you have a Lifetime Exemption. This means you can gift an amount equal to your Lifetime Exemption tax-free to whomever you wish. If you are married, you and your spouse can collectively shift an amount equal to each of your Lifetime Exemptions without any tax.

When you say that your Living Trust will reduce your death tax, you are probably referring to a special plan included in your Living Trust that preserves your Lifetime Exemption of the first spouse to die. But this plan is not an inherent part of the Living

Trust. If you want it, you must ask for it when you consult with an inheritance-planning lawyer.

I discuss this special plan further in chapter 36. However, as I discuss in chapter 36, you won't need to include this special plan in your Living Trust, unless you and your spouse have more than your combined $10,680,000 Lifetime Exemptions.

The Most Frequently Asked Questions

The following is a compilation of the most commonly asked questions I receive at my seminars about the Living Trust.

Q. *What is a Living Trust?*
A. The Living Trust is a predeath arrangement in which you set forth your instructions as to who gets your real estate and other assets following your death. The person who carries out your instructions is your out-of-the-grave agent, also known as your "Successor Trustee."

Q. *Who do I select as my Successor Trustee?*
A. Usually you designate one or more of your children.

Q. *What will my Successor Trustee do with my assets?*
A. Your Successor Trustee has the responsibility of transferring your Trust assets in accordance with your last wishes as set forth in your Living Trust.

Q. *Must I place all of my assets into the Trust?*
A. The benefit of probate avoidance will only be achieved to the extent your assets are transferred into your Living Trust.

Q. *Do I still own the assets I hold in my Living Trust?*
A. Yes. For all practical purposes, there is absolutely no change whatsoever in your property rights. You may do whatever you wish with your property. The only difference is that you own everything in your name as Trustee of your Living Trust.

Q. *Are there any changes in my income taxes after the Trust has been set up?*
A. No. The IRS does not require a separate tax number or a sep-

arate tax return. You continue to file the same personal income tax return as you did before you established a Living Trust.

Q. *Does this transfer trigger a property tax reassessment or other property-related taxes?*
A. No. There is no reassessment by transferring your real estate into your Trust if the transfer is done in a legally correct fashion.

Q. *Do I have to go through any special procedures if I want to deal with assets that I placed into my Living Trust?*
A. No. You are still the owner of your real estate and other assets. You may put assets into your Living Trust or take assets out of your Living Trust as often as you wish.

Q. *Once the Trust is created, can it be amended or revoked?*
A. Yes. Prior to your death, the Living Trust can be amended to include new instructions to be carried out by your Successor Trustee. You may also revoke your Living Trust at any time prior to your death.

Q. *What happens following the death of the first spouse?*
A. The surviving spouse automatically becomes the sole owner of all Trust assets (except for any portion set aside into what I call Dad's Tax-Free Trust Account, which I discuss in chapter 36). Following the death of the surviving spouse, the Successor Trustee has the authority to distribute your real estate and other assets in accordance with your wishes as set forth in your Living Trust.

Q. *May my Successor Trustee deviate from my wishes as set forth in my Trust?*
A. No. Your Successor Trustee is legally bound to adhere to your wishes as set forth in your Trust.

Q: *I already have a will. May I still set up a Living Trust?*
A. Yes. The Living Trust usually supersedes any prior Will.

Q. *What is the cost of a Living Trust?*
A. Compared to a probate proceeding, the cost of a Living Trust is minuscule. The fee is usually determined by the number of properties transferred into the Trust, the complexities of the Trust, and other estate and tax-planning needs.

Q: *How long does it take to set up a Living Trust?*

A. In nonemergency circumstances, it usually takes a few weeks. Setting up a Living Trust involves two or three consultations with the attorney in order to clearly define individual goals and determine which assets will be placed into the Trust. During this process, people often need time to make important decisions. It is an important process that usually gives a significant sense of satisfaction in having put things in order.

Q. *If the Living Trust has so many benefits, why hasn't it been popular in the past?*

A. The Living Trust has always been known to attorneys specializing in estate planning. However, because of the historical use of Wills and the probate courts as a means of transferring the family wealth, public acceptance and use by lawyers not specializing in estate planning has been somewhat slow.

Q. *I live in state ABC where I own real estate. I also own real estate in three other states. Can I use this Living Trust to avoid making probate lawyers in these states wealthier than they already are?*

A. Yes. If the Living Trust is good in one state, it's usually good in another, with the occasional exception of Louisiana.

Q. *Do I put the life insurance policy on my life in the Trust?*

A. No. Make the Living Trust a primary or secondary beneficiary of your life insurance policy.

Q. *Do I put my qualified pension plan and/or IRA in the Trust?*

A. No. Those are what I call self-executing assets. After you die, those assets will pass without probate to the prearranged beneficiary.

Q. *Do I put stocks in the Living Trust?*

A. Yes. However, every company will require you to fill out a number of documents so the stocks can be retitled into your name as Trustee. If you have shares in many different companies, this could be a big hassle. To keep it simple and hassle-free, you can open a stock account with a brokerage house in your name as Trustee and deposit your stock certificates into the account.

40

How Your Inheritance Instructions May Be Disregarded

or

Do You Trust Your Children to Carry Out Your Inheritance Plan?

You can have the greatest Living Trust in the world. You can spend thousands of dollars in legal fees making certain every "i" is dotted and every "t" is crossed. But if the persons whom you appoint to carry out your inheritance plan choose not to do so—for whatever reason—then you have no plan.

Now that I have your attention, allow me to explain the reasoning behind this statement.

In chapter 39, I explain that the chief purpose of establishing a Living Trust is to transfer your money and property to your children (or other heirs) without the expensive and time-consuming probate process. This benefit is achieved because the Living Trust allows you to appoint an after-death "agent" who will have the power to sign all documents that are necessary to transfer title of your real estate and other assets to your children or other heirs.

In the vast majority of cases, I advise clients to appoint all their children as the "agents." However, as I discuss in question 1 of chapter 5, if you have a child who poses a risk of loss to the

assets because of, for example, drug addiction, financial irresponsibility, mental disability, or family estrangement, administration of your Living Trust may be made less problematic if that
child is not appointed as a "co-agent."

You Know What They Say When You Assume

When I was a younger attorney drafting Wills and Living Trusts,
I always counted on the basic premise that a child will faithfully
carry out his parent's inheritance instructions. After all, an agent
is legally bound to follow those instructions. But with a child
serving as agent, this obligation becomes more than legal. The
instructions are his parent's voice from the grave, and the sense
of family duty creates a moral imperative to honor his parent's
last wishes.

However, having had the real experience of seeing the behavior
of children in the inheritance "arena" after their parents' deaths,
I no longer operate on the assumption that children will invariably and unfailingly carry out their parents' inheritance instructions. I now ask every prospective client whether they believe a
risk exists that a child appointed as "agent" will fail or refuse to
follow through.

Please do not be misled. Nine and a half times out of ten, a
child will faithfully follow his parent's inheritance instructions.
But during the years since this book's original publication in
1995, I have witnessed firsthand a wave of the other .5 percent.
I have seen a number of situations where clients died and their
inheritance instructions were casually disregarded by their children.

In the introduction of this book, I state that 95 percent of the
solution to any problem is recognizing the problem exists in the
first place. In keeping with that philosophy, I offer examples of
the most common situations that I have seen result in a client's
child deviating from a Living Trust's inheritance instructions. If
you "see yourself" in any of these scenarios, you can discuss

methods to resolve the problem with your inheritance-planning attorney.

1. I prepared a Living Trust for Norman Mount, which stated, in essence, the following: "When I die, my son will receive $100,000 as 'manager' for my grandson. When my grandson becomes thirty-five, my son will give my grandson the money."

Mr. Mount died when his grandson was twenty-five. Ten years later, the grandson came to my office and said to me, "I turned thirty-five yesterday. When I asked my father for the money, do you know what he said to me. He said, 'Where do you think we got the money to buy this house?' "

I did not believe Mr. Mount's son was an evil, money-grubbing person. He simply took the position that his son's money was family money, which he could use for the family without holding it specifically for his son. Nonetheless, the result was the same— Mr. Mount's grandson was out $100,000.

2. Almost every Living Trust I prepare provides a "backup" paragraph that states, in effect: "If one of our children dies before us, we leave that child's share to that child's children." Such was the case with the Living Trust I prepared for Frank and Janis Horowitz, who had two sons and a daughter. Mr. Horowitz died first. Shortly after his death, Mrs. Horowitz suffered the misfortune of the untimely death of her daughter, Lily, who was survived by a teenage daughter.

After Mrs. Horowitz's death fifteen years later, I met with her two surviving sons to advise them on the particulars of the administration and distribution of a Living Trust. As part of this process, I reviewed the document and reminded the sons of their legal duty to follow their parents' instructions and distribute one-third of their parents' estate to their now-adult niece.

The sons looked at each other then looked back at me. The oldest then stated in a most straightforward but relaxed manner: "Well, Mr. Condon, I'll tell you what we got here. We really haven't seen our niece for ten years. We can't stand the guy that she married and we let her know it. She just kind of disassociated herself from the family. So, we're just going to forget about the distribution to her. She'll never know about it anyway. And we'll just leave it at that."

3. I prepared a simple Living Trust for Sam Bottleman, which said, in a "nutshell," "Upon my death, I want $75,000 to go to my church, and everything else will pass to my son and daughter equally."

Sam's Living Trust appointed his children as his "agents." When Sam died and his children met with me for the usual information about trust administration, I reminded them they had to write a check to Sam's church. I'll never forget the response of the daughter: "Mr. Condon, that may have been my father's wish. But my brother and I talked it over, and you know something . . . it's not our wish."

4. I prepared a Living Trust for Leah Wolpert, an elderly widow with three children. The document provided that on her death, each of her grandchildren would receive, on reaching age eighteen, $25,000.

When Mrs. Wolpert died, she had eight grandchildren, all of whom were over eighteen years of age. Her three children (her "agents") were less than pleased at the news they had to part with $200,000 of "their" money. As Mrs. Wolpert's son said to me (actually, "shouted" is more accurate), "It's not going to happen. Not a chance. It's our money. It does not belong to our ———— kids, no matter what that ———— piece of paper says."

5. On another and similar occasion, Sean Weber's inheritance plan provided that his four grandchildren would split $100,000. When Mr. Weber died, his son (the grandchildren's father) stated this to me: "Well, I'm not going to write the checks right away. I'll probably write them at some point in the future. After all, they're my children and they're going to inherit from me anyway."

When I heard this from Mr. Weber's son, I realized that, for all practical purposes, the grandchildren would never see a dime of their grandfather's gifts.

6. Frank Hanson had two children, a son and a daughter, to whom he desired to leave his assets equally. But with Mr. Han-

son's son an inveterate gambler, it was obvious that his son could not receive his inheritance outright; rather, someone would have to manage it to prevent it from ending up with the casinos. Thus, when I prepared his Living Trust, I included a provision stating that on Mr. Hanson's death, his daughter would receive her brother's half and "manage" it for his benefit for the rest of his life.

One day, about six years following Mr. Hanson's death, I came to my office and saw a lady in my waiting room. I did not recognize her, but she introduced herself as Mr. Hanson's daughter. Without even waiting to be shown to my office, she reminded me of her father's Living Trust and that it had appointed her as her brother's "inheritance manager." Her eyes began to well with tears as she said to me, "Well, forget it, Mr. Condon. I want out. My brother is making my life absolutely miserable with his constant requests for money. We're no longer brother and sister. He just sees me as his checkbook. I'll tell you this—if you can't help me with this, then I'll just give him the money and that will be that."

I prepared the documents in which Mr. Hanson's daughter resigned as "manager." With no substitute manager in place, and no volunteers for the job, the son ultimately obtained full control over his half and proceeded to gamble it away.

When It Comes to Money, Legal Warnings Mean Nothing

In every one of these situations, I explained to each child the legal duty an "agent" has to carry out inheritance instructions, and the ramifications of noncompliance, such as lawsuits by aggrieved beneficiaries and criminal penalties. However, none were motivated to withdraw from their planned course of nonaction. And because of various laws on attorney ethics and standards that are too complex and technical to elaborate upon, I was prevented from informing the aggrieved beneficiaries of their losses.

Make an Informed Decision

Because of these and other experiences, I now ask my clients to make an informed decision as to whether they have any doubts that their child or children will faithfully carry out their inheritance instructions. On most occasions, the clients appreciate the thorough questioning and politely answer no. On the other hand, some persons have responded with an outright yes or with long and thoughtful silences as they seriously ponder this issue that they have never before considered.

As for you, the reader, do not lose sight that being forewarned is forearmed: 95 percent of the solution to any potential inheritance problem is first becoming aware of the problem. When you die and your children are "in charge" of distributing your Trust estate, there is no policeman looking over their shoulder. You have put them into a position to carry out your instructions exactly as you have provided, or to deviate from instructions.

If you consider there to be little to no risk of deviation by a child "agent," then you have made an informed decision. However, if you consider the risk to be too great too ignore, you can resolve the problem in your Living Trust, such as by appointing other "agents" whom you believe to be more trustworthy, such as another private individual or a corporate or bank Trustee. I discuss these alternatives in more depth in chapter 16 ("Who Should Be Your Child's Trustee?").

41

Don't Put Your House in Joint
Tenancy with Your Child

or

*How to Lose Your House to
Your Daughter's Creditors*

---

1. "When my husband died, I received his property without probate because we held everything in joint tenancy. Now I think I will put my daughter on title to my house as a joint tenant. When I die, she also won't have to go through probate."

Joint tenancy is the simplest and least expensive way to transfer your house and other assets to your daughter after you die. While you are alive, sign a deed that transfers your house to yourself and your child as joint tenants with right of survivorship (assuming your state recognizes this manner of holding title). When you die, your child will be the 100 percent owner of your house . . . without probate!

However, you have to be crazy to put your child's name on your house—or any other substantial asset.

When you put your child's name on the title to your assets, all you are thinking about is the convenience of avoiding probate after you die. But what you may fail to realize is that *you are making your child a co-owner of your assets!* You may not have intended to make a gift, but that is exactly what you have accomplished.

Is this bad? You bet it is! If you give your child a portion of your house, your house then becomes subject to your child's problems.

Mrs. Weldon learned this lesson the hard way.

"Mrs. Weldon . . . I Told You So"

I had just told Mrs. Weldon how a Living Trust would keep her children and property out of the probate court. But Mrs. Weldon did not like the fee. She told me she could save this fee and still avoid probate by putting title in joint tenancy with her daughter.

I told Mrs. Weldon what I tell all my clients who make such a proposition: Don't do it.

I paraded horror story after horror story to Mrs. Weldon to make my point. Mrs. Weldon, however, thought it would be different with her. She had absolute faith that her daughter would never have any financial problems.

Mrs. Weldon left my office without asking me to prepare a Will or Living Trust. I did not hear from her again until she called about five years later.

On the telephone, Mrs. Weldon was in a state of high panic. In fact, she was so hysterical that I failed to understand her. Finally, I was able to glean through her mutterings that "they" were going to take her house from her.

Mrs. Weldon was too panic-stricken to drive to my office, so I went to her home. When I arrived, she showed me a legal document she had received. It was a notification from the Bankruptcy Court that the bankruptcy estate was claiming one-half of *her* house and *her* apartment building.

What had happened was this: Mrs. Weldon put her daughter's name on the title to her real estate as a joint tenant. A few years later, her daughter and son-in-law had declared bankruptcy, and the Bankruptcy Court discovered the daughter owned 50 percent of Mrs. Weldon's house and apartment building. The Trustee then took control of these properties to pay the daughter and son-in-law's creditors.

After she appealed to the sympathies of the Bankruptcy Court, an agreement was eventually reached. Mrs. Weldon had to buy back her daughter's half for a substantial amount, all of which went to the creditors. In exchange, the court released its hold on Mrs. Weldon's real estate.

Do Not Subject Your House to Your Children's Problems

Almost weekly since my practice began, I have received inquiries from people who heard that joint tenancy with their child avoids probate. In all this time, my answer has remained the same: If you establish joint tenancy with your child, you are subjecting your house and other assets to your child's problems.

What kind of problems?

Creditors

If your daughter and/or her husband have creditor problems, their creditors could put a lien on your daughter's half of your house. The creditors then could force a sale of your home to turn their creditor's lien into cash.

Accidents

If your daughter and/or her husband are in a car accident and have insufficient liability coverage, the accident victim may go to court to get a judgment lien against your daughter's half of your house. The victim then could turn this judgment lien into cash by forcing a sale of your home.

Marital Problems

If your daughter and her husband divorce, her husband could claim that your daughter's half of your house is an asset that is subject to the division of marital assets.

IRS Problems

If your daughter and/or her husband incur any income tax liabilities, the first thing the IRS will do is attach a tax lien against any real property in either of their names, including your house if your daughter's name is on it.

Bankruptcy

If faced with significant business creditors, your daughter may declare bankruptcy without factoring in the effect it will have on your real estate. Why? Because she may not be aware, or may have completely forgotten, that you gave her 50 percent of your property.

Recall that when you put your daughter on the title, nothing was required of her. You went to the lawyer, you paid the lawyer, you had the deed recorded, and you kept the deed in your safety-deposit box. In fact, you may not have even told your daughter about the transaction.

So when she declares bankruptcy and the creditors come knocking at your door, your daughter may be just as surprised as you that your house is now subject to the bankruptcy proceedings.

The Solution

You can achieve the same goal of avoiding probate by using a simple Probate-Avoidance Trust. By this method, you retain the full ownership of your real estate, stock, and bank accounts without subjecting them to matters beyond your control. For more on the Living Trust, see chapter 39.

2. "I know it's a risk to put my son on the title to my house while I'm alive, but that's all right. If he ever gets into a divorce or if he has creditor problems, he will simply deed his half back to me."

Once you have made your child a joint tenant to your property, and your child subsequently incurs a creditor problem, your child cannot avoid the debt by retransferring the share back to you. The creditor can set aside that transfer and take your child's ex-share to satisfy the debt.

"Everyone Does It"

Mrs. Axelrod gave no second thought to putting Kim, her daughter, on title to her house as a joint tenant. Several years later, Kim was involved in a two-car accident and it appeared that she was at fault. Kim was not hurt, but the other driver suffered extensive medical injuries and auto damage.

Kim's auto insurance covered the repair bills, but not the victim's medical expenses. So to help her out, an attorney from Kim's insurance company slipped Kim a little tip: "Get rid of any assets in your name. If the victim sees that you do not own anything, he may not bother suing you for damages beyond your insurance coverage."

Kim wasted no time. The first thing she did was deed her 50 percent joint tenancy share back to her mother.

Several years went by and nothing happened. It seemed the plan worked to dissuade the victim from suing Kim. Then suddenly, from the proverbial left field, Mrs. Axelrod was served with lawsuit papers. She was being sued by *her daughter's accident victim*.

Why was the victim going after Mrs. Axelrod? Apparently, he hired a private investigator who discovered that at the time of the accident, Kim had a 50 percent interest in Mrs. Axelrod's property. Now the victim was going after Kim's ex-share.

The victim asked the court's permission to force a sale of Mrs. Axelrod's house. Once sold, he would take one-half of the proceeds to satisfy his judgment against her daughter.

Mrs. Axelrod thought she was protected when her daughter deeded it back to her. However, not only was she wrong, there was a substantial likelihood the victim would be successful in forcing a sale of one-half of the house. After all, courts do not favor people transferring their wealth to avoid creditors.

The Aftermath

I was able to make a deal with the victim to take $25,000 in lieu of proceeding with the lawsuit. Still, $25,000 was a substantial amount to Mrs. Axelrod. She had hoped to travel in her golden years, and now those plans had to be shelved. To come up with $25,000, she had to dip into her retirement savings.

As Ann Landers used to say, wake up and smell the coffee. You must realize that your child cannot defeat her creditors by deeding her joint tenancy share back to you.

---

3. "My daughter keeps telling me to put her as a joint tenant on my property so she can avoid probate when I die. She insists that none of the creditor problems you talk about will happen to her."

Children often lack the understanding and experience to realize that anything in life can happen. To them, it is absolutely unbelievable they could have an indebtedness problem. But as parents who have gone through the mill, we realize that those things in life that are not supposed to happen do happen. Maturity brings us experience that our children could not possibly envision.

Children can be very persuasive in convincing us to put their name on title to our property as joint tenants. However, do not succumb to your child's request. Your adult wisdom must prevail over your child's inexperience.

4. "My daughter said that if I put my house and apartment building in joint tenancy with her, she will pay less in death taxes after I die."

I am constantly amazed when people tell me they don't have to worry about the death tax because they put all their assets in joint tenancy with their children.

I remember one occasion when a client met with me on a real estate matter. He advised me that because he had put his $5 million of real estate into joint tenancy with his children, they would not have to pay anything in death taxes when he died.

This client was no dummy, but an astute businessman. But for whatever reason, he bought into the erroneous mindset that putting property in joint tenancy with children eliminates the death tax. As I point out in chapter 33 ("The Permanent Repeal of the Death Tax"), there is no death tax on estates of $5,340,000 or less. So, if your assets fall below that threshold level and you still somehow feel compelled to put your house in joint tenancy with your child, at least be informed that you should not doing so for death tax purposes.

The Hard Facts

As far as the IRS is concerned, any asset you owned jointly with anyone else is 100 percent yours. And as a 100 percent owner, the IRS will charge a death tax based on the full value of the jointly owned asset.

Certainly this tax seems unfair. Why should the IRS impose a death tax based on 100 percent of your property's value when you gave away 50 percent of it to your child? But when you think about it, the IRS's attitude does make sense. If the death tax could be avoided by giving property away, everyone would be doing just that, and the IRS would never get to impose a death tax.

Your child can challenge this treatment if she can show the IRS that she paid for her 50 percent share. However, unless you structured the transaction as a sale, your child will not be able to prove contribution.

Again, the IRS does not care how your wealth gets to your child. Whether she receives it through probate, joint tenancy, or Living Trust, the method of transfer is irrelevant. All the IRS wants to know is how much you owned when you died.

5. "I put my house into joint tenancy with my son years ago. Now I want to sell it. However, my son is giving me a hard time about signing the escrow papers."

Mrs. Hubbell put her son's name on title to her house as a joint tenant. She did so because she had heard that joint tenancy avoids probate.

Fifteen years later, Mrs. Hubbell wanted to sell her house so she could move into smaller quarters. After her broker had landed a buyer, Mrs. Hubbell received a phone call from the escrow officer, who said that since her son was on title to her house, her son's signature was needed on the title deed to the buyer.

Mrs. Hubbell's son, however, did not want to go along with the sale and gave his mother a hard time. Eventually, Mrs. Hubbell prevailed over her son, but only after threatening to cut him out of an inheritance.

Mrs. Hubbell thought that the worst was behind her, until she heard more news from the escrow officer. The title company now required the signature of *her son's wife!* Unless she signed the deed the title insurance company would not issue a title policy. And without a policy, there would be no sale.

Stunned by this information, Mrs. Hubbell called me. But all I could do for her was confirm everything she was told: If you want to sell your house, the title insurance company will not issue a title policy unless your spouse consents *in writing* to the sale, even if your spouse is not on the deed.

Easier said than done. When Mrs. Hubbell approached her daughter-in-law for her signature, she refused, explaining that she wanted to review the documents with an attorney before she signed them. Did the daughter-in-law ever make an appointment with an attorney? Of course not. She was too busy to find the time.

Ultimately, Mrs. Hubbell had to resort to the same threatening tactic she used with her son. Unless she signed off, her son would be cut off.

Under this pressure, her daughter-in-law finally signed the deed and other documents necessary for the sale. But look at the cost. Because of this dispute, Mrs. Hubbell has no contact with her son's family.

Solution: Just Don't Do It

The obvious solution to this problem is, quite simply, do not put your real estate in joint tenancy with your child. If you want to sell or refinance your real estate, you will have to go to your child for his signature and the signature of his spouse.

And they, being so smart and knowing what's best for you, may not sign.

6. "I put my daughter on title to my house and apartment building as a joint tenant. Since then, my daughter died in a car accident. Now, the IRS is claiming my daughter owned 100 percent of these assets. Unless I can prove I am the sole owner, I will have to pay a death tax on my own house and apartment building."

Dad put his daughter's name on title to his real estate as a joint tenant. After his death, she would be the 100 percent owner without any probate.

Unfortunately, Dad's daughter died first. His daughter's death was the biggest tragedy of his life, and he was further burdened by having to tangle with the IRS. Since his daughter was a joint tenant on Dad's real estate, the IRS presumed the real estate belonged *entirely to her*!

It was up to Dad to fight the proof battle. He had to show the IRS that he was the sole owner of the real estate and that he put his daughter on title only for probate-avoidance purposes. If Dad did not win, his properties would have been taxed in his daughter's estate—and taxed again when he dies!

It was an easy fight for Dad, as he had all the documents the IRS needed to see. However, the proof battle contributed significant additional stress to Dad's life.

Solution: Foresee the Unforeseeable

When parents put their child's name on title to real estate as a joint tenant; some of the risks to the property are foreseeable. But rare is the parent who factors in the risk of the child dying first and the surviving parent fighting the proof battle with the IRS.

When all the risks are added together, the probate-avoidance aspect of joint tenancy just doesn't compute. You can avoid these risks (and probate) by using a simple Living Trust to pass what you own to your children after you die.

---

7. "I thought I was being smart. I put my son and daughter on my house as joint tenants so they will avoid probate after I die. Unfortunately, my daughter died and now my son and I are the sole joint tenants. When I die, my son will get 100 percent of my house, with nothing to my daughter's children."

In fairness, your late daughter's share should go to her children. But when a joint tenant of property dies, the ones who usually inherit that property are the surviving joint tenants. The result is, your son will ultimately get 100 percent of your house (assuming, of course, that he outlives you).

You can always ask your son to leave a share to your daughter's children when he dies. What do you think he will say? If he says no, you can sever the joint tenancy with your son (if allowed by the state), which will free you to leave your half to your daughter's children.

Solution: The Living Trust

The ultimate solution to this problem would have been not to let it happen at all. A simple Living Trust could have accomplished the goal of probate avoidance. In addition, the Living Trust could have eliminated all risk of cutting out the children of your deceased daughter. Indeed, all you had to do was provide that your son and daughter are to receive your house when you die; and that if your daughter dies before you, her share is to go to her children, not your son.

8. "I own my house in joint tenancy with my only son. Who gets the house if, God forbid, he dies before me?"

If your son dies before you, his share will revert to you, leaving you as the 100 percent owner of the property. You will then need to establish a Will or Living Trust to designate who will receive your property after you die. If you don't set up an inheritance plan, the law will dictate who gets your property.

9. "I'm convinced that putting my daughter's name on title to my house is not such a great idea. But is it okay to put her name on my savings account, checking account, and certificates of deposit?"

As a practical matter, I do not discourage clients from putting their bank assets in joint ownership with their children. But if the cash asset is substantial, I would urge caution. It's one thing to risk losing a $1,000 checking account to your child's problems, but it is a completely different ball game to subject a $100,000 cash or brokerage asset to the same risk.

Part XIII

Inheritance Planning and Government Entitlements

42

Can You Leave Your Child an Inheritance Without Disqualifying Him from SSI?

or

How Your Child Can Inherit and Maintain His Government Entitlements

---

1. "I don't want my son's inheritance to disqualify him from SSI, Medicaid, or other entitlements."

Mr. and Mrs. Cook had three children, one of whom, Charles, was born somewhat mentally disabled. Charles was a loving son but, according to his parents, was a stressful element in their family life.

When Charles turned twenty-five, he moved to a residential facility that counsels the mentally disabled and steers them toward independent living. After a few years of group living, Charles was capable of living independently. He moved into an apartment in a nearby city and maintained a simple job at a sheltered workshop.

Charles received financial support from Supplementary Security Income (SSI), a program that guarantees a minimum income to a disabled child. But this income was barely enough to provide for his basic necessities: food, clothing, and shelter. For Charles to enjoy a more meaningful lifestyle, the Cooks supplemented

Charles's income with money for recreation, travel, and entertainment.

The Cooks felt at ease knowing their money afforded Charles a better standard of living. But, they wondered, what would happen to Charles after they died?

Would Charles only have an "SSI existence" for the rest of his life?

Would SSI benefits keep pace with inflation?

Government entitlement programs are always uncertain. Would the programs continue? If so, would Charles be able to support himself, or would he end up homeless?

The Cooks wanted absolute certainty that the lifestyle they provided for Charles would continue after they died. They wanted to leave Charles enough money to maintain that lifestyle. But they knew that if Charles received that money, he would be disqualified from SSI or other entitlements.

The Cooks wanted to know how to leave Charles an inheritance but, at the same time, keep his entitlements intact.

The Dilemma

Planning for families who have a disabled child is different from other types of inheritance planning. Decisions must be made about the disabled child's caregiver, living arrangements, financial needs, and preservation of entitlements.

Most entitlement programs are based on financial need. If Charles received his share of the inheritance, whether outright or in a Trust, he would no longer be needy enough to keep receiving government assistance.

I advised the Cooks of three alternatives to resolve their dilemma.

Choice Number 1: Forget the Entitlements—Just Leave the Disabled Child an Inheritance

One possibility was to leave money to Charles, forgetting the government entitlements. Let Charles participate in the inheritance and the lifestyle benefits it would bring.

If the inheritance is large enough, the loss of SSI and Medicaid may not be important. And if the inheritance is not sufficiently large, Charles could return to the entitlement programs after the inheritance was exhausted.

Of course, Charles could not receive his inheritance outright. If this plan was adopted, his inheritance would be left in a Protection Trust to provide for *all* his needs. The Trustee of this Trust would manage Charles's inheritance for the rest of his life, or until the money runs out. Chapter 10 is devoted entirely to this topic.

The Cooks dismissed this option. Although they wanted Charles to receive the benefits of his inheritance, they just could not stomach the idea of Charles losing his entitlements, particularly Medicaid.

Choice Number 2: Leave It to the Other Children and Hope for the Best

I advised the Cooks to leave Charles's share of the inheritance outright to their two daughters. With this plan, nothing would be on paper to show that Charles inherited anything, whether outright or in Trust. And by not inheriting, Charles would maintain his SSI benefits.

The Cooks immediately recognized the downside of this plan. Since their two daughters would be the owners of Charles's share, they could use it any way they wanted, with none of it being used for Charles's benefit.

The Cooks were correct. With their daughters receiving Charles's share, his inheritance would be at risk. They would have no legal obligation to use this money for his benefit. Nonetheless, this plan could be the answer to the Cooks' quandary. Granted, Charles's share would be owned by his sisters. But if his sisters recognized a duty to use that share for Charles's benefit, the risk of diversion would be minimal.

The Cooks trusted their two daughters to do the right thing, but there was no certainty. Charles could still end up on the street. They wanted a plan giving them greater assurance that Charles would be protected.

They could have this assurance with the Special Needs Trust.

Choice Number 3: The Special Needs Trust

SSI, Medicaid, and other government entitlements are designed to provide a disabled child with enough money for food, clothing, and shelter. But there is a plan that can provide the child with money to pay for things beyond those basic needs *without disqualifying the child from the entitlements.* This plan gives the disabled child the chance to experience life's extras: movies, travel, entertainment, recreation, sporting events, household appliances, and the like.

This plan is called the Special Needs Trust. A Special Needs Trust can be incorporated into the parents' Will or Living Trust and does not come into existence and is not funded until the parents' deaths.

The Special Needs Trust requires parents to leave a certain amount of money to a third-party Trustee. After the parents die, the Trustee can use the Trust money *only* for the disabled child's "special needs." If the Trustee uses the money for food, clothing, or shelter, the disabled child's entitlements may be reduced. Why? Because those basic needs are supposedly covered by the government entitlements.

How much money should parents leave to the Special Needs Trust? It depends. If the disabled child's housing has been taken care of, $50,000 to $100,000 may be sufficient, but because no one can predict the future availability of entitlement programs, greater amounts might be more sensible.

For the Cooks, the Special Needs Trust was the ultimate solution to their dilemma. They decided to incorporate this Trust in their inheritance plan and fund it with a small portion of their estate. They felt that this Trust would guarantee Charles more than a minimum standard of living without compromising his entitlements.

The Cooks left the balance to their daughters, hoping they would get involved in Charles's life and take care of any needs not covered by Charles's entitlements or the Special Needs Trust.

Part XIV

What Your Children Are Thinking . . . and You Live and You Learn

43

The Most Pressing Concerns
Your Children Have About
Your Will or Living Trust

or

Your Children Really *Want to
Ask About Their Inheritance . . .
but They Don't . . . Because
They're Afraid You Will Think
They Can't Wait for You to Die*

Your inheritance plan is your business and nobody else's. There is no legal obligation thrust upon you to tell your children about the existence or contents of your Will or Living Trust. After you bring it home from your lawyer's office, you can store it under lock and key and hide it from the world. If you are like most of my clients, your first instinct will be to do just that. As you place it in your safe-deposit box, you mutter aloud (perhaps with glee) that your children will never know about it or see it as long as you are alive.

In the last section of this book ("Final Thought"), I argue that you should run against that instinct and inform your children about your inheritance plan . . . and the size of their expected inheritance. I do not believe in your children waiting for the "reading of the Will" to learn that you have an inheritance plan and who gets what.

But, putting aside that admonition, let me inform you that if you are in your sixties and beyond, and if you have embargoed information about your inheritance plan, your children *are* curious about whether you have an inheritance plan and, if so, what it says about the distribution of the family money.

Actually, "curious" may not adequately describe some of your children's thought process over their share of inheritance. Try "preoccupied." Or "consumed." How do I know? Two out of every ten calls or meetings that I have during my normal work day are with children of clients with questions about their parents' inheritance plan. Of course, my lips are legally sealed from any such reveal (unless my clients authorize disclosure). But this anecdotal evidence highly suggests that children of aging parents have pressing inheritance questions and expectations on the brain.

Because these encounters consume a small part of my normal business day, I have devoted this chapter to the most commonly asked questions my clients' children have about their parents' inheritance plan. If you want to know what your children are thinking about your plan and their inheritance, here they are.

1. **"My dad feels he will die if he signs his Will or Trust. Of course, this doesn't make sense, but that is how he feels. How can I get him to do something?"**

You may feel your parents are the most rational people on earth. But when it comes to facing death issues, it is a whole new ball game. I have seen the most well-meaning and intelligent people equate signing their Will or Trust with impending death. If your parents are so death-minded, and you are attempting to get them past this illogical conclusion, let me save you some time. On an emotional level, you will not succeed. There is no way you can persuade your parents into thinking they will not die if they sign a Will or Trust.

To get them to do something, you have to hit them where they live.

Betty Talbert canceled for the fifth time the appointment she made for her parents. She complained that, once again, at the last minute, her parents broke their promise to see the lawyer about their inheritance plan. Her mother was agreeable, but her father was a "crusty old guy" who refused to deal with any death issues.

After five cancellations, I knew Betty would never get her parents into my office. So I moved the mountain to Mohammed. I thought I would have a better chance to overcome her father's stubbornness if he sat in the comfort of his own home.

As soon as I arrived at her parents' home, I could see that Betty was right. If you looked up *curmudgeon* in the dictionary, you would see her father's picture next to the definition. He did not shake my hand. He was bossy and pushy to his wife and daughter. He talked about how cheap everything was when he was younger. To top it off, he informed me that he hated lawyers and that I never earned an honest dollar in my life.

Although Betty's father talked a John Wayne lifestyle, the truth was that he was a coward. He simply could not hear any talk even remotely connected to death and dying. Still, there was "the Lawyer" standing in the middle of his living room, with his family present. That made it kind of hard for him to ignore me. I had barely started my spiel about the benefits of the Living Trust when he decided that he did not want to hear any more. "What did you say your name was? Condon? Condon, just bring me the damn papers!" he ordered.

Betty and I wasted no time. Two days later, she and I got his signatures, which took about ninety seconds, if that. Why so quick? Because the longer he spent with the inheritance documents, the longer he had to dwell on his mortality.

2. "I know for a fact that my parents have not done anything about establishing a Living Trust or any other kind of inheritance plan. I don't want to run into probate or estate taxes just because they

never got around to doing something. How do I get them to do something without coming across to them like a greedy bastard who can't wait for his parents to die?"

I used to believe that people would jump at the opportunity to save probate fees and estate taxes for their family. I once believed that "cutting out probate fees and taxes" were magic words that would spirit people to my office to establish a Living Trust or other inheritance plan. As a result, I have spoken those words to tens of thousands of people during my twenty-year practice at seminars, meetings, and consultations. If you count radio and television, the number of folks who have heard or watched me spread this gospel jumps to the hundreds of thousands.

Why, then, do I not have hundreds of thousands of Living Trust clients? Why do I not even have tens of thousands of Living Trust clients? Here's the truth I have gleaned after talking with so many client prospects during my practice: **People do care about the loss of their money to probate and estate taxes after they are gone, but not enough to pay a lawyer to do something about it.**

That's the truth, pure and simple. Paying a lawyer to do anything is out of the comfort zone for so many people, especially for those who have not had any prior dealings with lawyers.

People are not stupid. They recognize the benefits of the Living Trust and estate planning. But how much desire is there to pay for a product that produces a benefit that does not come into play until after their deaths? If your parents were to answer this question, they may answer, "Not a whole hell of a lot."

So, in the face of this "After Me, Who Cares" mindset, what can you do to get your parents to do something? Forget about the former magic words of "avoiding probate" and "saving estate taxes." Your parents have already heard them ad nauseam and have done nothing. Instead, use this three-step plan of attack:

1. Find a Living Trust lawyer and hire him or her to establish your own Living Trust. It does not matter if you need one or not.

That's not the point. The point is to be able to position yourself to say the words to your parents that appear in step 3, below.

2. While you are in the process of establishing your Living Trust, go to your parents' house and show them a draft of the document. Do not send it to them. Do not leave it on their front porch. You have to physically drop it in their laps.

3. While they are thumbing through the document, you then say these words:

> "Dad and Mom, I'm in the process of establishing my Living Trust, and it's great. When I'm gone, it's going to make things a lot easier for my family. And you know what? If I have one, you should have one. Let me make an appointment for you to see my lawyer. He's terrific. And if you're happy with him, let him do a Living Trust for you, and I'll pay."

With these steps, you will have removed from their path two obstacles that prevented them from establishing their Living Trust: finding a lawyer and paying a lawyer.

If that doesn't help, I suppose you can try gunpoint.

---

3. "My parents told me they have cut me out of their Will. They told me that if I get their money, I will spend it all on booze. I know I'm not the greatest son in the world, but I don't think it's fair that I get nothing. I'm doing the best I can to conquer my problem."

It is never too late for you to change, even if that change is motivated by money.

It is not uncommon for parents to disinherit a child because of their distress over some aspect of that child's lifestyle. But I have seen several situations where the child changed and his parents joyously redrafted their inheritance plan to include him.

On the other hand, you may know you will never change. Or you know that all the change in the world won't convince your parents to leave you a share of the inheritance. If that is the case, perhaps you can convince your parents that being cut out entirely is too severe a penalty. As an alternative, ask them to consider leaving you an inheritance in Trust. When they die, your inheritance will pass directly to a Trustee who will manage the money and pay you the income.

Your parents can even include a "motivation" provision for you. If you show the Trustee evidence indicating you no longer have the problem (letters from doctors, psychiatric reports, etc.), the Trustee can terminate the Trust and give you your inheritance share outright.

4. "Dad is dead and Mom is on her deathbed. Is there anything we can do?"

Almost weekly, I receive "the call." Mom is in the hospital, and the doctors say she is not going to make it. The caller is usually one of Mom's children. As Mom is about to breathe her last breath, the child asks, "Is there anything I should do?"

Why the call? Since I am not a doctor, I can only interpret it to mean that the child wants to know about the inheritance. The child, however, will not ask me any inheritance questions outright. That would be too crass. The blanket question "Is there anything I should do?" is a way of saving face.

Most likely, the child has one or both of the following concerns in mind.

"What Do I Have to Do to Get Mom's Money After She Dies?"

My answer depends on whether Mom has a Will or Living Trust. If she has a Will, you must go through probate to get your inheritance. If she has a Living Trust and it was properly funded, you can avoid probate. Or if Mom had your name on her assets as a joint tenant, you can acquire title simply by showing the asset holder Mom's death certificate.

"Mom Did Not Do Anything to Reduce the Death Tax. Is There Anything I Can Do on Her Behalf?"

Yes. The deathbed tax-planning strategy is: Mom must own less when she dies. The less she owns, the less there will be for the IRS to tax.

Mom can own less if she takes advantage of the $14,000 Annual Exclusion Gifts I discuss in chapter 37. For each $14,000 gift she makes, $5,600 may be saved in death taxes.

Earlier in her life, Mom may have refused to go along with this idea. Like many people, she may have felt uncomfortable parting with her money. On her deathbed, however, I am certain she would offer no objection.

If Mom is still able, she can write checks for $14,000 each, and the recipients must cash or deposit them *before Mom dies*. If Mom cannot sign the checks, it is usually too late to do any tax planning.

However, if Mom had signed a special Power of Attorney while she was competent, a third party (usually a child) may be able to make the Annual Exclusion Gifts on her behalf. If so, one of her children must bravely volunteer to move this plan into action, even if it means being absent from Mom's bedside during her final hours.

For more detailed information on this last-minute death-tax-reducing opportunity, see chapter 36.

5. "My brother is a successful doctor whom my parents put through medical school. They must have spent $250,000 on his education. My parents only spent $25,000 for my teaching degree. I love my parents and my brother dearly, but I think this is unfair. How can I get my parents to equalize?"

If Ann Landers were alive and responding to this question, she would say, "Get over it. It's your parents' money and they can do what they want." While Ms. Landers's philosophy may have found agreement with many of her readers, it does nothing to minimize the underlying threat that unequal financial treatment can destroy family relationships. My focus, on the other hand, is to resolve the problem so the family relationship is preserved when the inheritance is divided.

Money does funny things to people. You can know a person all your life, but you may never know a person's true nature until money becomes involved, whether through a gift, loan, or inheritance. As I say earlier in this book, it's as if a "money gene" deeply recessed in the human body rises to the surface to change a person's behavior in the money arena.

You say you love your brother and your parents, but it looks like this unequal financial treatment could cause some emotional distance between you and them. I don't blame you for your feelings. It's simple human nature to want "your share."

But look at it from your parents' perspective. Perhaps they were simply helping your brother at the time he needed help. If you had gone to medical school, I am certain that they would have paid for your "full ride." On the other hand, if your parents are to look at this situation from your viewpoint, they may understand that they have treated you financially unfairly.

It's a sensitive issue. You want fair treatment, but you do not want them to think of you as "money hungry."

What to do? Quite simply, approach them in a businesslike fashion. Explain to your parents how you feel. If they give you the Ann Landers response ("It's our money and we'll do what we want"), then you have your answer and you will simply have to live with it.

But if your parents, like most of my clients, cherish family harmony, they will work with you to ensure that you have received fairness. Perhaps they will establish (or amend) their inheritance plan to leave you an equal amount "off the top" before the rest of their estate is divided equally between you or your brother. Perhaps they will buy an insurance policy to pay the equalizing amount to you on their deaths. Or if they can afford it, perhaps they can simply write you a check.

Whatever their response, a discussion of this conflict with your parents is vital to its resolution.

---

6. "When I inherit my parents' wealth, will I need my own inheritance plan?"

When you inherit your parents' money and property, what are you going to do? Take a trip around the world? Buy a new car? Put a down payment on a house? Save for retirement? Pay off credit card debt? Go to Disneyland? Whatever you do, at some point you should consider establishing a Will or Living Trust for your inherited wealth.

Inherited Property Is Separate Property

The laws of most states say an inheritance is the separate property of the one who inherits. So if you are married when you inherit your parents' house or other assets, your spouse may not have any rights to your inheritance.

But if you are the conventional spouse, you will sign a deed or other transferring documents that put your spouse on title to your inherited money or property. With this transfer, your spouse will own one-half; if you die first, your spouse may own it all.

Why will you give your spouse one-half of your inheritance? Because, most likely, your spouse will ask you to. After all, as your spouse says, all married couples hold their property jointly . . . why not your inherited property as well?

Can you say no when your spouse asks you to put your inheritance in your joint names? Perhaps you can. But if you reject your spouse's suggestion, you risk sending the wrong message, because your spouse may think: "You don't love me," "You don't trust me," or "You don't think our marriage will last."

Is it so bad if your spouse ends up with your inherited wealth? To you, probably not. But what would your parents think? Most likely, they would want the family money they worked for all their lives to go to their grandchildren.

When a Man Loves a Woman . . .

When Jeff Collins's mother died, he was forty-two years old, married, and had one child. Jeff was the outright owner of all he inherited from his mother.

Would Jeff do the conventional thing and put his wife's name on title to his newly inherited wealth? I could just imagine his mother's reaction. As his late mother's friend and attorney, I felt duty-bound to tell Jeff what his mother would have liked him to do.

"Jeff, your mother did not leave you her money just so you could make your wife wealthy. If anything, providing for your wife is your job. If your mother were here, she would want you to take steps to ensure that your inheritance eventually passes to her grandson [Jeff's son]."

Solution: The Inherited Separate Property Trust

Jeff took my unsolicited advice quite favorably. He, too, realized that what was once his mother's should stay in the Collins bloodline. Jeff set up a Living Trust for his inherited property, leaving a small portion of his inheritance to his wife (if they were still married when he died) with the balance passing to his son.

The "Fallout"

Several weeks after Jeff signed his Living Trust, he phoned me. His voice was charged with emotion.

"My wife is mad as hell, Mr. Condon. When she read my Living Trust, she threatened to divorce me on the spot. She wants all my inheritance to go to her when I die."

To help take the heat off Jeff, I invited Jeff and his wife to meet with me. In front of both of them, I said that since I was the one who recommended the plan, I was responsible for their marital friction. I had considered the feelings of Jeff's dead mother over Jeff's live wife.

Resolving the Fallout: Leave Your Spouse a Substitute Inheritance

I then suggested how Jeff could be fair to his wife while remaining true to his mother's wish to keep her wealth in the Collins bloodline. Jeff could simply buy an insurance policy on his life with his wife as the beneficiary. When he dies, his wife would receive a large tax-free check from the insurance company, leaving Jeff free to leave his inherited wealth to his son.

This is a terrific way to balance the competing interests of Jeff and his wife, and I still believe that. Even the most irate spouse realizes that getting a comparable sum from the insurance company is a reasonable compromise.

However, Jeff's wife wanted more than a compromise. She wanted it all.

Jeff and his wife left my office saying they would think it over. About a week later, I received yet another emotion-packed phone call from Jeff.

"My wife has not stopped screaming at me. She says the only way she will forgive me is if I give her the insurance policy *plus* my inheritance. If I don't do it, I just know she is going to make good on her threat to divorce me." Once more, Jeff came down to my office. But this time I was not so accommodating.

"Jeff, I am your attorney, not your baby-sitter. Your wife is giving you a choice, so choose. Will you leave your mother's money to her, or will you leave it to your son? You are going to have to make up your mind and live with the decision you make."

Sometimes it is necessary to get tough with clients to get them to make tough decisions. Three months later, Jeff made his choice. "Mr. Condon, I have capitulated to my wife. I know it would be against my mother's wishes. But if that's the price I have to pay to avoid a divorce, so be it. I don't want to be a weekend father."

One week later, I met with Jeff and changed the terms of his Living Trust. All his inherited property will go to his wife when he dies. Before he left my office, he made one last request: He wanted an extra copy of his Trust. Why? Because his wife wanted immediate proof that he had really made the change.

Final Backup Solution: Pass the Buck to Your Parents

Like Jeff, you may also prefer to bypass your spouse and leave the wealth you inherited from your parents to your children. But as Jeff found, your spouse may have something to say about that.

How can you avoid this marital pressure? Tell your parents to keep you out of the decision-making loop and *let them decide* where their wealth goes when you die. This way, your dead parents, and not you, can take the heat from your spouse.

The buck is passed to your parents if they include the Transparent Trust in their Living Trust. I describe the Transparent Trust in detail in question 1 of chapter 9.

7. "I know I'm going to need some help managing my inherited money."

There will be no shortage of people who want to help you manage or invest your newly inherited wealth. In today's financial field, there is an abundance of financial planners, stockbrokers, and others offering to advise you on investments. If you need help managing your inheritance, give priority to a Trust Department of a local bank. The bank's Trust Department can provide you with whatever services you desire. It can pay the bills, collect the income, make your investment decisions, or share those responsibilities with you. As time goes by, you can diminish or enlarge these services as you see fit.

8. "My brother is my mother's caretaker. But I'm afraid he may take advantage of her weakened condition and gain access to her money. If he takes it all, there may be nothing left for me to inherit."

The next time your sibling asks for your help in taking care of Mom, remember this cardinal rule: The child who assumes the burden of Mom will get the lion's share of Mom's money when Mom dies.

Mrs. Roblin: For Love or Money?

Mrs. Roblin ran a restaurant with her husband for twenty-five years. When her husband died, she kept the business going for several more. Eventually, the business became too much for her, and she needed some help.

Mrs. Roblin had three children and looked to them to "carry the torch forward."

Her two daughters, Cherise and Chelsea, were not interested because, as they told their mother, they had lives of their own. With husbands, children, and social lives, they simply did not want to be saddled with the extra burden of running the business.

It was up to her son, Jack. If he said yes, he would be his mother's business partner; if he said no, the restaurant would close.

Jack said yes, but not on a volunteer basis. Running the restaurant, after all, would be a full-time job. So Jack instructed his mother to dip into her substantial savings and pay him a generous salary. Since Mrs. Roblin was so desperate for his help, she readily agreed.

Taking Over Mrs. Roblin

The job turned out to be more than Jack anticipated. Shortly after Jack took over, his mother became ill and incapacitated. Now, Jack was running the restaurant *and* providing for his mother's daily needs.

Because of the added burden, he felt justified in being paid more money. So Jack instructed his mother to increase his salary, and she complied.

Six years later, Mrs. Roblin died with her savings diminished to almost nothing. The only inheritance she could leave her three children was her house and a debt-laden restaurant business.

You Get What You Deserve

After their mother died, Cherise and Chelsea discovered for the first time how their brother had siphoned their mother's money under the guise of salary, and they were outraged. Off they went lawyer shopping, hoping to find one who would tear Jack apart in court and make him pay back all the money he took.

The Roblin sisters came to me. They told me their tale of woe, and I agreed with them. Their brother had taken advantage of Mom, and they suffered as a result. But if they thought they were getting a sympathetic ear from me, they were sadly mistaken.

As Cherise and Chelsea sat and listened to my little self-righteous speech, I could see them fuming at my every word:

"Cherise and Chelsea, I don't think you have any right to complain, because you have received a full benefit from your brother's efforts. While you were free to go about your normal lives, your brother was running the restaurant and taking care of your mother. While you visited your mother on occasion, it was Jack who drove your mother to the doctor, changed her diapers, bought her groceries, and did her laundry. Because of him, you lived without the burden of your mother on your shoulders.

"And now you have discovered the price of your freedom. Your brother drew out a large salary for his efforts. Because of it, your inheritance is significantly reduced.

"Cherise and Chelsea, there is an old proverb that I believe is so applicable here: The last one on the scene gets the money. And that is exactly what happened to your inheritance."

Having withstood my lecture (which I do not believe registered with them at all), the Roblin sisters then asked me their key question: Did they have recourse against their brother? Could they shake him down and make him give some of his salary back?

Not in their lifetime, I answered. Certainly, they could sue him and attempt to get a judgment. But unless their brother had assets to satisfy the judgment (which he did not), the judgment would be just a piece of paper. They cannot, after all, get blood from a stone.

The Roblin sisters were not appeased by my analysis and went to see other lawyers. However, their advice was the same: An expensive lawsuit was not justified unless they could find substantial assets in their brother's name.

Solution: Get Involved in Your Aged Parent's Affairs

If your sibling volunteers to care for your ill or aged parent, wise up! Question this sibling's motivation. Ask yourself: Is this gesture made out of love or money?

This question may sound cynical—and it is! But it is also justified. For thirty-five years, I have been on the front line and have seen this situation at least a hundred times. On most occasions, siblings have discovered that their on-the-scene sibling has usurped their parent's money or disposed of it in such a way that it could not be recovered.

When your parent becomes ill or aged, do not allow just one of your siblings to become your parent's sole caretaker—share the burden. Not only are you doing a kind thing for your parent, you can take steps to protect your own interests.

9. "My sister is taking care of Mom. I thought this was very kind of her, but now I'm not so sure. I think she is trying to control Mom's pocketbook."

It is never too late to volunteer to help your sister care for your ailing parent. But what if your sister won't let you help? About once a month, I receive a call like the one I received from Mr. Brenner:

"Mr. Condon, I think my sister is up to something. When Mom became ill, she was right there to be with her. I was glad to see her helping Mom out. But now I'm worried. If I try to visit Mom, my sister says Mom's not up to it. Whenever I call, my sister answers the phone and says that Mom can't talk right now."

Should Mr. Brenner be concerned? You better believe it! When his sister controls Mom, she also controls Mom's pocketbook. No one is around to stop the sister from forcing or tricking Mom into signing a Power of Attorney. No one can intervene when the sister forces Mom to make her the sole beneficiary of Mom's Will. No one can step in when the sister gets Mom to add her name to Mom's checking accounts.

If Your Sibling Won't Let You Share the Burden

If your sibling has already taken over and will not accept your help, be suspicious! The biggest indicator of something foul going on is being denied access to your parent. Your sibling may be sequestering your parent to get control of your parent's money.

What action can you take to gain access to your sequestered parent? Unfortunately, you can do nothing legally short of lawsuits.

A Warning About These Lawsuits

You must be careful how you perceive these lawsuits. It is easy for them to lull you into a false sense of security.

If your brother has sequestered Mom and you believe he is taking Mom's money, you may wind up doing nothing about it. Why? Because you overestimate the power of the lawsuit. You think to yourself, "Oh, well, I can always file a lawsuit later."

These lawsuits, however, should never be your first line of offense. Not because you may lose (which you probably will), but because a lawsuit after the fact is no substitute for being intimately involved in your aged parent's life.

A lawsuit should only be used as a final offensive against your controlling sibling.

The Conservatorship Lawsuit

While your parent is alive, you can go to court and ask the judge to appoint you (or a third party) as conservator over your parent. As conservator, you may wrest your controlling sibling's hand from your parent's affairs and try to undo the financial damage done.

Of course, establishing a conservatorship is like any lawsuit. It involves time, money, lawyers, and it will take an emotional toll on you. And after all is said and done, you may lose.

The Undue Influence Lawsuit

If your parent dies with a Will or Living Trust that names the controlling sibling as sole beneficiary, consider bringing an undue influence lawsuit against your controlling sibling. If you win, the judge will force him to return all the money he siphoned from your mother. In this lawsuit, you tell the court four things.

First, before your mother died, she was physically and/or mentally weakened.

Second, while in her weakened state, your controlling sibling was your mother's last caretaker.

Third, you attempted to gain access to your mother, but you were denied by your controlling sibling.

Fourth, your controlling sibling coerced your mother into doing things she would not have normally done, and your mother did not have the strength of mind to fight back.

Proving that your controlling sibling unduly influenced your parent is extremely difficult. To increase your chances of winning, start preparing for the lawsuit while your sequestered parent is alive. Keep a diary of all controlling or coercive acts exercised by your controlling sibling. On the witness stand, you may be able to recite those written observations for the jury.

Also, consider hiring a private detective to tail your controlling sibling. He or she may be able to dig up some more dirt that can help you in your litigious future.

44

Cautionary Tales from the Inheritance Arena

or

Read About . . . and Learn From . . . My Previous Mistakes and the Mistakes of My Clients

Legal knowledge about Living Trusts is not enough to prevent problems from occurring in the Inheritance Arena. Like the medical doctor who gains experience on the ills and bodies of patients, so it is with the Living Trust attorney who gains wisdom, understanding, and sensitivity to forecasting potential problems by seeing "what happens" when money and property passes from a deceased person to a spouse, children, grandchildren, and others.

The stories in this chapter are true. Each is representative of "things gone wrong" because of the failure to foresee consequences in the process of money and property going from the dead to the living. They are incidents from which I gained experience to better advise clients on the "right way" of transferring money and property after death.

With these stories, you will gain invaluable information and insight about your own Living Trust or other inheritance plan that only comes from "being there" when assets go from the dead to the living.

With these stories, you will see that unintended consequences are inherent in the Inheritance Arena.

With these stories, you will benefit from my many years of observing the hurt that occurs when a mistake is made in the Living Trust or the Inheritance Arena.

Cautionary Tale 1: Probate Is the "Lawyers' Retirement Fund"

Lesson to be learned: If you have real estate . . . you need a Living Trust to transfer that real estate after your death.

Mr. Schultz was a cantankerous eighty-year-old man who told me with pride, "Condon, I've always gotten along pretty good without having to pay a lawyer for anything."

So what brought Mr. Schultz to my office? He got remarried . . . and he was feeling the pressure from new wife to go along with a new inheritance plan.

Mr. Schultz continued, "When my first wife died five years ago, I became the 100 percent owner of our house. When I remarried, I planned to keep it that way. But, my new wife wants us to sell our houses and pool all the money into a new house for the both of us. Since we're each putting up one-half of the cash, I want to keep one-half of the new house in my name."

Not such a great idea. To put it mildly, it's a tricky proposition for "second time around" spouses with children from their respective first marriages to own property jointly.

If Mr. and Mrs. Schultz take title to the new house as "tenants-in-common" (also known as "tenancy-by-the-entirety" in some states), the half of the first spouse to die will belong to whomever he or she leaves it. So . . . if the new Mrs. Schultz dies first and her inheritance plan leaves her half to her children from her first marriage, those children would be partners in the house with Mr. Schultz's.

What's wrong with that? Because one co-owner (the new Mrs. Schultz's "first children") can always bring a legal action to boot the other co-owner (Mr. Schultz) out of occupancy and force a sale. If Mr. Schultz plans on staying in that house, this is not a pleasant scenario.

Of course, this is a goose/gander scenario, as Mr. Schultz's "first children" could do the booting to the new Mrs. Schultz if he dies first. Still . . . doesn't Mr. Schultz want the relief of knowing that he won't get the boot from the house if he is the survivor? And doesn't Mr. Schultz want to have the satisfaction of knowing that his new wife will be able to live in the house for the rest of her life if he dies first?

These are not rhetorical or academic questions. This is real life with real consequences. I put these questions to Mr. Schultz and he responded, "Do I look like an idiot, Condon? Do I want to get evicted by my new wife's kids? No! And do I want to be sure that my kids won't kick out my new wife if I die first? No! So . . . what else is there we can do?"

I then told Mr. Schulz about another "joint owner" option, which was for them to take title to their new house as "joint tenants with right of survivorship." With this method, the surviving spouse automatically inherits the half of the first spouse to die. That surviving spouse then owns the entire house and will be free to leave it all to his or her "first children"—completely cutting out the "first children" of the one who died first.

In the context of "second time around" spouses, this is also not such a great way to take title to property. The spouse who dies last ""wins" the entire property. And so do the children of the spouse who dies last. Not exactly a pleasant prospect for both spouses.

In any event, after my little speech about these downsides of joint ownership, I started my usual spiel of how a Living Trust could be used to prevent those problems while avoiding the probate process, but Mr. Schultz interrupted me with the usual exasperated client refrain: "Sounds too complicated. I'll just do the tenants-in-common thing that you talked about first."

"Okay, I replied. "I'm not sure that's the best thing for both of you. But, if that's what you want, then just tell the escrow that you want to take title in your names as tenants-in-common. But, since you'll own your share in your sole name; you must have a Will or a Living Trust that says who gets your half of the house on your death, and your new wife needs to do the same." But, when I quoted him the fees for the Living Trust packages, he muttered aloud something about a Will being cheaper, stood up, thanked me for my time, and left.

I get that a lot after my price quotes—the "thanks-for-your-time-I'll-get-back-to-you-but-not-really" routine. I'm used to it. Still . . . I could do without the muttering aloud, which I have always found more than slightly grating.

Mr. Schultz never got back to me—but his second wife called me after he died. At our meeting, Mrs. Schultz presented me with a page torn out of a letter-size notebook. This page, according to her, was in this handwriting. It had words sounding like a Will that said, in essence, that it was his wish that his share of the house would go to Mrs. Schultz.

"Is this valid?" she asked me with a quiet sense of desperation. To her great relief, I informed her that it was a valid California holographic Will . . . written, signed and dated entirely in the handwriting of her husband. But, this Will was not self-executing. In order to carry out Mr. Schultz's wishes, the Will had to be submitted to court for "probate," which, in a nutshell, is the court-supervised process of transferring assets from the dead to the living. The probate process took about thirteen months and about $12,000 in court costs and attorneys' fees . . . but she ultimately ended up with the entire house.

End of a fairly dry story? Not quite. At some point during the probate process, I advised Mrs. Schultz that now that she owned the entire house, she should have a Living Trust. With a Living Trust, she retains ownership and control of the house during her life. On her death, the Living Trust then transfers the ownership of the house to her children without that probate court non-sense. But like her husband, Mrs. Schultz did not warm too kindly to my price quote: Actually, her reaction was somewhat aghast: "Mr. Condon, I can get that same Living Trust for half the price from one of those outfits that advertises in the *Los Angeles Times*. You just got thousands of dollars from me from probate—and now you want more money from me for my Living Trust? You should do it for free!"

A frustrated client insisting that I should do free legal work? I think I would have preferred the muttering aloud.

But, as with her husband, Mrs. Schultz left my office . . . never to return. But who did I see about a year later? Mrs. Schultz's children! Who informed me that their mother died before completing her Living Trust—and who hired me to engage in yet another probate process to transfer the house from their deceased mother to them.

More fees for me? Of course! Another probate = more attorney services = more money for the attorney. If I'm not getting paid, I might as well be at the beach.

But this time, the fees would be double! Why? Because the probate fees are based upon a percentage of the value of the assets going through the probate process. The $12,000 I received from Mr. Schultz's probate was based on the value of half the house . . . because it was only his half that went through probate. Now . . . with Mrs. Schultz being the owner of the WHOLE house—and with the WHOLE house now subject to the probate process—my fees would be based on the value of the WHOLE house!

Silently, I thanked my deceased clients for not doing a Living Trust and unwittingly contributing to my retirement fund.

Post-Cautionary Tale Comment: There are actually two points to take from this Cautionary Tale. First, and quite simply, if you own real estate and don't use a Living Trust to transfer that real estate after your death, you will have diminished your assets by the amount of money consumed by probate costs and fees.

Could you avoid the Living Trust *and* probate by adding your children on title to your real property as joint tenants with right of survivorship? Sure! They would automatically receive ownership after you die. However, by putting your children on title to your house, you subject your house to your children's problems. Your children file bankruptcy? Your children get a divorce? Your children cause an accident and have insufficient insurance? Your children have tax problems? Your children pile up the creditors? Quite possibly, your house can be sold during your life to resolve those problems.

Bonus Second Point . . . As Promised! In these "new start" situations where remarried spouses sell their respective houses and pool the funds for a new house, a Living Trust is essential to ensure that the survivor can remain in the home until the survivor's death without the fear of getting the boot from the family of the first spouse to die.

If title is held as "joint tenancy, with right of survivorship" (or as a "tenancy in the entirety"), the survivor will be the 100 percent owner and the survivor can direct who shall receive the entire property, such as children from a prior marriage, or even a new spouse.

In a community property state, such as California, taking title as "community property" or as "tenants-in-common" gives the first spouse to die the power to bequeath by Will or Trust his/her one-share directly to that spouse's "side." However, the "side" of that deceased spouse becomes "partners" with the survivor, and any partner can always force the end of that partnership by forcing a sale of that house, which potentially puts the survivivor out on the proverbial street.

The only solution? The "newlyweds" should establish a Living Trust, put title to the new house in the Living Trust, and put instructions in the Living Trust that say, in essence, the survivor is in control of the entire property for the rest of his or her life, and the house (or the sale proceeds) shall be distributed equally to each "side" after the survivor dies.

Cautionary Tale 2: "I Don't Want Him!"

Lesson to be learned: You have to predict the future about the nature of the relationship between Trustee and Beneficiary.

I've heard a lot of grumbling from my colleagues about having to make "field trips" to meet with clients. Which has always mystified me. It almost goes without saying that an integral part of this job is meeting with elderly and infirm people in their homes. Besides . . . who doesn't relish the opportunity to get out of the office during the workday for a few hours? One can't make a quick side trip to Wild Oats for their incredible oatmeal-chocolate chip cookies if one is chained to a desk.

It was at such a "house call" that I came upon Mrs. Clancy. Her caretaker opened the front door and ushered me into the main bedroom, where Mrs. Clancy was propped up in her bed. I started to introduce myself, but Mrs. Clancy appeared to be in no mood for pleasantries, as she shouted, "I don't want him! Get rid of him!"

I stopped in my tracks. Already this was not the typical housecall where I encounter a docile and infirm elderly person. Though 87 and bedridden, Mrs. Clancy appeared to have a residue of strength and full mental acuity. And I'm not usually greeted by the occupant with a loud demand to do something.

"Who don't you want, and why don't you want him?" I asked Mrs. Clancy, who then proceeded to enlighten me. Her husband died a few months prior to my visit. They established their Living Trust some years ago with another attorney. She didn't pay much attention to the documents. Her husband hired the attorney. He made the arrangements. She went where he went. She signed what he signed.

Now that she was alone, the words in that Living Trust came to reality. Their Living Trust provided that if Mr. Clancy died first, a third party would be in charge of their assets in the Living

Trust—their money and property—for the rest of her life. This shocked Mrs. Clancy to her core, as she had no idea that this was the plan that her husband had arranged.

I don't think that Mr. Clancy was attempting to "get" his wife by removing her from control of the family assets if he died first. In light of his wife's physical infirmity, I am reasonably certain that he was looking out for her best interest by arranging for a third-party trustee to manage their assets for her benefit, which would leave her free to focus solely on her health.

Eventually, Mrs. Clancy did come around to that line of thought. The big problem that she had—and the reason for my being summoned to her bedside—was that she hated, nay, LOATHED the person her husband selected as the Trustee: the attorney who drafted their Living Trust.

I knew this attorney. Somewhat of an abrupt, impatient, "no bedside manner" type. The first time Mrs. Clancy learned of the attorney's new role in her life was when he showed up for the funeral. As Mrs. Clancy said, "It went downhill from there."

I suppose Mr. Clancy must have had faith in his attorney. But it is unusual for the drafting attorney to want this "job" because it is often difficult to sustain a law practice while engaging in the daily rigors of managing, administering, and distributing the assets of someone else. I figured that the attorney accepted this responsibility for the obvious reason—fees. Their Living Trust said that the attorney would get a yearly salary of 2 percent of the value of the trust estate for his trustee services. Which is way more than the usual and customary trustee fee of 1 percent!

"I feel like a beggar asking him for my money," Mrs. Clancy continued. "It's like it's his money. One time I said I needed one of those automatic pillows that you can adjust with buttons. He said that I could make do with the pillows that I have. But it hurts when I move and I told him that. But that son-of-a-bitch didn't care! I want him out, Condon! I'll take anyone else—but I want him gone".

This wasn't my first rodeo with a beneficiary and a trustee not seeing eye-to-eye. Usually I can smooth out the conflicts by calling a meeting to bring both parties in the same room, where each side has the opportunity to "air" their differences, which I can then resolve with old-fashioned problem-resolution. But, when the trustee-beneficiary relationship turns poisonous and, for whatever reasons, cannot be paved over with my skill set, the trustee typically resigns . . . often graciously . . . sometimes grudgingly.

But, in this case, the attorney refused to resign. I called him after my meeting with Mrs. Clancy. I explained how displeased she was with his curt and "know-it-all" manner, how she adamantly believed he was not responsive to her most basic of needs, and how vehement she was in ridding herself of his control over her and her assets.

I then said something that, upon reflection, must have come across as patronizing, especially to a fellow professional: "C'mon, buddy. I can't see how you would want to keep being trustee in such a poisonous atmosphere. If I was in your shoes, I wouldn't want to wake up every single day with the knowledge that I have to deal with someone that hates me. Life is so short . . . too short to be around such negative energy. So what do you say? Let's give both you and Mrs. Clancy a break from each other and each of you will live a happier life".

Well, whether he was a control freak, or whether he wanted to maintain his trustee fees, or whether he was miffed by my borderline-insulting commentary, he declined, mumbling something about "loyalty to the husband."

When I gave the bad news to Mrs. Clancy, she wanted to know what else could be done to bounce him as trustee. I told her that she could bring an action in court to have him removed, but that there was little chance of success. Why? Because being a jerk is not enough to get a trustee booted. If we could prove that he embezzled or mismanaged the trust estate, then sure, he would certainly get the court-ordered removal. But, without those facts, there was nothing Mrs. Clancy could do.

Or was there? "%$# him!" she said to me. "He doesn't give

one %$# about my husband or his wishes. He just wants money. So that's what I'll do. I'll just offer that piece of @$% some money to resign.

So . . . Mrs. Clancy offered him money to resign, something that I did not even consider. Did he take it? You bet he did! He took that $25,000 and signed the resignation documents so quickly that I conjectured that he must have had creditors chasing after him.

Post-Cautionary Tale Comment: Two comments, actually.

First, if you signed your Living Trust without reading it because you had faith in your spouse to make the right decisions, you should really take a look at the "who-gets-what" and "how-they-get-it" sections before the first one of you dies. If you don't, you, like Mrs. Clancy, may be shocked to find yourself in a situation that was unimaginable to you.

Second, getting the right trustee to manage the family money and property for the surviving spouse's benefit is a very important choice. If the surviving spouse and the trustee can't get along, problems and unhappiness will arise.

Putting a private person in charge of one's money and property is dangerous. Sometimes "faith" is not enough. The private person is not bonded. There is no policeman looking over that person's shoulder. There is no one around to say "No." The money and property goes into that person's name, which empowers that person to do what he/she wishes with the assets. The private person will charge the same, if not more than the bank or corporate trustee and may not do as good a job.

My personal preference is the professional trustee, which is contrary to most clients' decisions. If a personality or management-driven conflict arises between the beneficiary and the individual assigned by the bank or other institutional trustee to interact with the beneficiary, a different person can be assigned. However, if a private person is chosen as trustee after the first spouse dies, and that choice causes great stress to the surviving spouse, it will be more difficult to substitute that trustee without court involvement—if at all.

CAUTIONARY TALE 3: "SI, SI, COMMUNITY PROPERTY"

Lesson to be learned: Terminate the economic connection between your "first children" and your second spouse.

At age 65, Boyd was the model of the conventional family man with a successful building contracting business, two children, and a long-standing reputation for civic and community service. His wife had passed away, and he often talked of meeting someone new, perhaps a young woman from South America, where his business often required him to be.

Well, one day he came to my office and introduced me to his new wife, Carmen, a 35-year-old woman from Costa Rica . . . who was holding their one-year-old baby girl. After my initial incredulousness dissipated, I admit I quietly snickered at Boyd for having to struggle with the installation and use of baby car seats and strollers at age 65.

My silent dubiosity, however, turned into quiet admiration for Boyd as I engaged in light banter with Carmen, who was just learning to speak English. She was charming and though she was much younger than he was, her affection for Boyd seemed sincere. Carmen turned out to be a blessing to Boyd because during those years, I never saw him look so good and have so much energy.

What brought them to my office was the baby. Boyd wanted a plan that would leave something for his "first children" and also take care of his new wife and child.

The "first children–second wife" scenario is a most difficult one to handle unless there is great wealth to satisfy and placate both sides. Boyd did not have great wealth and, thus, could not accomplish the goal of making everyone happy. Still, Boyd was insistent that his "first children"—his two sons—and new family each receive an inheritance in a way that would satisfy all concerned.

I advised Boyd that he could achieve that end by giving money to his sons to purchase an insurance policy on his life, with Boyd continuing to give his children money for the annual premium payments. By doing this, his children would receive the insurance proceeds on his death with no tax obligation. Also, Boyd could put provisions in his Living Trust that establish a "sub-trust" for Carmen where she would have the use of his assets for the rest of her life, and which upon her death would be distributed to their new daughter.

Boyd then insisted I explain this plan to Carmen in a way that she could understand. In my best Spanglish, I explained that if Boyd dies first, his money and property would provide for her and her child. She stared at me blankly and said, "Si, si, community property."

Well, that response was inaccurate and irrelevant, and compelled me to somehow convey that Boyd's assets were the separate property of Boyd, not the community property of Boyd and Carmen. In my best broken Spanish, I said, "Lo siento, Carmen. La Casa de Boyd. Y el dinero de Boyd. Solamente the separada propiedad de Boyd." (Don't laugh! With four years of high school Spanish being a distant memory, I thought that was a fairly decent stab at it.)

Boyd liked the plan I suggested—and that's what he did. He gifted the money to his "first children" for them to purchase a $1,000,000 life insurance policy on his life and additional funds each year for the premium payments. He also amended his Living Trust to provide the sub-trust for Carmen and their daughter.

A few times over the next fifteen years, Boyd stopped by to see me and make slight trust revisions. Carmen's English became much better, if not profoundly so. Their daughter was growing up as a California surfing girl, and it was easy to see she was Boyd's delight.

I heard nothing further about his "first children" nor did I see them until it became apparent Boyd was terminal. They came to my office to see me to find out if they would receive any inheritance from their father. Of course, as Boyd's attorney, I could not disclose that privileged information. I asked them if they had been to see their father, and one of them said, "No. We just want to know about the money."

I was a bit taken aback by the boldness of their statement. Usually when I meet the estranged children of my clients, there is some attempt to summon a modicum of sincere concern for their parents, even though everyone in room knows that the inheritance (or lack thereof) is the main motivation for their visit. But with Boyd's "first children," there was no such attempt at disguise. Nonetheless, being unable to give them the response they had sought, I simply told them, "I'm sure your ailing father would like to see you. Have a nice day." They shuffled silently out of my office.

From time to time, Carmen called to apprise me of Boyd's condition. I'm sure it wasn't easy for her to take care of Boyd through the periods of chemotherapy; the radiation, the weight loss and changing of diapers. "Not once," she said, "did his sons come and see him."

How ironic. Boyd's friends and associates (including myself) initially condemned his "May-December" marriage as a stereotypical old-man fantasy arrangement. While his "first children" couldn't give a damn about their father. Carmen and their daughter turned out to be the the best things that ever happened to him, giving him life's greatest joy.

Post-Cautionary Tale Comment: To arrange the insurance policy for his "first children," Boyd and his sons must have had, at least, some basic communication with each other. Therefore, those children would have some knowledge and expectation about their windfall prior to their father's death. So when they came to my office, they must have been aware of their expected insurance windfall. Yet they still were asking me about the money. Apparently, the $1,000,000 policy was not satisfactory to them. Personally, in light of how happy his new family made him, I think those sons were lucky to get anything.

Still, the point of this story is that a client with two families used an insurance policy to provide a monetary inheritance for his "first children," and you can too if you are on your second time around and you want to ensure that both sides are taken care of in the inheritance arena.

I know, I know. Just the word "insurance" makes your eyes (and mine) glaze over. But keep it simple. When you purchase a policy as a device to provide an inheritance for both your "first children" and second family, you don't need to know about cash value or where you fall in the actuarial tables. All you are thinking is how much that policy will cost to provide one side (either the "first children" or the second spouse) with an amount that is reasonably comparable to the inheritance that the other side will receive.

Cautionary Tale 4: "I Only Have the Children I Choose to Tell You About"

> Lesson to be learned: A child that you want to exclude from an inheritance may still inherit from you.

When I realized that I had screwed up, I must not have been able to disguise the fear of failure—and of being sued—on my face. Because Josh reassuringly said to me, "Don't worry, Mr. Condon. I'm not planning to make any claim." Fortunately for me, Josh was not the litigious type.

About 20 years prior to this meeting with Josh, I established a Living Trust for my client, Mr. Warburton. Josh introduced himself as the son of Mr. Warburton, who died about two months before.

As Josh and I met, I perused the Warburton file and saw my handwritten notes next to the usual litany of questions an inheritance lawyer asks a first-time client. One of those standard questions was: Do you have any children of your current marriage or prior marriage? My note next to this question recorded Mr. Warburton's response: "Two children from marriage, Henry and Denise. No prior marriages. No other children."

I assumed Josh was one of those two children who were here for advice on the administration of the Warburtons' Living Trust until I noticed that Josh wasn't Henry or Denise. "Josh," I asked, "do you also go by 'Henry'? To that Josh replied, "No, Mr. Condon. My name is Josh, and I just found out a few months ago that Warburton was my biological father".

It was math that drove me to law school, but I now had to engage in some math to process the information that Josh just presented to me. Mr. Warburton was married for 55 years before his death. Josh was 63. Which means that Mr. Warburton would have been around 19 when Josh was born. In light of what I remembered about Mr. Warburton, an unassuming and conventional business-and-family type, I thought it unlikely that he sired a child out of wedlock while still a teenager.

The stuff of cinema, yes? Well . . . it can also be the stuff of real life, as Josh so informed me.

"That's about it, Mr. Condon. It was at the beginning of World War II. Warburton was in the Navy. About to go overseas. Met my mother who was only 18. Had their fling. He left. She never saw him again. After I was born, my mother met and married a guy named Dan Balter. I thought Dan was my father. He and my mom raised me. Dan died about a month ago. And for whatever reason my mom felt compelled to tell me that Dan was not my biological father."

Here was Josh, Mr. Warburton's unacknowledged yet biological child. And here was Mr. Warburton's Living Trust . . . which made no mention of Josh. With these two elements present, Josh could make a claim against Mr. Warburton's estate to receive an equal share.

Why was Josh entitled to an equal share? Most states have certain laws that state, in effect, that if a parent has a child at the time that person executes his inheritance plan . . . **and that child is not expressly omitted as a beneficiary,** then that child STILL gets a piece of that parent's estate. Even if the parent did not intend to leave any piece to that child! This is the law of "pretermission," which is in effect in most states. Basically, if your inheritance plan fails to mention or make any reference to your child, we shall presume that failure was accidental and the child should not be penalized because of that inadvertent omission.

However, there is a way around this law; if a parent want to cut out a child, the parent merely has to state in the Living Trust that the child is cut out. It's that simple.

This is why I felt myself becoming nervous when Josh told me his soap-opera story. Mr. Warburton's Living Trust made no mention of Josh or cutting out Josh. As a result, Josh could file a claim demanding one-third of Mr. Warburton's estate. It matters not whether Mr. Warburton knew about Josh's existence at the time he established his Living Trust. The law is the law. And because I was the attorney who drafted that document, Mr. Warburton's two other children could come after me for failing to include a provision cutting out Josh.

Sure, I relied on the response of Mr. Warburton when he said that he had no children other than Hank and Denise. But, since when has common sense stopped anyone from suing the "deep-pockets" attorney?

Well, it turns out Josh was a good guy who had no interest in creating any trouble for anyone. Josh was a physician with his own family—a wife and two children. He didn't want to meet his two half-siblings and he didn't want to make any claim against Mr. Warburton's estate as an "accidentally-cut-out-child." (Besides, Josh had twice the money that Mr. Warburton had.) When Josh's mother told him the truth about Mr. Warburton being his biological father, naturally Josh wanted to find out more about him.

When Josh finally tracked him down, he found that he had died about a month before. Bad timing. So Josh was left with talking with his father's old "cronies" to discover more about that man. And that's why Josh came to my office. Not for money, but for memories.

Post-Cautionary Tale Comment: A physician cannot fully or accurately diagnose and treat a patient who is less than forthcoming about his medical history. The same holds true in the context of attorneys and their clients. In order for attorneys to give the best and most salient advice possible, they have to know everything relevant about that client. Which is why there is an attorney-client confidentiality privilege. And there is nothing more relevant in the inheritance planning field than the existence of a child.

If a child was born before the parent executed an inheritance plan that does not mention that child, then that "omitted child" may be entitled to take a portion of that parent's estate. The underlying legal philosophy is that failing to mention the "omitted child" must have been an oversight and the law will correct that oversight by treating that "omitted child," for inheritance purposes, as a child who is entitled to participate equally with the decedent's other legitimate children.

However, if the parent signs an inheritance plan after birth of the "omitted child" and mentions or specifically disinherits the child, the child has no inheritance rights.

Cautionary Tale 5: "You Can Take This Painting— and Shove It!"

Lesson to be learned: The one who gets the valued item may also get the death tax bill on that item.

My secretary buzzed me and said, "There's a cowboy in the office and he wants to see you." He had no appointment, but so what? After years and years of dealing with the same type of client, I wanted to see the Cowboy! And there he appeared in my office in all his cowboy glory—boots, hat, plaid shirt.

Why did he come to see me? I'll let him say.

"I visited my granduncle years ago at his home in Beverly Hills. He had this painting of a cowboy scene. I casually mentioned that I liked it. Well, he died about two months ago. At his funeral one of his sons told me that he had left the painting to me in his Will. Well, I was the first one back at my granduncle's house for the funeral reception, so I just took it off the wall and put it in my truck and went back to Texas.

"Then about two months ago, I got this letter from some lawyer saying that I got to pay $80,000 because of that painting. I called that lawyer and said I'd give it back, but he said it was mine and no one else wanted it. Then I tried to sell it, but no takers. So I jumped back in my truck, drove on out here, and tried to make them take it back. They threatened to call the cops on me if I didn't back off. So I looked up my own estate lawyer to see if I really gotta pay this thing. That's you, Mr. Condon."

I never asked the Cowboy why he felt compelled to drive all the way from Texas to California when he could have simply called any estate lawyer to handle this matter for him. But, I figured, his "get-up-and-go" reaction seemed part of the stereotypical Cowboy Way: Don't think . . . don't talk . . . just do.

The Cowboy showed me the letter. It wasn't a typical "demand letter" where the lawyer passionately makes his case and makes all kinds of legal threats unless the Cowboy ponies up (pun intended) the dough. Rather, the lawyer dispassionately pointed out the painting was appraised at $450,000 and requested that he remit a $80,000 check for his share of the death tax within 30 days of the date of the letter. The lawyer concluded by saying that if that check was not received within 30 days of the date of the letter, a collection lawsuit would be instituted against him.

As I read the letter, the Cowboy commented, "They could take the picture and shove it up their wahoos! I don't have that kind of money and even if I did, I wouldn't spend it on a tax for a picture that I didn't ask for. That's why I'm here. I don't want to be sued and I don't want this picture if I'm stuck with the tax on it."

With the Cowboy in my office, I called the lawyer who wrote that letter and offered to have the painting returned. That was a non-starter. Like the Cowboy said, nobody else in the family wanted it. I then asked the lawyer to send me a copy of the Cowboy's granduncle's Living Trust, which he faxed to me a few minutes later.

It's a good thing the Cowboy sought my help. Because as I

perused his granduncle's Living Trust, I immediately recognized that it contained provisions that would completely absolve the Cowboy from having to pay any estate tax on that picture. In fact, any inheritance attorney with any modicum of experience would have come to the same conclusion. Was this lawyer just stupid— or was he trying to pull a fast one on the Cowboy? I suppose I'll never know.

But I digress. Let's focus on the really exciting tax provisions of the Cowboy's granduncle's Living Trust.

Specifically, the person who drafted his granduncle's Living Trust used a standard form that said that the estate tax would be paid from the "residue of the estate." In English, this means that recipients of the specific bequests (like the Cowboy with the painting) inherit those gifts tax-free. And all death taxes that are due on those specific gifts are paid from the assets inherited by the beneficiaries who receive the rest (or "residue") of the estate . . . such as the granduncle's own children. In other words, the granduncle's children had to pay the death tax attributable to the Cowboy's painting.

If the drafter of this Living Trust had thought about it, he or she would probably have changed that provision so that *all* recipients—of specific gifts and residuary gifts—pay their proportionate share of the estate tax based upon the value of the assets they inherit. I know I would have made that change. But, the drafter simply left it in there . . . probably without thinking.

A common mistake, but one that got my cowboy client off the tax hook. I told the Cowboy the good news that had no death tax liability, and that he could take his painting and go back home, which he did. The only time I heard from him again was when he called me to tell me that he refused to pay the bill I sent him. Why? Because according to the Cowboy, since his granduncle's Living Trust spared him from any tax responsibility, I didn't do anything for him other than tell him that he had no such responsibility.

Abraham Lincoln once said, "A lawyer's time and advice is his stock in trade." It was my years of experience in the inheritance arena that ultimately brought relief to the Cowboy. But that's not how he saw it. The lawyer didn't do anything so the lawyer shouldn't get paid. Maybe it's me . . . but I never thought that chintzing out of a bill for legitimate and effective legal services rendered was part of the Cowboy Logic.

Post-Cautionary Tale Comment: Who pays the death tax is an often overlooked issue that may have profound unintended consequences. In the typical Living Trust, the children inherit the entire estate and the death tax is borne equally by them. Each child receives an equal share of the estate, thus each child contributes equally to pay the death tax.

The "tax allocation" problem arises when one child or non-child is to receive a specific itemized gift. A house to the son who lives in that house. Cash to a daughter of a prior marriage. Insurance proceeds to a prior spouse. The jewelry in the safe-deposit box to the daughter. And on and on. As with the story of the Cowboy and the painting, the issue of who pays the tax on a specific gift is not thought about . . . and the Living Trust may have a "Tax Payment Provision" that would be contrary to the parents' intent, resulting in an imposition of an unintended burden on the "wrong persons".

This scenario arises most frequently when parents have, say, three children and leave their house to one child, with everything else (the residue) going to all three children. Assuming a date of death market value of $500,000 and a pro-rata death tax on that house of $50,000, who pays the $50,000 tax? The child receiving that house from his own money . . . or all three children from the residue of the estate?

Well, when a lawyer is asked a question, he answers with another question, which is: What does the Living Trust's tax allocation provision say? In MOST cases, it will not have been addressed by the lawyer who drafted the instrument and that provision will most likely say that the estate tax on that house shall be borne by ALL three children. Which means not only that the "house child" gets the house, but the $50,000 estate tax attributable to that house is shared by all three of them.

Is that what the parents wanted? Perhaps, but probably not. What parent would leave a house to one child and then intentionally say that all his children shall pick up the estate tax tab? It doesn't make sense.

Thus, the "who pays the death tax" issue is a very important one and must be carefully considered before the Living Trust is signed.

Cautionary Tale 6: "Screw the Whole Bunch of Them!

Lesson to be learned: If you object to your family member's gay or lesbian lifestyle, you may find yourself cut out of the Living Trust.

I practice in Santa Monica, which is miles and worlds away from West Hollywood and Silverlake, two areas of Los Angeles County that have a significant gay population, Nevertheless, I seem to have attracted a bevy of upscale and financially successful gay-couple clients from those cities. Why? Because of this one exchange with my first gay clients many years ago:

Gay Couple: Mr. Condon, do you get any gay couples in your office for Living Trusts?

Me: No. I must admit, you are my first.

Gay Couple: Are you bothered by the fact that we are a gay couple?

Me: No. I say, live and let live. Just as long as you don't smoke.

That one line sent them into hysterics. They became my clients and told their many friends in the gay community about the funny and non-judgmental lawyer in Santa Monica.

Among those new clients were Robert and Tom.

Robert was a very successful real estate investor who, except for Tom, had no family. No children, parents, siblings, uncles, aunts, cousins . . . no one. Tom, on the other hand, had two brothers and five nieces and nephews. All raised as Mormons in Salt Lake City.

When they first conferred with me about Living Trusts, Robert's net worth was about $10 million . . . with no one to leave it to except Tom, his longtime partner. Tom, in turn, wanted a Living Trust leaving his assets, which were nowhere near Robert's level, to Robert. Also fine.

The discussion then turned to the "back-up" beneficiaries. If Tom died first, Robert's assets would have to go to someone other than Tom, and vice versa.

In Tom's Living Trust, Tom could name his family as his "back-ups" if Robert died first. An easy choice.

But in Robert's Living Trust, who would Robert name as "back-ups" if Tom died before him? Since Robert was 10 years older than Tom, the naming of "back-ups" in Robert's Trust became a most compelling matter. I suggested charities as the back-ups, but that did not fly with Robert. Finally, Robert said he had a friendly relationship with Tom's siblings and their children, and he would name them as the "back-ups."

Robert died about 5 years later, survived by Tom, who inherited Robert's assets. I attended Robert's funeral and was struck by the amazing turnout—which did NOT include any members of Tom's family.

A few years later, I had the occasion to run into Tom, who was now the owner of Robert's lifetime of accumulations. He seemed to be taking Robert's death pretty hard. Trying to make some attempt at conversation, I said to Tom that I could not help but be surprised that none of his family had attended Robert's funeral. For an estate planning attorney jaded from years of clients' deaths, that constitutes small talk.

With this one random statement, Tom seemed to change before my eyes, from depressed to living. He then said, "Nope. None showed up. I was surprised too. About nine months ago, I went home for a change of scenery and to visit my family. Do you know what they told me? They said that did not attend the funeral because they did not want to give their fellow Mormons the impression that they approved of gay couples or the gay lifestyle. Can you imagine that? They never told me anything like that before."

Tom added that running into me reminded him that he wanted to change his Living Trust to cut out his relatives, based solely on that slight. "Screw the whole bunch of them, Jeff. How fast can you change my Living Trust to leave everything to those charities you mentioned when Robert and I were first in your office?"

Years later, Tom died. After his funeral, which his relatives did attend, his brother called me, saying that he assumed he was named as a beneficiary in Tom's Living Trust and asking me how long it would take for him to receive his share. That's when I told him, "You got cut out after Robert's funeral. Your big no-show and your inability to keep your Mormon opinion to yourselves cost you and your family about $30 million in real estate."

Post-Cautionary Tale Comment: What comment can I make to this story other than the obvious? In terms of the size of the loss, the failure to tolerate an alternative lifestyle may have been the biggest mistake I have ever encountered in my practice.

Cautionary Tale 7: "I Don't Want to Be a Weekend Father"

Lesson to be learned: Never leave an inheritance outright to a child.

"If I sign a Living Trust that leaves my inherited house to my kids, my leaving the house to my children, my wife will divorce me!" In all the excuses I've heard to justify not establishing a Living Trust, this one from a man named Daniel Slosberg was the topper.

Daniel was in his early 40s, married with two daughters, ages 3 and 5. He and his wife lived in a 50-year-old home he inherited from his mother. His parents bought the house in 1952 for $20,000 with the help of the G.I Bill, and which, 50 years later, was worth over $1,000,000 due to inflation, and being in the prime residential area within walking distance of the beach.

I established Daniel's parents' Living Trust, which said, in essence, that Daniel (their only child) would inherit the house after both died. Daniel's father died first, and now Daniel was in my office to confer with me shortly after his mother's death.

At first, Daniel lauded the services I rendered for his parents. He was delighted that the Living Trust would avoid a costly and time-consuming probate process. All Daniel had to do to receive ownership of the house was to sign a deed in which Daniel, as the Successor Trustee of his parents' Living Trust, transfers the house to Daniel, in his individual capacity.

If this transfer had taken place in a probate context, it would have taken 9 months and cost thousands of dollars. With the Living Trust, it would take just $750.00 and the time necessary to prepare the transfer deed . . . about 20 minutes.

As my secretary typed the deed, I casually mentioned to Daniel that he should have his own Living Trust to leave his inherited house to his children. With that, Daniel stopped singing my praises and berated me for what he perceived to be a money grab: "Some racket you have going on here, Condon! You charged my parents for their Living Trust to transfer their house to me. How come I now have to pay you another fee for doing the same kind of Living Trust for the same house?

I'm only human. I can only take so much from people taking umbrage at paying me for my services without responding adversely. So, I kind of lost it. I stood up and said (yelled, actually), "We're starting over, Daniel! That was your parents' Living Trust! Now we're talking about your Living Trust! A new Living Trust means a new fee! What part of that don't you understand?!"

I fully expected Daniel to run from the room, but to my surprise, he stayed put. Too shocked to move from being witness to such unprofessional conduct? Perhaps, but he was also one of those types who admire people who have the temerity to tell them off. Daniel then hired me to prepare his Living Trust. Maybe I should yell at my clients more often.

After our meeting (shouting contest?), I prepared Daniel's Living Trust, which provided that his inherited house would, on his death, be distributed to his two daughters. I met with Daniel a few weeks later so he could review the first draft and to schedule the signing appointment for the following week.

During the review appointment, Daniel asked whether he should leave the house to his wife instead of his children. I replied, "Daniel, if you leave it to her, there is no guarantee that she'll leave it to your children. Just do this my way."

Do you take issue with your doctor when he gives you medical advice? Probably not, and you probably comply as well with the advice your lawyer bestows upon you, as did Daniel. He left his Living Trust the way I drafted it, and we scheduled the date for the signing appointment.

The day of the signing meeting came, but no Daniel. My secretary called him to reschedule. We rescheduled; but, another no-show. Another call, another reschedule, another no-show. This routine went on about three more times. During each rescheduling call my secretary made to him, he came up with the same excuse: "family problems."

Daniel finally showed up for the signing appointment on the sixth go-round. He looked drawn, tired, exasperated. "What's bothering you?" I asked him.

And he sure told me . . . with that same antagonism as before.

"You almost destroyed my marriage, Condon! I brought the draft home and my wife saw it. She picked it up and read the part about the house going to our children instead of her. She started hyperventilating. I thought she was going to have a heart attack. She gave me look of death and said, 'I always thought I would get the house if you die. Looks like I won't. I may as well as divorce you now!' "

"Listen, Daniel," I said. "Your wife has no right to that house. It's not community property, it's separate property. It's YOUR separate property. There is no rule that says you have to leave it to your wife. You can leave it to whomever you want. And I'm sure that your parents didn't intend to have the family home end up out of the bloodline."

To that, Daniel yelled, "It's my life, Condon! Not yours! I'm not signing. I know my wife and she'll do just what she says. I am not going to be one of those guys who see their kids every other weekend! So &#! your Living Trust . . . and @#&! you while you're at it!"

He got up and stormed out, never to come back . . . and never to pay me for any of the services I rendered in preparing the final draft.

Was I a bit brazen about dismissing Daniel's slight initial suggestion to initially leave the house to his wife? Sure. But I was also in the right. If Daniel died first, and his wife remarried, it is entirely possible that his parents' house could end up with their ex-daughter-in-law's children from her new husband's first marriage. Hey, don't laugh! This has happened more times than you'll ever know!

Somehow, I did find out later that Daniel complied with his wife's wishes by signing a deed that transferred the house from his parents Living Trust to himself as his separate property, and then signing another deed that transferred the house to him and his wife as their community property. If he dies first, she gets the whole thing.

Post-Cautionary Tale Comment: Even though I believe my advice to Daniel during the signing appointment was right, Daniel was also right. I could not live his life for him. His parents were dead, the house was his to do with as he pleased, and he had the absolute right to do what he needed to do to keep his family together.

And on sober second thought, I was really bothered by the fact that advice I had given so casually almost caused a divorce.

You live, you learn. I now prevent that marriage-destruction scenario by not giving people who inherit (like Daniel) the choice of whether to leave the inherited house to their children or their spouses. I now leave that choice with their parents.

Specifically, if I was drafting Daniel's parents' Living Trust now, I would provide that when the last parent dies, the family home stays in the parents' Living Trust in a "sub-trust," which I call the "Protection Trust." This "Protection Trust" would act just like the

Living Trust that I prepared for Daniel that he never signed. By leaving the house to Daniel in the Protection Trust, Daniel would own and control the house. And when Daniel dies, the terms of his Protection Trust would state that the house must go to Daniel's daughters.

The use of this sub-trust is like getting two Living Trusts for the price of one. The first one is Daniel's parents' Living Trust, which transfers the house to him, and the second one is the Protection Trust, which leaves the house to Daniel's children.

And even more important, the decision of ultimately leaving the house to Daniel's children would have been made by Daniel's parents, not Daniel. So when Daniel's wife would shimmy up to her husband and "suggest" that he leave the house to her, he could retort with something like, "Honey, you know I would love to. But my hands are tied. My parents left it to me in trust for the kids."

Cautionary Tale 8: "I Lost the Bet"

Lesson to be learned: When you own your home with your spouse as "joint tenants with right of survivorship," you expect to own the whole house if you outlive your spouse. Well . . . maybe not.

I didn't mean to be flippant with Mrs. Barber. But when she told me her husband "screwed her," I said "I hope so!" I know. Very unprofessional. But the opportunity to use that line was served up to me like a tennis lob, and I just couldn't resist the smash. I don't think Mrs. Barber noticed, though. She was too involved with her own thought process to notice my lack of decorum.

Mrs. Barber was in her mid-70s. Married twice. She had two children of her first marriage, which ended in divorce.

Mrs. Barber's second marriage was to a man 10 years older than her with a son from his first marriage. She was the housewife with little business knowledge. He was one of those business executive types. Her second marriage lasted for 20 years until her second husband's recent death. No children from that second marriage.

Shortly after Mrs. Barber entered her second marriage, they sold their separate houses and combined the funds into one new home to get a fresh start. When it came to deciding how to take title to their new home, the escrow lady suggested "joint tenancy with right of survivorship." Sounded good to her. With her second husband being 10 years older, and with women statistically having a longer life expectancy than men, she assumed that he would die first and then she would own the entire house.

Later, they bought an apartment building together and took title the same way—joint tenancy with right of survivorship. As Mrs. Barber said, "We talked it over and he agreed that if he died first, the house and the apartment building would be mine; and the apartment building would throw off enough rents to take care of me."

Just as Mrs. Barber assumed, her second husband died first. But contrary to her expectation of receiving her second husband's half of the house and apartment building, his shares went to someone else. That's why she was meeting with me and why she said she got screwed.

I had a fairly decent idea of what happened. After I checked out the title to the properties from the county recorder's office, it turned out that I was right. A few months before Mrs. Barber's second husband died, he terminated the "right of survivorship." This was easy to do. He simply signed a deed that "severed" the joint tenancy by transferring his one half from himself as a joint tenant to himself as a tenant-in-common. As a result, the second husband was free to leave his half to anyone he wanted.

And he sure did. The second husband then transferred his halves of the properties to a separate Living Trust that Mrs. Barber never knew existed. After his death, Mrs. Barber discovered this Living Trust and that it left those halves to . . . here it comes . . . his secretary!

The second husband's secretary and Mrs. Barber were now

equal co-owners of the properties. Partners! Like out of a movie, yes? But true!

What a shock this was to Mrs. Barber. A triple shock, actually. Her second husband dies unexpectedly. She discovers he has a longtime mistress. Then she learns that the mistress will be getting what she assumed she would get.

Then the fourth shock arrives in the form of a letter from the mistresses' lawyer. To paraphrase the contents: "Mrs. Barber, my client is now the co-owner of the house and the building. She offers to sell you her half of those properties at fair market value. If you don't elect to purchase those halves, we will go to court to get an order forcing you to join in with my client to list those properties on the market for sale."

"Can she do that, Mr. Condon? Can she force me to sell them if I don't buy her out?" I felt like the doctor who faced the task of telling his patient he had a life-threatening sickness. "Yes," I said mournfully. "She can."

Sometimes the doctor can offer the hope of a possible cure. But there was no cure for Mrs. Barber's condition. She made the fatal mistake of assuming joint tenancy would protect her, and she was wrong.

Mrs. Barber did not want to lose her home or the rents from the apartment building, but she didn't have the resources to buy the secretary's half. So she was forced to sell. Today, Mrs. Barber resides with one of her children in another state, a far cry from the social and financially independent life she envisioned.

Maybe Mrs. Barber's second husband loved her. After all, he married her and their marriage lasted for 20 years. And in light of his extravagant gift to his secretary, I figure he must have loved his secretary equally. Or more. But being a sophisticated business type, Mrs. Barber's second husband must have known that such a gift would make his wife and his mistress partners in the same assets. How can a man possess such love toward those two women and still intentionally create a chain of events that places those mortal combatants in the same plane?

I still have not reconciled that one.

Post-Cautionary Tale Comment: Actually, more of a warning than a comment.

Husbands and wives commonly take title to real estate as joint tenants with right of survivorship. With joint tenancy, the expectation is that the surviving joint tenant will be the 100 percent owner, and life goes on.

But, as seen with the Barber Family Saga, that expectation can be a fallacy. Any joint tenant can terminate the joint tenancy, which leaves each former joint tenant with the power to leave his share to anyone he desires without the knowledge or consent of the other former joint tenants.

The solution is for husbands and wives to own real estate in a Living Trust. If a spouse desires to move his half of the property out of the Living Trust, he cannot do so without first obtaining the knowledge, consent, and signature of the other spouse.

Cautionary Tale 9: "My Husband Stole Our Property"

> Lesson to be learned: Beware the provision in a Husband-Wife Living Trust that allows the signature of only one spouse to bind both spouses to any transaction.

As one would imagine, I get a lot of panicky phone calls from clients and their children about a demise or impending death in the family. Of course, these are not spiritually based inquiries, but more of the "what-happens-now" and "is-there-anything-I-should-be-doing" variety. Which is fine. Any inheritance lawyer worth his salt should always "be there" for clients any time they have pressing questions while they experience these most solemn and intense hallmark times in their family history.

One would think that after all these years in this business, I would have found some magic words that effectively assuage those who have lost a loved one. But, even with all my years of dealing with surviving spouses and children, I still find that the usual words of consolation ("I'm sorry for your loss") sound trite and meaningless. Today, I simply listen while the bereaved regale me with their stories of the Last Days. I then begin to talk to them about the first steps of administration of the Living Trust.

But on this occasion, the panicky phone call wasn't from a client but from a divorce lawyer who told me that Mr. Courtney had sold the real estate and disappeared with the money.

I had prepared a Living Trust for Mr. and Mrs. Courtney about ten years prior to this call. I recalled that Mr. Courtney was one of those rare clients that read every word of the Living Trust and ask an endless array of questions. Which is very rare, as most of my clients only read the "who gets what" part and rely on my "nutshell" explanations of the really boring boilerplate provisions.

For the flat fee I charge for my Living Trust services, my clients may spend as much time with me as they wish without fear of that fee increasing if our trust review sessions run into multiple hours. Mr. Courtney took this to the extreme. We had about eight meetings and four extensive phone conversations before he and his wife signed their Living Trust and transferred all their major assets to themselves as Trustees. He asked me the meaning and impact of practically every word in the extensive document that wasn't "the" or "and." When the Courtneys finally signed their Living Trust and exited my office, I collapsed in happy exhaustion.

In any event, the panicky divorce lawyer told me that he represented Mrs. Courtney in their divorce and that two sinister events had taken place prior to this call. One, Mr. Courtney disappeared suddenly and with the proverbial no trace. Two, a man appeared at Mrs. Courtney's home and informed her that he had just bought her house and wanted to know when he could expect her to start packing.

Put the two events together and you have what happened: Mr. Courtney sold the house without Mrs. Courtney's knowledge and disappeared with the sale proceeds. We later discovered that he arranged to send the proceeds to himself overseas.

Initially, this math did not compute. Even though the Courtneys' assets were contained in their Living Trust, those assets were STILL the joint assets of Mr. and Mrs. Courtney, just as jointly as the assets would have been outside their Living Trust. And with joint ownership comes the requirement that BOTH spouses must execute all documents that are necessary to transact. For their Living Trust assets to be sold, exchanged, encumbered, gifted, whatever—and Mr. and Mrs. Courtney would BOTH have to participate.

With all this in mind, I asked the divorce attorney how Mr. Courtney could sell the jointly owned house. He said, "That's what I want to know." But as soon as I uttered my question, I realized how Mr. Courtney could unilaterally and without notice engage in that sale transaction. And then I felt my face and body become warm and clammy, the symptom that usually befalls me if ever I am exposed to my possible legal screw-ups.

With the Courtneys being among my earlier Living Trust clients, they executed a Living Trust model that had not been put through the wringer of real life. After many years of seeing certain provisions in my earlier verstions unintentionally create family conflict or financial devastation after the clients' deaths, I would remove or change those offending provisions. Because of that trial-and-error process, the model I use today is more aware as it addresses the innumerable potential problems that I now recognize could arise in the inheritance arena.

This is why the practice of law is called a "practice." We lawyers get to practice this stuff until we get it right.

But my New-and-Improved model came too late for Mrs. Courtney because there was something in the Courtneys' early Living Trust format that allowed Mr. Courtney to perpetrate divorce fraud. Hidden in the boilerplate "Powers of the Trustees" section was this one small and seemingly innocuous sentence: "Either co-trustee may execute all deeds and other documents on behalf of the trust . . ."

And that's what Mr. Courtney did. As a co-trustee of the Living Trust, he executed all the documents necessary: listing agreement, escrow instructions, financial information, disclosures, deed on behalf of the owner, the Courtneys' Living Trust. All the real estate broker and title company needed to see to recognize Mr. Courtney's sole authority to sell the house was that "little" provision.

With Mr. Courtney somehow finding a way to keep secret all aspects of that sale, he sold the home and their apartment building and commercial property, pocketed the cash, and took off.

No client has ever sued me for malpractice, and I was almost physically overcome with the thought of Mrs. Courtney being the first. My rookie mistake had placed Mr. Courtney in the position to steal. I placed this one-signature provision in their Living Trust to be consistent with the typical husband-and-wife custom of one spouse's signature binding both spouses to a transaction, such as writing checks from a joint account. But the words "deeds and all other documents" gave one spouse carte blanche with the jointly held Living Trust assets.

With my mind racing with thoughts of spending time in the Litigation Hell Zone (depositions, pre-trial procedures, attorneys fees, mediation attempts), I still had a job to do to prevent further abuses by Mr. Courtney. Every Living Trust has provisions that authorize one spouse to revoke it if that spouse, for whatever reason, wants to cancel it. Usually in cases of divorce where the divorcing spouses no longer want an inheritance plan that leaves their respective halves to each other. I told the divorce attorney that Mrs. Courtney needed to "pull the plug" on this Living Trust by signing a Revocation. With that document and the "publication" of that document to the account representatives of their remaining assets we could prevent Mr. Courtney's further access into the Living Trust assets. Yes, the damage was done, but we could still do something to stop the bleeding.

Mrs. Courtney came to my office the next day and signed the Revocation I had prepared. I was prepared for an onslaught of finger-pointing and blame, but she practically said nothing. Still numb from the stunning discovery that her house and other real estate had been sold right out from under her, she had to find a new place to live.

After Mrs. Courtney signed the Revocation, I immediately sent it to each bank and brokerage firm at which the Courtneys' Living Trust still had assets with a Letter of Warning that stated: "Mrs. Courtney has revoked the Courtneys' Living Trust. It no longer exists. Freeze the Living Trust accounts. Disregard all future attempts by Mr. Courtney to unilaterally withdraw or access assets in those accounts." Just in time. The Courtneys' primary brokerage representative called me to advise that Mr. Courtney sent them from afar an instruction to make a complete account liquidation and electronic transmittal of the net sale proceeds.

And he also told me that this instruction was accompanied by the page in their Living Trust that evidenced his authority to make such a unilateral request. Once again, I felt the warm and clammy hand of guilt on my shoulder and visions of spending hours with lawyers preparing for my deposition flooded my head.

Post-Cautionary Tale Comment: To say this was a learning experience is a severe understatement. I had to live with the knowledge that I unwittingly had a hand in Mr. Courtney's nefarious scheme and with the prospect of being sued for malpractice for my carelessness in incorporating that boilerplate provision.

Spouses almost always have both names on title to their family home, brokerage assets, and other assets, and the participation and signatures of both spouses must be obtained in order to make any transaction with those assets. When those assets are transferred to the spouses' Living Trust, the spouses now own those assets as co-trustees. Still, those assets are still considered to be owned jointly, and the assumption is that those spouses STILL want any sale or other disposition to require both signatures.

However, as seen with the Courtney Family Saga, sometimes that assumption doesn't work its way into the Living Trust document. There may be a provision hidden in the section called "Trustee's Powers" that allows one spouse, as a co-trustee, to execute all documents that "bind" the trust estate. This boilerplate section typically does not get extensive review or any review at all. It's just there. And it may not be what the spouses want unless one of them elects to exploit it to pursue clandestine theft.

Of course, there are exceptions. I typically provide that only one spouse's signature is necessary for checks, which is consistent with the everyday practice of husband-and-wife joint checking accounts. Also, one spouse's impending diminishing mental incapacity coupled with a long-term marriage justifies an entry into the "only-one-signature" world. But in situations where the customary and reasonable expectation of the clients is that both signatures are necessary, then the Living Trust will follow that expectation.

But, rest assured, I would never again allow my Living Trusts to include a sweeping power for one co-trustee/spouse to empower one spouse to singularly execute "all deeds and other documents" on behalf of the Living Trust.

Final Thought:

"Should I Tell My Children About My Inheritance Plan?"

I never cease to be amazed how often clients ask this question when common sense dictates it is the right thing to do. Nevertheless, clients seem loath to discuss inheritance issues with their children, leaving their children in a mystery as to the contents of their parents' inheritance plan.

Why do parents persist on keeping their children in the dark? In most cases, they simply want to avoid conflict. Parents often feel that disclosing their inheritance plans may generate disputes between their children. By deferring this disclosure until after their deaths, they can enjoy their lives without the aggravation of their children's complaints.

In other words, the less their children know, parents believe, the better.

Avoiding conflict is not the only reason. Some parents simply believe their inheritance plan is a private matter, for their eyes only. And, of course, there are those parents who fear their children will do nothing productive with their lives if they know in advance who gets what.

Whatever the reasons, my clients always expect me to be supportive. They believe their lawyer should validate their decision not to bring their children into the inheritance-planning process.

However, when it comes to this issue, as personal and private as it is, I am anything but supportive. I can perceive no worthwhile justification for not telling your children about the nature, extent, quality, and quantity of your assets—and how those assets will be shared after you die.

A full and frank discussion between you and your children about your inheritance plan is the foremost tool in avoiding inheritance problems. As you have noted throughout this book, I highly recommend the family inheritance meeting as the ultimate solution to particular inheritance problems.

Even if discussing inheritance issues with your children goes against your grain, I strongly encourage you to do it anyway. If you care enough, this is the true solution to potential conflicts and the simplest way to their resolution.

"You don't know my children. If I convene a family inheritance meeting, I just know it will go sour and leave everyone angry and combative."

If you believe your family inheritance meeting will end on a sour note, I still believe you should throw out your inheritance issues on the table for discussion. My philosophy has always been, better your children be distressed now than after you die. While you are alive, you have the potential to defuse the anger. You can explain the reasons for the particular measures you have taken in your inheritance plan.

This potential to clear the air, of course, extinguishes following your death. If your children first learn what you have done at the reading of your Will, you will have left behind a legacy of conflict and chaos.

However, if you think raising a particular concern will lead to trouble, I believe you are in for a pleasant surprise. I have convened hundreds of family inheritance meetings among my clients and their children. The overwhelming majority of them have been positive.

In this meeting, you will have the opportunity to get off your chest inheritance issues that you have been considering for some time. And most likely, you will find that your children have been thinking about the same issues. Finally, they say as they sigh with relief, you have gotten around to them as well.

And to your pleasant surprise, your children may have sophisticated input as to how to resolve your particular inheritance concern.

Index

AB Trusts. *See* Living Trusts
Accident claims, 409, 410–11
Accountants, 231, 250
Annual Exclusion Gifts, 175, 184–85, 360–62, 383
  Deathbed Power of Attorney and, 376–78, 435
  Family Limited Partnerships and, 372–75
  to grandchildren, 284–86, 290–91, 388
Annuities, 328–30
Appraisal, real estate, 347
Attorney-in-Fact, 377–78
Attorneys, 45, 61, 231, 323–24, 353–54
  fees for, 432–34, 451, 470, 472, 477
  inheritance contests, 108–10
  probate and, 15–16, 395, 454

B Trusts, 365–70
Bank accounts, 306, 346, 348, 359, 417, 481
Bank Trustees, 87, 306–7, 330, 406, 440
  as child's trustee, 148–56
  as Co-trustees, 156–57, 249–51, 260
  for minor children, 163, 164
  pet care oversight, 315–17
  as Special Trustees, 154–55, 221
  surviving spouse and, 234–36, 238, 243–44
Bankruptcy, 100–101, 408–10

Beneficiaries
  "back-up," 467–69
  Trustee relationship with, 453–56
Boards of Directors, 187
Bonds, Guardian, 166
Businesses, 39, 102, 177–88, 261, 347

Capital gains taxes, 184, 188–89, 225, 327, 328
  stepped-up basis, 289
Caretakers, 225–29, 238–44, 441–46
Charitable Remainder Trusts, 328–32, 375
Charities, 132–33, 316–32, 375
Children, 3–6
  allocation of death taxes, 463–67
  bankruptcy of, 100–101, 408–10
  business succession and, 177–88
  as caretakers, 225–29, 441–46
  childless, 88–90
  community property, 457–60
  as conservators, 231
  as Co-trustees, 156–57, 235, 248–49, 275
  creditors of, 58, 99–104, 156–57, 409–12
  Death Inventory concerns, 348–50
  death tax payment, 338–44, 351, 381–85
  disabled. *See* Disabled children
  disinheritance of, 104, 107–20, 134, 433–34, 467–69
  disregard of inheritance plans, 401–6

Children (*cont.*)
    divorced, 59, 77, 350, 410
    with Durable Power of Attorney,
        232–33, 238
    "early inheritance" seekers, 215,
        217–29, 267–68
    equal inheritances. *See*
        Equalization, Inheritance
    estranged, 127, 459
    excluded, 460–63
    as Executors or Successor
        Trustees, 10–11, 34–36, 190–91,
        401–6
    financially immature, 65–75,
        155–56
    from first marriage, 154–55,
        200–206, 265–70, 276–80,
        457–60
    grandchildren bequests and,
        299–308
    inheritance condition imposition
        on, 136–41
    inheritance expectations of,
        129–35
    inheritance mismanagement by,
        58, 65
    inheritance planning by, 437–40
    inheritance problems of, 6–7
    inheritance size effect on, 121–28
    joint ownership with, 395–96,
        407–17
    leaving valuables and household
        contents to, 169–76
    Living Trust establishment by,
        432–34
    as Living Trust Trustees, 233–34
    loans to, 42–53
    management power-sharing,
        38–40
    medical decision making by,
        237
    minor, 127, 158–66, 361, 374, 383
    as Money Managers, 91–95
    outright inheritance for, 469–73
    as own Trustees, 156–57

    parents' inheritance planning,
        430–37, 483–85
    with personal problems, 9–10, 58,
        62, 64, 118–20, 127, 145, 156–57,
        401–2, 409–11
    remarriage of, 59
    from second marriage, 277–80
    of second spouses, 271–80, 448
    Sibling Trustees, 146–47
    spouses of, 76–90, 157, 190–91,
        301, 437–40
    Surviving Spouse Life Estate
        Trusts and, 261–62, 279–80
    telling children about Living
        Trusts, 429–30, 483–85
Co-trustees, 156, 190, 235, 248–51,
    260, 275, 480, 481
Community Foundations, 326–27
Community property, 452, 457–60,
    472
Competency
    determination of, 70, 98, 120, 231,
        234
    document validity and, 109, 110,
        232–33
Conservators, 159, 230–34, 242, 258,
    445–46
Convalescent care, 236–38
Corporate Trustees, 91, 95–96, 330,
    406
Credit Bypass Trust, 365–70
Creditors, 58, 99–104, 157, 409–12
Crosby, Lindsay, 73–74
Custodians, 294, 361

Dad's Tax-Free Trust Account,
    365–70, 399
Death benefits, 347. *See also specific
    types*
Death Inventory, 342, 344, 345–51
Death taxes, 12–13, 130, 335–44,
    353–56, 463–67
    allocation of, 463–67
    Annual Exclusion Gift benefits,
        284, 285–86, 360–62, 435

Death Inventory and, 342, 344, 345–51
discussions about repeal of, 335–40
on family businesses, 182–85
on grandchildren's inheritance, 13, 288–89
on homes, 222–23
joint ownership with children and, 413, 415–16
life insurance as payment source, 375, 381–85, 388
Lifetime Exemption. See Lifetime Exemption
Living Trusts and, 396
on real estate, 328, 331
reduction strategies, 299, 303, 357–80, 386–90, 435
scenarios about, 340–44
on valuables, 174, 463–67
Deathbed Power of Attorney, 374, 376, 435
Deathbed promises, 277–78
Disabled children, 91–98, 118–20, 127, 196–98, 421–25
Disclaimers, 104
Disinheritance, 104, 107–20, 134, 433–34, 467–69
Divorce, 59, 77, 350, 410, 479
Durable Power of Attorney, 232–33, 238
for Health Care, 233, 237–38, 244

Education, 139–40, 290–91, 324–25, 362, 388
Education Trusts, 139–40, 291–92
Employment, 74–75, 140–41
Equalization, 21–33, 117, 435–37
Annual Exclusion Gifts, 283–87
Co-executors/Co-trustees, 34–36
family businesses, 180–91
family homes, 196–98
grandchildren bequests, 301–3
inheritance, 9

life insurance and, 29–30, 186–87, 188, 199
loan forgiveness, 45–46, 49–50, 52–53
real estate, 30–33, 40–41, 209–11
valuables and household items, 170–71
Estate Guardians, 159, 164–66
Estate Tax Returns, 346
Estate taxes. See Death taxes
Executors, 10–11, 34–35, 177
Exemption Trusts, 365–70

Family Incentive Trusts, 123
Family Limited Partnerships, 102, 185, 294–95, 372–75
Family Trusts. See Living Trusts
Federal Savings and Loan Insurance Corporation, 100
Fees
inheritance contests, 109, 110
Living Trust, 399, 451, 470, 472, 477
probate-related, 16, 395, 432
Trustee, 95, 148, 152–53, 163, 454
Foreign country Protection Trusts, 102–3
Foundations, 133, 326–27

Gay lifestyle, 467–69
Generation Skip Amount, 389
Gifts, 25–29, 77, 463–67
annual. See Annual Exclusion Gifts
of businesses, 184–85
Death Inventory, 348–50
Death taxes and, 463–67
to grandchildren, 283–95
homes as, 224–25
jewelry, 174–76
life insurance policies as, 384
Lifetime Exemption and, 338, 339
loans as, 45, 52–53
paintings as, 463–67
Glavine, Tom, 123

Government entitlements, 421–25
Grandchildren, 50–53, 79, 86,
        136–41, 191
    bequests to, 296–308
    death taxes and, 13, 288–89
    gifts to, 283–95, 388
    inheritance protection for, 10,
        57–64, 88
    Transparent Trusts, 82, 84
Grantor Retained Trusts, 379
Guardians, 158–66, 306

Health care, 233, 236–38, 244
Heirship Agreements, 115–16
Home, 192–206
    death taxes on, 222–23, 389–90
    disabled children living in,
        196–98
    "early inheritance" seekers and,
        218–19, 268
    gifting of, 224–25
    House Trusts, 370–72
    household contents, 169–76
    joint ownership with children,
        407–17
    Living Trusts and, 194, 219,
        469–73
    purchase option plans, 199–200
    second wives/husbands and,
        200–206, 268–69
    Skip Trusts and, 390
Hospitals, bequests to, 325–27
House Trusts, 370–72
Household contents, 169–76

Incentive-based inheritance plans,
        123–28, 137
Incentive Trusts, 134–35, 140–41
Income taxes
    on annuities, 330–31
    audits of, 350–51
    investment life insurance and,
        291
    joint ownership concerns, 410
    Living Trusts and, 398

Surviving Spouse Life Estate
        Trusts and, 261
Individual Retirement Accounts,
        385, 400
Inheritance plans
    business succession and,
        190–91
    charity bequests, 325–27
    of children, 437–40
    children from all marriages and,
        279–80
    as control mechanism, 136–41
    dispute-resolution mechanisms,
        39, 186–87, 308
    disregarding of, 401–6
    family home and, 198–200,
        203–4, 469–73
    grandchildren's inclusion in,
        296–308
    guardianship and, 158–66
    incentive-based, 123–28, 137
    income vs. growth goals, 154–55
    informing children about, 429–30,
        434, 483–85
    key objectives, 8–14
    loan forgiveness issues, 49–50,
        52–53
    parents' avoidance of, 430–37
    personal and household item
        bequests, 171, 173–74
    and Personal Property
        Memorandum (PPM), 171
    pet-related concerns, 311–12
    procrastination and, 15–17
    safeguard programs, 68–71
    Side Letters and, 171–72
    Special Needs Trusts, 424–25
    See also Living Trusts; Wills
Inherited Separate Property Trusts,
        437–40
Installment Notes, 183–84, 188,
        328–29, 379–80
Insurance. See Life insurance
Inter Vivos Trusts. See Living
        Trusts

Internal Revenue Service, 12–13, 342, 343, 410. *See also* Death taxes; Income taxes
Interval Allocation, 66–67
Inventories, 177, 345–51
Investment life insurance, 291
Investments, 246–51, 261, 266–67, 275–76
Irrevocable Trusts, 293, 303–4, 361
  Insurance, 383
  Protection, 64, 85–90, 97–98, 102, 119–20

"Jackal protection," 176–77
Jewelry, 174–76
Joint bank accounts, 306, 348, 417, 481
Joint ownership, 348, 434
  with children, 395–96, 407–17
  by children's spouses, 77, 82–83, 437–38
  Lifetime Exemption and, 365–70
  surviving spouses and, 11, 115, 215, 255, 271–73, 277–78, 394, 449–50, 452, 473–76
  survivorship rights, 77, 115–18, 215, 273, 277, 407, 449–50, 452, 473–76
  termination of, 116–18, 273, 416, 476–81

Landers, Ann, 44, 412, 435–36
Lawsuits, 108–11, 124–25, 148, 227–29, 395, 445–46
Leases, sweetheart, 187–88
Letter of Warning, 480
Life Insurance
  as backup inheritance, 262, 458, 460
  charity trusts and, 331
  for children from first marriage, 204–5, 269–70, 276, 458, 460
  for children's spouses, 439–40
  death tax payment using, 375, 381–85, 388

for disinherited children, 118
equalization strategies and, 29–30, 186, 188, 199
investment, 291
Living Trust as beneficiary, 400
needier children as beneficiaries, 25–26
Lifetime Exemption, 336–44, 383, 390, 397
  Annual Exclusion Gifts and, 284, 291, 360
  Death Inventory and, 244, 342, 345, 346, 348–49
  gifts and, 338, 339
  proposals concerning changes in, 337–40
  scenarios concerning, 340–44
  serial marriage and, 344
  single people and, 340
  surviving spouses and, 340–44
  tax-reduction strategies and, 362–70
Lifetime gifts, 25–30, 283–95
Limited Partnerships, 347. *See also* Family Limited Partnerships
Living Trusts, 16, 177, 434
  asset management, 248–51
  "back-up" beneficiaries, 467–69
  beneficiary-trustee relationship, 453–56
  bequests, 33, 171, 463–67
  business succession plans, 190–91
  bypassing of spouse, 260, 439–40
  cautionary tales about, 447–81
  for children from all marriages, 278
  children's disregard of, 401–6
  children's establishment of, 432–34
  community property, 452, 457–60
  contesting of, 108–11
  Co-trustees, 190, 235, 248–49
  disabled children and, 92–94
  Education Trusts, 291–92

Living Trusts (cont.)
  employment motivation and,
    74–75
  estranged children, 459
  excluded children, 460–63
  grandchildren's inheritances, 306
  homes held in, 194, 219, 448–52
  inheritance conditions, 139
  for inherited property, 437–40
  Irrevocable Protection Trusts, 102
  outright inheritance to child,
    469–73
  Personal Property Memorandum
    (PPM), 177–79
  pets, 313–14
  probate avoidance and, 222,
    393–406, 410–11, 417, 448–52,
    470
  Protection Trusts, 59–64, 458,
    472–73
  Revocable, 85, 479–80
  right of survivorship, 473–77
  signatures of spouses on,
    476–81
  Special Trustees, 219, 220–21
  Successor Trustees, 10–11, 34–36,
    177–79, 190, 194, 398, 399,
    401–6, 470
  surviving spouse establishment
    of, 219–22, 278, 448–52
  surviving spouse incapacitation
    and, 233–34, 240–41, 243–44,
    481
  Surviving Spouse Life Estate
    Trusts, 260
  Transparent Trusts, 81–82, 84–85,
    440
  videotaping of signing, 110
  Wills and, 399, 450
  See also Disinheritance
Loans to children, 42–53

Marriage, 59, 138–39, 344. See also
    Remarriage
Medicaid, 224–25, 423, 424

Medical expense payments, 362,
    388
Minor children, 127, 158–66, 361,
    374, 383
Money Managers, 91–96, 119, 123,
    125, 127, 147
Mortgages, as loan collateral, 45,
    49–50

"Pay over on death" bank accounts,
    306
Pension plans, 400
Perot, Ross, 131
Person Guardians, 159, 164–65
Personal property, 169–76, 347
Personal Property Memorandum
    (PPM)
  and bequests, 171, 177–79
  Living Trusts, 177–79
Pets, 309–17
Photo journals, 162, 177
Pooled Trusts, 331–32
Power of Attorney
  Deathbed, 374, 376–78, 435
  Durable, 232–33, 238
  for health care, 233, 237–38, 244
  Living Trusts and, 396–97
  nonrelated caretakers with, 242
"Pretermission," law of, 461–62
Probate, 13–14, 393–417, 434
  conservatorship process, 231, 242
  fees, 451
  Guardians and, 164, 166
  Living Trusts and, 222, 393–406,
    417, 448–52, 470
Probate-Avoidance Trusts. See
    Living Trusts
Promissory Notes, 45, 46
Property taxes, 399
Protection Trusts, 59–64, 107, 115,
    423, 458, 472–73
  foreign country, 102–3
  Interval Allocation, 66–67
  Irrevocable, 64, 85–90, 97–98,
    102, 119–20

Revocable, 102
Trustees, 60–61, 66–70, 73, 74, 145–57
Protectors, 69–71, 87, 96, 157, 163

Real estate
  bank Trustees and, 153–54
  business, 186–89
  charitable bequests, 327–32, 375
  co-ownership concerns, 39–40, 475–76
  Death Inventory, 347, 348
  division of investments, 207–11
  equalization strategies and, 30–33, 40–41, 209–11
  Family Limited Partnerships, 102, 372–75
  as grandchildren's inheritance, 307, 469–72
  held in trust, 37–38
  Interval Allocation and, 67
  joint ownership termination, 273, 416, 473–77
  Living Trusts and, 398–99, 400, 448–52, 469–72, 473–77
  management power-sharing, 38–39
  outright inheritance for children, 469–73
  Retained Income Trusts, 378–79
  and signatures on Living Trusts, 476–81
  title insurance, 83–84
  Transparent Trusts and, 83–84
  See also Home
Religion, 138, 162–63
Remarriage, 12, 59, 200–206, 256–59, 262–80, 344, 448–51, 457–60, 472, 473–76
Retained Income Trusts, 378–79
Revocable Living Trusts, 85, 479–80
Revocable Protection Trusts, 102
Rotating choice distribution, 173

Safe-deposit boxes, 175–76, 347
Scholarships, 324–25

Securities, 31, 346, 400
Self-canceling Notes, 379–80
Sibling Trustees, 146–47
Side Letters, 171–72
Signatures, for Living Trusts, 476–81
Single people, 176, 340
Skip Trusts, 379, 389–90
Special Bank Trustees, 154, 221
Special Needs Trusts, 424–25
Special Trustees, 219, 220–21
Spousal inheritance. See Surviving spouse
Stepped-up tax basis, 289, 379–80
Stocks. See Securities
Sub-trusts. See Protection Trust
Successor Trustees, 177–79, 194, 398, 399
  children as, 10–11, 34–36, 190, 401–6, 470
Supplementary Security Income, 421–25
Support Trusts, 263
Surviving spouse
  asset management, 11–12, 215, 246–51
  bank Trustees for, 154–55, 221
  childless, 238–44, 468–69
  community property, 457–60
  conservators for, 230–31, 242
  diversion of family money by, 255–64
  "early inheritance" seekers and, 215, 217–29, 267–68
  Heirship Agreements, 115–16
  incapacitated/incompetent, 215, 225–45
  inheritance plan changes by, 69, 97–98
  inheritance problems of, 6
  joint ownership and, 11, 115, 215, 255, 271–73, 277–78, 365–70, 394, 449–50
  Life Estate Trusts, 260–62, 269, 273–76, 279–80

Surviving spouse (*cont.*)
    Lifetime Exemption and, 340–44
    Living Trusts and, 399, 448–52,
        457–60, 467–69, 473–76
    lump-sum bequests to, 264
    outright inheritance to child,
        469–73
    remarriage of, 12, 200–206,
        256–59, 262–70, 448–51, 473–76
    second spouse's children,
        271–80, 448–49, 473
    Support Trusts, 263
    survivorship right termination
        and, 116–18, 273, 476–81
    Trustee relationship with, 453–56
    as Will heir, 77
Survivorship, right of, 77, 115–18,
    215, 273, 277, 407, 474–77
Sweetheart leases, 187–88

Taxes. *See* Death taxes; Income
    taxes
Tenancy in the entirety, 452
Tenants-in-common, 448–49, 450,
    452, 474–77
Third-party Trustees, 453–56
Thomas, Danny, 323–24
Title insurance, 83–84
Titles to homes, 218, 219, 224–25,
    348, 370–71
    joint tenancy with children,
        407–17
Transparent Trusts, 64, 81–85,
    88–89, 157, 440

Trust Deeds, as loan collateral, 45,
    49–50
Trustees, 95, 117, 139, 145–57, 163,
    306–7, 406, 453–56, 476–81. *See
    also* Bank trustees
Trusts, 59–64, 102, 260, 291–92
    real estate held in, 37–38
    terminating provisions, 98
    See also Living Trusts; Protection
        Trusts

Undue influence lawsuits, 445–46
Uniform Transfers to Minors Act,
    374

Valuables, 169–76, 347, 463–67

Wills, 16, 77, 434
    bequests, 33, 171
    bypassing of spouse, 260
    contesting of, 108–11, 227–29
    employment motivation and,
        74–75
    Executors, 10–11, 34–35, 177
    grandchildren's inheritances,
        306
    Guardian designation, 158–59,
        164
    Living Trusts and, 399, 450
    revisions to, 32–33
    telling children about, 429–30
    trusts, 59–64, 102, 260, 291–92
    videotaping of signing, 110
    See also Disinheritance

Jeffrey J. Condon welcomes your comments about any of the information in *Beyond the Grave: The Right Way and the Wrong Way of Leaving Money to Your Children (and Others)* and is pleased to—without charge—respond to brief general questions you may have. The contact information is:

Jeffrey J. Condon, Esq.
Mailing Address:
3435 Ocean Park Boulevard
Santa Monica, California 90405
Telephone (310) 393–0701
email: jeff@condonandcondon.net

When communicating with Jeffrey, please follow the following guidelines:

1. For the most immediate response, your questions or comments should be made by telephone. When calling, please state that you are making a "Book Call."
2. Jeffrey cannot accept any collect calls.
3. If Jeffrey is unavailable to speak with you, you may leave your name and telephone number to receive a return call.
4. Jeffrey will, most likely, respond to all e-mail communications by telephone. Therefore, all e-mail communications to Jeffrey should include a telephone number for a return call.

All communications from Jeffrey are made with the understanding that he is not engaged in rendering legal, accounting, or other professional service by responding to your comments or questions. If you need legal assistance, you are required to (1) retain Jeffrey as your attorney or (2) retain the services of other competent attorneys who emphasize a practice in estate and/or inheritance planning.

About the Author

Jeffrey L. Condon is an attorney who has practiced in the field of trusts and estates since 1987. He received his Bachelor of Arts in English Literature at UCLA (Class of '83) and his law degree from Whittier of College School of Law in 1987. He presently practices at the Law Offices of Condon & Condon in Santa Monica, California.

With his late father, Gerald M. Condon, Jeffrey is the co-author of *Beyond The Grave: The Right Way and Wrong Way of Leaving Money to Your Children (and Others)*. Published in 1996 and revised in 2001, the *Wall Street Journal* has called Jeffrey's first book "the best estate planning book in America." In 2008, Jeffrey authored *The Living Trust Advisor: Everything You Need to Know About Your Living Trust* (John Wiley & Sons).

He has been cited as a source for over 100 newspaper and magazine articles discussing inheritance planning, including *New York Times*, *Los Angeles Times*, *Washington Post*, *Wall Street Journal*, *Time*, *Kiplinger's* and *Business Week*. The topics in this area are so many and diverse, he has been quoted in periodicals ranging from *Fortune* to *DogWorld*.

Jeffrey has discussed various inheritance planning issues on over 70 radio call-in shows throughout the United States, and on numerous television programs including "The Money Club" (C-NBC), "Primetime News" (CNN), "The 700 Club (CBN), "One on One with John McLaughlin (NBC) and "The Dr. Laura Show (CBS).

He has conducted over 200 talks and seminars on the living trust and family inheritance planning throughout the United States for numerous financial institutions, insurance companies, charities, civic groups, service clubs, real estate companies, trust companies, and conventions.

Outside the legal world, Jeffrey is an avid swimmer who swims 3000 meters a day and participates in long-distance ocean races during the summer. He also enjoys obsessing over food and dining, spending down time at home with his daughters and their friends, and attending his daughters' high school and college softball games (Santa Monica High School and Sonoma State University). Jeffrey recently retired from a 15-year stint coaching in a youth girls' softball league that he misses tremendously. Jeffrey considers "Breaking Bad" to be the best television show ever, that Melanie C is a seriously underrated recording artist, and that it's perfectly okay for a grown middle-aged man to enjoy watching "Hannah Montana," "High School Musical" and "iCarly" with your young kids.